The Russian Intelligentsia

The Bloomsbury History of Modern Russia Series

Series Editors: Jonathan D. Smele (Queen Mary, University of London, UK) and Michael Melancon (Auburn University, USA)

This ambitious and unique series offers readers the latest views on aspects of the modern history of what has been and remains one of the most powerful and important countries in the world. In a series of books aimed at students, leading academics and experts from across the world portray, in a thematic manner, a broad variety of aspects of the Russian experience, over extended periods of time, from the reign of Peter the Great in the early eighteenth century to the Putin era at the beginning of the twenty-first.

Published:

Peasants in Russia from Serfdom to Stalin: Accommodation, Survival, Resistance, Boris B. Gorshkov (2018)
Crime and Punishment in Russia: A Comparative History from Peter the Great to Vladimir Putin, Jonathan Daly (2018)
Marx and Russia: The Fate of a Doctrine, James D. White (2018)
A Modern History of Russian Childhood, Elizabeth White (2020)
Marriage, Household and Home in Modern Russia: From Peter the Great to Vladimir Putin, Barbara Alpern Engel (2021)
A History of Education in Modern Russia, Wayne Dowler (2021)
Russian Populism: A History, Christopher Ely (2022)

Forthcoming:

The Russian Military and the Creation of Empire, John Steinberg (2023)
The History of the Russian Worker: Life and Change from Peter the Great to Vladimir Putin, Alice Pate
Gender in Modern Russia, Aaron B. Retish

The Russian Intelligentsia

From the Monastery to the Mir Space Station

By
Christopher Read

BLOOMSBURY ACADEMIC
LONDON • NEW YORK • OXFORD • NEW DELHI • SYDNEY

BLOOMSBURY ACADEMIC
Bloomsbury Publishing Plc
50 Bedford Square, London, WC1B 3DP, UK
1385 Broadway, New York, NY 10018, USA
29 Earlsfort Terrace, Dublin 2, Ireland

BLOOMSBURY, BLOOMSBURY ACADEMIC and the Diana logo are
trademarks of Bloomsbury Publishing Plc

First published in Great Britain 2024

A catalogue record for this book is available from the British Library.

A catalog record for this book is available from the Library of Congress.

ISBN: HB: 978-1-3500-3539-3
ePDF: 978-1-3500-3583-6
eBook: 978-1-3500-3540-9

Typeset by Integra Software Services Pvt. Ltd.

To find out more about our authors and books visit www.bloomsbury.com
and sign up for our newsletters.

Contents

Foreword

The task undertaken in this book might be considered impossible – to give a more than superficial account of one of humanity's most diverse, talented and unclassifiable groups of women and men. The project arose out of the happy idea of the series editors that they would encourage assessments of important Russian social groups over longer time spans than usual and crossing over divides – tsarist, Soviet, post-Soviet, for example. Their initiative met up with my own aspiration to investigate the intelligentsia from the perspective of breadth rather than depth and the belief that a longitudinal study would bring out features that might be undervalued in a more detailed approach. The reader will judge whether the following account bears out these hopes. Even within the context of the series, the time span of the present volume is very extended, stretching from the rise of Muscovy to the present. The title was conceived some time ago but the persistent reader will be rewarded with a fairly recent symbolic event in which the historical imagination has been underpinned by a quirk of reality. The long span was chosen because it has become more and more apparent that, despite its great fractures – the Tatar or Mongol yoke, the Time of Troubles, the Great Schism, pre-Petrine and Imperial periods, serf emancipation, the 1917 revolution and the 1991 collapse of the communist project – Russian history shows great continuity within and beyond those moments of turbulence. For the intelligentsia, many of whom were intensely aware of Russia's past in which they found both inspiration and impediment, it seemed necessary to go back to medieval Muscovy (the Moscow city-state) to trace its earliest sparks. Conventionally, the intelligentsia tends to be seen to have begun in the late-eighteenth century in the person of Radishchev or Novikov, with, perhaps, a backward glance to the extraordinary figure of Grigorii Skovoroda, all of whom play key parts in our story. However, it seemed necessary to at least sketch the forerunners and that is where this study begins, in the monasteries which have long been so important to Russia's intellectual, artistic and spiritual development, and have, to the surprise of many, become so again since 1991. The Muscovy period was also significant for being the first time the actual names of individual artists have come down to us.

The early period also shows forerunners in science and technology which are also central to intelligentsia achievement. In particular, the state, with its demands for military equipment and expertise, and the expansion of Russia to the east, which awoke an ongoing geographic, ethnic and scientific engagement with its borderlands from the Arctic and the Pacific to the Tien Shan and Caucasus mountains, have continued to shape the intelligentsia and its interests down to the present moment. Military might, Russia's defensive substitute for natural borders, and Eurasian ideas continue to depend on the intelligentsia.

It needs to be acknowledged that two intertwined elements have gone to make up the subject of this study. Due respect has been paid to the 'traditional' concept of an *intelligent* as an educated person who devotes a substantial part of their life and talent to 'serving the people'. However, this can rarely be clearly separated from the notion of an intellectual, defined in the sociological sense as a 'brain-worker' as opposed to a manual worker (though each category, of course, enfolds elements of the other) or as a recipient of higher education. The distinction becomes even harder in the twentieth century because the post-revolutionary definition of the intelligentsia combines them both. Service of the people was expected by the party in Soviet Russia but the revolution, affecting all industrial economies, which put a premium on the human brain as a key factor in production through advanced skills in science, technology, administration and so on, meant the two categories became fused together even more. In Russian, the term '*intelligent*' still has priority and there is no commonly used separate term derived from 'intellectual'. What's more, it still has connotations of special status and group identity, though, as will be discussed later, it has lost most of its sense of duty to 'the people', the *narod* in Russian. Throughout this account a broad understanding of the intelligentsia is pervasive, encompassing revolutionaries, reformers, scientists, technologists and creative figures across all the arts, including some performers as well as creators. It even touches on those working within the state system, even though many *intelligenty* ((plural form)) considered, and still do, that to belong to the group they must oppose the state.

This leads to a further complication. The social function of the intelligentsia is, in large part, to be the creators and bearers of 'culture', itself a notoriously slippery term. This pulls the account into aspects of Russia's cultural development. Attention is paid to the expansion of Russia's skills and knowledge base and its cultural evolution as important drivers of intelligentsia development. In many cases 'intellectual history' and early forms of 'cultural history' tended to exam their subjects and topics in something of a void, minimizing their links to the broader society around them and its current level of development. The realm of ideas is often presented as though it was self-sufficient. The present study tries to balance the 'impersonal' structural elements forming the intelligentsia as well as paying due attention to the individuals who made it up, though this is where the impossibility of the study lies. There are hundreds, even thousands, of individuals who deserve our attention. The importance of individuals as the foundation of the group has to be acknowledged even though it is, of course, inevitable that many individuals will be given short shrift. Some will only have a brief mention, some a few paragraphs, a few will have a page or two of attention. Of course, where sources are available, every one of these figures could merit a study as long as this entire book. In defence, all that can be said is that, in many cases, such studies already exist and it is the present writer's hope that readers might be stimulated to plunge more deeply into the high-quality studies of these extraordinary personalities which have been published in many languages. It is also hoped that the present approach compensates for sketchy consideration of individuals by throwing light on interactions, persistence of issues, oversimplifications of standard categorizations like 'westernizer' and 'slavophile' and so on which are often marginalized in more detailed accounts.

Finally, it needs to be said that the individuals who do appear are often taken up for their own sake. 'Eccentric' thinkers like Nikolai Fyodorov, to take one example, are given more attention than some major figures like Pushkin, partly because the former are less well known but also because they may illustrate something different and original more helpfully than repeating ideas about the more prominent figures. For that reason among others, this is not a textbook in the sense of being a comprehensive and systematic relation of fact nor a comprehensive cultural history of Russia. Rather it aims to be an interpretative, analytical, hopefully challenging at times, account of the development of an extraordinary group of people. The most satisfying effect would be to stimulate the reader to want to know more about them and to fulfil the hope that the reader enjoys reading this book as much as the author has enjoyed writing it.

Note: The term 'Russian' has been used throughout to describe the intelligentsia of the tsarist and Soviet periods. The explosion of successor states after 1991 has added further complications but, by and large the term holds together because, apart from some examples noted in the text, the people referred to mainly transmitted their ideas through the medium of the Russian language. In fact, many *intelligenty* were Jewish, Polish, Finnish, Ukrainian, Armenian, Georgian and so on by ethnicity. In many ways, the most complicated case is that of Ukraine. Culturally, Ukraine and Russia are inextricably intertwined. To deprive Russia of its cultural components of Ukrainian origin – Berdyaev, Vernadsky, Gogol', Trotsky – or to try to invent a Ukrainian culture separate from Russian culture are undesirable and impossible. There are difficult cases. Vernadsky was born in St Petersburg, for example, and Skovoroda, who wrote in both languages and travelled throughout Russia (he died in St Petersburg) and Ukraine and was accepted in both. The Russian language has two adjectival forms for 'Russian' – *Russkii* and *rossiiskii* – sometimes translated as 'Russian' and 'All-Russian' respectively since the former applies to ethnic Russians, the latter to the broader entity, the 'Russian world'. British citizens have an equivalent in distinguishing British from its Welsh, Irish, English and Scottish components. Apart from items published in the minority languages, to entirely separate a shared culture makes little sense. Great figures of Scottish culture – such as Adam Smith, David Hume, Walter Scott and so on – wrote in English, contributed to British culture, frequented London, were published by presses in England indistinguishably from Scotland. Scots who became British Prime Ministers from the Earl of Bute down to Tony Blair and Gordon Brown operated in a single British political space as did many Irish and Welsh politicians such as Lloyd George. British culture cannot usefully be torn into separate minority components nor can Ukrainian and Russian culture. Clearly, each region has its own characteristics and style but, with the possible exception of items in the minority language, they operate in a shared space. Unless otherwise stated the term Russian is used in its wider meaning of all-Russian rather than ethnic Russian throughout.

Acknowledgements

A sweeping account like this needs not only to draw on the author's own lifetime of engagement with the subject but also on the vast number of other writers who have also engaged with the topic and those who are an integral part of the intelligentsia itself. I owe them all an immense debt of gratitude. The influence of too many people runs through this volume for me to pick out individuals. Instead I want to thank all those belonging to the wonderful collectives, which it has been my privilege to be a small part of The foundation of it all has been my family who have been essential to everything. Then come those to whom I am indebted for my education in schools, St Mary and St John and St Chad's College in my home town of Wolverhampton, and universities, especially the historians at Keele University in the 1960s, the Soviet Institute in Glasgow and the Government Department at LSE. Since then I have had bedrock support from many friends around the world, you know who you are, and especially colleagues in the History Department of the University of Warwick. The Study Group on the Russian Revolution, now almost fifty years old, has been a constant source of stimulus. CREES in Birmingham, the Southern Conference of ASEEES, the Irish Association for Russian, Central and East European Studies and the Russia's Great War and Revolution project have provided a particularly rich supply of friends and colleagues. I have also been fortunate enough to work in many wonderful libraries and archives in London, Leningrad as was, Moscow, Tartu, Oxford, New York, Boston, Berkeley and Palo Alto. Above all, my Estonian and Russian friends mentioned in Chapter Nine have sustained me through thick and thin on my many visits to the Soviet Union and Russia and helped me understand more than they will ever realize. It was, therefore, with great sadness that I learned of the death of Slava Nemodruk on 7 July 2023 as I was putting the finishing touches to this book which I dedicate to Slava and his family – Lucy, Julia and Lev – and all my Russian and Estonian friends with my unquenchable love and affection.

Introduction – What is the intelligentsia? Towards a definition

From the middle of the nineteenth century to the present the question '*chto takoe intelligentsiia*?' has cascaded through the generations of Russian thought and has even created animated debate in Russia today. What were the identifying characteristics of this group? Where did it fit in class society? Was there even such a thing? And was it unique to Russia? As we will see, much ink was spilled on all these issues. However, before embarking on our more detailed study it might be helpful to meditate on some of these debates to draw out some of the aspects of those identifying as members of the intelligentsia, considered to be defining of the group.

Closely associated with this are the conditions in which it developed, namely an increasingly educated and increasingly complex society in which the knowledge and skills base was not just expanding exponentially but moving into the limelight as a key, possibly the key, factor of modern economic and industrial production. Since the mid-eighteenth century the importance of mental labour has risen, at first slowly and later very rapidly. The first industrial revolution was driven, literally, by steam plus coal and iron. Inventions were crucial but the contribution of mental creativity remained limited. In the last third of the nineteenth century, the second industrial revolution – based on chemicals, electricity, steel and oil, knowledge and creativity – emanating from new social groups such as scientists (who retreated from the real world to laboratories at this time), engineers and managers, and skilled mental labour was a key driver. The third industrial revolution, whose roots go back to the Second World War, is the digital revolution through which we are now living. It depends on human ingenuity more than any other single component. In the first industrial revolution the machines were large and the mental labour input relatively small. In the digital industrial revolution the machines are small and light by comparison (silicon chips and computers) and the mental input enormous. The three revolutions did not succeed one another but lie on top of each other like a layer cake. There are plenty of enormous machines today – think of diesel engines, the largest of which weighs 2,300 tons, which power giant ships – but the digital revolution increasingly underlies almost everything. Alongside these revolutions societies have become ever more complex, the largest urban centres comprise tens of millions of inhabitants. Transport and communication networks link the globe by air, land, sea and fibre optic cable. Management of such a world has become increasingly difficult and the imperative for global management of shared problems of climate emergency, pandemics, nuclear power and weapons of mass destruction, which threaten humanity almost to the point of extinction, poses an unprecedented challenge to human creativity and co-operation which may not be successfully met. In all these ways, mental labour and intelligentsias, which point to problems, analyse social, political, economic and identity issues and propose and debate solutions, have moved from the margins of social élites to become the crucial component in modern society, including its economic output. Since the late eighteenth century, the steam engine has been replaced by the human brain as the driver of industry and society.

Although it has not been in the forefront of industrializing powers in terms of wealth, for a variety of reasons Russia has had a special place in the development and interpretation of the intellectual class in modern society. In fact, not being in the forefront may be a decisive factor in the emergence of the Russian intelligentsia in its classic form as a group driven by moral concerns to 'serve the people' and, in a situation of an autocracy which was increasingly unfit for the purpose of governing Russia, to consider itself to be the 'mind, honour and conscience' of the country, a large not to say presumptuous claim first made around 1870. These were the bedrocks of the intelligentsia identity which began to emerge in Russia after the 1861 emancipation of the serfs proved to be a disappointment. It left the peasants, while not exactly impoverished, certainly as much poorer than almost every other social class. It has been Russia's fate, in the recent centuries of global uplift of wealth, to occupy a position below the wealthiest, hovering at around one-third to one-half of US per capita national wealth but ahead of the poorest 'underdeveloped' nations. In the 1950s the notion of a first world and a third world came into use. The Communist world, including Russia at that time, was deemed to be a second world pinned between the other two. This perfectly expresses Russia's situation over the last 250 or so years. How does that contribute to the emergence of the Russian intelligentsia around the 1850s and 1860s?

The intelligentsia, by and large, showed an awareness of Russia's 'backwardness' (*otstalost'*) and set out from that basis to critique its political, social and economic structures and commit to liberating the chief victims, the peasantry at that time plus workers later. Since the corollary of 'backwardness' is 'forwardness', only a country in Russia's position was likely to throw up such an intelligentsia. It provoked unfavourable comparisons with the more advanced world but that could only happen in a society which already had a degree of cultural development in which that insight could be formulated, developed and, of course, resisted by those like the Slavophiles, who largely rejected the premiss that Russia had anything to learn from anyone else. In that sense having an intelligentsia of this type might well characterize a more 'backward' society but it was also a signifier of awareness of that backwardness and also of a desire to change that status by 'catching up' with the more economically wealthier societies. In that sense it was an indicator of a first step out of backwardness.

Similar social formations and individuals, from José Marti to Che Guevara and Fidel Castro, emerged in areas like Latin America, where the comparison with the United States was especially acute. Liberal and left-wing movements, like their counterparts in nineteenth and early-twentieth-century Russia, tended to look to models resembling, and often supposedly improving on, those provided by the 'advanced' societies. Since the sometimes overlooked revolution of the late 1970s, fundamentalisms of many kinds – capitalist, Christian, Jewish, Hindu, Muslim, various nationalisms – have emerged all around the globe, even in the advanced western nations themselves. They have challenged the narrative of 'global' development and proposed following different, indigenous paths of development. This echoes what was called *samobytnost'* by Russian slavophile *intelligenty*. The term refers to a distinct national path of development, different from that of other peoples, a unique identity, exceptionalism. The term echoes the German '*sonderweg*' which has no direct equivalent in English.

Analysis of the Russian intelligentsia as a social group has been complicated by several factors but two further complications have made the deepest mark. On one hand there is the special Russian notion of a 'monastic order' committed to social justice and, on the other, the broader definition of the intelligentsia as 'mental labourers'. The former obviously prioritizes subjective ideas and beliefs, while the latter is based on objective social position and occupation. Second, like the Russian intelligentsia, many western intellectuals tended to associate themselves with social justice and socialism. This led to right-wing intellectuals feeling beleaguered and coming up with very politically charged definitions, including the view that left-wing intellectuals were alienated misfits and that is why they protested against the status quo, or that they were driven by psychological compulsion. Others argued that, while they have social prestige, capitalism undervalues their work and that is why they criticize capitalism.[1] However, the terms 'intellectual' and '*intelligent*' (pronounced with a hard g as in 'get') do not map precisely on to each other. Perhaps the key difference is that intellectuals are individuals and even when referred to collectively – the intellectuals – it is understood more as a group of diverse individuals. The term '*intelligent*', on the other hand, tends to have connotations of being part of a group with shared characteristics even though it might also embrace people with very different worldviews.

In English the word 'intellectual' was used occasionally in the early nineteenth century, usually in a disparaging way which has often clung to it ever since in the UK. However, the term 'intellectual' gained real traction in France at the time of the Dreyfus affair in 1898 when the country's leading novelist of the age, Émile Zola, accused the French government of being anti-semitic in imposing a heavy sentence on a Jewish army officer on a trumped up charge of spying. The affair raised an outcry and those from the literary, artistic and scientific circles who spoke out in defence of Zola came to be known as '*les intellectuelles*', still in a dismissive way. It was only in the twentieth century that it came to be a term of respect. The attention of Max Weber, the great German sociologist, was drawn towards it and he, and the French pioneering sociologist Émile Durkheim, was one of the first to grapple with defining and analysing it and investigating its social role. Weber's recognition of the social role of intellectuals was linked to his insights into the growing importance of managerial bureaucracies in modern society and the increasing importance of mental labour, science and rationalism which had, amongst other things, 'disenchanted' the world by marginalizing mystery, the metaphysical and the religious.[2] In the new world intellectuals replace the priesthood as organizers and developers of knowledge using reason rather than faith as their basic tool.

In Russia around this time the term 'intelligentsia' was also coming under scrutiny from three directions. In 1903 the Polish radical Jan Vaclav Machajski (1866–1926.

Makhaev in Russian. Pseudonym: A Vol'skii.) put forward the provocative theory that the intelligentsia embraced socialism because it was the ideological embodiment of their group interests. A socialist society, so Machajski argued, would be managed and regulated from above and this was a task which would be accomplished by the educated class, the mental labourers, who would become the ruling élite in a technocratic socialist society. According to Trotsky (1879–1940), who was in internal political exile after 1905, the idea had a degree of support from his fellow prisoners. However, the idea re-emerged in different forms at different times. It partly influenced Trotsky himself who claimed after 1917 that the revolution was failing because the bureaucracy was using the state for its own interests rather than those of workers. After the Second World War, the Yugoslav communist Milovan Djilas, who does not appear to have read Machajski, came up with a similar notion that the educated bureaucracy of socialist societies constituted what he termed *The New Class*. The concept spread widely in the Cold War. Other writers and dissidents in eastern Europe took it up, for example the Hungarian thinker George Konrad in *Intellectuals on the Road to Class Power*. Of course, in reality, it was only when communist power collapsed that figures from the old bureaucratic apparatus were able to convert their restricted power and property-holding under communism into real power and undreamed of personal wealth to form a new oligarchic, real class power.

The second Russian debate on the intelligentsia took place among the emerging Marxist intellectuals. Marx himself had died in 1883 before the awareness of the intelligentsia as a distinct group had really developed. Insofar as Marx thought about them, they were considered to be the articulators of the interests of the main classes of society. Establishment intellectuals supported ruling class bourgeois values, radical intellectuals spoke for worker and peasant classes. Obviously Marx spoke for the workers but, like so many who followed, he was clearly not working class by birth, upbringing or style of life. He never really drew out the implications of this anomaly though he was insistent that 'the emancipation of the working class is the task of the workers themselves';[3] that is, outside support by intellectuals and middle-class sympathizers might be helpful, but was only marginal. In Russia, prior to Lenin (1870–1924), the radical movement comprised *intelligenty* rather than peasants and workers. Lenin's views on the role of intellectuals in the workers' movement became somewhat confusing. A letter from him to Gorky of 1919 is often quoted. In it he crudely fulminated to Gorky that the intelligentsia considered itself to be the brains of society but it was actually society's shit.[4] This seems pretty unequivocal. However, in his breakthrough pamphlet *What Is to Be Done?* (1902) he assigned an important role in party formation and development to intellectuals like himself in the form of what he calls 'professional revolutionaries'. By 1904 he is, possibly under the workerist influence of his newly found ally A.A. Bogdanov, partially rowing back on this and re-asserting the pre-eminence of workers in the party.[5] However, the rest of the much-quoted letter to Gorky shows clearly that this is not a general condemnation of intellectuals. He divides them into 'the intellectual forces of the people' who bring science and enlightenment to the masses and 'whom we pay a higher salary' and those who are 'lackeys of the bourgeoisie' whom he scorns so crudely. For what it's worth he clearly distinguishes the two groups: 'It is wrong to confuse the "intellectual forces" of the people with the "forces" of bourgeois intellectuals.'[6] For Lenin it was the political orientation of the educated classes which was important so, to that extent, he was following Marxist precedent. He did, however, come to share the fear that bureaucracy was stifling the revolution. Several times he complained about the revolution becoming entrapped in red tape and in his last article prioritized the problem but put forward a completely inadequate solution of having fewer but better officials in the Central Committee. Neither Lenin nor Trotsky acknowledged the real problem, which was that their type of revolution, with strong guidance from the centre by an enlightened élite, could only be accomplished by a bureaucratic control apparatus that was only partially understood and which was the antithesis of democracy, the oxygen of which the revolution needed to avoid suffocation. Bureaucracy emerged as a key, widespread problem in both capitalist and communist contexts and beyond in the twentieth century and still, in the twenty-first, no real solutions have been implemented.

The third source of analysis, which was more hostile in attacking the otherwise sacrosanct intelligentsia tradition, came, in 1909, from the authors of a collection of articles entitled *Vekhi* (*Landmarks* or perhaps, in our age of the GPS, *Waypoints*), whose key argument was that by prioritizing social action over personal self-improvement, and opposition to the state rather than improving the life of the country by working within the state structures, the intelligentsia had chosen counter-productive paths. The intelligentsia of all political colours shrugged it off, though in the 1920s its influence was felt by a few of the Bolsheviks' White opponents and numerous engineers and others in the form of *Smena vekh* (*Changing Landmarks*) and National Bolshevism which encouraged non-communists to work within the Soviet system rather than engage in risky and pointless opposition. Interestingly, when Mikhail Agursky revived interest in National Bolshevism around 1970, he, with the support of Solzhenitsyn, edited a collection of essays entitled *Iz pod glyb* (*From under the Rubble*) which self-consciously saw itself as a continuation of the sequence of *Vekhi* (1909) and its confiscated successor *Iz glubiny* (*Out of the Depths*) (1919) which will be referred to later.

Intelligenty and Intellectuals

A final cluster of preliminary thoughts. If the reader will permit, a brief look at non-Russian arguments about intellectuals will help to deepen our appreciation of the distinctiveness, if any, of the Russian concept. *Vekhi* had little or no impact outside the Russian-speaking world, although an early international controversy about intellectuals did reflect some of its points. In 1927, Julien Benda published his short, sharp and still relevant critique of intellectuals entitled *La Trahison des Clercs*.[7] At the heart of his argument was an accusation that the intellectuals (*les clercs* i.e. clergy) had abandoned enlightenment reason and, especially, objective detachment, in favour of commitment to nationalism, fascism and communism. The task of intellectuals, for Benda, was the pursuit of reason and truth for their own sake. However, a very different critique emerged in 1941. James Burnham, who had been a supporter of Trotsky in the mid-1930s but went over to US Republican conservatism, published a book entitled *The Managerial Revolution*[8] in which he argued that bureaucratic state systems, with the US New Deal in the forefront, were squashing individual rights in favour of state priorities. In comments shared by many conservative thinkers, he rejected 'the stress on the state as against the individual; planning as against private enterprise; jobs (even if relief jobs) against opportunities; security against initiative' and, most tellingly and more openly than later conservatives, denied the priority of '"human rights" against "property rights"'.[9] Other commentators had similar ideas. The Italian anti-fascist Bruno Rizzi had written about *La Bureaucratisation du Monde* (*The Bureaucratisation of the World*)[10] and in 1943 the radical thinker Simone Weil pointed out in her brilliant essay *L'Enracinement*[11] (*The Need for Roots*) the individual-crushing similarities of international statist developments, not only of communism and fascism, but also of the New Deal and the French Popular Front. In less fraught times the idea underpinned convergence theory in the 1960s which argued that industrial societies were drawn to similar structures (factories, cities, managerial authority and so on) irrespective of ideology and that this would lead to capitalist and socialist societies converging.[12]

Convergence theory was an exception in a period of Cold War which permeated intellectual life in liberal capitalist societies from top to bottom and was more concerned to separate out and vilify the enemy, not prophesy increasing similarities. Analysis of intellectuals themselves was in the frontline of Cold War thinking. Rafts of protest movements over the decades in the western world pitched radical intellectuals against their own national governments and ruling élites. Protests were made about many causes, including the Chinese revolution, Korean War, US-sponsored regime changes in Iraq, Egypt (failed), Guatemala, Cuba (failed) and many other places, plus the long-running conflict in Vietnam (1946–73) and burning issues of nuclear weapons and global inequality. Western 'dissidents' such as Noam Chomsky, who revealed the imperial underpinnings of American foreign policy, and Bertrand Russell, who devoted his last years to the Campaign for Nuclear Disarmament, took the intellectual initiative away from conservatives. Right-wing analysts worked hard to explain away the concerted intellectual opposition to capitalism and related causes. In 1998, a decade after the end of the Cold War, the distinguished Harvard professor Robert Nozick continued to pose the question in an unusual way:

> It is surprising that intellectuals oppose capitalism so. Other groups of comparable socio-economic status do not show the same degree of opposition in the same proportions. Statistically, then, intellectuals are an anomaly. Not all intellectuals are on the "left." Like other groups, their opinions are spread along a curve. But in their case, the curve is shifted and skewed to the political left.

His explanation for this 'statistical anomaly' is astonishing.

> Schools have already given the academically most gifted the message that they are most valuable and deserving of the greatest rewards, and later these very pupils with the highest encouragement and hopes see others of their peers, whom they know and saw to be less meritorious, rising higher than they themselves, taking

> the foremost rewards to which they themselves felt themselves entitled. Is it any wonder they bear that society an animus?

Nozick was very contented with his solution: 'We have found, I think, an explanatory factor that (once stated) is so obvious that we must believe it explains some real phenomenon.'[13] Left-wing protest is driven by frustrated self-interest and relatively low pay. The main thrust of such a naïve, 'materialist' explanation is to deprive protest of any legitimacy and to imply that protest only comes from self-interest, this last being, of course, the dominant human motivation for self-described libertarian capitalists. The moral imperative which runs so clearly through the nineteenth-century Russian intelligentsia was just a response to their blocked upward social mobility.

By 1998, Nozick had spent a long career developing such ideas. Another leading light in establishing conservative views of the role of intellectuals was Chicago professor, Edward Shils. In a much more sophisticated, brilliant and engaging essay Shils, like Nozick, professed puzzlement: 'Why did writers, historians, philosophers and other intellectuals, some great and all interesting, feel such revulsion for their own societies, for the institutions through which they were ruled and the persons who ruled them?'[14] His answer was that they were influenced by factors such as populism, apocalyptic notions of social transformation and other moral impulsions, initially derived from religious searching, which had been partially secularized into the pursuit of reason and truth since the Reformation and Enlightenment. In a sense, Shils still saw the radical intellectual being driven by personal self-fulfilment though he had considerable respect for their moral commitment. The idea of committing to social justice does not enter the consciousness of Shils, let alone Nozick. However, Shils analysis allows intellectuals all kinds of social roles from being advisers to the sovereign power or key components of the political system itself such as judges and jurists, to being revolutionaries in political and/or cultural senses.

Shils planted his flag at the head of what was a very influential group of 'conservative' analysts of intellectuals and intelligentsias. Some very prominent western intellectuals, with a smattering of star exhibit dissidents from the communist world, agonized over why comfortably-off beneficiaries of middle-class living standards and life opportunities wanted to protest and even join radical movements, even armed and 'terrorist' factions, dedicated to bringing down that class and social order in which they were so privileged. Many of them considered intellectuals to be 'alienated', to be social outcasts and misfits simply expressing personal frustrations and inadequacies. Liberal conservatives who argued along these lines included Raymond Aron, Leszek Kolakowski, Seymour Martin Lipset, L.Coser, Shlomo Avineri and many who focused on Russia, notably Richard Pipes, Martin Malia, Leonard Schapiro, Alain Besançon, Michael Confino, Tibor Szamuely and others.[15] It would take us too far from our current focus to follow up this fascinating debate but there are several points worth making briefly. Much of this literature seemed targeted at the newly minted phenomenon of 'student protest', especially against the Vietnam War and '1968' without giving weight to the idea that that war was innately unjust and unwinnable so that the causes of opposition to it did not require deep reflection. The commentators who linked it to Russian intellectuals equally overlooked that one hardly needed to be an alien misfit to fight against the evils of tsarism, although devotion to that struggle might turn them into that. Second, they tended to confine the definition of an 'intellectual' to politically committed radicals, ignoring many groups and classes – composers, writers, artists, teachers and so on – whom we shall be looking at in this study. Finally, to turn round a cheap gibe several of them aimed at Marx and his followers – notably that his theory of class struggle held no place for bourgeois intellectual sympathizers like Marx and middle-class Marxists to side with the proletariat – these theorists of intellectual alienation were, of course, comfortably settled intellectuals themselves.

Since the Cold War the English-speaking world, with only a few exceptions,[16] moved on from discussing intellectuals and intelligentsias although lively discussions continue down to the present in France.[17] Perhaps only one aspect is clear in both the Russian and western debates about intellectuals. There are almost as many explanations of intellectual behaviour as there are intellectuals. Disagreement is the norm, consensus, far away.

Part One

The roots of the intelligentsia

1

The birth of the Russian soul

As medieval extortionists went the Mongols were not the worst. Their raids were cruel and vicious but their permanent presence was light. In 1237 the invaders razed many Russian cities including Ryazan, Kolomna, Moscow, Vladimir, Suzdal, Rostov, Uglich, Yaroslavl, Kostroma, Gorodets, Galich, Pereslavl-Zalessky, Yuriev-Polsky, Volokolamsk, Tver and Torzhok. Finally, in 1240, they reached and razed the capital, Kiev/Kyiv. Novgorod, one of the most northerly cities, survived by judiciously surrendering rather than fighting to the death. The victors let local rulers continue in power but demanded tribute (*dan* in Russian) from them in the form of gold, money, valuables, slaves and women for sexual servitude. If the local tributary paid up, the Mongol khans were satisfied. Default brought hideous debt extraction. The so-called 'Mongol yoke' influenced the entire future of Russia but it was not just the oppression which was formative. The process by which a new Russia emerged from under the yoke was crucial. In order to understand the emergence of Russian ideas, knowledge, culture and, ultimately, its intelligentsia, we need to remember some of these large, shaping factors and enduring characteristics of 'Russia'.

The impact of the Mongol invasion has long been controversial and in recent times has become extensively so, as it has become deeply absorbed into the now-competing revision of foundation myths of contemporary Ukraine and Russia. This tragic division has caused increasing and immensely regrettable bitterness. For our purposes, however, perhaps we can identify important features that are less contestable. In the first place, the Mongols were culturally tolerant. They did not seek to impose their religion and way of life on the tribute territories. The khans even permitted a Russian Orthodox cathedral to be built in their capital of Sarai. They were shamanistic pagans[1] when they began the invasion but later, despite being in conflict with the Ottoman Empire, adopted its Islamic faith. But Russian Orthodoxy remained unchallenged and was re-inforced as a key foundation of Russian identity. This did not prevent a degree of assimilation. The principality of Muscovy (Moscow) became the chief ally/vassal state of the Mongols and court figures adopted the Tatar language, fashions of clothing and even names. The Russian language adopted many words from their overlords, usually connected to state and judicial practices which they adopted including organized tax-gathering (*nalog* is the modern Russian term for tax), basic transport via post routes and severe punishments including capital and corporal punishment (recalled in the loan-word *knut'* the knout or whip).[2]

We should also note that, in choosing Moscow, and to a lesser extent Novgorod, as its partners, the Mongol rulers had caused the centre of gravity of early Russian/Rus civilization to move northwards from its original centre in Kiev/Kyiv. According to some historians today this also brought a decisive break between Russia and Ukraine (and even Belarus in some versions) but the Russian/Rus world was manifestly harmoniously united for most of the period we will be considering in that for educated intellectuals it was not very important to be Ukrainian, Belarussian or Russian. The Russian language was the lingua franca of this group and the Ukrainian and Belarussian versions were largely considered to be peasant dialects, an assumption which is fiercely contested today. However, the degree of dialogue between the elite and the khans did promote changes in the Russian identity which have had an unexpected resurgence in the twenty-first century. Although Russia remained unshaken in its adoption of the Orthodox faith dating back virtually to the initial emergence of Kievan Rus in 988, it did evolve certain features that have led to the theory that Russians have a composite Eurasian identity. The drift north and then the opening to the west are seen to have created an identity dispute to which we will frequently return. Some rejected the Eurasian interpretation in favour of a specifically Slavic identity but, as links with western Europe also evolved from the fifteenth century, there was also a tendency towards westernization, particularly of the focus of the present study, the intelligentsia. A major debate between westernizers (*zapadniki*) and slavophiles (*slavianofili*) seized hold of them in the second half of the nineteenth century. Not only have Russians been unsure of their identity, their neighbours have shared their puzzlement. By and large, Russia has not been seen as fully European by Europeans or Asian by Asians though it is often seen from outside as a distinctive Slavic culture of its own.

A third set of influences derived from the Mongol years have exerted an even less tangible but no less vital set of shaping forces. These were the consequence of the way Russia freed itself of Mongol rule. While it is true the Mongol empire collapsed and withdrew from its European vassal states, the emancipation struggle of those states gave them a specific form. Muscovy led the way and emerged as the core of a renewed Russia. The circumstances of its re-birth, however, left deep imprints still visible today. In the first place, military power and state power became even more closely fused than in any other state of that time. The relatively small population put a premium on forcing everyone, including those at the top, into the service of the state cause. State rule was harsh for everyone and its cause of liberation required oppressive taxation from wherever it could be raised to pay for the military. Harshness engendered resistance. Resistance engendered tough enforcement. An elite of boyars[3] became the superenforcers of the states will.

As Russia fought back against the Mongols after its initial major victory at Kulikovo in 1380, another persistent problem emerged. What were its borders? There was no naturally defined homeland bordered by mountains, rivers or seas. Muscovy/Russia developed on a vast plain from the Baltic to the Black Sea, to the Urals and to the Caucasus. In the fifteenth century only a central core of this area was Russian. Russia was defined not by its ‘homeland’ territory, actual or historic, but by its Orthodox culture, ethnicity and its current state boundaries defined by its military capacity.

A final shaping factor meant that, in this fluid and undefined vastness of territory one of the ways to evade the harshness of the state was to flee into the unorganized spaces. This was especially significant in the case of two groups, one important to our study, the other less so. Monasteries were a favourite source of state requisition since many were successful in becoming not only self-sustaining but surplus-producing institutions. Some churches and monasteries accumulated wealth and land which the state envied. To escape its attacks monks moved eastwards into the wildernesses beyond its borders towards the Arctic, the Urals and western Siberia to regain their independence. The second group was the peasantry. This weakness of the rising Muscovite state, that it had ill-defined and ill-controlled borders, tempted peasants to flee also from the harsh conditions imposed on them by the state and the boyars. This threatened the whole project. If the labour force were to disappear, the land would not be tilled and the few but crucial armaments manufacturies would lack workers. There were still some slaves but enslaving the whole of the masses was not an option. Instead, the institution of serfdom was expanded. Serfdom differs from slavery in that most serfs do not become personal possessions as such but they are linked to the land. If the land changes hands the peasants go with it. In exchange for working on the landowners land the peasants had their own allotment which they could treat as their own. However, they lost the status of being free, independent farmers. As the system weighed more heavily upon them more and more took the option of simply fleeing into the wide open spaces, particularly of the steppe lands of the south-east which were beyond the reach of the state. Best known of these former runaways are those who formed themselves into the Cossacks who set up their own semi-'democratic' culture and customs separate from the state, at least for the time being. Now the irony of these mass flights was that eventually, instead of freeing them from state oppression, the state came after them and re-absorbed them. Russia's post-Mongol dynamic saw an expansion of territories worked by the peasants followed by re-absorption into the state. Russian peasants cultivated more and more of the vast spaces of eastern Europe to the Urals, the Black Sea and the also somewhat indeterminate boundaries of the Turkic peoples of Central Asia and the Ottoman Empire. They also trickled into the much harsher environment of Siberia which also became an attraction to fur hunters who eventually reached the Pacific Coast and even hopped the Bering Strait and continued pursuing bears and sea otters. They reached as far south as today's Northern California before the Spanish missionaries advancing from Mexico and long before the Anglo-Americans from the East Coast.

Although these developments took centuries to accomplish the birthmarks remain, arguably to the present. Lacking a clearly defined natural territory and accepted ethnic or other borders 'Russia' has been defined by its state (together with a closely allied church) in which the military was the central institution to an even greater extent than most other states. The state and military defined and defended the borders which neighbours constantly encroached upon. This led to the unresolved dilemma, which took different shapes at different times, of whether Russia and its central military were defensive or aggressive. Russians naturally tended to see the army as protectors from a series of invaders – from Mongols, Teutonic Knights, Lithuanians, Poles, Turks, Napoleon, the Kaiser, Hitler and so on – while their neighbours saw them as imperialists of the first water. It is not our task to resolve this issue but we should note that a heavily militarized state has characterized Russia, almost continuously, from Muscovy to the present. At moments when the state weakened – from the Time of Troubles in the seventeenth century to the collapse of the USSR – chaos and disintegration have followed. In a more emphatic way than elsewhere, Russia depended on its military, its state and its church for its existence. A second set of implications followed. Maintaining the army was costly and that re-inforced the harshness of the state and its repressive apparatus in squeezing people, produce and money from the population. It would not be fanciful to see here the birth of state, collective, priority over individual rights which so distinguishes Russia from western Europe. Tsar Peter the Great proclaimed that everyone, including himself, was a servant of the state and set up a Table of Ranks to reinforce it. In Russia serving the state was supposed to take precedence over service of the self. It is often mistakenly thought that Russian collectivism was introduced by the Soviet authorities. Like so much of the argument about Russia it makes more sense to attribute many supposed features of the Soviet era to deeper Russian traditions. Russia did not become communist/statist then collectivist but being statist and collectivist opened the way to a particular form of communism, lazily defined and dismissed as 'Stalinism'.[4] Finally, it is obvious but sometimes overlooked that this path of development put Russia on a very different course from the west. The breakdown of powerful monarchies in western Europe began with the powerful tier of 'barons' asserting themselves at the expense of monarchy. The English parliament was set up by nobles and gentry as a check on monarchy. In Russia, the monarch was subduing the nobility. As Russia was expanding serfdom, in Europe it was disappearing and more flexible forms of labour emerged as capitalist development speeded up. Free market capitalism has never been present in Russia until quite recently though even now the state still plays a big role in an economy which is part casino, part command. Processes like the Reformation and the Renaissance, which were underpinned by growing ideas of individualism and the individual conscience, had no counterpart in Russia. The Enlightenment had some impact on the tiny but growing educated class in the Russia of Catherine the Great and after, but it led not to deep changes in Russian life but, arguably, created a gulf between the educated class and the wider population.

The consequence of these features is that, despite deep, internal transformations – the Great Schism; the reforms of Peter the Great; the abolition of serfdom; the revolution of 1917; the collapse of the Soviet state – the old intangible forces have often re-asserted themselves. Russia remains today a strongly centralized state with a powerful defensive military and controversial borders with Ukraine, China, Japan and smaller conflicts like with Georgia over the status of Ossetia and Abkhazia and with independence forces as in Chechnya. It is one in which individual rights remain weak and state demands powerful and strictly enforced. Today, popular fear of chaos has been re-inforced by the disasters of the 1990s and the spectacle of Ukraine's never-ending time of troubles over the last thirty years. Even today, many Russians are prepared to pay for stability with their individual rights. The heavy hand of the authoritarian state has lain unchallenged over successive governmental systems. Flight, most recently by national minorities including Ukraine from the collapsed USSR, has been the primordial response. Challenges to the state have been sadly limited. No baronial class has emerged to challenge it. Where powerful potential challengers have emerged, from landowners to oligarchs, they have tended to prefer to look to the state to use its power in their own interests rather than to replace it with their own, and, with few exceptions, the state, in very different ways from Ivan the Terrible to Putin, has been vigilant to nip their challenge in the bud.

It was under these long-lasting influences that Russian culture fermented. The present study concentrates on the elite but mass, that is overwhelmingly peasant, culture has fascinating characteristics of its own – partial self-government through the *obshchina*/village commune; village and family rather than individual landowning including the ability to agree periodic re-distribution. In the words of one of its most perceptive historians the Russian peasantry is one of the most successful entities in human history in terms of its cultivation of more of the earth's surface than any other and its size in terms of numbers.[5]

Like any human society, Muscovite Russia was underpinned by its knowledge base. Compared to what came after, that knowledge was simple and distributed. Compared to what came before, it was increasingly complex because human societies accumulate and expand knowledge but at very different rates. Under feudalism, reproduction was more the norm than enhancement. Reproduction of what had gone before was the best guarantee of survival in that it had at least got society where it was, often under challenging conditions. Russia was a case in point, especially the North, with its harsh climate and four to six months growing season. The classic triad of feudalism – the peasants labour; the clergy pray; the nobility fight – held more or less true. The peasants were largely self-sufficient with their own building, craft and clothing and textile working abilities. Most important they were the holders of the most crucial knowledge, that which provided the food supply. Without it arable and livestock production would have come to a halt. This did not prevent them from being deeply repressed and exploited by those who depended on them. In the growing urban settlements – Moscow having possibly 100,000 inhabitants in the sixteenth century and Velikii Novgorod maybe 25,000–30,000 – the peasantry was replaced by a labouring and artisanal class or tradespeople – butchers, carpenters, builders, etc. – who embodied the knowledge and skills and labour power/physical strength to keep the cities going. Soldiers and officers had their own roles while peasant labourers, often having the status of serfs, provided the skilled and unskilled labour for factories, such as the state arsenals like the Moscow Cannon Yard, and for mining and other industrial occupations. Iron casting was very advanced. Many other skilled groups were necessary in sixteenth-century Moscow. State administrators (up to the level of the ruling councils and the ruler himself), merchants and clerks expanded in number. As Russia itself grew, expertise in forest crafts, fur trapping and so on became increasingly important and contributed greatly to the wealth of the country. Trade routes required river boat construction and navigation.

Culture, in the sense of artistic and other forms of creativity, was highly developed and each class and group had its own favoured formats. In many cases the artistry was tied up with crafts. In particular, peasants had many skills from wood carving, to embellish domestic utensils and the structures of wooden houses, to dyeing and weaving and embroidery to provide spectacular clothing for special occasions. A lively tradition of wandering minstrels, *skomorokhi*, stretched from Kievan Rus (and earlier) through to the mid-seventeenth century. With stringed instruments like the gusli, a kind of zither, they sang songs based on legends, folk stories and historical myths. They joined up with others and with wandering groups of players to perform simple dramas based on similar themes which might also echo biblical stories and ancient Greek and Roman myths and legends. They were very popular in secular society but often drew the wrath of the church for their 'pagan' origins and inspiration and for their association with 'unseemly' popular festivals and carnivals which were denounced for their association with drunkenness and sexual license. In 1648 they were outlawed but the tradition was not entirely repressed.[6] These troubadors were song and story writers as well as performers but could only be considered as distant forerunners of an intelligentsia, which was later to become identified primarily by its role in the development and application of ideas and knowledge.

No specialized group devoted to thinking and critical analysis had separated itself out in Russia by the beginning of the eighteenth century. Nonetheless, important forerunners began to shape what were, much later, to become characteristics of the intelligentsia. One indicator is that, for the first time, creators began to attach their names to what they produced and, for the first time, it is possible to dimly recognize emerging individual creators. They were not necessarily performers and singers. For example, key practitioners like Kashpir Ganusov and Andrei Chokhov became well-known names as a result of their skill in casting large bells and giant cannon. Chokhov's 39 ton 'Tsar Cannon' of 1586, one of the largest in the world at the time, can still be seen in the grounds of the Moscow Kremlin. Chokhov and Ganusov might be considered distant forerunners of the technical intelligentsia. Not untypically they worked in the armaments industry.

However, the most important institution for the early development of Russian culture was the church. Orthodox services, buildings and artefacts became the most advanced stimulants of artistic and cultural activity. To name but a few areas of material cultural production, spectacular churches and cathedrals drew on the skills of architects, stonemasons, plasterers, carpenters, woodcarvers and painters. Services focused on superb music and choral and solo singing of choirs and clergy. The tradition of the iconostasis created a great demand for skilled painters. It consisted of a wooden screen between the main body of the church and the part of the altar where the most sacred part of the ritual was enacted, a screen with strict canonical requirements for depiction in icons of Christ, the apostles, scenes from the gospels and the lives of the saints, making the icons illustrated texts for telling sacred histories. Every church had its iconostasis and the great cathedrals of Moscow, Vladimir, Rostov Velikii, Novgorod, Suzdal and many others had icons and frescoes of great skill and insight. The interiors of the domes, which themselves represented heaven, were decorated with enormous, striking images of Christ the Redeemer or Mary the Mother of God, looking down on the earthly congregation below. Rural churches had simpler, more folk-oriented styles. Individual icons, of local patron saints, of the *Bogomater'* (Mary, the mother of God) and the leading church fathers and favourite saints revered by the orthodox church – Grigorii, Vasilii, Afanasii, Ioann Zlatoust (John Chrysostom), Nikolai – embellished columns and side-altars. The walls themselves were usually covered in frescoes of the same range of subjects. But it was not only music and painting which were called upon to testify to the adoration of God. Illuminated manuscripts, books such as the Bible, separate Gospels, manuals for liturgy and so on were essential. These little known artefacts were often produced in a simple folk style far from the detailed depictions and brilliant colour palette of western manuscript artists.[7] Items used in rituals such as incense burners, monstrances, chalices and candle-holders and altar lights, called on the skills of metalworkers, as did the pectoral crosses, rings and other religious objects worn by clergy and faithful alike. The elaborate tunics, stoles, mantles, mitres and other liturgical vestments demanded highly skilled embroiderers and tailors.

Speculatively but plausibly it can be argued that the nature of the Russian Orthodox church and its services made a crucial and long-lasting contribution to the distinctiveness of the Russian soul. In the Russian tradition, faith is transmitted through the beauty of the churches and the rituals rather than through theological argument (though there was plenty of that, too). While the well-known chronicle telling the tale of the reason for the adoption of Christianity as the religion of the early Slavs in 988 may be a mythical retelling of the event rather than a literal account, it does possibly contain a persistent emotional/aesthetic truth. According to the chronicle, delegations were sent to report on the religions of nearby civilizations, Muslims, Jews and both eastern and western branches of Christianity. The Byzantine emperor pulled out all the stops to impress the visitors:

> The emperor sent a message to the patriarch to inform him that a Russian delegation had arrived to examine the Greek faith, and directed him to prepare the church and the clergy, and to array himself in his sacerdotal robes, so that the Russians might behold the glory of the God of the Greeks. When the patriarch received these commands, he bade the clergy assemble, and they performed the customary rites. They burned incense, and the choirs sang hymns. The emperor accompanied the Russians to the church, and placed them in a wide space, calling their attention to the beauty of the edifice, the chanting, and the offices of the archpriest and the ministry of the deacons, while he explained to them the worship of his God. The Russians were astonished, and in their wonder praised the Greek ceremonial.

The Emperor's plan worked. When they returned

> the envoys reported: "When we journeyed among the Bulgars, we beheld how they worship in their temple, called a mosque, while they stand ungirt. The Bulgarian bows, sits down, looks hither and thither like one possessed, and there is no happiness among them, but instead only sorrow and a dreadful stench. Their religion is not good. Then we went among the Germans, and saw them performing many ceremonies in their temples; but we beheld no glory there. Then we went on to Greece, and the Greeks led us to the edifices where they worship their God, and we knew not whether we were in heaven or on earth. For on earth there is

> no such splendour or such beauty, and we are at a loss how to describe it. We know only that God dwells there among men, and their service is fairer than the ceremonies of other nations. For we cannot forget that beauty. Every man, after tasting something sweet, is afterward unwilling to accept that which is bitter, and therefore we cannot dwell longer here."[8]

According to this account the key feature that distinguished the Orthodox religion from Islam and western Christianity (the Germans) was the direct perception of God and heaven through sensual perception of beauty. Indeed, the chroniclers' conclusion that, when they stood in the Cathedral of the Holy Wisdom (Hagia Sophia) in Constantinople, so beautiful was the church, the singing and the ritual that they could not tell if they were in heaven or on earth, affirmed a deep element in Russian culture. Whether the aesthetic uplift was new to the Russians or whether the Orthodox ritual appealed to a pre-existing sensibility cannot be definitively known but a foundation had been laid, or confirmed, which resonates to the present day in Russian culture. Bearing in mind that Russia did not put Christian thinkers like St Augustine of Hippo or St Thomas Aquinas in its main canon and was peripheral to great western forward leaps of reason and individualism in the Reformation, Renaissance and Enlightenment, it can be argued Russian spiritual and intellectual evolution took a very different path from that of its western neighbours.

From 988 and after, Orthodox Christianity, *Pravoslavie* in Russian, which literally means 'praise of truth', became central to Russian culture. Today it is an ideological rock of the Russian state. More broadly 'praising truth', in the form of strenuously defending beliefs and 'truths' and denouncing 'others' as heretics to be, figuratively but sometimes literally, eliminated has been an important dimension of the structure of Russian thought. Russia certainly has no monopoly on intolerance but tolerance and dialogue have often been hard to find in its élite culture. The sense of having a truth to defend rather than seek or construct through reason has shaped religious and secular elements of Russian culture. The marginal impact of the Renaissance and the Enlightenment is perhaps partly attributable to this feature and also accounts for its persistence. As we will see, even the secular intelligentsia was riven with bitter disputes and mutual denunciations which seem to have outdone even their western European counterparts who were themselves no strangers to factionalism.

It was from within the growing institutions of the church that the first glimmerings of an intelligentsia class can be dimly discerned. The artistic and practical skills associated with the church, depicted above, were often acquired by members of the clergy or, more frequently, monks and nuns whose service for God was conducted through producing sacred items or building, maintaining and decorating churches. Thus the men and women who devoted their lives to the church, especially in monasteries and convents, need to be considered briefly for their influence and pioneering role.

As well as being centres for prayer and contemplation Russian monasteries in this period were powerhouses of cultural development and sometimes the advance guard of Russian expansion. Monks sought a life separate from the rest of society and constructed monasteries in more and more inhospitable places in order to cut themselves off from secular life and also from the depredations of the state which sought to tax their enterprise and encroach on their land. Monastic complexes dotted the Russian north from Vologda to the Solovetsky islands in the White Sea, almost within the Arctic Circle. They also spread eastward into the endless forest where they made clearings and built up arable and livestock agriculture and vegetable plots. Monasteries aimed to be self-sufficient and spurred minor economic revolutions in the areas they occupied by changing the landscape and bringing secular labour – free and unfree – in their wake. They also elicited tithes and donations from wealthier supporters and monasteries could become relatively rich, hence the state's desire to tax them and the monks desire to get away from its grasping hands. However, a favourable sovereign might lavish money and privileges on a chosen few convents and monasteries, though successors might eye it greedily and take it back. Monasteries and other ecclesiastical institutions were also great centres of education and learning, amassing libraries (of manuscripts, of course in the early stages) of sacred texts and later of classical and philosophical texts.

The best known of these monastic forerunners of the intelligentsia were three great icon painters – Andrei Rublev, Dionisii and Feofan Grek (Theophanes the Greek). They stand out, not only because their names have come down to us, but also because their painting had distinguishing qualities elevating their work above the norms of the time. Much of the knowledge, culture and skills of this period were based on rote learning and repetition of skills. These three icon painters were especially adept at adding a personal style and personal touches to the accepted canon. More spectacular and personal choice of colours, greater delicacy of line and form and deeper spiritual content made their work distinctive. They were much sought-after in their day and admired down to the present. Very little is known about them personally but their story begins with Feofan. He arrived in Novgorod from his home city of Constantinople in 1370 when he was about thirty or forty years old. He painted the frescoes in the cathedral, among many other items, although precise attributions are disputed. Critics have pointed out that his use of relatively few and darker, earthy colours – green, brown, yellow – stood out and were indicative of a growing sense of individual influence beginning to emerge. He was also noted for his philosophical knowledge and for applying new, more complex thought to his icons. One critic put it very succinctly:

> Theophanes was described by the Muscovites as "learned in philosophy", a reflection on his broad education and erudition. A hint of this might be gathered from his panel icon of the Transfiguration of Jesus, where the arresting geometry and brilliance of the figure of Christ is balanced against the ordered disarray of the earthbound Apostles, strewn about doll-like in the uncreated Light of Mount Tabor. The balance of mathematical harmony in line and shape, wed to a master's use of an earthtone palette and precious gold leaf, evokes a spirituality that is immensely powerful, and speaks to the genius of this relatively unknown painter.[9]

Though his style was very different, Andrei Rublev was a pupil of Feofan who, together with his associate and friend Danil Chorny, further revolutionized icon painting by introducing more personal elements. For example, Rublev did not use the 'dull' colour palette of Feofan but turned to white, red, bright blue and gold. He also developed the depiction of near-translucent veils and haloes and he elongated figures more than was usual, a feature conventionally emphasizing their spirituality. He followed Feofan in depicting full-length figures in the main section of his separate icons.[10] The tradition was continued by Dionisii (1440/50-1503/08) and his sons. He was also an indicator of changing times in that he was the first secular icon painter. He painted many icons and frescoes. His best-known work was a large series of commissions at the Joseph–Volokolamsk Monastery and at Beloozero and the Nativity Cathedral of Ferapontovo Monastery.

Joseph of Volokolamsk (also known as Joseph Volotsky) has one more claim to our attention. As is quite common elsewhere, monasticism in Russia was subject to cycles of strict discipline which might slacken over the decades towards laxity in various degrees followed by zealots who aimed to restore discipline. Joseph was devoted to restoring monastic order in the church. So was another monk Nil Sorsky. The problem was that each of them had a different approach. Sorsky wanted to establish the pre-eminence of spiritual values and divest the monasteries of much of their material and practical dimensions. This meant, among other things, abandoning their land. By some calculations the monasteries between them owned a third of the land in Muscovy. Much of it was from patrons, some of whom were wealthy landowners who donated whole villages (including their serfs) to a chosen monastery. Sorsky and his supporters became known as the 'non-possessors (*nestiazhateli*)'. The opposition to Sorsky was led by Joseph of Volokolamsk who defended the self-sufficiency of monasteries and wanted to revive spiritual devotion through veneration of material objects like icons such as the works of Dionisii and by devoting practical talents to the service of God.[11]

The precise details of the struggle, in which Joseph prevailed at the Church Council (*Sobor*) of 1503, need not detain us here but we might note that the debate showed new kinds of thinking, a debate between the spiritual and the material and a winner-takes-all mentality which were to be found in Russian thought and socio-political practice and theory centuries later. Joseph and Sorsky were not social and political critics, though Joseph did defend the concept of a tsar, a title used more frequently as the Grand Prince of Muscovy increasingly asserted his primacy over the princes of the other city-states. Joseph asserted that while the ruler was a man, his power came from God and his authority was only legitimate insofar as the tsar adhered to Christian principles. Like serfdom, the entanglement of religion and the state was growing at a time when, in western Europe, the opposite was happening. Serfdom was disappearing and the first signs of conflict and separation were appearing and rulers were taking control of churches after the beginning of the Reformation in 1517. In Russia, serfdom was only finally abolished in 1861 and the entanglement of church and state, creating what even twentieth-century critics called a theocracy,[12] was a key feature in Russia until 1917, although, in 1721, Peter the Great amalgamated church and state on the state's terms by abolishing the office of patriarch, the head of the church, and adding it to the powers of the autocrat.

Before moving on from these early forerunners of the intelligentsia, the achievements of one more remarkable figure, a follower and supporter of Joseph, need to be considered for a moment. Makarii (1482–1563), the Metropolitan (Archbishop) of Moscow, was a remarkable polymathic figure. He is one of the earliest known authors of Russian books and a founder of Russian historiography, who wrote the twelve volumes of lives of the Russian saints known as the *Great Menaion Reader*. He also, astutely, worked on a genealogy of Ivan the Terrible, known as the *Stepenaiai kniga* or *The Book of Degrees of the Royal Genealogy*, conveniently tracing his lineage, with a little help from the imagination, back to a fictitious brother of Caesar Augustus. He was a supporter of the first Russian printing press and contributed to the chronicle of his era, *Chronicle of the Beginning of Tsardom of Tsar and Grand Prince Ivan Vasiliyevich* (that is Ivan IV, or Ivan the Terrible). It was a time of great political intrigue and of cultural and imperial self-assertion and Makarii was at the heart of it all. He even acted as regent, minding the shop while Ivan was away on his campaign against Kazan'. In political life he was noted for a rather rare ability to reconcile conflicting factions. Makarii also assisted in the painting of St Basil's Cathedral in Red Square (he is believed to have already painted icons in his former bishopric of Novgorod). In his later years he stepped back from politics and devoted himself to more writing and cultural activities such as support for the first Russian publishing house The Moscow Print Yard established in 1553 by Ivan Fyodorov in the Kitai gorod area of central Moscow. In particular, the new technique had to be defended against manuscript writers and illustrators whose way of life was threatened by the new technology. While it is hard to know exactly how many of these achievements were his and how much they were exaggerated by admirers and aided by subordinates, it is clear that Makarii was man of many talents and of great vision and an important author and defender of nascent print culture. Clearly he had characteristics which would later resemble those of the modern intelligentsia.

By the end of the sixteenth century, while there was certainly no intelligentsia in the modern sense, the knowledge and skills base of Russian society was getting ever more complex. Lasting characteristics of the Russian state – authoritarianism; autocracy; militarization; entanglement with the church and the Christian religion; expansion; great cultural achievements – were already asserting themselves. In the cultural sphere, an orthodoxy versus heresy mentality was developing and much elite culture was still tied in to religion. Renaissance humanism was not an influence, nor was the developing individualism of the west. Nonetheless, religion, with its close association with the existential questions of life, death and meaning, was beginning to prise open the post-Mongol Russian mind and to shape the foundations of the 'Russian Soul'. Russia was embarked on its own journey of intellectual and cultural development.

2

Encountering reason, science and the secular

The Muscovite foundation of Russian culture proved robust and enduring, surviving, in part at least, to the present. But the paradox was that, despite having its origins in a dialogue between Russian and Mongol elements, the more successful it became the more it expanded and expansion brought it into greater and greater contact with more diverse influences. As the Mongols retreated eastward, so Muscovy began to exert its power in more northerly, westerly and southerly directions. Our current purpose is to trace the history of the intelligentsia, not to produce a comprehensive cultural history of Russia, though the two are obviously intertwined. There are, however, a number of features of the period between the initial emancipation of Muscovy and the emergence of a modern intelligentsia which need to be noted.

After its enforced and defining interaction with the Mongols, Muscovy's most important outside connection was with Constantinople, until its fall in 1453, and Mount Athos as the spiritual powerhouse of Orthodox Christianity. They, in turn, had greater interaction with western Christianity, obviously Catholicism up to 1517 and Protestantism as well, as the Reformation evolved. Prelates and others of Greek origin (we have already met the influential icon painter Feofan) had already migrated to Russia and several church leaders and patriarchs were Greek by birth. Successive waves of refugees from advancing Islam fled Bulgaria and Serbia and sought shelter in Moscow. More important links with the Protestant world followed on from Muscovy's northern advance. In 1478 it overcame its rival, Novgorod, which had proved itself a wily trading city which had appeased the Mongols without a fight, thereby saving the city from destruction. Situated away from the coast but on the Baltic trade route which penetrated Russia by its great river systems, it formed links with the Germanic Hanseatic League and even had a significant Hanseatic quarter on the opposite bank of the river from the Russian city. Thus, it had close links not only with North European trade but also technology and ideas. When Moscow took over, on its journey to becoming Russia, it inherited and profited from these links.

However, the most important entanglement in the North and West was with Poland and its associated state, Lithuania. Both were strongly Catholic and imbued with the spirit of counterreformation Catholicism. Briefly, Poland/Lithuania challenged the very existence of Russia at the turn of the sixteenth and seventeenth centuries. The outcome was, essentially for the first time, the embroilment of Russia in the political and cultural processes of central and western Europe. Though its situation is often overlooked, Russia was a major participant in the seventeenth-century religious wars.

It was, despite not having a reformation as such, also part of the political revolution of the seventeenth century which saw titanic struggles between church and state resulting in the emergence of the inaccurately named secular state. The dynastic states of the era, Russia above all, were far from secular but, in various ways, they all underwent a transition in which the church no longer claimed authority over the sovereign. The original Muscovy, a society permeated with religion promoted by a religious state, foundered on this emerging rock. At the beginning of the seventeenth century, under threat of invasion by the militantly imperialist Catholic Polish-Lithuanian Commonwealth, Russia collapsed into a Time of Troubles (1598–1613) during which the very survival of Russia was at stake. The Romanov dynasty, which came to power in 1613, began a process of re-assertion of the Russian state. Disputes shook the church and church and state came into conflict themselves in the latter part of the century. The high point of the church/state conflict came in 1721 when Peter I (the Great) (1672–1725) abolished the Patriarchate which, ironically, was only revived in the first weeks of Bolshevik power in 1917, when the new, militantly atheist, authorities were not sufficiently established to do anything about it, or even to see it as a priority. Although severely persecuted in the 1920s and 1930s, the Patriarchate remained in existence throughout the Soviet era, even though the position was effectively vacant from 1925 to 1943. Nonetheless, Patriarch Sergius was brought into political play to assist with the war effort in 1943–5. The celebration of the millennium of Christianity in Russia in 1988 was warmly supported by the last Soviet leader, Mikhail Gorbachev, and the church once again, as we shall see, played a significant role in Russian cultural and political life. Secularism is not the right term to describe the Russian situation then or now. This aspect of the Muscovite foundation remained.

Although less extensive than other interactions it should be noted that the complex intertwining of Jewish and Russian cultures was a significant feature of the Muscovite period. Contact with ancient Jewish communities in Crimea and the Caucasus brought the all-too-frequent cycling of relations between occasional fruitful dialogue, near-permanent confrontation and outbursts of violent anti-semitism. The expulsion of Jews from Spain brought many refugees into the Slavic world and Eastern Poland and Western Russia became the main centre of world Jewish life and culture. The dominant anti-semitic response from the Slavic population has, according to some historians, notably James Billington,[1] served to conceal a significant Jewish contribution to the formation of early Russian culture, traceable in a few loan words but, especially in the post-Mongol period, in a popular tradition of Old Testament apocalypticism, expressed in an outburst of sectarianism, and messianic expectation, culminating in the well-known concept of Moscow as the Third Rome, a Russian equivalent to being a Chosen People.

The growing multiplication of contacts and the religious and practical challenges they brought meant that Late Muscovy was the scene of vibrant and often bitter intellectual disputes, normally expressed in the theological language of the era. For the first time, following Nil Sorsky and Joseph of Volokolamsk, individual theologians and religious thinker/prophets engaged in scholarly intellectual debates on key issues of faith and Russian identity. Identifiable individuals emerged as did new means of communication, notably printed books and libraries.

A few examples can give the flavour of these discussions. Often, behind the forbidding theological terminology there lay concealed debates about social and personal issues. Take, for example, the debate about hesychasm. The word itself means 'stillness' or 'tranquility' and can be roughly compared to the notion of 'meditation'. Like their near-contemporary Protestants in the west, the hesychasts, with Nil Sorsky in the forefront, argued that God could be perceived directly, from inner silence and contemplation, as well as through the increasingly lengthy and elaborate rituals of the Orthodox eucharist and so on. The discussion became entrenched and the two schools went on side by side. It is no coincidence that even on the cusp of the twentieth century Tolstoy could tell us that *The Kingdom of God Is within You.*[2] Also, at almost the same time, a group of intellectuals argued that the intelligentsia would serve the people best by pursuing self-perfection rather than social and institutional redemption. Echoes of the division can be found throughout the intellectual history of Russia.

Foreign influences were often channelled through key individuals, not least in the case of Greek and Renaissance contacts. Maxim the Greek (1470–1556) embodied both. Born and brought up in western Greece he studied in Italy and retired to Mount Athos for a life of study and contemplation. He was plucked from his monastic cocoon by a summons to Moscow where he spent the last thirty-eight years of his life, contributing to and presiding over great religious/cultural/intellectual endeavours. He had been called to translate classical and other texts into Russian but he added many commentaries of his own, bringing the sceptical eye of the Renaissance humanist to bear on the Muscovite church's superstitions, scholasticism and inaccuracy in its translations of sacred texts. In their place, Maxim preached the importance of God-given reason rather than fanaticism and sided with the non-possessors and hesychasts. He urged repentance on the wealthy and compassion for the poor, though he was no critic of the social order itself. Rather, each person needed to pursue personal moral perfection and use that to play their allotted social role justly. In Maxim, the concept of reason made its first serious inroads into the thinking of the Russian elite. One of his followers, Ermolai-Erazm (*c.*1505–50), was more radical in that he produced a book, whose indicative title showed that he was modestly producing a *Guide for the Government of the State and the Measurement of Land, for the Well-wishing Tsar* (1549). In it, he proposed a perfected social order based on freeing peasants from their tax burdens, promoting land reform and instituting the reign of a natural peasant-based economy and Christian love.[3] While there is no suggestion Ermolai was aware of it, Thomas More's *Utopia* had been published in 1516. It might be stretching too far to suggest Ermolai was the founder of Russian social criticism, but his work was clear evidence that Russian thought was opening up this dimension.

Ermolai had been preceded by the lay merchant, Afanasy Nikitin (1433–72) who, in *Journey beyond Three Seas*,[4] described his travels in the Middle East and India between 1466 and 1472. His account was only the second European description of India. Among other things he came up with the view that all the great religions were equal and related to the same God. While Nikitin did not offer consistent proposals for social re-organization, his outlook bears testimony to a new critical and rational spirit being focused on questions of traditional religion and also on society. He commented widely on the institutions, behaviours, economic practices and governing systems he came across. He was no sceptic or rationalist, let alone atheist, but his thought was a significant break with acceptance of traditional dogmatism. Trade, travel and increasing international contact were stimulating new ideas and comparisons.

While the religious framework of Russian thought and culture was creaking, it still had a long way to go. The time after Ivan IV became increasingly chaotic. Already, Catholic influence had peaked when his grandmother, Sophia Palaiologina (1449–1503), a member of the fallen ruling family of Byzantium who had been brought up in Rome under the personal supervision of Pope Sixtus IV, became Ivan III's second wife in 1472 after a long negotiation. Papal hopes of a Roman Catholic breakthrough were dashed when Sophia, a redoubtable and influential figure who refused to be confined to the women's quarter (the terem) of the Kremlin, quickly asserted her commitment to Orthodoxy rather than Catholicism. She also appears to have modified the protocol of the Russian court along Byzantine lines to make it appropriate for the ruler of the Third Rome. Nonetheless, she was a formidable conduit of a modified westernization, perhaps best symbolized by the fact that the most quintessential of Muscovite buildings in Moscow, the Kremlin wall and two of its cathedrals, were built in this era by Italian Renaissance architects. A Latin inscription on the Spassky Tower gives the name of its chief constructor Petrus Antonius Solarius. Marcus Ruffus designed the Tsar's new palace within the walls. In this way, the new parts of the Kremlin represent a new fusion of Latin and Muscovite influences blending western expertise with Muscovite style. Muscovy was no longer in thrall to its neighbours but was dealing with them on a more equal basis. By the time the construction of the stunningly unique St Basil's Cathedral began in 1555, German skills and Italian styles were incorporated as a matter of course and English craftsmen may also have been involved, though little is known about its architects. It was consecrated in 1561. Although the dominant influence and style were obviously Muscovite this astonishing building was a tribute to the fruitfulness of collaboration and dialogue between Russia and its western neighbours. Under Ivan IV and Alexis in particular, the inward absorption of western ideas, technologies and military and government practices, continued apace. Political disruption and Polish/Lithuanian invasion both halted the process and stimulated it. Not for the first or last time Russia learned from its invaders, not least how to overcome them.

The last major Muscovite upheaval came in the late seventeenth century and produced the Great Schism in the Orthodox church. Two great figures in the old Muscovite tradition, Patriarch Nikon (1605–81) and Archpriest Avvakum (1620/21–82), confronted each other with charges of heresy. The story of the Great Schism has been told many times and this is not the place to rehearse it in full once more. It does, however, have implications for our story and we will focus on them. The underlying cause of the dispute was a conflict between the attempts of Patriarch Nikon to follow the efforts of predecessors such as Maxim to tidy up errors and anomalies in Orthodox texts and rituals.

Two themes stand out for us from the dispute. First, though neither protagonist could be considered to be a scholar or intellectual, the issue was partly precipitated by books and certainly focused around them. Nikon's reforms were encapsulated, in the years 1655–9, in correcting errors in a new psalter (a book of psalms and other liturgical materials) and the production of new service books. This was at the heart of the process to which Avvakum objected on the grounds that it was innovatory and thereby weakened the truth of faith and was also indirectly the outcome of foreign influence. Nikon, no less than Avvakum, was opposed to foreign, notably Catholic, influence and other books of the period, notably the *Book of the One True and Orthodox Faith* (1648) asserted a strongly Orthodox line by, respectively, engaging in bitter polemic against Jews and Uniates (an orthodox splinter group which acknowledged papal authority but retained orthodox practices). However, a more ambiguous figure is cut by Metropolitan Peter Mogila whose *Catechism* (1649) and *The Helmsman's Handbook (Kormchaia kniga)* (1650) were also published at this time. The former provided a manual for the instruction of the faithful and the latter was a systematizing of canon law.[5] Mogila (Mohyla in Ukrainian) (1596–1647) was Metropolitan (Archbishop) of Kyiv and Halich who wrote a number of influential works. His *Catechism* was adopted by many Orthodox patriarchates. A text in Latin from the Vatican archives, apparently by him, was first published in 1928. In it he acknowledges his own acceptance of papal supremacy and proposes a plan for bringing the eastern and western branches of Christianity back together. His sympathy, or at least ambiguity, towards Uniates has led some leading church historians, notably George Florovosky, to see him as a pioneering westernizer.[6] He has become a figure against whom harsh polemics have been targeted in current Orthodox theological wars.

The second theme was that, following on from the powerful Patriarch Philaret, Nikon supported the Muscovite idea of a shared reign by Tsar and Patriarch. Under the personal influence of the striking personality of Nikon, the young Tsar Alexis was enthralled and even put Nikon in charge when he was away waging war. All the more surprising that the two should part ways in 1657. After several snubs on administrative issues in 1658 one of the tsar's officials physically assaulted Nikon's representative at court. Nikon awaited an apology from the tsar which never came. In protest, Nikon withdrew to his newly founded monastery of New Jerusalem on the outskirts of Moscow. He remained there for eight years. The eventual summons from Alexis which Nikon was awaiting was not the one he had hoped for. In 1668 he was called to face the Church Council of 1667–8, which deposed him and banished him to Ferapontovo Monastery in the distant North. The main cause of his downfall was his continuing insistence on the power of the church within the state. Alexis, whose reign was characterized not only by war in the west with Poland but also continued import of knowledge and skills, had come round to a clear assertion of the supremacy of state power over the church. Though not formally connected, this mirrored the emerging practice in western Europe and the conclusion of the Thirty Years' War in the Treaty of Westphalia in 1648 which supported the right of the Sovereign to choose the official religion of the country. Russia did not, however, follow the second major principle of Westphalia, that all other non-official denominations of Christianity should be tolerated. The Pope's vehement condemnation of the treaty as 'null, void, invalid, iniquitous, unjust, damnable, reprobate, inane, empty of meaning and effect for all time' could well have been uttered by Nikon in the face of his defeat.

However, Nikon's banishment did not mean the victory of Avvakum and his followers who took a more fundamentalist line and rejected most of Nikon's liturgical and ritual reforms. In a supreme irony, in 1667 the same council that condemned

Nikon affirmed most of his changes. It also condemned Avvakum and banished him to a distant monastery. While, eventually, Nikon was partially pardoned and allowed to return to New Jerusalem when he was dying in 1681 (though he actually died on the journey), Avvakum spent the last fourteen years of his life imprisoned in a zemlianka (a dugout dwelling with a straw roof) and was burned at the stake in 1682. Avvakum's resistance to the new ways of doing things did not die with him and he left a legacy of followers who came to be known as Old Believers, communities of which survive down to the present, often in the areas to which they had fled to avoid persecution. They were particularly prominent among the traditional merchants of Moscow and Nizhnyi Novgorod.

Both sides were, in an important sense, defeated. The winner was the tsarist state. Both sides represented a Muscovite approach and, indeed, the differences were about what was rightfully Muscovite. Instead, the state condemned both men and asserted its own authority. In that respect a form of westernization was victorious. Alexis was a proponent of cultural borrowing and his eventual successor, Peter the Great (1672–1725), has become a byword for westernization of Russia's government, its military and the landed elite. The founding of the 'window on the west', St Petersburg in 1703, is the best-known symbol but, in many ways, his suppression of the office of Patriarch, in 1721, was more startling. The state took firm hold of church administration so that even in the early twentieth century, one prominent intellectual described the autocracy as a form of theocracy in which the temporal power had usurped the spiritual power.[7] But while the Muscovite principle was seriously weakened it was far from dead and it has remained as a component of Russian culture down to the present, but its dominance was definitively over.

The enlightenment and the emergence of the first Russian intellectuals

By the eighteenth century Russia was, in many but by no means all respects, in a very different intellectual and cultural place from the Principality which had fought off the Mongols. The elite had been socially transformed and even had a radically different physical appearance as the court style of Versailles became the Romanov norm. The architecture of St Petersburg would not have been out of place anywhere in the Baltic, or even much of the rest of Europe. The knowledge base of society had expanded exponentially in terms of practical skills, and seamanship and a navy had become integrated into the state structure. Proto-industrial processes and the first modern factories began to appear, unsurprisingly associated in large part with armaments. The Tula Arms Factory was founded by Peter in 1712 and, as well as being Russia's leading producer of guns, cannon and swords, it was consistently one of the most technically advanced factories in Russia and one of the most important in the world. Culturally, the élite spoke French and German as easily as Russian. As we shall see, intellectual debate, for the secular (i.e. those not in holy orders but not necessarily non-religious) educated class, revolved around the same themes as in western Europe whose influence continued to flow in. It should, of course, be noted that the entity described as 'the west' was itself in the process of transforming itself through the Enlightenment and the proto-industrial revolution. Global trade and science were having deep impacts. Reason, scepticism and cultural relativism were increasingly influential.

As far as Russia is concerned, it would be easy to overestimate the degree of change. As Russian cities went, St Petersburg was a complete anomaly. Many other towns and cities still comprised mostly traditional wooden buildings. In any case, the urban population was only about 7 per cent of an estimated total of 14 million. Provincial and rural Russia remained very traditional. Large landowners modernized their style and even language, especially if they were accepted at the royal court, and lesser gentry aped their style but the mass of the population remained little changed. Serfdom held sway throughout the eighteenth and first half of the nineteenth centuries. The peasants, whose skill and labour were crucial to the survival of the élite, remained repressed and farmed in the traditional manner. The Orthodox church remained central to rural (and urban) life and a multitude of religious festivals punctuated the working year. The peasant commune remained strong in most parts of European Russia. Peasants were not inert. Large-scale rebellions occurred, often in support of supposedly legitimate claimants to the throne who were fighting against the supposedly usurping incumbent. Such was the case for supporters of the 'false Dmitrii' during the Time of Troubles (1598–1613) and in the revolts of Stenka Razin (1670–71) and, perhaps the most threatening, that of Pugachev in 1785. They showed not only the potential rebelliousness of a severely oppressed class but also the curious amalgam of legitimacy and revolt which characterized peasant action at least down to the abolition of serfdom. This mixture has often led observers to consider peasants to be 'conservative', but if conservatism can lead to uprising it would appear to be the wrong term. Peasant culture was itself vivid and deeply rooted. Styles of izba (wooden village house) construction only evolved slowly. The religious icon corner was ubiquitous. Similar clothing styles were reproduced from generation to generation. Pagan, animist songs and tales of water sprites and shape-shifting animals and trees, of drowned cities and miraculous past kingdoms were passed down. Choral and solo singing were ubiquitous. Traditional musical instruments that might be heard among urban workers and peasants included stringed instruments such as the balalaika, domra and the ancient gusli; the bayan, a kind of accordion, and improvised items equivalent of washboards, wooden spoons and various forms of tambourine. The *skomorokh* tradition was weak but, from the eighteenth century, fairground booths (*balagany*) began to circulate with singers and other performers. The peasants and urban poor remain exceptions to our story of transformation. The pace of change in the village was much slower.

However, it should not be passed over that peasants often were drawn to an increasing number of religious sects in these years. Ironically, these apparently characteristically Russian groups were given a major stimulus from the radical reformation in the west. A German sectarian, Quirinus Kuhlmann (1651–89), transferred his fading hopes of a radical reformation in Germany and western Europe to Russia. He travelled there in April 1689 to persuade Tsar Ivan V to join his hoped for alliance of Protestant powers and the Ottomans to destroy Catholicism once and for all and establish the reign of Jesus. Not only did he fail to persuade, he was denounced by a Lutheran cleric in the

German Quarter of Moscow, arrested and burned at the stake as a heretic on 4 October. Despite the brevity of his visit he did spread knowledge of his own writings and those of Jacob Boehme whose influence was also felt among Russian intellectuals 200 years later. Sectarianism and millenarianism, with or without Kuhlmann, flourished among parts of the peasantry. While the peasantry lived a life very different from that of the élite, they did become important in the formulation of the early generations of the intelligentsia itself in the mid-nineteenth century. Their culture increasingly impinged on that of the intelligentsia. Much of that, however, lay well into the future and we will return to the peasantry later.

Peter's suppression of the patriarchate was a symbolic cultural act of the greatest importance. A second, equally significant action, was the founding, in 1724, of the St Petersburg Academy of Sciences. It went through a number of changes of name but, in essence, it has survived to the present day and, from its foundation, it has been a key institution in the formation of the scientific, technical and academic intelligentsia of Russia. It was the Trojan Horse which smuggled western Enlightenment rationalism and science into eighteenth-century Russia. Although Peter died before the Academy was actually set up, it was, in many ways improbably, a part of his reforms. Peter himself had no claims to being an intellectual. Like many of his successors he was more inclined to the active and the practical than to reflection and philosophical analysis. He was, famously, the man who taught Russians to sail and this is a practical skill which calls upon numerous additional requirements such as marine architecture based on calculations of buoyancy and dealing with a wide range of weather phenomena, and navigation which was based on astronomical observation and measurement and mathematical calculation. The last two became major elements in the new academy and have remained deeply etched in Russian science down to the present, notably in the form of the space programme.

Commerce and the military also needed better geographical, geological, biological and botanical knowledge. Since the seventeenth century science, commerce and the military had formed close attachments to one another. The immediate foundation of the Russian Academy, however, was Peter the Great's interest in the freakish, the bizarre and the exotic and unusual. He had, as one historian puts it, a 'disturbing' by modern standards fascination with little people, who were gathered together at court to provide amusement for average height guests and the colossal 6'7" tsar.[8] He also had a collection of curiosities. One part was made up of malformed animal and human foetuses from all over Russia, displayed to disprove superstitious theories of monsters and show that deformities were nothing more than accidents of nature. His agents also acquired collections of gemstones and other rocks and minerals and scientific equipment from several private collectors in Danzig and Amsterdam. A building was constructed for these collections on the banks of the Neva in the new capital of St Petersburg and the new museum was called the Kunstkammer, a term of Dutch origin meaning Art Room or Hall. It was completed in 1727. The museum still exists today and has some 2,000,000, mostly anthropological, items in its collection. It was closely intertwined with the emerging Academy and their histories remained interconnected. For a while, in Soviet times, they were merged but the museum regained its full independence in 1992.

From its early days the Academy took on features which it retained even down to the present day in some cases. It had very strong links with foreign scholars, especially German and Dutch with a sprinkling of British and French. Originally there were three main directions of research, mathematical, physical (natural science) and humanities. 'As it expanded (it) soon included the scientific and cultural riches of the country' including the holdings of the Kunstkammer. It added an anatomical theatre, a Geography department, an astronomical observatory, Physics and Mineralogical workrooms (*kabinety*), a Botanical garden and an equipment workshop.[9] Although it expanded steadily over the next three centuries to the present, the title of 'Academician' was reserved for only a small number of stellar achievers. There were fifteen at the outset, all non-Russian, and by 1918 there were still only forty-five, though there was an explosion of membership in the Stalin years. It quickly became an integral part of European scholarship, providing a nurturing ground for great foreign scientists, including the leading mathematician of the era, L. Eiler, who founded a brilliant tradition of mathematical thought in Russia. It also made Europe aware of great Russian scholars, like the polymath Mikhail Lomonosov, in the middle of the eighteenth century. The peak of early internationalization came in 1761 when a team, including Lomonosov, and British and French participants, collaborated in observing the transit of Venus across the face of the sun from a variety of points around the globe. There was already a practice of setting up expeditions to extend knowledge of the geology, topography, flora and fauna and so on of undocumented areas of the Russian Empire and some of its neighbours. One major result was the completion of the first comprehensive map of the country, published in 1745 as the *Russian Atlas*.[10]

It should be noted that a major driver of the Academy's research was practical application. Academy scientists provided, according to one authoritative account, 'the bases for mining, metalworking and other branches of Russian industry'.[11] By the middle years of the eighteenth century the Academy had developed its own press and publications which included items on medicine, history, natural sciences and the arts including plays, opera and literature. In 1747 it was renamed the Imperial Academy of Sciences and the Arts. The latter categories were strengthened by the founding in 1785 of a completely separate Russian Academy which focused on language, linguistics and literature which eventually merged with the broader institution in 1841. The development of a more educated civil society elite was indicated by the development of versions of the academy's activities and publications directed at the non-specialist and, from 1785 to1802, public lectures on scholarly and scientific topics in St Petersburg.[12] These lectures were given in Russian. Early publications had been in Latin, the lingua franca of European scholarship at that time. Indicative of the developments of the age, the first scientific treatise published in Russian was *Writings on the Land of Kamchatka* by the first Russian Academician, S.P. Krasheninnikov (1711–55), appointed as an adjunct in 1745. It also symbolizes the moment in that Krasheninnikov had been part of Vitus Bering's second Kamchatka expedition. Bering himself was a Dutch citizen by birth working in the service of the Russian Navy. Despite having been long preceded in entering the strait that now bears his name by a Russian named Simon Dezhnev in 1648 and by another, Mikhail Gvozdev in 1732, with the latter being the first Russian to cross the strait and sight the west coast of the American mainland, it was Bering whose name was chosen by Captain Cook to designate the area and also several of its features, including the island where Bering died and was buried. Many of the findings of these expeditions were kept as closely guarded secrets, another reminder that military and state power was increasingly entwined with modern scholarship and science.

Imperial patronage was important to these developments. Few of the tsars of the eighteenth century had intellectual or artistic inclinations but it was a happy accident that the most influential ruler of the time, Catherine the Great, did. Like many of the leading lights in the Academy, she was German and brought her western heritage intact into the business of governing her empire. It is well known that she corresponded with Voltaire, assuring him, among other things, that Russian serfs were well looked after and ate chicken every day. As is also well known she constructed model villages to demonstrate the fact to foreigners. Ever since, foreign visitors to Russia who deviate from the normative, often russophobic, discourse, have been accused of being deceived by similar ploys in the tsarist, Soviet and even Post-soviet period where they have the added accolade of being 'useful idiots'. In fact, few foreigners were deceived in such a crude way. Catherine built up a persona of being an up-to-date and modern reforming ruler in line with continental standards. The ruthless suppression of the Pugachev rebellion in 1784 and the grisly fate of Pugachev himself, who was brought to Moscow in a cage in 1785, and displayed in public before being decapitated, drawn and quartered, suggested older cultures still lurked beneath the modern western veneer. Confirmation that a Voltairean reign of reason was far away came when the French revolution broke out and new, rationalist ideas were blamed by many for its occurrence. Catherine turned away from dabbling with them and returned to the good old instruments of repression. But this was not only a turning-point for Catherine, the moment also marked what is often seen as the birth of the critical intelligentsia. In particular, two individuals are seen as its forerunners, its storm petrels. They are N.I. Novikov (1744–1818) and Alexander Radishchev (1749–1802).

Novikov and Radishchev differed from earlier forerunners of the intelligentsia because of the obvious influence on them of the enlightenment and of western, especially German, philosophy. Indeed, Radishchev's book *On Man, His Mortality, His Immortality* was considered to be one of Russia's pioneering philosophical texts. Later scrutiny has suggested that it contained a good deal of paraphrase from Herder, the immensely influential German theologian and philosopher.[13] That, of course, confirms the influence. But it is not this text that Radishchev's admirers consider to be the one which stakes his claim to be the first *intelligent*.[14] That honour is reserved for a remarkable journey he made and the observations it gave rise to. As we have seen, scientific expeditions to Kamchatka and Alaska were a feature of Russian science/exploration/imperialism, but Radishchev's expedition was not in pursuit of any transit of Venus. Its title was self-explanatory. It was simply a *Journey from Saint Petersburg to Moscow* a mundane, non-exotic voyage undertaken by thousands of his contemporaries.[15] It is suggested that this helped it pass the lethargic censors of the day who thought it was a guidebook and passed it without reading it. In actual fact, the book is not based on an actual single journey but consists of stories, anecdotes and observations gathered together in St Petersburg over several years. What made it so distinctive was that it brought Radishchev into the purview of the Empress who, in horror at what she saw, not only decreed his arrest but described him as a 'worse rebel than Pugachev'? Nearly all copies of his book were gathered up and pulped. It was banned by the tsarist regime until the collapse of censorship in 1905 though it was widely known and circulated unofficially as one of Russia's prototype examples of *samizdat*.[16] Radishchev's main 'offence' was to have given a frank account of what he saw and what was actually happening in the Russian countryside. In particular, his book gently exploded myths of happy serfs and unexploited peasants. Reading his text today it seems very mild. It is no political manifesto. It does not contain any denunciations of authority. It is not even a sounding board for peasant diatribes against their situation or against their landowners. What it does portray, unequivocally, is the massive inequality he found in the Russian countryside. Members of his own class lived leisured, westernized, lives. Their peasants lived lives of unremitting labour. In one case, Radishchev recounts an encounter with a peasant busy with harvest who, uncomplainingly, explained that he worked sixteen hours a day at that time of year to maintain a meagre living standard for himself and his family. Radishchev was not shouting from the rooftops. Quite the opposite. But he had made a fatal transgression of a kind that got others into trouble later. He had treated the serfs as human beings. He had drawn attention to their plight. But there was one phrase in particular that later intellectuals considered the founding moment of the intelligentsia. His motivation for undertaking the trip was that 'I looked around me – my soul was wounded by the suffering of humanity.' This simple formulation resounded for over a century and was considered by Berdyaev to be the moment of birth of the Russian intelligentsia. Radishchev was arrested in 1790, the year his book was published. He was sentenced to death but this was commuted to ten years of Siberian exile. He served six, during which he studied Herder and produced his book *On Man, His Mortality, His Immortality* before being freed and allowed to return to the capital.

Nikolai Novikov was also steeped in the western European Enlightenment. Novikov's contribution was very different. Habermas has pointed out that in late-eighteenth-century Europe what he terms a 'public sphere' arose in which educated individuals began to communicate with each other without the intervention of state or church. Coffee houses, newspapers, journals, books, libraries, archive collections, secular schools built up. Novikov, though he came from a military family and set out on a military career himself, was heavily involved in bringing all these things to Russia, or to St Petersburg to be precise. He edited journals, promoted publishing projects, set up schools, brought together an important archive of Old Russia. He was a founder of Russian journalism. He, too, eventually fell foul of the empress and was consigned to fifteen years in the Schlüsselberg Fortress near the capital, one of the first of many distinguished social critics who were sent there in the next century and beyond.

Why had thinking critical minds like those of Novikov and Radishchev fallen so far from Catherine's favour? The answer is simple: the French Revolution had broken out. Catherine had terminated her political and intellectual flirtations with Voltaire and come to believe the spread of enlightenment principles had undermined the French *ancien régime* and she was not going to take the same chances. She transited from promoter of ideas to persecutor, setting a precedent that even today's Russian leadership has not thrown off. For the remainder of her reign and that of her successor, the emerging public sphere was stifled and traditional ideas were mobilized in the dominant feature of the next twenty years, the struggle against the French Revolution and Napoleon.

Before moving into the nineteenth century there are several points about the earlier period which we need to note. Despite being heavily influenced by western rationalism, both Radishchev and Novikov retained a religious-mystical dimension in their intellectual world. In a way echoing earlier German sectarianism, Novikov was heavily influenced by the esoteric mystical movements of Rosicrucianism, Martinism and Freemasonry. He also had an interest in alchemy and gathered together the sources in the Hermeneutic Library. Radishchev also combined rationalism with a fascination with the metaphysical as the title of his philosophical work indicates. The concept of immortality was in the centre of his focus. Neither of the pair was religious in the conventional sense, but like Russian predecessors (and other enlightenment thinkers) they did not make a full break with religion and were not atheists.

One of the most unpredictable twists in Radishchev's life was that in 1801 the new tsar, Alexander II, appointed him to a royal commission to study reform of Russian law and constitution. This reminds us that, although in Soviet times he was a designated 'forerunner of Bolshevism' and his *Journey* was widely available and taught in schools, Radishchev and Novikov were no revolutionaries. The dividing line between state officials like them who were involved in commissions for reform and unacceptable (to the authorities of the time) radicalism was very fine. Traditionally, bureaucratic reformers of the late eighteenth and nineteenth centuries are not considered to be true members of the intelligentsia but they were, at least, second cousins. They were also intellectuals engaged in social critical activity. As Berdyaev implied, the defining characteristic of an *intelligent* was not just education or social position but a moral inclination to reform and especially to improve the lot of the peasantry. Before 1861 this meant amelioration of the outdated, demoralizing, inefficient and anachronistic system of serfdom but even after 1861 the plight of the peasantry remained in the forefront of the focus of the critical intelligentsia.

Before leaving this era there is one more forerunner to consider, the extraordinary Grigorii/Hrihory Skovoroda (1722–94). Skovoroda came to combine several aspects of traditional Russo-Ukrainian culture.[17] He spent his later life as a wandering holy man reliant on strangers and acquaintances for food and shelter. In what is usually described as a Socratic manner, Skovoroda 'taught' philosophy in roadside and marketplace conversations with whoever happened to be present. Like Socrates, he believed that philosophy was a search for truth and the basis of it was to know oneself. Unlike Socrates, Skovoroda was deeply religious, in a personal and unorthodox, even heretical, fashion arguing that the kingdom of God could be found within the self. Skovoroda was born in the Ukrainian Cossack region and wrote primarily in a personal linguistic amalgam of the dialect of his village, standard Ukrainian, Old Church Slavonic, Russian and a smattering of other languages such as Greek and Latin.[18] In addition to his philosophical works he wrote religious songs and poems sometimes compared in style to the works of wandering singers known as kozbars who were descendants of the earlier skomorokhi. Even before his decades of wandering Skovoroda did not hold down any fixed occupations for very long. He became the embodiment of his philosophy and his ideas. He is often acknowledged as Russia and Ukraine's first philosopher and was, by chance, an ancestor of the later philosopher Vladimir Solov'ev whom we will encounter again. Unlike many influential western philosophers of the time Skovoroda was clearly deeply religious though in very personal and unconventional ways. In this respect he was the first of many Russian philosophers like Solov'ev, Lossky, Ern and others from the late nineteenth and early twentieth centuries. He also influenced many writers including Tolstoy – who also wrote that *The Kingdom of God Is within You* (1908) – and Dostoevsky. Even down to Solzhenitsyn Russian writers could be deeply religious and Skovoroda exemplified how, in the Russian context, classical rationalism co-existed with a religious dimension whereas western rationalists were moving quickly into deism, agnosticism and atheism and theology was becoming a distinctive channel of thought. Once again, distinctive features of Russian thought and culture today can be seen to have very deep roots.

3

From Speransky to Belinsky – Reformers, Decembrists, Slavophiles and Westernizers

Russia in the early nineteenth century had developed features which were unrecognizable compared to one hundred years earlier. Western styles of dress had taken over for the court, the aristocracy and the educated elite. The army wore uniforms in the same style as the other armies of Europe and followed a national flag adapted by Peter from the Dutch original. A navy was beginning to make an impact in northern waters and commercial fleets in what were to become major maritime trading routes, from the Baltic ports to Germany, Scandinavia and Britain and from Odessa to the Mediterranean. Industries, notably mining, metalworking and textiles, had begun modest expansion. The knowledge base had expanded mightily. The scientific advances and scientific exploration revealed vastly more than had been known before about the territory of the Russian Empire, especially its geology, geography, flora and fauna. Siberia had been absorbed and the first landings had been made on the North American continent. Territorially, wars against Turkey, Sweden and France and the carve-up of Poland between Russia, Austria and Prussia had secured large new possessions. They brought further cultural diversity, including significant Protestant, Catholic and Jewish minorities. Jews were increasingly hemmed around with regulations limiting the areas in which they could live (the Pale of Settlement) and quotas were imposed on numbers allowed in towns and, by the end of the nineteenth century when it became more significant, on the proportion allowed to study in universities. Violent persecution was rare in the early decades but it did become a major blight on the empire from 1881 onwards. At times, the developing cultural diversity was welcomed. In 1773 Pope Clement XIV issued a Bull suppressing the Jesuit order. In the period before their restoration in 1814 Russia was a major refuge. Catherine had welcomed them, especially their skills as educators, and many members of the elite were educated by Jesuits. Alexander I eventually took up a more traditional anti-Catholic attitude and expelled them from Russia in 1820. This was shortly after the papal ban was reversed but, ironically, Russia had been an unlikely island (along with Prussia, China and the United States) on which the Jesuits had survived in the period of suppression.[1] Alexander I seems to have been influenced by anti-Catholic feeling which had endured from the times of earlier encounters such as, the 1572 visit of Antonio Possevino which upset Ivan IV. The Orthodox church was always highly suspicious of any Catholic presence in its areas of dominance and accused the Catholic church and, in this case the Jesuits, of trying to gain converts. There was little evidence to support it. It was only in 1843 that Prince Ivan Gagarin did convert to Catholicism and joined the order as the first Russian Jesuit. True, he speculated about whether Russia should become Roman Catholic[2] and Catholicism attracted later figures whom we will encounter like Vladimir Soloviev and Vyacheslav Ivanov, but the predominant feeling in Russia was, and remains, anti-Catholic. As the century progressed, it was increasingly re-inforced by the adherence of the highly unsettled Polish population of the empire to a brand of militant Catholicism which emphasized their separate identity from their Russian Slavic cousins. There were also significant numbers of Catholics in Lithuania and western Russia (Belarus). The newly incorporated territories in the west had also brought Russia directly into the European power game as a major player. What had been an insecure toehold when it was founded on Swedish-claimed territory in 1704, Peter's 'window on the west', had become a large forecourt embracing parts of Poland, plus Finland, Latvia, Estonia and Lithuania and had secured the merging of Ukraine in the Russian Empire.

However, it must be emphasized that in many respects the innovations were an elite veneer and the vast mass of Russians were only marginally affected. Diversity of territory brought diversity of custom which went beyond religion and included key elements such as landholding and institutions of governance, education and so on. By and large, Russian institutions were laid over the local differences and, for example, the division of the country into so-called *guberniias*, administrative divisions considerably larger than an average English county but much smaller than most US states, incorporated all the territories of European Russia and even much of Siberia where they were vast and underpopulated like the region itself. But in the traditional Russian heartland the rural areas, apart from a modernization of gentry culture which, though she might have found it crude and often alcohol-soaked, would have been somewhat familiar to Jane Austen, life was little changed for the serfs and other peasants. They still comprised over 90 per cent of the ethnic Russian/Ukrainian population. The new territories did not have serfs and customs varied between large Swedish-owned (for the most part) estates in Estonia and Finland to small independent peasant holdings which could be found in parts of Poland, the other Baltic states and among free Cossack communities in Ukraine and South Russia. Only in the major cities such as St Petersburg, Moscow, Kyiv and Odessa, were the transformations visible and even here much of the artisanal and working-class women and men lived lives little changed over the eighteenth century. Only after 1850 did knowledge-driven innovation begin to make a mark on them.

As we have seen, for Peter the Great 'western' influence focused on the shipyards of Deptford and Amsterdam, in practical issues of craft and organization with largely German 'science' emerging in the final years. By the time of Catherine, it was French influence that was pouring in and transforming the aristocracy which even took up the language in preference to Russian. French influence was less about practicalities, more about style, ideas and artistic expression. Russian Imperial palaces imitated Versailles. Court splendour followed French precedent. St Petersburg was, in the late eighteenth century, awash with theatrical performance – operas and plays with Catherine herself contributing mediocre examples of the latter. Enlightenment philosophy was à la mode. The first brilliant figure in modern Russian literature emerged in the form of the playwright Denis Fonvizin (1745–92). This was all well and good and Catherine had immersed herself in it. However, from 1789 the influence of quite a different, revolutionary, France began to replace aristocratic luxury and Catherine retreated rapidly from her philosophical dabblings. Radishchev, though he was little influenced by French revolutionary ideas, was one of the first victims of Catherine's change of heart. However, the early trickle of influence became a flood. Russia became drawn into the revolutionary and Napoleonic wars, at first signing a humiliating peace at Tilsit (1807) after defeat at Austerlitz (1805) had opened the way to the complete defeat of Prussia by France. Russia's tepid implementation of the treaties and continued secret trading with Britain, with whom Russia was technically at war, tried Napoleon's patience until he decided to attack Moscow. His epic defeat drew large Russian armies pursuing the retreating invader deep into western Europe, arriving in Paris for the first time in 1814 and, along with its allies, forcing Napoleon's surrender. Alexander I participated personally in a victory parade in the city. As with other countries engaged with and occupied by Napoleon, the experience stimulated not only resistance but also imitation. German intellectuals began to dream of a united, liberal German nation. Groups in Italy and Spain followed suit. Even in unoccupied Britain radical ideas emerged and came into conflict with traditional toryism. Tom Paine became a deputy in the revolutionary French Convention. Russia underwent comparable processes and, although they were less extensive than further west, seeds had been planted. Not only Russia spawned new radical ideas, Polish nationalism was also inspired by Napoleonic examples and experience since the French had re-constituted a unified grand Duchy of Poland.

As we have already remarked, it was not only radicals who were enamoured of ideas of reform. Conservatives, too, were becoming critical of state structures and, for a variety of reasons, of serfdom. Russia was the last holdout, though, of course, the United States still had active slavery. At this point, one of Russia's most celebrated reformers, Mikhail Speransky (1772–1839), emerged. In a sense, Speransky embodied the enlightenment Russia developing under Catherine but, unlike Catherine, Speransky continued to advocate energizing reforms and found a fellow-spirit in Tsar Alexander I. Speransky proposed constitutional reform based on setting up a series of local, regional and national councils (dumas), each one electing the one above. A State Council nominated by the Tsar would provide a check. Over the course of the next hundred years aspects of Speransky's vision were enacted but it was only in 1905 that anything even vaguely resembling constitutional government emerged. Speransky also wanted to apply his somewhat liberal principles to freeing serfs and landowners, both classes being 'enslaved' as he saw it:

> So, instead of all the magnificent divisions of the free Russian people into the freest classes of the nobility, merchants, and so on, I find two states in Russia: the sovereign's slaves and the landlord's slaves. The former are called free only in relation to the latter, but there are really no free people in Russia except beggars and philosophers.
>
> (from Speransky's treatise: *The Fundamental Laws of the State*)

These were, indeed, radical ideas and, when he proposed reforming the masonic order and using it to educate the Orthodox clergy he went a step too far. His proposals leaked out, he made an enemy of the church and he was dropped by the tsar in 1812. He did have a second career after 1816 but was nowhere near as influential and his ideas were set aside.

The next major tsarist strategist put forward a quite different proposition reflecting the mood of the next reign, that of Nicholas I. In place of Speransky's vision of a kind of liberal freedom the new tsar was looking for counterweights to the inrush of western ideas. He found his man in the shape of Sergei Uvarov (1786–1855). In place of constitutional innovations, Uvarov looked to prop up Russia's traditional bulwarks of tsar, church and nation. The centrepiece was the emergence of the triple slogan that dominated the reign of Nicholas and beyond – Orthodoxy; Autocracy; Nationality.[3] As Minister of Education from 1832 to 1849 he based what limited education there was on these three principles.[4] The supporting philosophy was rejection of the west. Russia had its own ways which were suited to itself and superior to those of the west. The task of Russian culture was to nurture its own principles – embodied in the triple slogan – and eschew foreign notions of freedom, reason and so on.

From our point of view, few people have suggested either Speransky or Uvarov was a member of the intelligentsia. However, they do remind us that the dividing line between an *intelligent* and an intellectual civil servant was not absolute. Even widely acknowledged forerunners such as Radishchev and Novikov straddled this line. All reformers were social critics of a kind, a central feature of the intelligentsia. The conflicting proposals had also brought to the fore what, from then on, was a fundamental split in Russian cultural life between those who sought inspiration from western Europe and those who tried to limit western influence in favour of the supposedly superior virtues of Russia's own specific destiny and supposed cultural and moral self-sufficiency. Westernizers and Slavophiles were already emerging. All four were social critics, with very different perspectives, but only Novikov and Radishchev mainly inhabited the fragile public sphere, another key aspect of an *intelligent*. But, though they were state officials, Speransky and Uvarov did have a considerable influence on the emerging intelligentsia.

The great leap forward of conservative thinking under Nicholas I was not only the result of growing resistance in many parts of Russia's ruling elite to liberalism since 1789 and the trauma of the Napoleonic invasion of 1812, but also, more immediately, of the first radical uprising of the nineteenth century. Not, as was the case earlier, a peasant rebellion, but a radical attempt at constitutional reform – the Decembrist revolt of 1825. It had many striking features. First, its social composition. It was largely made up of elite army officers. The majority belonged to the guards regiments and had seen active, sometimes heroic, service in the Napoleonic wars. Second, despite its origins among a tiny elite minority, it had a very radical agenda. Though it lacked a single, unified programme, one group within its membership was explicitly republican, the remainder being constitutional monarchists. These two outstanding features help us to identify its origins. It was a movement inspired by interaction with Napoleonic France. Army officers who had pursued Napoleon to his Parisian lair had seen the glittering capital of European culture, style and radicalism and compared Russia unfavourably to it. They had also been exposed to Paris's radical ideas and some of them saw a republic as the essence of the modern in place of an anachronistic medieval autocracy which had, as we have seen, evolved to fulfil quite different functions from those of the nineteenth century state. The republican Decembrists were among the first Russians to argue that the autocracy had outlived its usefulness and was now the problem, not the solution.

The name Decembrist originates from their endgame. The movement began informally around 1815 when there was an atmosphere of reform and a breath of liberal air floating into Russia from the west. It was not only Speransky's constitutional proposals which had had official sanction but pressure was building against serfdom, a feeling driven for the Decembrists by close observation of the tribulations of the soldiers under their command during the war. In 1816 to 1819 it was abolished in the Baltic States. This was a largely symbolic gesture by the authorities as there were few serfs in these more recently acquired areas compared to the Russian/Ukrainian heartland. In order to facilitate this it would be necessary, they correctly observed, to establish new relations between state, landowner and peasant, which would require a constitution. Even in the moments of official contemplation of reform and a constitution such radical ideas as those of the Decembrists had to be discussed secretly. Two centres emerged. One, in St Petersburg, initially called itself the Union of Salvation (and also, at times, the Union of the Faithful and True Sons of Russia) and another, based in the small garrison town of Tulchin in Ukraine, called itself the Union of Prosperity, though they are now better known as the Northern Society and the Southern Society respectively. Numbers involved were very small. It is thought there were about 200 or so active members in each of the Societies, a drop in the ocean of Russia's 35 million population at the time. The leader in the north was Nikita Murav'ev (1796–1843), in the south Pavel Pestel' (1793–1826). The former was more liberal and moderate in outlook while the latter was more influenced by French Jacobins like Robespierre and believed that only decisive, violent action would wrest power from the hands of the autocracy and its supporters. Discussion proceeded and some very radical ideas emerged. Murav'ev proposed a constitutional monarchy but the more radical Pestel' and the Southern Society contemplated the abolition of the autocracy altogether in favour of a republic. That was not all. They even supported regicide as a necessary step to the achievement of their goals.

Plans were one thing, implementing them was quite another, a dilemma faced by all *intelligenty* reformers and revolutionaries everywhere. However, they thought fate had presented them with an unmissable opportunity in December 1825, from which their name was derived. Alexander I died and his son Constantine declined the succession in favour of his brother Nicholas. The Decembrists sensed a moment of uncertainty and weakness in the autocracy and brought out troops to Senate Square in the centre of St Petersburg to demand a constitution. Their support was too limited and they were quickly arrested, tried and, in many cases, exiled to Siberia. Five leaders were executed and others had death sentences commuted to exile. Class principles ruled even in punishment. The largely aristocratic leaders were treated relatively leniently, travelling openly to designated, relatively undemanding places of exile where they could read, write, meet and interact with the local population. Some assisted with welfare relief, some set up village schools. By comparison, ordinary soldiers who were convicted were transported in chains and sent to arduous forced labour camps.

They had been bold and courageous but tragically naïve in thinking they only had to proclaim freedom for the country to turn and follow them, an illusion that persists to the present, especially among liberals inside and outside Russia. Despite being small, short-lived and unsuccessful, the movement showed characteristics which recurred for over a century in radical and revolutionary intelligentsia groups. There was disagreement on principle between 'moderates', who believed it was necessary to advance by small steps and revolutionaries demanding rapid change and a deep break with the status quo. Most were liberal but some were socialist and even communist. The Southern Society, for example, called for half of serf land to be taken over by the state, the rest given to the serfs. They were already suffering one of the key weaknesses of all reformist and revolutionary movements. A shared desire for substantial change rarely led to an equally shared view of objectives. The 'moderate'/'extremist' split, with many hybrid varieties in between, has been a crucial weakness in many reformist movements. Disagreement on tactics – the degree of justified violence if any and the crucial problem of enlisting support in hostile and repressive environments – caused additional differences, often described as 'splits'. Splits over objectives and tactics have been the Achilles heel of most modern radical movements. It is far from uncommon to see members within the same radical movements engaging in more vitriolic arguments with fellow members than with the shared enemy. We will encounter many later Russian movements which show obvious examples of this. Any movement based on principle is open to endless discussion of the nature of those principles and their consequences. By comparison, upholders of the status quo, for all their gathering round themselves the banners of principle, are usually united by the stronger bonds of self-interest, privilege and power. Usually, it is only when those interests conflict that serious breaches open up in the social fabric. The Decembrists learned this the hard way but many later groups suffered from the same problem. Like their successors, including the Bolsheviks who admired and honoured the Decembrists, they found it expedient to combine legal and illegal activity. In addition to their secret political core they opened up legal channels of change via societies and clubs with literary, charitable and educational objectives.

The Decembrists, and even the reformists like Speransky and Uvarov, were showing signs of a kind of shop window effect. It was not an entirely new phenomenon but the impact of gazing into and learning about and even experiencing, the existence of wealthier, freer more 'advanced' societies, notably to the west, was beginning to have a more corrosive effect. This aspect became much more acute by the mid-century but it is interesting that it was already having a significant impact. Its deep root is related to what has become known to historians as the 'Great Divergence'.[5] From around 1700 certain societies, mainly in western Europe and North America, began to enjoy an unprecedented increase in wealth. Up to that point, global societies had existed at comparatively similar levels of living standard and technology resulting in a wealth disparity between 'rich' and 'poor' countries of about 3 to 1. By 1800, and even more so by 1900, newly industrializing countries were exponentially increasing their wealth and, often, admitting wider social circles into the governing classes and even beginning to toy with 'democracy' and freedom. As a result, wealth disparities soared into ratios of 10 to 1 and much more in the twentieth century. While this broad process is beyond our present scope it is important to note that in countries 'left behind' in this process the knowledge of better-off and freer societies was corrosive of the status quo. Russia was a pioneer in this. By the mid-century a discourse of 'backwardness' had taken hold of the intelligentsia. But it was already incipient in 1825 in the ideas of the Decembrists. Observations of the anachronistic nature of the key institutions of Russia at that time – autocracy and serfdom – were powerful drivers of 'progressive' ideas. It should be noted that this affects conservatives as well as reformers since the former are as much at pains to deflect the impact of foreign influences as the latter are to adapt and import them.

Finally, two more aspects of the Decembrist experience foreshadowed later developments. The extreme narrowness of the Russian elite of the period is brought home by the interconnectedness of leading Decembrists with figures in broader cultural and social circles. Among the leading Decembrists was Prince Trubetskoi, the first of several family members down to 1917 who associated with liberalism. Another leader, Mikhail Fonvizin (1788–1854), was a relative of the playwright Denis Fonvizin. Mikhail Fonvizin was an early exponent of socialism and later of Marxist communism about which he wrote one of the first pamphlets in Russia.[6] In his later years, around 1848, he associated himself with the Petrashevsky Circle, one of Russia's first actively socialist groups, in which a young man named Fyodor Dostoevsky, a giant influence from the 1860s onwards, also participated bringing, between them, almost a century of intelligentsia radicalism into direct contact. Other writers and intellectuals of the day were close to the Decembrists even where they did not participate. The educated Russian elite was, indeed, very small at this time and the number of landowners, gentry and urban upper classes was also very small. Even by 1850 the entire urban population was still below 10 per cent of the total.

In many respects the Decembrists already exemplified features of the classic Russian intelligentsia. Above all, perhaps, like Radishchev, they exemplified the moral roots of their political and social engagement. Their generation is commonly labelled as being one of 'repentant noblemen'. In a way this demeans them. They were not simply assuaging a personal sense of guilt. They were moved by the plight of the oppressed groups, especially serfs, and were prepared to sacrifice themselves in order to create greater justice and fairness in society. They were not driven by personal self-interest. Their personal interests dictated they should do as the majority of their fellow nobles did and simply enjoy their privileges. But they did not. It was not selfishness that shaped this. Later descriptions of the intelligentsia, as we shall see, described them as being something like a religious order and, in certain respects, the Decembrists shared certain characteristics. They had a moral commitment and, for some, an ultimately heroic degree of self-sacrifice. The army officer and poet Kondraty Ryleev (1795–1826) was a well-known example. In one of his poems he put words into the mouth of one of the characters that are generally thought to apply to himself as he foresaw that his commitment to the cause would bring execution.

I know full well the dire fate
Which must upon the patriot wait
Who first dare rise against the foe
And at the tyrant aim the blow.[7]

Ryleev was hanged on 13 July 1826 along with four other Decembrist leaders for his part in the revolt. Where others cracked and informed on fellow conspirators, Ryleev held firm and proposed that he alone should be executed, one of the first to offer to sacrifice himself for the sake of other supporters of the cause. He carried a copy of Byron's poetry with him to the scaffold.

The Decembrists were forerunners of the intelligentsia but had significant distinctions from the purer examples of subsequent decades. They were not fulltime radicals; they were senior officers in the military elite and lived on, sometimes very substantial, private means. Many were major landowners. They were an integral part of the elite against which they protested. However, they led the way in honourable moral commitment and heroism despite, like later *intelligenty*, being tactically naïve and isolated from the peasant and serf groups in whose interests they believed they were acting. Their legacy was considerable. They were remembered in paintings, poetry, plays and stories. In Soviet times, streets and bridges were renamed in their honour. The self-sacrifice of several wives following their husbands into Siberian exile became symbolic. Ironically, perhaps the most intriguing part of their legacy might have been the element that was never realized. One of Tolstoy's earliest projects was to have been a major novel about the Decembrists. Only three chapters were written but it was in the course of preparing them that Tolstoy began his research on 1812, which he believed was the key to the Decembrists, but was distracted into writing about the Napoleonic experience instead, the result being *War and Peace*. From the completed fragments one can surmise that Pierre and Natasha Bezukhov are the prototypes of what would have been a Decembrist couple. What Tolstoy would ultimately have made of them we cannot know. Nonetheless, the Decembrists have come to have an honoured place in Russian political and intellectual history.

Although the numbers involved were small and the movement was easily crushed the Decembrist revolt was one of the key shaping influences of the reign of Tsar Nicholas (1825–55). Their revolt created concern at the highest level out of all proportion to its actual effect. It created an atmosphere of retrenchment and conservatism around the throne. The revolt was attributed, as was often the case in later generations, to a dangerous dabbling with liberal reforms rather than the true cause which was the absence of such reforms. Conservatives began to shore up (or even invent) Russian 'traditions' in order to fend off change. It was no accident that Uvarov and his ultra-conservative triple slogan of conservative nationalism emerged at this time as a major ideological prop for reaction.

There was a second influence deeply interacting with the first to shape the mentality of the autocracy. The defeat of Napoleon was taken as a sign that not only did Russia not need to imitate the west it was, in fact, superior. This led to a wave of triumphalism and national self-satisfaction which gradually turned into complacency. This was a dangerous cocktail. It deeply discouraged innovation and it led to a build-up of internal economic, social and political problems. Rather like the so-called 'years of stagnation' in the Brezhnev era, or even the 'dull' 1950s in the United States, external appearances concealed the continued motion of life and ideas under the carapace of immobility and resistance to change. In all three cases repression led to explosions – perestroika after Brezhnev; the 'sixties' after the 1950s in the United States and, in Russia's case, the humiliation of the Crimean War (1854–6), which blew the complacent sense of superiority to pieces and necessitated the rapid and partial 'Great Reforms' of the 1860s. The foundations of those explosions were being laid down during the moments of stagnation. In Russia's case the slowness of political, social and economic development belied the emergence of a vivid expansion of literature, the beginning of Russia's 'Golden Age', focused on Alexander Pushkin (1799–1837) who had been on the fringes of the Decembrist movement. Great magicians of the Russian language like Fyodor Tiutchev (1803–73) and Afanasy Fet (1820–92) bewitched their readers. One of the great themes of the day was investigation of Russian national identity. The great conflicting schools of westernizers and Slavophiles took shape. Historians and social thinkers took centre stage. Chaadaev and Khomyakov were the leading advocates on each side. Many human societies depict their identities through stories of their past. In ancient societies myths, epics, sagas and chronicles told of heroes and heroic deeds. Imagination dominated with, at most, a thin layer of fact. The acts of real individuals were embellished beyond recognition. Russia was no different. Chronicles told of the adoption of Christianity and the destruction of Kyiv. *The Lay of Igor's Host* immortalized an unsuccessful battle against the Polovtsy. Only in the early nineteenth century did a genuine history, based on documentary research, put in an appearance.[8] Its author was Nikolai Karamzin (1766–1826).

There is a story that Karamzin had witnessed the Decembrists action in Sennaya Square in St Petersburg.[9] If true it would be ironic in that he had also been in Paris in the early stages of the French Revolution and he would probably have been extremely alarmed to see what might have been the first stage in a repetition of what he saw as the repellent events of the French Revolution recurring in his own country. Karamzin, along with Novikov and Radishchev, was an important figure in the late-eighteenth-century appearance of a fragile public sphere in Russia. Like them, he was not only a writer but also an editor and publisher, absolutely crucial activities in the emergence of the intelligentsia as a separate social entity. After a brief stint as a guards officer Karamzin turned to a literary career. He became a very successful poet and storyteller in the prevailing style of sentimentalism.[10] He travelled to western Europe, visiting Immanuel Kant in Königsberg and witnessing the early stages of the French Revolution in Paris, which he wrote about in an account of his travels. He was also highly accomplished in philology and, somewhat ironically for a conservative who warned against change, is credited with a number of modifications to the Russian alphabet and vocabulary. In 1791–2 he also edited one of the earliest intelligentsia journals, *The Moscow Journal (Moskovskii Vestnik)* and in 1793–4 pioneered a format of collected essays from various authors known in Russian as an *al'manakh* or *sbornik*. This became a very popular format for publication of views, usually by like-minded authors but sometimes containing clashing opinions. Without books and newspapers it would not have been possible to conduct discussion with ever wider, albeit still elite, participation.

His expertise and knowledge covered so many fields that he might be considered to be one of a number of figures of the late eighteenth-century world about whom it was said that they, almost literally, 'knew everything' worth knowing at that time. On 31 October 1803, he was appointed by Tsar Alexander personally as official historian of the Russian state. He soon turned to this fulltime and in 1818 the first four volumes of his *History of the Russian State* were published. The edition of 3000 copies sold out within three months. Karamzin read it to the emperor. Seven more volumes were completed and published and an unfinished twelfth volume came out posthumously, taking the story to the early years of the Romanov dynasty (1613). Unsurprisingly, for an official historian appointed by the tsar, who befriended the tsar and read his work to him, Karamzin's interpretation supported the autocracy as a vital centrepiece of Russian life. He bitterly opposed interference with it and was hostile to Speransky's proposed reforms. To emphasize the point, in 1812 he wrote *A Memoir of Ancient and New Russia*, for Alexander I pointing out what he saw as the dangers of interfering with the existing arrangements. It became one of the most influential statements of its time and beyond of the conservative and Slavophile principle. He had, in effect, made himself the state ideologist of autocracy.

Karamzin had thrown down a gauntlet. He might well have been surprised by the energy with which it was taken up and his ideas refuted. The most passionate challenger was Pyotr Chaadaev (1794–1856). Between 1826 and 1831 Chaadaev penned eight *Lettres Philosophiques* (*Philosophical Letters*). They circulated in manuscript at first until the one and only publication in Chaadaev's lifetime of the first letter in 1836. Publication brought the wrath of the authorities down upon him. The rule of law, for once, just about held up and the authorities could find no crime with which to charge him. Instead, they responded in a way that was much more extensively revived in the 1970s. He was declared insane and ordered to undergo psychiatric treatment. Unlike that of his twentieth-century successors, Chaadaev's punishment did not involve imprisonment beyond a period of house arrest. Once again, his status as a gentleman of the elite protected him from a worse fate. In response Chaadaev was able to produce an *Apologie d'un Fou* (1837) which was not published in his lifetime. The title is usually translated into English as *Apology of a Madman*. However, although some of the nuances of his argument were modified compared to the *Letters*, Chaadaev was not saying sorry to anyone. He was using the term in the theological sense of 'apologetics' – that is, an explanation and defence of a philosophical proposition or propositions. What had he said that had so ruffled the feathers of tsar, government and, perhaps especially, the church?

Chaadaev did not mince words. His basic proposition was that Russia was a pariah among nations which had never contributed one single thing to broader human civilization.

> It is one of the most deplorable traits of our strange civilization that we are still discovering truths that are commonplace even among peoples much less advanced than we. This is because we have never moved in concert with the other peoples. We are not a part of any of the great families of the human race; we are neither of the West nor of the East, and we have not the traditions of either. We stand, as it were, outside of time, the universal education of mankind has not touched us.

Even worse, Russia existed, he said, only to act as an example to more civilized countries. 'We are an exception among people. We belong to those who are not an integral part of humanity but exist only to teach the world some type of great lesson.'[11] The implication was that it would be an example of how not to do things. It was the reverse of Russia's tendency to messianism and seeing itself as the 'Third Rome' – a beacon for lesser nations. Clearly such ideas would resonate and Chaadaev split the educated elite. To underline his point, Chaadaev did not even use the Russian language. The letters were written and published in French.

Tsar Nicholas was not prepared to turn a blind eye to such an attack. As we have established, the twin pillars of 'traditional' Russia were the autocracy and the church. Chaadaev had particularly scandalized the church by suggesting that the secret of the west's success was its formation under the influence of the Christian rationalism, as he saw it, of the Roman Catholic church. Chaadaev recommended that Russia should return to Catholicism. The Great Schism of 1054 had, he argued, begun Russia's journey to isolation and insignificance. Personally, Chaadaev took no steps towards personal conversion and died within the bosom and funeral rites of Orthodoxy. Nonetheless, he had struck the church's ultra-sensitive anti-Catholic nerve. The year following the publication of the first of the *Philosophical Letters* Chaadaev responded to his critics and the sanctions against him in his apologetics. In the words of modern press conferences he 'clarified' certain points on which he might be said to have rowed back but the main tone was defiance and the addition of nuance to his main propositions. *Apologie d'un Fou* was also written and published in French.

Chaadaev is often considered one of Russia's first philosophers. One of the countries most critical minds wrote, in 1909, that philosophy was like a clock, lost by an explorer in Africa, which was found and worshipped by an indigenous tribe who had no idea how it worked or what it was for. It even, Izgoev continued, became a token around which factions fought. 'Just such a clock is philosophy among the Russians.'[12] Chaadaev did, indeed, write treatises in the Schellingian manner but, like many others in Russia, the purely philosophical elements were seldom original and have been considered marginal to the mainstream of European and world philosophy. Without being a cultural determinist, it is reasonable to say that the Russian soul, as it developed, was less keen on pure abstraction than its western equivalents. Russian thought excelled where it was linked to life either through social criticism, literature or religion. Russian thought tended to focus on science, social problems or on what, around the 1840s, came to be called the 'cursed questions' (*prokliatie voprosy*) associated with the meaning of life, the existence of God and the supernatural. It was less comfortable with pure abstraction. In the words of one of its most pre-eminent and internationally respected practitioners, Nicholas Berdyaev (who was an associate of Izgoev), Russia produced what he called 'concrete idealism'.[13] He was referring to it being embedded in life, in experience. It is no accident that he was admired by French existentialist philosophers, who shared this characteristic. Berdyaev had influence on them in his own right during his post-1917 exile in Paris, but he was also acknowledged to have introduced them to another great influence, Dostoevsky.[14] Chaadaev's philosophical writing, like a number of successors, was important in spreading philosophical ideas among the Russian élite but it was not very original. So where did Chaadaev's ideas come from?

The strength of his ideas was more related to the social aspects. It also needs to be born in mind that two great issues were behind the social criticism of the era – autocracy and serfdom. Even Catherine the Great had tinkered with serfdom and it began to play on the conscience of part of the élite. Contact with the west had stimulated dissatisfaction with autocracy. Chaadayev had travelled extensively in western Europe, including visiting Rome, and it was experience and observation which had played a great role in the evolution of his ideas. He had links with the Decembrists but the narrowness of the thinking élite must be borne in mind. Many of them were personally acquainted. Chaadaev, for example, met Decembrists in the house of Karamzin. It also needs to be remembered that, partly as a result of this close mutual interaction, the categories usually applied to Russian thinkers do not fit neatly and, as we shall see, most of them crossed over the boundaries of the various schools of thought rather than living neatly within them. This led to many paradoxes. Despite having sympathy for the Decembrists, Chaadaev was certainly no revolutionary. He was influenced more by French Catholic conservatives, like de Maistre, Chateaubriand and other critics of the revolutionary extremes. It is also the case that, inexplicably, Karamzin, the archpriest of the cult of autocracy in Russian life, declared that, at heart, he was a republican. Similar refusals to be categorized are common. Even the great split into westernizers and Slavophiles was not a clean break. Both sides sympathized with peasants. Both were fiercely patriotic in that the fate and future of Russia was at the heart of both schools. Chaadaev himself illustrated some of the ambiguity. Despite having written, in the first *Lettre Philosophique* the most excoriating description of Russia's nullity on the world scale and having insisted that if it was an example to humanity it was an admonitory one, showing the world how not to do things, in *Apologie d'un fou* he, somewhat inexplicably, claimed that: 'We [Russians] are called to resolve the great problems of the social order ....to respond to the most important questions which occupy the attention of humanity.' Here Chaadaev sounds rather like an exponent of the Russia as Third Rome idea, Russia as a beacon to save the world.

The heated debate around Chaadaev's challenge showed a number of these characteristics, especially the difficulty of clearly separating westernizers from Slavophiles. In particular, there was sometimes a shared critique of serfdom and autocracy and an underlying love of Russia which manifested itself, at one extreme, with a certain complacency about its problems and, at the other, in a fierce desire to put things right.

Chaadaev published nothing after his *Apologie* but what he had published stimulated a storm of opposition feeding into a golden age of Slavophilism. Three younger generation writers came to the fore, Aleksey Khomyakov (1804–60), Ivan Kireyevsky (1806–56) and Konstantin Aksakov (1817–60). None of them was old enough to have more than childhood memories of the Napoleonic invasion.

The main proposition of the Slavophiles was that Russia had its own path of development which differed from all other nations. At the heart of its special nature was Russian Orthodoxy and the Russian Orthodox Church. 'Russian' values clustered around it, notably the fundamental religious-social concept of *sobornost'*, a term so special that translators have not found a universally agreed term for it in English and many other languages. It has a meaning that references collectivism and ecumenism (the drawing together of humanity round a single spiritual focus). To translate it as 'togetherness' is too trite, 'collectivism' is too abstract. In particular, admirers of *sobornost'* saw it as the antithesis of liberal individualism which they hated for splitting society into competing atoms, a critique of liberalism they shared, surprisingly perhaps, with the early Marx. In place of individualism they idealized a strong collectivity focused on church and national state. The roots of Russian collectivism lay, so they believed, in the peasantry. Focused on the village commune (*obshchina*) peasant life involved shared values, shared control over land and a local system of elementary justice. Such values, based on the village commune and its urban equivalent the *artel'*, a workshop based on an association of artisans and labourers, were the models for Russian society. Like many western romantics the Slavophiles were horrified by the growth of industrial enterprises. They led to the formation of oversized, dirty, disease-ridden cities inhabited by a drug and alcohol – addicted impoverished population of forgotten souls. Such people were, the Slavophiles argued, abandoned to exploitation by wealthier society. In the Russian equivalent, organic ties of family, kinship and love would unite all in a mutually co-operating and mutually dependent, though by no means equal, society. Everyone would have a place and the weak would be protected by the strong. Small-scale 'human-sized' institutions like the *obshchina* and *artel'* would be the basic production units of Russian society. There would be very few, or even no, sizeable factories. Output was secondary to social cohesion and mutual assistance.

A touchstone of the Slavophile attitude was the reforms of Peter the Great, around whom a great debate began to rage. Did Peter betray Russia's essential nature as defined by the Slavophiles, or were they a necessary step along the path of 'modernization' which would lead to an ever-increasing degree of convergence between Russia and the Great Powers of western Europe? It should not be assumed that Slavophiles admired full-blooded autocratic rule. Some did, but the figure of Peter complicated that picture. Did his reforms mean that the actually existing autocracy was an heretical version and it was necessary to row back from westernization? For others, the existing autocracy risked failing in a key element of its duty which was to rule in the interests of all subjects and to defend the weak. It did not need a parliament but did need the advice of a traditional assembly, a revived *Zemskii sobor* (*Assembly of the Land*)[15] to keep it on the correct path. This could resemble a peculiarly Russian form of constitutional monarchy. These considerations meant that even 'supporting the autocracy' was not the straightforward proposition it seemed to be on the surface.

There were also complications arising from the panslavist movement emerging from Slavophile circles. The core element was that there should be a union of all the Slavic peoples. Unification of all the Slavic territories and the reconquest of Constantinople (significantly known as Tsargrad in Russian) were ultimate dreams for the more starry-eyed, although acquiring Constantinople remained a key foreign policy objective as late as the First World War. Such ambitions caused multiple problems. The most obvious was an endless series of wars with Turkey going back to the seventeenth century. A less obvious but more intractable problem was that independent Slavic nations were, to say the least, not always keen on Russian domination. Poles were especially hostile. Despite being Slavs they were fiercely Catholic, had engaged in bitter conflicts with Russia for centuries and had even abandoned the Cyrillic (Russian) alphabet. In varying degrees increasing national consciousness made White Russians (Belarussians) and 'Little Russians' (*Malorossianiny*, better known as Ukrainians and Cossacks) reluctant to see themselves simply as sub-branches of Russia itself. Some Slavic subgroups, notably Serbians, Bulgarians, Czechs and Slovaks, were more inclined to see Russia as a big brother who might help in their own projects of independence whether from Habsburg or Ottoman domination. However, panslavism was little more than an archaic and romantic dream.

It was Khomyakov who became the most influential prophet of Slavophilism in the 1840s, supported by Kireyevsky, Aksakov and others. Although our study is focused on the socio-political roots and development of the Russian intelligentsia rather than the cultural and intellectual history of the country, the two are, of course, closely intertwined and there are a number of further comments we could make about the early Slavophiles in order to illuminate our main theme. To see Slavophiles as being purely anti-western is too simplistic, not least because the term 'western' has no defined meaning. In some ways they showed that all thinking sections of Russian society were influenced by and borrowed from the 'west'. For example, although they were stoutly anti-Roman Catholic they were less anatagonistic to Protestantism. Khomyakov made well-known comments that Catholicism placed reason above mystery and also valued order above freedom while Protestantism placed freedom above order compared to the supposedly happy balance between these features found in the *sobornost'* of Orthodoxy. Nonetheless, there was a tendency to see Protestantism as being closer to Orthodoxy as, Khomyakov argued, they both emphasized freedom whereas Catholicism was imprisoned in the net of human reason and papal authority. Many Protestants might express some surprise at this since they tend to see the Catholic church, rather than themselves, wrapping itself in obscurantist mysteries. Khomyakov and Russian thinkers more widely were, perhaps, less sensitive to this because Protestant mystics and evangelicals had, as we have seen, had significant influence in Russia in earlier centuries. In any case, it warns us again not to make simplified judgments about the assumptions of Russian thinkers. Similarly, the binary of freedom and mystery versus hard reason is traced back by Khomyakov and other Slavophiles to the impeccably 'western' sources of Plato for the former and Aristotle for the latter. Orthodoxy and Protestantism were Platonic. Catholicism was Aristotelian.[16]

Slavophilism was not uniform in outlook. There were significant discrepancies and disagreements. One of the most unexpected, in many ways, was about Hegel. It is, perhaps, surprising that Slavophiles read Hegel at all since he was the centrepiece of German and European philosophy and the most complete exemplar of mistrusted reason. Kireyevsky was inspired by Hegel. Khomyakov was also influenced, especially in his early years, but more critical later on. To some extent Hegel and the concept of 'world spirit' could be seen to acknowledge the limits of pure reason. Kant had also provided a critique of pure reason. Hegel was also known for deeply influencing those who rejected, or at least deeply disagreed, with him like the Young Hegelians of the early to mid-nineteenth century. The best known among them, Karl Marx, claimed he had found Hegel standing on his head and he, Marx, had turned him the right way up. It is also the case that the idea of a special national distinctiveness (*Sonderweg*) and even national mission was developing among German liberals and philosophical idealists including Hegel. Indeed, emerging liberal nationalism and imperialism often included this concept in one form or another. Russia was not as alone as the Slavophiles thought in proclaiming a special path of national development. They were among the earliest to do this because of Russia's own situation of being, to varying degrees, 'backward' compared to the western powers.[17] Nonetheless, concepts such as *Sonderweg* in Germany and even Manifest Destiny later in the United States had distinct similarities to Slavophile views of *samobytnost'* (cultural distinctiveness). Finally, while most Slavophiles were careful not to construct a bygone paradise, a Russian equivalent of 'Merrie England', some of them, like Yuri Samarin (1819–76) and, to a lesser extent, Ivan Kireyevsky, looked to an ideal pre-Petrine past for inspiration. In fact, as Russian nationalism imbued more and more of the arts, there were increasing numbers of writers, artists and composers who were inspired by and reproduced idealized versions of the Russian past. Perhaps unexpectedly, such views did not prevent Samarin, like most Slavophiles, calling for reform of two fundamental pre-Petrine institutions, autocracy and serfdom.

Whatever the precise differences among the early Slavophiles they show that clear divisions are the exception even within intellectual schools. Before looking at the rival westernizer school, we should note some important aspects of the condition of intellectual life and the emergence of the public sphere and the increasingly rapid expansion of the country's knowledge base. The years of the long reign of Nicholas I (1825–55) were very ambiguous. At one level there was an explosion of ideas and literature. Alexander Pushkin (1799–1837) was the most celebrated but many other great writers flourished, Nikolai Gogol' (1809–52), Mikhail Lermontov (1814–41), Ivan Goncharov (1812–91), Afanasy Fet' (1820–92), Fyodor Tiutchev (1803–73) and Ivan Turgenev (1818–83) to name but a few. Russian science was also making great strides. The best known and most influential was probably Nikolai Lobachevsky (1792–1856) who pioneered non-Euclidean geometry. Less well-known is the engineer Vasily Semyenov (1801–63) who, in 1846, inspired by the ideas of Nikolai Voskoboinikov (1801–60), drilled the first modern oil well in the Caspian oil field. On the other hand, Nicholas imposed a heavy hand over the intellectual world. Pushkin was under surveillance. Lermontov was exiled. Turgenev was put under house arrest. In 1849 the young Dostoevsky was condemned to death, a sentence commuted to hard labour. There was also suspicion of broader modernization symbolized by an extreme reluctance to build railways. The opposition was, ostensibly, strategic. The post-Napoleonic triumphalism and complacency still existed and it was thought dangerous to build railways which would open up viable routes for any future invader. This would nullify Russia's supposed advantage of vast spaces to fall back into as had happened in 1812. They were to discover in the Crimean War (1854–6) that lack of viable routes also severely hampered Russia from deploying its own large army. There were also other considerations. Railways brought mobility and change which risked instability. The landowning elite were worried by this and preferred not to have to pay taxes for such schemes when they wanted the money to go into agriculture and traditional projects. The outcome was that, as railways snaked across more and more of western Europe and the United States, by the mid-century, Russia only had a skeleton railway network, much of which was shoddily constructed and single track.[18] In 1855 Russia had less than 1,000 km of track, mainly on two routes – St Petersburg to Moscow and St Petersburg to Warsaw and then Vienna. By 1849, there were over 5,000 km of track in Germany and 2,467 km in France. The fears of Russian anti-modernizers were being borne out in that railways were great agents of economic and social change and helped integrate countries internally, heavily influencing, for example, the unification of Germany.

The ambiguity of the reign, especially as it affected the intelligentsia, is well-symbolized by the career of Sergei Uvarov as Minister of Education (1833–49).[19] He instilled the triad slogan of official nationality – Orthodoxy, Autocracy, Nationality – across the education system. Fearing disruption from free and critical thinking, he carefully restricted the size of the universities. But at the same time there was some growth and increasing numbers of emancipated serfs and other non-gentry classes (all male at this time) were recruited. However, the university system, comprising universities in St Petersburg, Moscow, Kiev, Dorpat (Tartu) and Kazan, had approximately 1,500 students in 1836 rising to 2,500 in 1844 and 3,400 in 1848. In the words of one historian the increase 'troubled Nicholas'. The author goes on to point out that

> Rising total numbers obviously meant a larger number of students from "low classes" each year, yet the social composition of the student bodies changed hardly at all – the "free" classes provided the clear majority of students. For example, … … gentry and officers made up 66.9% of the students in 1836 and 67% in 1848. There were wide differences between universities, but these also were constant over time. For example, after 1835 at Moscow University, gentry were never less than 45% of the students but never as much as 50%, while at Kiev the gentry were never less than 75%. At the other extreme, at Kazan, gentry were never less than 25% of the students but never as much as 30%.[20]

It seems almost inconceivable today that such small numbers should elicit concern but Nicholas was always questioning Uvarov's strategy and trying to reduce the numbers of non-gentry students. The tsar referred to them as *raznochintsy*, namely those from 'various ranks' at the lower end of the social ranking system introduced by Peter the Great. The explanation, however, is relatively simple. Nicholas's outlook, throughout his reign, was clouded by the experience of the Decembrist rebellion, an affair of only a few hundred leaders at most. Nicholas believed small numbers could be very disruptive.

The final years of his reign, from 1848 to his death in 1855, were a tumultuous coda. In 1848/9 western Europe was being rocked by social protests in Berlin, Vienna, Paris, Milan, London and other major cities. Nicholas's reactionary instincts were stimulated. He strengthened censorship, clamped down on dissenting intellectuals, extended control over schools and universities. Uvarov was replaced and he died shortly after. At the request of the Habsburg Emperor, Nicholas sent troops to help quell the unrest, which Nicholas was prepared to do in the hope the infection would not spread to Russia, which was silent as the grave by comparison. So far so good, it might be thought. Nicholas's Russia was the arbiter of Central European politics and a rock of reaction. However, there was to be a rude awakening in 1854 in the Crimean War. Russian diplomacy had blundered into allowing its chief rival, Turkey, to enlist the British and the French in its service in the Black Sea. Habsburg Emperor Franz Joseph, whose territory and possibly throne, had been saved by 140,000 Russian troops in 1849, refused to return the favour by helping the tsar. As a result, Russia had to maintain forces in Poland to prevent an Austrian-inspired uprising from breaking out. After a number of relatively desultory battles against a highly inefficient foe, Russia had to admit defeat. Coincidentally, Nicholas died in 1855. A peace agreement was brokered in 1856 which restricted Russia's ambitions in the Black Sea. Defeat brought a major reappraisal of the strategies of Nicholas's reign. In particular, the self-satisfaction engendered by the events of 1812 and 1848 had dissipated and been replaced by a desire for strengthening the state and country through reform. The Crimean War, limited though it was as a military struggle, was an important turning point in Russia's social, intellectual and, to a much lesser degree, political evolution.

By this crucial moment an intelligentsia as a self-conscious group rather than scattered groups was on the verge of appearing. The intellectual ferment and creativity had been hampered by official restrictions. Censorship of published materials operated in such a way that a journal that transgressed could be shut down, creating not only an intellectual threat but also an economic one to the publisher. This bred a degree of caution and reluctance to push boundaries. Books might also be confiscated. Leading writers were put under surveillance or worse. Universities were restricted in their growth though even this caused anxiety for Nicholas. Widespread opposition to serfdom and heavy-handed governance by the autocracy grew but, as has so often been the case in Russia in the last two centuries, had only limited scope for legal expression. How did the thinking classes react in the later decades of Nicholas's reign?

The tiny public sphere of the 1780s had grown but still remained small. Its members looked, first of all, to the printed word as the medium for as broad a discussion and dissemination of ideas and literature as possible. One of the great achievements of Russian intellectuals, the brilliant *tolstye zhurnali* (literally 'fat journals' perhaps best translated as heavy journals) were set up by leading figures such as Karamzin and Radishchev before 1800. Great publications like *Evropeets* (*The European*), *Telegraf* (*The Telegraph*), *Russkaia beseda* (*Russian Conversation*) and many others held a distinguished if sometimes short-lived place in cultural life in the first half of the nineteenth century.

Another innovative format was the emergence of intellectual *kruzhki* (circles) where groups gathered for intense discussions. They began in the 1760s on the model of French salons of the period. They still existed in the early twentieth century but their heyday was probably the 1830s and 1840s. They usually met under the patronage of, and in the town houses of leading aristocrats. They were small and not especially influential but their devotees were very committed. Their main activity was discussion of literature and many fashionable metropolitan writers took part. They did not confine themselves to literature but used it as a launching pad for discussing morality, philosophy and social questions in some cases. They were also notable for the significant participation of a number of women, some of whom, as in pre-revolutionary France, hosted a *kruzhok*.

One of the most outstanding and sought-after participants in such gatherings was Vissarion Belinsky (1811–48) whose short life burned with intellectual intensity. The most indicative anecdote is Turgenev's account of several hours of deep discussion which brought from Turgenev the tentative suggestion they should have a break. Belinsky's retort – 'We haven't even settled the question of the existence of God yet and you want to have dinner' – has become one of the most popular quotes from this era.[21] It was not for nothing that Russians referred to such 'eternal questions' as the existence of God and the meaning of life as *prokliatye voprosy* (cursed questions). Belinsky's ravenous intellectual appetite and burning desire to seek truth (a very different thing from finding it) drew him into science, literature, theology all on a basis of German idealist philosophy. He is usually described as a 'literary critic' and he was but we need to note that institutions like heavy journals and intellectual circles were not the only ways in which cultural and intellectual life circumvented the encumbering restrictions. One of the most important was the displacement of banned political discussion into forms literature and abstract philosophy. This was known as using Aesopian language from the ancient Greek writer of fables, like the hare and the tortoise, which remain popular even today. Aesop wrapped a comment about life in a seemingly innocuous story. Russian political ideas were expressed in a similar fashion. Many Russian writers were (and remain) deeply involved in analysing the society in which they lived. Pushkin wrote a sharply pointed epigram *On Karamzin* (1818) who, Pushkin claimed:

> … proved to us
> The need for autocracy
> And the charms of the whip.[22]

Tiutchev also made politically charged comments from time to time. One of them has become widespread among Russians

> Who would grasp Russia with the mind?
> For her no yardstick was created:
> Her soul is of a special kind,
> By faith alone appreciated.[23]

The authorities were not blind to this and many writers fell under official sanction for sailing too close to the political wind. Lermontov was demoted in his military rank and exiled to the Caucasus for his poem *Death of a Poet* subtitled *A Call for Revolution* which concluded with direct accusations of government complicity in bringing about the death of Pushkin. There could be no clearer example of the fusion of literature and politics. His exile only gave him further fuel for his wonderful novel *A Hero of Our Time*, which remains a favourite to the present day. Pushkin was suspected by Nicholas from early on as he had consorted with, but never joined, the Decembrists. He was too popular a writer for the usual sanctions so someone had the brilliant idea of summoning him to court where he would be under the personal eye of the tsar. Both he and Lermontov died young as a result of duels, among the earliest of suspicious deaths which are often adjudged to have been officially inspired, a sad tradition which continues down to the era of President Putin. Nothing spontaneous, it sometimes seems, ever happens in Russia. More directly, Ivan Turgenev (1818–83) had his collection of stories *Zapiski Okhotnika* (*A Hunter's Notebook*)[24] confiscated in 1849 and he was exiled to his country estate, a sanction he circumvented eventually by leaving Russia for good and spending much of the rest of his life in Paris. More dramatically, in 1848/9 the young Fyodor Dostoevsky (1821–81) was also arrested but, by unequivocal state action, sentenced to death for belonging to one of the first socialist groups in Russia, the Petrashevsky Circle in St Petersburg. He was accused, among other things, of reading Belinsky's banned *Letter to Gogol'* in which Belinsky called for an end to serfdom and denounced Gogol' for abandoning the cause of raising the masses from their imposed ignorance and oppression. The sentence was commuted but not before a bizarre mock execution was carried out which went as far as putting Dostoevsky and his fellow condemned circle members in front of a public firing squad and blindfolding him before announcing a commutation of the sentence to one of ten years hard labour, of which he served four before reprieve. The increasing fierceness with which writers were treated reflected the growing fear of instability aroused in government circles by the widespread rebellions of 1848/9 in almost the whole of western and central Europe and the desire to ensure they did not spill over Russia's arbitrarily defined, fragile borders into the Empire's ethnic jigsaw puzzle.

Even though the circumstances were much grimmer, Dostoevsky followed Lermontov in using his punishment as grist to the mill of his writing in his memorable *House of the Dead* about his Siberian experiences, turning his sentence into an enduring indictment of those who had imposed it. The chronicler of later labour camps, Alexander Solzhenitsyn (1918–2008), put into the mouth of one of his characters the view that 'For a country to have a great writer is to have a second government'.[25] Of nowhere was this more true than Russia, where such a situation was already well-established by the 1850s and embraced not only a few great writers but a broad spectrum of intellectuals. Lermontov's work was closely associated with a critique of Russian rule in the Caucasus and a sympathy for the fierce mountain tribes which held out against it. Turgenev's book of stories reads, today, as a charming series of accounts of encounters with the serfs on his estate which alludes to their cultural life of animist spirits in ponds and woods, to the wonderful singers among them and to the harsh conditions of their daily lives. However, in the eyes of the authorities he had transgressed by portraying the serfs as human beings with lives and culture of their own, a revelation which cut at the very foundations of autocratic paternalism which considered peasants and serfs to be children needing the guidance of the autocrat/parent. Dostoevsky was not condemned for his writing but for his, at that time, socialist ideas. As we shall see, his later works were considered conservative and Slavophile.

The crossovers and interactions in the Russian intellectual sphere were not getting any more simple, a fact that continues to mislead many amateur analysts of Russian life down to the present. But the last years of Nicholas from the 1848 revolutions to the Crimean defeat were, indeed, a turning point. They were also a turning point in the life of one individual. Like so many of the intelligentsia forerunners we have encountered including Radishchev, Novikov, Karamzin, Khomyakov, Kireyevsky, Aksakov, Samarin, Lermontov as well, of course, as the Decembrists he was an army officer. In 1854 he was serving in Crimea. He had been a hard-drinking, woman-chasing, gambling-addicted member of the gentry and army officer in the conventional style, frequenting balls and social occasions. His dangerous drunken exploits were replicated by many young men of his social position. In the Crimea, he carefully observed the brutality of war at first hand and began to record what he saw. A series of stories, including *The Raid* depicting fighting, courage, death and atrocities on a small-scale, thereby making it even more meaningless and repellent, and three short novels based on his experiences, announced the arrival of a great force. *Childhood* (1852), *Boyhood* (1854) and *Youth* (1856) and *Sebastopol' Sketches* (1855) were the first publications by Lev Tolstoy (1828–1910).

In 1855, when Nicholas died, various potential futures lay in front of Russia. Only one would prevail and it could not be predicted which one it would be.

Part Two

The intelligentsia matures

4

From reform to revolution

Once again Russia's stability and development had been rudely interrupted by foreign intrusion. The deep problems revealed by Russia's inept performance in Crimea rocked the elite and were to provoke changes that touched everyone in the country. The complacency of the glories of 1812 was obliterated by the stalemate at Sebastopol'. As many writers have shown, the war efforts of Russia's enemies – Turkey, France and Britain – were riven with corruption, incompetence and disunity. One account summarized the war as 'notoriously incompetent international butchery'.[1] In British folklore it was the heroically tragic and wasteful 'Charge of the Light Brigade' which came to symbolize the disaster. The figures that emerged as heroes were not the generals – Lord Raglan occasionally referred to the enemy as 'the damned French' alongside whom he was fighting – but the healers Mary Seacole and Florence Nightingale who tended to the wounded. Even so, fighting on their own soil, the Russian forces were even more incompetent. Battles were won but no decisive breakthrough came and the powers agreed a peace. The blame game began on all sides. In Russia it was clear that the neglect of modernization and complacent assumptions of invulnerability and isolation were having destructive consequences. The year 1812 had opened one window for Russians to compare themselves with the ever-more rapidly expanding and developing western powers. The Crimean War opened all such windows and doors and allowed a gale to blast away decades of inaction and lost opportunities. The need for reform was plain for all the elite to see. For once, and crucially, the new tsar, Alexander II (1818–81; reigned 1855–81), understood changes were necessary. It was, of course, one thing to have a broad consensus that change was necessary but quite another to agree on exactly what those changes should be.

The conjuncture of events, ideas and forces which prevailed in Russia in the mid-century amounted, for our purposes, to a perfect storm in which the intelligentsia proper emerged and matured. The components of that storm were the national debate about reform of key institutions, notably serfdom but for many also the autocratic system itself. Secondly, behind this debate, was a powerful sense that Russia was losing critical ground to its rivals in terms of economic as well as social development. The emergence of a very powerful term – *otstalost'* (backwardness) – had implications not only for the state structure but for the economy and the social and cultural spheres. For civil society it was the lack of a real rule of law, absence of a constitution and other limitations on freedom which were highlighted. It was also clear to many that serfdom was inhuman, anachronistic and inefficient. For the government it was, as it had been for centuries, the power of Russia's armed forces and its ability to defend itself which was in question. If Russian military planners wanted an example of what happened if you fell behind they needed to look no further than their traditional foe, the Ottoman Empire (essentially Turkey), which was being picked apart by new, vigorous, increasingly industrialized strains of capitalist imperialism generated in Britain and France. As the century moved to its conclusion the example of the Habsburg Empire, which was being reduced to a stalking horse for rapidly-growing German power, added to the lesson. The state structure and the serfdom which had shaped it needed reform. But that was not all. Power rested on weapons. Weapons rested on industry. To stay strong Russia needed armaments. To stay independent it needed to manufacture its own. Any effort to industrialize and modernize needed to be underpinned by several crucial foundation elements, such as good organization, sufficient tax income, and a vast expansion of the national skill set, which implied education and training on a hitherto unprecedented scale.

The instincts of the tsar and his supporters were for the autocracy and society to stay as unchanged as possible. However, 'backwardness' highlighted the danger of not changing at all. The autocracy was being driven into an ever more acute, even intractable, dilemma based on a serious contradiction. The autocracy needed to reform, to change, in order to stay the same – an impossible position. It also needed to expand education and training, which also went against its most basic instincts. We have seen how Nicholas I had a deep distrust of education, fearing, correctly, that it would encourage the growth of critical thought in Russia. The distrust was shared by his successors but Alexander and his advisers realized it had to be expanded if Russia was to remain strong and competitive. There was another unsettling (for the government at least) consequence of this. Russia's ruling elite of gentry and service nobles who worked for the state in the civil service and as senior armed forces was very narrow. Any expansion would push recruitment beyond the traditionally loyal and reliable elite social groups. People of lower rank, so-called *raznochintsy* (meaning people from lower positions, *chin*, on the official Table of Ranks), would have to be recruited into responsible positions in the military, civil service and the growing market economy which needed traders, entrepreneurs, financial experts and so on far beyond the old sources of traditional merchants and owners of serf-operated factories and the like. As an illustration, the number of army officers grew rapidly. In 1879 there were approximately 15,600 army officers. By 1897, according to the first census, there were 44,000 officers in military service.[2] This meant less politically reliable groups were being drawn into a new elite, or at least sub-elite. The new intelligentsia was an area which drew in *raznochintsy* on a large scale, including a disproportionate number of sons of priests. It is unclear why boys from clerical families evolved into radicals in disproportionate numbers but it probably had something to do with several aspects of their upbringing. Married clergy were at the bottom of the clerical heap since only the celibate could rise to the higher levels. They were neglected by the church and often resented by their parishioners who had to pay them for sacred ceremonies from land blessing to rites of passage. They were often seen as rural parasites, people who had chosen an easier, lazier, less demanding path than that of the peasants themselves.[3] For their children – though their situation might be expected to make them hostile to the peasants – the combination of clerical poverty, close observation of the hardships of their peasant neighbours and a secularization of Christian principles such as love of neighbour plus a modicum of educational opportunity open to them more than to most peasants perhaps were the factors which opened the road to radicalism for a minority. The number who became radicals was small, but their proportion within the, as yet, small group of radicals as a whole was distinctive.[4]

Thirdly, it was not just the social and industrial structures which made up the perfect storm. The cultural and intellectual conjunctures complemented them perfectly. The main elements here were the influence of the Pan European unrest of 1848/9, the impact of the Crimean War in provoking major rethinking, the debate about how and on what terms serfdom should be reformed or abolished, the related reforms which would be needed to underpin such a fundamental reform and the wide sense of disappointment when the emancipation of the serfs was decreed and, in the view of many, the associated reforms only scratched the surface. In particular, there was total silence from above on the key issue of a constitution, a word Alexander refused to acknowledge in official documents. He supposedly went so far as to cross it out should it have inadvertently been used in items presented to him. The outcome here was that the disillusioned intellectuals turned to more radical solutions. But in doing so they unearthed a dilemma of their own. It was one thing to have bright ideas, it was another to garner a political force to implement them. The radical intelligentsia was only a tiny group. Even in 1900 it had only some 25,000 core members in a population of 100 million. From 1861 onwards an important feature of the radical intelligentsia was its search for a social group with which it could ally to realize its dreams.

In this perfect storm the intelligentsia proper emerged, developing many features from their repentant noblemen predecessors but adding new elements, not least the conscious elaboration of schemes not just for reform but also for revolution.

Reform – 1. Emancipation of the serfs

Centuries came and centuries went. Dynasties came and dynasties went. Eventually, even revolutions came and went. But the shaping features of Russian state and society persisted. Indeterminate borders were constantly encroached on by neigbouring powers. A large military was needed to defend them. A large military needed soldiers but also taxes which were hard to squeeze out of a country with harsh agricultural conditions and few readily exploitable resources. Nonetheless, the peasants were very successful in reproducing their lives and culture over the centuries and even drifted, by a kind of osmosis, into even less densely populated areas to the south and east of the Moscow/Kyiv heartland. As well as this migratory imperialism, the rise and decline of European neighbours brought expansion in the Baltic north west and Poland. These expansions added to the problem as there was more territory to be defended and borders conflicted even more with the ethnic and geographical elements that defined many other states. Tougher military impositions, including taxation to pay for it, stimulated flight and evasion so serfdom persisted to keep peasants in the harsh heartland. This was the set-up which had been found to be not fit for purpose in the wake of the Crimean War. While there was broad support for doing something about serfdom it could not be dealt with alone. Like a giant game of jenga, removing one piece could bring the rest crashing down. The interconnectedness of autocracy, serfdom, landownership, law, justice and the armed forces presented a vast range of dilemmas. It is to the credit of the authorities and the civil servants that they were able to produce a serviceable reform five years after the end of the war. It was less praiseworthy that the solutions in a number of crucial areas did not match the problems. How did these developments impinge on the maturing intelligentsia?

A key requirement for a successful emancipation was something for which Russia was not famous – organization. The 1857 census gave a total population of 61 million of whom 50 million were classed as peasants. Twenty-three million peasants were enserfed. There were 609,000 hereditary nobles. According to figures for 1877–8, there were 114,000 landowners. It was easier to deal with serfs in domestic or industrial service but for those attached to land every estate and peasant plot had to be surveyed. This demanded technical expertise in quantities Russia was short of. The technical challenge had to be met by an army of trained land surveyors.[5] But there was also the socio-political challenge. How would the countryside be structured after emancipation? In theory, under the serf system peasants were allocated plots in return for service to the landowner. If they were liberated from tied service what would happen to the land? Many landowners believed it should all revert to them. Naturally, the peasants were of the opposite view. They had an instinctive social justice, possibly derived from the Bible, that the land belonged to whoever worked it and that those who did not work should not eat. They had a precedent on their side. The largest serfowner was the state, including the monarch. State serfs had been liberated and given land. Since this was done with the consent of the tsar it was much less challenging than dealing with private aristocratic and gentry landowners. They argued that they had no obligation to the serfs if labour services were curtailed, transformed or ended. The land should revert to them in its entirety. The peasants asserted a claim that it should go to them. Neither extreme suited the Ministry of the Interior which believed that either one would undermine Russia's precarious social stability. If the peasants were dispossessed they would become a rootless and possibly wandering, vagrant, dangerous class. The existence of such a class was believed to be a root cause of the French Revolution.[6] If the landowners were dispossessed they would have no way to sustain their elite and privileged position. For the autocracy such an outcome threatened disaster since the autocracy rested on the support of this very class. There was a danger that the autocracy might saw off the branch on which it sat.

The outcome was that larger portions of the land were, unsurprisingly, given to the landowners who were also 'compensated' by the state for the land and labour they 'lost', while the peasants held on to most of their plots but had to compensate the state for it through redemption dues. The settlement left roughly 25 per cent of the land in the hands of 114,000 landowners and 75 per cent or so held by 63 million peasants. Other reforms had to follow in quick succession. The serfowner had been the chief dispenser of 'justice' to his (and occasionally her) serfs. That control had to be replaced and a new legal system, including trial by jury, was set up. Peasants still tried lesser crimes (land disputes and family settlements, petty theft and what was considered minor violence such as drunken brawls and, depressingly, most incidences of wife-beating) in their own peasant courts. Serfowners had also had responsibilities for welfare services and maintaining the basic infrastructure on estates – bridges, pathways and so on. These functions were passed on to elected local administrative bodies called *zemstva* (that is *zemstvo* in the singular). Military service was also modified. Before the reform conscription had fallen on peasants selected by the landowner who were condemned to what had been more or less lifelong service of twenty-five years. From 1874 conscription became universal for all males at the age of twenty, who served for six years followed by nine years in the reserve.

This was a massive package of reforms and created new relationships between state, landowner and peasant. How did the various stakeholders feel about the changes? From the state's point of view an ancient drag on Russian progress appeared to have been lifted. Peasant unrest eventually died away after the announcement of the emancipation, made at the beginning of Lent in 1861 in the hope of catching the peasants in penitential mood. Interestingly, in the period immediately after the proclamation, a number of rebellions in which leaders claimed to have 'Golden Charters' did break out. The dissatisfaction of the peasantry was evident in that the charters claimed to be the true emancipation terms, much more favourable to the peasants than the official ones. Former serfowners were blamed for suppressing these 'true' charters and hoodwinking the tsar by substituting the terms which were, so the fable went, proclaimed without his knowledge. At that time, it seems, fake news and conspiracies only influenced the unlettered and unschooled. However, these rebellions died away and there was a somewhat disillusioned peace and stability in the village as the new situation was phased in. After 1870, rising rural population and, a decade later, falling agricultural prices made peasants feel as badly off as they had been before 1861. They had lost what they considered to be their land and now had to pay for it from static or declining incomes. They were also resentful that the overwhelming amount of disputed demarcations of boundaries between landowners and peasants had been adjudicated in favour of the landowners by supposedly neutral assessors. The parcels of land lost in this way were fire branded into the peasant sense of injustice, so firmly that even fifty-five years later, in 1917, they were the first target of peasant land seizure.

Peasant dissatisfaction did not mean the former serfowners were happy. They had lost a huge amount of free labour and also a great deal of what they thought of as their land. They did, unlike the peasantry who were slated to foot the bill, have a pocket full of state bonds. Nonetheless, in the post-emancipation era, it must be borne in mind that the landowners were in crisis as well as the peasantry. The traditional foundations of estate life had been blown up. Estates had to be run through paid labour, rent and capital investment not by simply ordering peasants to get on with tasks. True, exchange of labour was sometimes resorted to in lieu of rent, since peasants had little or no actual money in the 1860s, which resembled an adjusted form of serfdom, but there were big changes. In essence, rural society was leaping from quasi-feudal to quasi-capitalist forms in the space of one or two decades. One crucial aspect was that traditional aristocratic and gentry society was geared to leisure and luxury not self-denial and capital investment. Following the example of Dostoevsky in his fictional characters as well as his actual life, elite Russian males with a stash of cash headed for the wine merchants, the casinos of western Europe and the brothels, local and foreign, in pursuit of pleasure. New ploughs, steam machinery, painstaking learning of the latest agricultural methods, was much less attractive. Despite the state attempting to help stave off landowner bankruptcy by loaning them money via the Nobles' Bank at cheaper rates than those available to peasants, the class was, for the most part, in decline. Despite overall population growth the 114,000 landowners of 1877 had become 107,000 by 1905. Chekhov's depictions of three sisters pining to leave the declining estate and head for Moscow or a fading gentry family having to sell its last piece of land, the cherry orchard, could be replicated many times over in real life. The table below shows the decline in the overall number of landowners and of the area they owned. The landowners with the smallest holdings increase in number and percentage of land owned showing how significant numbers were sinking down the hierarchy while many were leaving the countryside altogether (see Table 1).

In the short term, the state was happy with the outcome. It had undertaken a major reform, the scale of which should not be overlooked, without uncontrollable protest. The village had gone quiet, the military could recruit healthier and more reliable soldiers. However, rural Russia was falling into the grip of a slow-burning economic crisis. This could not but alarm the autocratic leadership since they were dependent on rural harmony and a healthy gentry. There was also disquiet in certain circles, as we shall see, because the system of governance – the autocracy itself – remained untouched. The opportunity for moving towards a constitutional form of government was there and it was completely ignored. This was particularly painful for liberals because, not only did

Table 1 Landholding in Russia 1877 and 1905.[7]

Landholding 1877 and 1905

Size of Landholding	Number and Percentage of Total Per Category		Area Owned Per Category (1,000S of Dessiatinas) 1 Dessiatina = 2.7 Acres/1.09 Hectares	
		1877		
Up to 100 des	56,551	49.3%	1,924.4	2.6%
101–1,000 des	44,827	34%	16,264.7	22.2%
Over 1,000 des	13,388	11.7%	54,976.4	75%
Total 1877	**114,766**	**100%**	**73,163**	**100%**
		1905		
Up to 100 des	60,910	56.8	1,662.6	3.1%
101–1,000 des	37,003	34.8%	13,218.8	24.9%
Over 1,000	9,324	8.7%	38,290.9	72%
Total 1,905	**107,237**	**100%**	**53,172.3**	**100%**

From Spring, David (ed.), *Landed Elites in Nineteenth Century Europe*, Johns Hopkins University Press, Baltimore and London 1977 p. 87.

Nicholas I, of all people, grant a constitution to Poland in 1830 but Alexander himself, towards the end of his reign, granted one to the newly established ally, Bulgaria, in 1878 as it shook off Ottoman rule.

Reforms – 2. The tsarist dilemma – *otstalost'*, industrialization and the demand for education

The reforms constituted the opening of Act II in the drama of Russia's perennial struggle to keep up with the wealthiest and best-armed powers and overcome 'backwardness' (*otstalost'*), a campaign begun by Peter. It was in the crisis from 1848 to emancipation in 1861 and its aftermath that the intelligentsia, in the specific Russian sense, emerged.[8] Arguably, the link with 'backwardness' helped to define the Russian intelligentsia as a dedicated, almost religious, sisterhood and brotherhood devoted to the development of greater equality and freedom in Russia and its component minority nationalities. Two of the basic prerequisites of backwardness are the existence of 'advanced' countries for comparison but also there needs to be a perception of lagging behind. The intelligentsia were the embodiment of that perception. Ironically, they were also an indicator of progress in that they were themselves a sign, through their education and culture, that Russia had taken its first steps on the path of development. It was perhaps the first such country in which a significant number of educated people realized that there was a gap. To an extent, other 'second division' European powers in terms of wealth and industrialization, like Spain and southern Italy, began to share similar perceptions. Later, Latin America showed similar debates, as did other major victims of the advanced and imperial powers like India. China retained its 'eternal' complacency into the twentieth century but then catching up and overtaking became, as in Russia, a nationalist and, later, communist party mantra. In all these cases a cultural and political intelligentsia devoted itself to overcoming backwardness. They differed in style from the Russian example but the 'uniqueness' of the Russian intelligentsia, often adduced by comparing it with the advanced societies, looks less unique in comparison with other countries lower down the league table of wealth and 'modernization'. One might say that the truly 'backward' countries were those which did not realize they were behind. Perception of being behind was one of the first steps towards advancing.[9]

As already noted, by and large, those advocating learning from and following the example of western Europe (to which the United States was an increasingly important but unspoken extension) became known as 'westernizers' (*zapadniki*). But the idea of Russian backwardness and the need to follow, learn from or adapt western practices was not, it should be noted, a concept confined to the radical intelligentsia. Liberals, constitutional monarchists, 'non-political' writers, composers and artists came closer to Britain, France, Germany and Italy in their intellectual make-up and felt ever closer integration with the west was inevitable. Even Tsarist reformers could be and were also deeply influenced by it as we have seen with Speransky and even Uvarov, not to mention Tsar Peter himself. Elements of it can be found in many influential forerunners of the intelligentsia identified in previous chapters who combined intelligentsia characteristics with state service, including the military, or with literary careers and so on. As we have seen, there were even the 'repentant noblemen' who, like Radishchev, were not prepared to stand by in the face of peasant suffering and were ready even to sacrifice their personal material interests in the name of helping to alleviate it. The preparation for the emancipation owed a great deal to several figures built in the semi-*intelligent* and semi-state-official mould like Speransky and even Uvarov. Dmitrii Miliutin and, perhaps surprisingly since Slavophiles are often considered to be defenders of the status quo, Yuri Samarin played a major part in drawing up proposals for reform. The participation of the latter reminds us that Slavophiles did not unconditionally defend autocracy or serfdom. The autocracy was often criticized by them as having been polluted by Peter the Great's reforms and serfdom, some of them claimed, held Russians in an unworthy subjection and was a disfigurement on Russia's reputation and moral character. Without straining the reader's patience, it is important to remember, yet again, that the slavophile/westernizer split was not so much a clean break as a spectrum on which individuals and groups were located. Westernizers had 'slavophile' characteristics which might include a patriotic love of Russia, an acknowledgement of the uniqueness and superiority of some of its institutions, such as the peasant commune for populists, and a distaste for large-scale western industrialization, urbanization and factories which, some radicals hoped, might take smaller-scale and more human forms based on traditional Russian *artely* (co-operative workshops) and small towns rather than vast cities. On the other hand, Slavophilism itself was inspired by western ideas, Schelling for example from whom Karamzin borrowed its fundamental idea of a separate national path. Also there were Slavophiles who despised nineteenth-century Russia because its institutions had been polluted by Peter the Great and by already existing western intrusions such as capitalist industry and democracy. In many crucial areas there were crossovers and mutual influences. Few Russians, including westernizers, achieved, or even sought to achieve, full integration with foreign role models and remained proudly Russian even after generations of emigration. Even Russians expressing a radical critique of autocratic Russia and traditional Russianness failed to be perceived as anything but Russian – not just as members of the nation but as people of a distinctly different culture. Despite loudly proclaiming their internationalist credentials, Lenin and many Bolsheviks were seen by westerners as deeply Russian. This was a tendency which stretched back at least to the First Working Men's International of 1864 in which Marx clashed with 'the Russians' led by Bakunin. Throughout the late nineteenth century western European socialists considered much of the radical Russian left to be distinctive in its fanaticism and terrorism.

One of the chief architects of emancipation was the landowner/serfowner and state administrator, Nikolai Miliutin (1818–72). He came from an impeccably aristocratic lineage. He was also Slavophile in outlook but that did not prevent him from being a reformer as well and as such he exemplifies the fuzziness of the borders of Russia's intellectual groupings. His motivation towards reform was the parlous state of the peasantry and the post-Crimea shock. Incidentally, his brother, Dmitrii Miliutin (1816–1912), was Minister for War (1861–81) and supervised the reforms of the army. In his memoirs Nikolai Miliutin mentioned his revulsion from the casual cruelty with which his father treated serfs on his estate, brutally flogging them to keep them in order. Such, Miliutin said, was the normal practice of the age. However, Miliutin became a repentant nobleman himself and oversaw the process of reform and drafted the emancipation Manifesto which made the radical change public in February 1861.

The Miliutin brothers were not alone. In many respects the reform moment was a peak of influence for conservative reformers from the élite. A group of them clustered around the cause of liberal constitutionalism. In their view, Russia needed the rule of law, effective over government as well as society, and a constitution to modify, define and codify the powers of government at central, regional and local level. The forerunner of Russian liberalism was Timofei Granovsky (1813–55) a medievalist historian from a moderately wealthy gentry family, who, unlike most followers of that speciality, was a liberal westernizer who used his knowledge to undermine not only the shared Slavophile views of the specificity of Russian history but also the populist assumption about the uniqueness of the Russian peasant commune (*obshchina*), discussed below. He was able to do this because, as a scholar studying western Europe, he was able to demonstrate that Slavophile assumptions about it were incorrect. For Granovsky, Russia was not so different after all. In his view, history moved, as Hegel had shown, via contradictions of thesis and antithesis towards the unity of the world spirit. His lectures were very popular and influential, standing out in the age of official nationalism and harsh censorship. His early death deprived Russia of a very perceptive, original and scholarly thinker. In the reform decade itself the most influential constitutionalist and jurist was Boris Chicherin (1828–1904). In his view a strong but constitutionally constrained centralized state was needed as a basis for Russia's development. The legal reforms of the mid-1860s were important steps, but without the overarching framework of a constitution and the rule of law the task was only half done. For most of his long life he lobbied for these principles and became their foremost proponent. However, in what became the autocracy's long-drawn-out death wish, Alexander II, like his two final successors, refused to contemplate any weakening of the autocratic principle. Bolstered by conservative Slavophiles and proponents of official nationality, Alexander baulked when it came to the decisive reform that might have changed the survival prospects of his dynasty. Rather than reform it he and his successors were firmly of the opinion that full-blooded autocracy was the only way of government for Russia and was ordained by God. Why did Russia need the 'cold' legal prescriptions of democracy when it had the 'warm' paternalistic myth of the Russian family gathered around its *tsar-batiushka* (little father) to whom all were allowed to petition for the righting of wrongs? Followers of Granovsky knew that this myth, far from being unique to Russia, had been widespread in medieval Europe and had been wiped away as modernization proceeded. Russia had a similar choice. Modify or languish. It was the besetting failure, from the point of view of the autocracy, that the last three tsars could barely distinguish conservative defenders of a monarchy they wished to strengthen through reform, from radicals advocating much deeper changes. Chicherin more or less withdrew from public life in 1868 as a protest against increasing repression and, from his estate, sent out a series of brilliant scholarly works including a widely admired history of political ideas and four volumes of memoirs. However, at no point in his later life, or beyond to 1917, did the autocracy ever come closer to an opportunity to follow his proposals than was the case in the early 1860s. The conjuncture was never so favourable again and the autocracy could not be deflected from its path of self-destruction.

However, while the 1860s was their moment, the liberal constitutionalists were not the dominant group in the intelligentsia. The term 'people of the sixties' (*shestidesiatniki*) has become associated with a much more radical and socially diverse intelligentsia. Between the 1840s and 1860s political opinion swung to the left and new social groups emerged holding these more radical ideas. The growth points of Russian thought were slipping out of the control of the old elites. Even so, the godfathers of this new shift themselves belonged to the elite and emerged from the usual elite channels. Though shortlived, one of the most influential of the intellectual powerhouses of the 1830s was the Stankevich Circle (*kruzhok*) centred in Moscow. Despite the fact that the focus of the circle, Nikolai Stankevich (1813–40), died of tuberculosis while in Italy at the tragically early age of twenty-six, his ideas permeated the seminal figures of the next intelligentsia generation. Liberals like Granovsky took part but, for the future of the intelligentsia, the ultimately contrasting figures of Alexander Herzen (1812–70) and Mikhail Bakunin (1814–76) came to define not only the next generation but, arguably, the next epoch in Russian socio-political and intellectual history. In fact, neither could be said to have subscribed to Stankevich's ideas. He posited the importance of love as the centre of human existence, a force pushing the individual to self-fulfillment and linking God and humanity. Sexual love and love of neighbour were, for Stankevich, the foundations of life and of human social action. Sadly, he did not have time to elaborate his ideas. Both Herzen and Bakunin developed away from a youthful flirtation with the idealism of Stankevich and the inevitable Hegel towards a more revolutionary and socialist perspective. Both of them were influenced by the 1848 revolutions in Europe which they both experienced personally as they had exiled themselves from the stifling atmosphere of Nicholas I and Uvarov's Russia. Bakunin assisted revolutionary action wherever he found it and was finally arrested in Dresden during the 1849 disturbances and handed over to Russia in 1851.

Herzen was less hands-on. He was and remained a writer rather than activist. He participated in the key *kruzhki* of the time, having one which revolved around himself and his long-term friend and associate, Nikolai Ogarev, as well as participating in the Stankevich circle and even travelling to St Petersburg on occasions to join meetings of Belinsky's circle. Proposals and writings emerging from these groups brought him to official attention and he passed most of the 1830s and early 1840s in internal exile. Eventually in 1847 he left Russia for good and set up a thick journal called *Kolokol* (*The Bell*) around which he centred the rest of his life. Herzen was an ardent westernizer, becoming the founding father, alongside his mentor Belinsky, of the tendency even though he was not the first. He was inspired by the French Revolution, by western constitutionalism and also ideas of personal freedom. Russia's future, Herzen advocated, lay ineluctably along this path. At the heart of Herzen's ideas were humanism, on a materialist and atheist foundation, and republicanism. His attitude to nationalism was more ambiguous. He detested Russian official nationalism and the Slavophile mystique but clearly had a love for Russia and sympathy with liberal and republican liberation struggles in other countries and hoped to see them take root in

Russia itself. The ambiguity is encapsulated in one of his writings which, during the Crimean War, he wrote in admiration of the heroes behind the defence of Sebastopol' which became the centrepiece of Russian nationalism at the time but subverted it by calling on the hero-defenders to change sides and fight with the British and French to overthrow the autocracy. His popularity was severely undermined in 1863 when he came out in unequivocal support of the Polish Uprising of that year which embodied his core political principles of republican constitutionalism and basic civil rights. Even his radical Russian audience found it hard to support his pro-Polish position.

Inevitably, Bakunin and Herzen were influenced by Hegel but by the mid-century Hegelianism itself had moved on. Feuerbach had become influential and he had undercut a great deal of the idealist underpinning of Hegel with a more materialist position encapsulated in his radical critique of religion. It was not, he argued, God who created man, but man who had created God. For Feuerbach, humanity had a tendency to build what he called fetishes. By this he meant that humanity would develop an idea but, in a sense, lose control over it so that an idea which had originated in the service of humanity ended up as something seen as a constraint. The idea of God corresponded to human understanding of the world in the absence of reason and science but, instead of serving man, the concept of God had become an absolute which humanity feared and worshipped rather than controlled. His critique also extended to other phenomena and to other Hegelian 'absolutes'. For example, Hegel had argued that the modern state, specifically the Prussian model, was 'the end of history', the final point of human political development and could not be improved upon further. For the Young Hegelians these conservative conclusions were unacceptable. In the words of one of them, Hegel had been upside down and it was necessary to turn him the right way up, to reject his conservative conclusions but to build on his assumptions in a radical direction.

The narrowness of the social circles of mid-century radicals, already seen in the Russian salons and circles, also applied in part in their western exile as well. Herzen and Bakunin both participated in and attended meetings of the International Working Men's Association (also known as The First International) set up in London in 1864. There they also met the Young Hegelian who advocated turning Hegel the right way up – Karl Marx (1818–83). In this symbolic encounter it is possible to see the foundations of more than fifty years of the Russian intelligentsia's future development and the beginnings of the ideology which dominated Russia for seventy-four post-revolutionary years. Herzen himself had moved on from the largely liberal outlook of his early years and instead, following Feuerbach and French socialist thinkers like Prudhon, St-Simon and Fourier, had come to realize that individual freedom could only be realized through socialism. He had also (like the Slavophiles he despised) come to see the Russian peasant commune as a potential base for a future Russian socialist society. The result was that Herzen stood for a not-very-well-defined 'moderate' socialism, though in Russian conditions of the absence of any permitted oppositional politics, this was inevitably revolutionary. He was also significant for focusing, like Radishchev, on the plight of the poorest and most oppressed members of society. This was also the case with Bakunin who arrived back in western Europe in 1861 after escaping from a period of cruel and vindictive imprisonment. He had been extradited from Austria in 1851 at the request of Nicholas I and treated with great harshness since the government was ultra-nervous about stability after 1848. He was detained in the St Peter and Paul and Shlüsselburg prisons up to 1857 until his sentence was commuted to Siberian exile for life by the new tsar. Not surprisingly, for Bakunin the chief repressive forces holding humanity back were the state and the church. One can see that Russian conditions of the time, especially the official ideology of Orthodoxy, Autocracy and Nationality and the close relationship of state and church, could inspire such thoughts in those who opposed the resulting near-theocracy. Bakunin adhered firmly to anarchist principles of which he became, and remains, one of the leading exponents in the modern world. This brought about a deep intellectual conflict with Marx for whom labour and the related division of society into classes were the keys to social analysis and liberation. Class struggle, not Bakuninst direct assaults on the state and church, was the path of revolutionary transformation. The currently oppressed class, the working proletariat, would realize they were being oppressed by the system, not simply by individual employers, and rise up to take over the factories, banks, land and capital on which the power of the bourgeoisie rested. Marx also emphasized, following Feuerbach, that humanity had a tendency to fetishize and worship its own creations. Money and the market, for example, had evolved to serve human needs but had developed into juggernauts which crushed those who had created it. For Marx, money and the market had to be turned back into servants, not masters and ultimately be superseded. He also repeated Feuerbach's assertion, which applied to all these activists, that philosophers had only interpreted the world, the point, however, was to change it.

The Russian intelligentsia was ready and willing to do exactly that. Of the three influential figures, Herzen had fallen in popularity after 1863, Marx was as yet unknown in Russia but Bakunin was at the peak of his influence. His determined revolutionary commitment, including violence, and his central focus on the state and the idea of God, which supposedly assisted the ruling class in their suppression of the masses by means of the church, appealed to many. He was the first prominent intelligentsia figure to promote the idea of mass popular uprising to achieve a complete revolution. He represented the birth of revolutionary consciousness in Russia. The intelligentsia in the 1860s was following Bakunin's prescriptions. It embodied their appeal but also soon found out their limitations. The atmosphere in Russia after the Crimean War and the accession of Alexander II was one of increasing expectation, tension and apprehension. Not for the first time or the last, a vague feeling of apocalypse could be felt from the peasantry to the élite. Peasant disturbances began to increase in number and size. Alexander was able to use this to his advantage. In a much-quoted sentence, spoken at a gathering of gentry, the tsar warned the assembled landowners that if serfdom was not banished from above it would begin to abolish itself from below. In other words, Alexander was putting pressure on those most likely to actively oppose emancipation. He implied that emancipation was coming and the only choice was between state-led orderly transformation or the unleashing of a peasant jacquerie of unpredictable dimensions, something most landowners deeply feared. In fact, as we have seen, the emancipation proclamation failed to immediately quell peasant uprisings which took the new and ingenious form we have noted of claiming to support supposedly genuine 'golden charters' containing the true terms of the emancipation which the landowners had subverted, concealing their deception from the tsar, who, as little father of his people, would, the peasants believed, surely have looked after their interests better.

Although the protests died out without serious threat, the mood of apocalyptic expectation was replaced by one of apocalyptic disappointment, which was keenly felt among the new generation of the intelligentsia. Bakunin, with his stern, violent action against the state, captured the atmosphere of the moment. For Bakunin, 'the passion for destruction is also creative' by which he meant that, in a Darwinian fashion, whatever existed should be subject to challenge so healthy tendencies could emerge and sickly ones be pushed aside.[10] Many young people heeded his call and, firstly as an insult, they were termed nihilists (*nigilisty*), those who stood for nothing and against everything. They were embodied in real life and in literary figures, the latter being more influential and better known. The archetype was Bazarov in Turgenev's novel of 1862, *Fathers and Children* (*Otsy i deti* traditionally but incorrectly known as *Fathers and Sons*). Bazarov advocated the new ideas and, though Turgenev was not at all sympathetic to them and Turgenev subverted them through depicting Bazarov falling in love, an experience he could not account for in his philosophy, the novel was widely popular and spread the new ideas as much as it criticized them. The title also captured the sense of a change of generations which was very much a preoccupation of that moment.

A second literary exploration of nihilism came a decade later in Dostoevsky's chaotic, profoundly disturbing, tragic and dazzling novel *The Devils* (*Besy*).[11] At its heart are much darker forms of Turgenev's themes of changing generations, from the gentlemanly liberal Hegelians of the 1840s to the more ruthless young nihilist revolutionaries of the 1860s and 1870s. Dostoevsky's characters embody various philosophical and religious positions. One is a liberal landowner of the 1840s (Stepan Verkhovensky who resembled in part Granovsky and Herzen) while others represent a form of Slavophilism known as *pochvenichestvo* (meaning rooted in the soil) (the character Shatov), while another is an idealistic socialist and atheist engineer who plans a cathartic act of suicide intended to dispel humanity's fear of death, which he attributes to belief in God (Kirillov). The simple-minded, childlike Mariia Lebiadkina has features resembling those of a traditional 'holy fool'. In the character of Pyotr Verkhovensky, the son of Stepan, Dostoevsky presents a darker and much more extreme representation of a nihilist than Turgenev's Bazarov. The younger Verkhovensky deludes his fellow conspirators into believing they are one cell of a vast, empire-wide revolutionary network waiting for a signal to rise up and overthrow the autocracy. To bind them together in an unbreakable bond he proposes they jointly commit the murder of Shatov, who represents the opposite of Verkhovensky's western, rational, atheist, humanist, revolutionary views.

If this seems a little extreme, even by Dostoevsky's standards, it is doubly disturbing to know that the character of Verkhovensky and the bonding-by-murder plot were based on the actually existing quintessential nihilist Sergei Nechaev (1847–82). Unlike most of the *intelligenty* we have so far encountered, he did not come from the wealthy urban or gentry élite but from a family of workers and ex-serfs. His father was a waiter and Nechaev himself worked as a waiter in his early adolescent years. Nonetheless, he was provided with tutors and was able to qualify as a teacher though he never attended university. After a period of intellectual search, he concluded that the only ethical principle should be that anything that promoted revolution was permissible and strove to carry it out in practice. He wrote a *Catechism of a Revolutionary* (1869) in which he elaborated the idea that revolution was 'the single passion' to which all else – including family, love, religion, ethics – must be submitted. It was on this basis that he developed a real-life murder plot. He and his associates killed a dissenting member of the group in November 1869, the dreadful event on which Dostoevsky based the central incident in his novel. So Bakuninist was Nechaev's *Catechism* that for a long time it was believed to have been Bakunin's work. It was not, even though the two did collaborate but Nechaev's extreme adherence to his extraordinary principles drew him into isolation. Even Bakunin eventually split from him and referred to him as a fanatic. Nechaev spent the last ten years of his life (1872–82) under the harsh regime of prison and hard labour which he endured without complaint or weakness. He continued to be as active as conditions allowed in pursuing the ultimate goal of revolution. In his way he was a deeply misguided saint of the revolutionary cause.

Nihilism itself proved to be an intellectual cul-de-sac. Devoted and energetic as its real-life and fictional embodiments were, it came up against the insuperable problem of implementation of its revolutionary task. It proved impotent. No amount of pretence at nationwide conspiracies and concealed supporters could make up for the fact that, though it was an intellectual sensation, it did not convince or incorporate many supporters. As mentioned, even Bakunin found Nechaev's mixture a little too rich. Nonetheless, the notion of total devotion to the revolution did not die out and remained inspirational for other revolutionaries, even if they disagreed with Nechaev's indefensible excesses. Nihilism was the birth, in Russia, of the idea of revolution. Its failure presented a challenge. How could a small, devoted group of intellectuals attach their dream to a social force capable of implementing it? Already, in the 1860s, other revolutionaries were pondering this dilemma.

'What is to be done?' was a question, alongside 'who is to blame?', which echoed through the rest of the century after emancipation. In 1862 a young journalist and writer, named Nikolai Chernyshevsky (1828–89), was arrested. He never saw freedom again, apart from a few last weeks when he was allowed back to his home town of Saratov to die. Up to the moment of his arrest he had been a thorn in the regime's side as editor of one of the finest thick journals of the time entitled *Sovremennik* (*The Contemporary*). After his arrest he was initially kept in solitary confinement in the notorious Alexeevsky Ravelin of the St Peter and Paul Fortress in St Petersburg, spending ten days on hunger strike protesting his conditions. In 1864 he was sentenced to mock execution and hard labour. He spent the rest of his life in the exile sites of Usol'e near Irkutsk and then Nerchinsk, Aleksandrovskii Zavod and Viliuisk all in Eastern Siberia and the Far East. Although the initial hard labour element of his sentence was reduced from fourteen to seven years by Tsar Alexander, all later attempts to free him were to no avail until 1889 when he was allowed to return to his home town of Saratov to die at the age of sixty-one. What had he done to deserve such harsh punishment? In addition to being under surveillance for being a prominent critic, writer and editor he was suspected of being the author of an item entitled *A Bow to the Landlord's Peasants, from Their Wellwishers* (*Barskim krest'ianam ot ikh dobrozhelatelei poklon*) which was, in effect, a counter-manifesto to the official emancipation charter. It denounced the terms of the emancipation and made radical proposals for revolutionary action to replace them with something more favourable to the peasantry. Chernyshevsky's authorship of the document is still contested but he was the one who took the responsibility. Despite the harshness of his sentence he was able to continue writing, supposedly turning out some four thousand pages during a seven month spell in the Peter-Paul fortress. However much it was that he actually produced, the most influential outcome was a novel precisely entitled *What Is to Be Done?* (*Chto delat'*?). Even more significant was its often-overlooked subtitle, *Stories of the New People*. The novel depicted its new people as rational egoists who recognized that their own interests would only be fulfilled when they co-operated with others and even, paradoxically, to defer to the interests of others, as one character gracefully does when his wife falls in love with another man. The figure that grabbed the imagination of generations of Russians was Rakhmetov, a young revolutionary who devoted his life and energy to making himself mentally and physically tough enough to fight for the revolution. To this end he worked with the barge-haulers of the Volga, the most downtrodden but toughest workers in Russia. He slept on a bed of nails. In this way Chernyshevsky's work was not just a story but a parable, a pointer to exemplary revolutionary behaviour. Some literary critics despised it. Unsurprisingly, Turgenev was one since Chernyshevsky was taking aim at Turgenev's depiction of Bazarov, who had (like Turgenev for better or worse) succumbed to the softness of love rather than the harshness of political struggle. Also unsurprisingly, one of Russia's finest literary stylists, the poet Afanasii Fet, deplored its unsubtle, direct, simple language. Dostoevsky was pushed to retaliate to it in his 1864 novella *Notes from the Underground,* denouncing its assumption of the rationality of humanity as the illusion of an innocent babe in the woods. Nonetheless, it was immensely influential. It was admired by Marx and Engels who described its author as a great Russian writer and critic[12] and, according to a friend of Lenin, the latter said that reading Chernyshevsky in his teens had 'plowed him over'[13] turning him from a conventional middle-class child into a budding revolutionary. He was not the only one. In a fascinating and controversial article, it has even been suggested Chernyshevsky was a key influence on a young Russian student born in 1905 named Alisa Rosenbaum (1905–82), better known to the world as the neoliberal conservative guru Ayn Rand.[14] Be that as it may, Chernyshevsky's novel was a landmark and a rallying cry. From the usual influences – the French Enlightenment, Hegel, Feuerbach, Fourier, Belinsky, Herzen – he derived not only his ethical doctrine of rational egoism but also his, apparently contradictory, socialism (since it was usually associated with altruism rather than egoism) and identification of the peasantry and the commune as the bedrocks of revolutionary change. The name populism (*narodnichestvo* from the Russian word *narod* meaning the people) became attached to this emerging set of ideas.[15] Chernyshevsky was its founding prophet and his vision of the future enthralled several intelligentsia generations.

As a prisoner and exile Chernyshevsky, for better or worse, could only contribute to the intellectual development of the movement. The consolidation of it as an intelligentsia-based social movement was in other hands. In the forefront were a former army officer-turned social analyst, editor and publicist, Pyotr Lavrov (1823–1900) and the literary critic and social analyst Nikolai Mikhailovsky (1842–1904). Mikhailovsky became one of the main theorists of populism, establishing some fundamental tenets which resounded down the generations. None of his statements was more influential than his assertion that the intelligentsia's 'awareness of the universal truth could only have been reached at the cost of the age-old suffering of the people. We are the people's debtors and this debt weighs down on our conscience'.[16] He was one of the first to formulate the specifically Russian notion of the intelligentsia as members of the wealthier and more privileged classes, distinct from the mass of peasants, workers and artisans, who listened to their conscience and devoted their lives to acting on the consequences, namely working for the good of the *narod* (the people). He also had complex sociological ideas about subjectivism (sometimes translated as individualism) being the high point of developmental progress. In contrast to Darwin he argued that human evolution was driven by higher levels of social organization emerging, which produced individual action to control and adapt the environment. Darwin, he objected, had considered the relationship to be the other way round, in which the environment shaped the individual. There was also a sense of willed action (voluntarism) in Mikhailovsky which opposed the more deterministic views of other positivists and of some Social Darwinists and other materialist schools. This led him to formulate another notion which echoed through populism. Although Western Europe had reached a higher level of development it was a society divided by the division of labour and (though Mikhailovsky seemed less aware of this) competition whereas Russia was less developed but had a higher level of organization. Where was that higher level of organization? It manifested itself in the deep-rooted collectivism of the peasant commune. The door was open for a key question which grew in acuteness as the century unwound. Could Russia convert itself into a socialist society more easily than western Europe? Could it build on what populists and others saw as its basic socialist, co-operative foundation and avoid having to trudge through the much-criticized inhuman, exploitative process of capitalism, which reduced workers to objects and herded them into insanitary cities where they succumbed to malnutrition, alcoholism, drugs and early death.

In the long context in which we have been tracing the rise of the intelligentsia we might make two comments about Mikhailovsky and the influential ideas he expressed. Although he was very much in the materialist, atheist and positivist mindset of the mid-nineteenth century, in that for him science and reason were the definitive guides and society was shaped by laws of the kind he believed he was enunciating, one can detect the faded footprint of much earlier thought, notably the impulse to what he called 'solidarity' as the highest social principle. It resembled the ancient idea of *sobornost'*, the gathering together of the whole people, the overcoming of social divisions. Second, though Mikhailovsky and his followers would have summarily rejected the idea, idealizing the commune, suggesting a path for Russian development which differed from the west and promoting an element of Russian superiority, it could also be found embedded in the ideas of the Slavophiles. Mikhailovsky and the populists had no time for mystical notions of Slavic destiny or religious illusions, as they saw them. They considered themselves confirmed westernizers but, once again, we find crucial overlap between radically different schools which make simple characterization difficult.

Lavrov shared many of the assumptions of Mikhailovsky though the latter's 'subjective sociology', as it came to be called, remained controversial. However, the idealization of the commune and the hope to avoid the capitalist stage of development remained in the forefront of the ideas of most populists. Lavrov engaged in the debate but his own contribution came more in the sphere of tactics. It was all very well to feel guilty in the face of peasant poverty but how could one do anything about it? What was to be done? Lavrov argued that the answer was for the intelligentsia to educate the peasantry to understand their plight. If the peasants could be brought to realize it was not just the local landowner who oppressed them but the system itself, and that this system pressed down on the vast majority, the peasants could be helped to understand that, through coming together (Mikhailovsky's 'solidarity' chimed in here), they would exert an unstoppable power. They would be able to overthrow the oppressive system and rebuild Russia along the lines of small-scale rural and urban workshops and enterprises based on co-operative forms of labour, such as the peasant commune (*obshchina*) and its urban equivalent the *artel'* (communal workshop).

This was only half an answer. It begged the question of how the intelligentsia might reach the peasantry in order to perform this task of education. The obstacles were enormous. Once again the intelligentsia was confronted with the fundamental difficulty of finding a social force to implement their ideas. The intelligentsia was a very small group, tens of thousands at the most. The peasants were some 70 million around 1870.[17] The intelligentsia were urban, the peasants spread across a vast landscape. The intelligentsia were educated, the peasants barely literate so how could the populists communicate with them? The intelligentsia, even the less privileged ones, were from a social group whom the peasants considered part of the elite and therefore untrustworthy. On top of that, the government was highly suspicious and hunted down populists for sedition, sending many to jail or exile. Lavrov's tactic seemed to be an impossible dream. Nonetheless, in the 1870s, the call went out for populist sympathizers to go into the villages and try to persuade the peasants to rebel. Hundreds, mainly university students, heeded the call. From 1873 to 1876 they ventured into the villages. The sudden appearance of strangers, who appeared to the peasants to come from the landowning classes, startled the tradition-bound villages. The new arrivals were treated with a vast range of responses. Some were listened to but most were not. Worse, many were attacked and others handed over to the police by the peasants. The rationalism, atheism and republicanism of many of the young populists drove a major wedge between them and the loyalist, religious peasants. By and large the movement was a disaster ending up in mass trials of hundreds of participants. It should also be noted that women played a significant part in the emerging populist movement. For the moment, let it suffice to say that their presence among the populist emissaries only served to alienate the misogynistic, patriarchal peasantry. Nonetheless, here and there, seeds of co-operation were laid especially by the more humble populist missionaries who took on a less admonitory, less pedagogic tone and began to merge themselves into peasant life for the long haul task of winning their confidence. Indeed, in the 1880s, there was a turn towards 'small deeds' and the ideas of its leading advocate, Iakov Abramov (1858–1906). Observing the failure of the apocalyptic approach embodied in the 'going to the people' Abramov began to advocate 'serving the people' in more mundane ways – helping with practical problems, teaching literacy and so on. In the 1880s, he called upon rural doctors and teachers and other educated people who worked among the peasantry to use their influence on the peasants to improve their lives.

For most, however, the failure of the two excursions into the countryside created a deep shock. Some concluded, like Lavrov himself, that the participants had been too optimistic, had underestimated the task of winning the peasants confidence and were guilty of confusing them with sudden exposure of what were alien ideas. In the eyes of some populists, the fiasco had underlined the significance of an entirely different approach, the use of physical force. They believed it was now necessary to move on from 'propaganda by the word' to a proactive 'propaganda by the deed', to terrorism.

In his 1970 Nobel Literature Prize Lecture the Soviet-era dissident, novelist, chronicler of the gulag, Slavophile and ultimately Putin supporter Alexander Solzhenitsyn (1918–2008) argued that Russians had preceded the rest of the world in evolving modern revolutionary and terrorist tactics and strategy.

> Dostoevsky's DEVILS – apparently a provincial nightmare fantasy of the last century – are crawling across the whole world in front of our very eyes, infesting countries where they could not have been dreamed of; and by means of the hijackings, kidnappings, explosions and fires of recent years they are announcing their determination to shake and destroy civilization! And they may well succeed. The young, at an age when they have not yet any experience other than sexual, when they do not yet have years of personal suffering and personal understanding behind them, are jubilantly repeating our depraved Russian blunders of the Nineteenth Century, under the impression that they are discovering something new.[18]

The brilliant, still definitive, account of the revolutionary movement in Russia in this period (1848–81) runs to almost 1,000 pages.[19] Revolutionary thought had taken on an explosive growth in this period. Violence had been considered an unfortunate but unavoidable part of the revolutionary process by many radical thinkers but the idea of terrorism as tactic was not widespread. Bakunin advocated violent resistance and proposed a kind of Darwinian social competition in which, so he thought, the fittest would survive.[20] However, terrorism was different. It was seen as a tactic to bring about revolution rather than a consequence of it. The first Russian terrorist of this era was Dmitrii Karakozov (1840–66), who fired a pistol shot at the tsar in 1866. The main outcome of this isolated act was a heightening of Alexander's security and a change of political approach which brought an end to reform and greater defensive vigilance on the part of the government. If there were even the faintest hopes of a constitution, Karakozov's shot had killed them off. Karakozov was executed (an unusual punishment in Russia where the death penalty was considered morally unacceptable and was only invoked for extreme offences). The organization to which he belonged, led by his cousin Nikolai Ishutin (1840–79), was broken up and ten supposed associates were sentenced to hard labour while, in a tribute to the independence of courts and juries at this time, twenty-five were acquitted. Ishutin, despite only being active for four or five years, was the prototype terrorist. Alongside the growing utopian socialism and working with the people – which led him to set up a sewing co-operative and a small free school – Ishutin believed, that in the disappointment of the post-emancipation years, only conspiracy, violence and terror would bring down tsarism. He participated in a number of fleeting organizations, notably Land and Liberty (*Zemliia i voliia*) and his own conspiratorial groups The Organisation (*Organizatsiia*) and Hell (*Ad*). He and his associates were swept up in the police roundup following Karakozov's *attentat*. He suffered mental breakdown under the pressure of solitary confinement in the Shlüsselberg prison fortress but, despite this, he was moved to exile and hard labour in Siberia for the rest of his life. He was a forerunner but it was only in the mid-1870s that terror became a serious threat even though the numbers involved directly were probably in the very low hundreds.

The next wave of terrorism was a response to the, according to some, failure of the Going to the People. A few populists decided it was time to follow other paths for radicalizing the peasants. In 1876, under the guidance of Mark Natanson (1851–1919), a former member of Land and Liberty, a group formed a new political movement called The People's Freedom (*Narodnaia voliia* also known as The People's Will in English). Believing it was impossible in Russian conditions to organize even semi-openly and democratically the group used a cell structure in which only one or two members knew anyone from another cell. This meant that, even if the police broke up a cell, it would not necessarily lead them to another. It also had a permanent central executive committee., which included, among others Alexander Mikhailov (1855–84), Andrei Zhelyabov (1851–81), Sophia Perovskaya (1853–81), Vera Figner (1852–1942), Nikolai Morozov (1854–1946), Mikhail Frolenko (1848–1938), Aaron Zundelevich (1852–1923), Savely Zlatopolsky (1855–85) and Lev Tikhomirov (1852–1923). This form of organization was influential on several later movements including Lenin's Bolshevik faction.

The leadership quickly evolved the aim of killing the tsar as its central policy as well as carrying out assassinations of government officials, usually very high-ranking police chiefs. Several attempts were made to kill Alexander. In one case, a carpenter, named Khalturin, succeeded in gaining employment in the Winter Palace which allowed him to smuggle in small quantities of dynamite on a regular basis. When he had assembled enough he detonated it under a reception room where the tsar was scheduled to host élite guests. The tsar was delayed and was not in attendance when the bomb exploded. Attempts to blow up his train also failed to catch him. The imaginative enterprise of building a tunnel under the main street of the city, Nevsky Prospekt, also failed as, for security reasons, the tsar was kept away from the main thoroughfares. It was on a side street running beside the Ekaterinskii Canal that Alexander's good luck ran out. A bomb thrower was waiting for just such an opportunity and threw his bomb at the royal carriage. The tsar himself was uninjured and stepped down from his carriage when a second bomber threw his device and fatally injured the tsar who died within hours on 1 (13) March 1881.

The concept behind the tactic of terror was that it would demonstrate the vulnerability of the oppressors and show the peasants that they could strike them down. It was hoped that a spontaneous nationwide uprising would follow a successful assassination. In this, the terrorists were disappointed. Few disturbances took place. Rather, the country, including the peasantry, was stunned by the unexpected development. The authorities moved with speed to arrest the group and execute its leading figures, including Sofia Perovskaia, Andrei Zheliabov, Nikolai Kibalchich, Nikolai Rysakov and Timofei Mikhailov. In addition, Ignaty Grinevitsky died in the action, Nikolai Sablin was shot dead while being arrested, and Gesia Gelf'man's execution was postponed because of her pregnancy but medical aid was withheld when she gave birth and she died of sepsis. The arrests and executions liquidated the St Petersburg branch. Further terrorist acts were conducted in the 1880s in Moscow, Kyiv and the provinces and three would-be regicides were executed in 1887 for a plot against Alexander III. One of the martyrs was Alexander Ulianov whose brother Vladimir became known to the world as Lenin.

Rather than demonstrate the state's weakness the acts of terror mainly served to reinforce the repressive reaction of the state. The new tsar quickly brought in so-called Temporary Regulations reversing some of the reforms and putting more authority back in the hands of the gentry. One of the first major outbursts of anti-semitism was orchestrated by the authorities to turn social hostility away from the authorities and blame the Jewish population of Russia for the attacks. For the next almost twenty-five years, a new *éminence grise*, Konstantin Pobedonostsev (1827–1907), became the chief architect of political strategy for Alexander III and his son Nicholas II. Pobedonostsev was an arch-reactionary who firmly promoted the uniqueness of autocracy, its special suitability for Russia and denounced all notions of democracy as imports of a morally rotten and corrupt western society. He published his views in a collection of essays entitled *Moskovskii sbornik* (Literally *Moscow Collection* but translated under the title *Reflections of a Russian Statesman*).[21] Fatefully, Pobedonostsev not only took an ultra-Slavophile line. He argued that the best way to bring the diverse Russian Empire together was to assert the values of the largest group, Russians, over the literally hundreds of ethnic and linguistic minorities. Rather than repress the minorities, Russification policies stirred deep resentments in them. The 1881 assassination had not sparked off any significant uprisings but it had precipitated an unshakeable opposition to reform in the minds of the last two tsars, a renewed wave of repression and a suicidal policy of enforced Russification. Inadvertently, they had exposed a very different effect of terrorism, the stimulation of governmental reaction and overreaction which, in turn, created greater and greater popular resentment. Perhaps, after all, the intelligentsia martyr/assassins of 1881 would have their revenge in the long run. The political situation had altered beyond recognition. Alexander's reforms were as dead as the Tsar Liberator himself. Pobedonostsev and the governing circles saw them as the cause of unrest and terrorism and vowed never to repeat the supposed error. Their intended beneficiaries, the peasants, saw only their inadequacy as their economy stalled after 1881. The gentry were in unexpected decline. Although the 1880s was a decade of rampant government reaction, revolutionary intellectuals began to sense new openings, new opportunities and came up with new strategies. Inadvertently, the autocracy after 1881 had set the compass heading in the direction of revolution.

The intelligentsia in the mid-nineteenth century

It was in the sixties and early seventies that the term 'intelligentsia' began to catch on. The first appearances of the word, which, although it later came to be applied mainly to the Russian group, most authorities consider to be a derivative from the German 'intelligenz' (intelligence), itself derived from the Latin *intelligentia*. Its first use in Russia has been attributed to Belinsky and Ogarev and others around 1850. From the beginning, definition became somewhat confused. It was originally meant to distinguish what was, at the time, a uniquely Russian phenomenon of members of the educated élite abandoning their own careers and interests and adhering to the cause of modernizing Russia, i.e. helping to overcome 'backwardness', through methods which would produce a fairer, more equal and more just society. Such impulses could be less dramatically expressed in the partially democratic and liberal societies of the west through political writing, political agitation, union organization, being a progressive educator and even being elected to a public office. None of these was open to the political opposition in Russia. Even conservative reformers, the most likely people to be able to save the autocracy, were treated with suspicion by the last four tsars. Constitutions were granted to Poland and Bulgaria through autocratic patronage but any mention of the word in connection with Russia was considered seditious. It has been suggested that the assassination in March 1881 not only turned the tide against reform on a large scale but that it also frustrated it more directly. At the moment of his assassination Alexander was on his way home from a formal meeting where he had agreed that a set of proposals, which some see as a potential constitution, drawn up by Count Loris-Melikov, should be discussed at the Council of Ministers. In fact, the proposals were very mild, simply slightly broadening the scope of recruitment to advisory bodies and leaving all legislative power firmly in autocratic hands. The new tsar, Alexander III (1845–94: reigned 1881 to 1894), immediately jettisoned the proposals and dismissed Loris-Melikov, compounding the error that reforms rather than lack of reforms were at the root of Russia's political crises. It is vital to remember that, with increased repression after 1881 and tighter censorship, even loyal critics of autocracy had little legal space for manoeuvre. Radical criticism came directly up against the state apparatus and all forms of political organization and protest were illegal. Participants were liable to arrest and imprisonment. The absence of legal space for opposition strengthened earlier tendencies of Aesopian language, diversion of political discussion into fictional literary forms and self-imposed foreign exile. In addition, censorship could also be undermined by discussing topics in technical language, for instance, economics. Famously, Marx's *Das Kapital* was translated into Russian and passed by the censorship in 1872, because it was deemed too difficult for the average reader to understand. One of the two censors assigned to it reported that 'It can be confidently stated, that in Russia few will read it and even fewer will understand it.'[22] It was under these unpromising, difficult and dangerous conditions that the Russian intelligentsia formed itself and challenged the autocracy, which hung on for twenty-three more years until, on the cusp of the twentieth century, its increasingly rigid structures cracked in many crucial places.

Such challenging conditions were vital to the formation of the intelligentsia's sense of a special identity and mission. The mission was the easier part to define and the simple concept of 'serving the people' took root and many *intelligenty* associated themselves with it. Peter Lavrov came up with one of the first definitions of the intelligentsia itself describing its members as 'critically thinking people'. A slogan emerged which stated that the intelligentsia was 'the mind, honour and conscience of the people' (*Um, chest' i sovest' naroda*), a phrase that not only resounded through the late nineteenth century but was also used by the Soviet Communist Party as a self-description, even in its final decades when it could be seen prominently displayed on the road from the main international airport, Moscow Sheremet'evo, to the city. Observers at the time often compared the intelligentsia to a monastic order on account of its devotion to a crusading chivalry. To belong was considered a great honour and from early on a favourite exercise of its members was to decide who was in and who was out. Any senior state official was out. Conservatives and Slavophiles were considered to be out. Less overtly political writers, artists and composers were out. Dostoevsky was an outsider. Tolstoy ruled himself out, as did others. However, such fine discrimination to the point of hair-splitting is unhelpful.

The problem was compounded by the emergence over time of intellectuals fitting a more sociological definition as workers by the brain as opposed to the view of the intelligentsia as the servants of the people. However, it is necessary to acknowledge the way the two groups overlap. Few intellectuals, especially in the creative field, were completely non-political. Many of them were the audiences for the writings of leading *intelligenty*. Many scientists and engineers followed their profession with a view to 'serving the people' in a practical way, linked to what was called a 'small deeds' approach, meaning immediate practical gains were prioritized over large, sometimes nebulous, schemes, for reform and revolution. While the 'managerial revolution' lay in the future, the scope of intellectual labour was expanding and important elements of those involved were as much part of the fight for a new and better Russia as were the political *intelligenty*.

As a result, the social milieu in which the intelligentsia was developing was becoming broader (as was the intelligentsia itself) and much more complex in response to changing social and economic demands. Although still few in number and with small student enrollments, universities were becoming the main recruiting ground for *intelligenty* and intellectuals in the broader sense. The forerunners, up to and including Tolstoy and Lavrov, had been military officers rather than university students. From the 1860s onwards only a few men of military background could be found in the intelligentsia. For what it is worth, Lavrov was one of the last *intelligenty* who had been educated primarily as an army officer and Chernyshevsky was one of the first to have been a seminarian. While they were not able to access university education in anything like the scope offered to men,[23] it is obvious that an important minority of women were increasingly active in the political intelligentsia even to the point of carrying out assassinations, like Sophie Perovskaia and Vera Zasulich (1851–1919) who shot and severely injured General Trepov, the police chief of St Petersburg in 1878. Despite being caught literally with a smoking gun the jury acquitted her because they considered it to be a justified act. The decision pretty much sounded the death knell for jury trials in Russian Imperial courts.

Why was the importance of students and universities growing? Although outshone by its western neighbours, the Russian economy was growing at its own pace. In particular, factories were spreading and raw material, transport and trading resources were expanding in proportion. This brought a rapid expansion, though perhaps not an explosion, in the knowledge base. New skills, ideas, practices had to be mastered. To take a few key examples, industrial society hastened urbanization, called for increasingly complex organizational skills, required new raw materials which demanded, for example, mining skills plus geological and geographical expertise. Construction needed site supervisors, architects, building materials and access. Theoretical and practical sciences and engineering were at a premium. Development had to be financed. Where the state was involved, as it had been for centuries, new sources of taxation or, later, international borrowing needed financial, accounting and clerical skills. Private investment needed a sound system of banks and trustworthy credit backed by enforceable civil and criminal law. All of these demands were based on the expansion of technical and scientific education. Increasing numbers of educated people brought about new cultural markets for leisure activities including theatre, opera, journals, newspapers, books and tourism among many other things. These, in turn, stimulated art schools, drama, literature and scholarship. The emergence of most of these things put additional pressure on Russia's creaking political institutions. Educated people tend to be more resentful of restrictions on their freedom and growing sense of social self-importance. To add to the socio-economic and political pressures, in 1881 Russia was still trying to catch up with the first, coal and steam driven, industrial revolution while the 'advanced' world was on the cusp of a second phase based on electricity, steel and chemicals (including explosives). Russia's survival and, more specifically, the autocracy's prospects demanded not falling behind. The example of the Ottoman Empire, in its increasingly abject submission to British and French imperialism and internal dissolution under pressures of modernization, continued to be a powerful warning of the cost of failure. Nonetheless, industrialization and modernization, far from being government priorities, were treated until the end with immense suspicion by the autocracy. New classes of workers and middle-class capitalists, professionals and industrialists were not only not welcomed but treated with great wariness by senior state officials.[24]

Railways and, inevitably, armaments were key drivers of change in mid- and late-nineteenth-century Russia. These in turn brought great demands and fostered extensive, often unintended but inevitable, consequences. Railways were the internet of the middle and late nineteenth century. They demanded extensive new skill sets from engineering and construction to the complexities of timetabling, pricing and ticketing. Demand for coal, firewood, steel and locomotive, freight waggon and passenger carriage construction increased exponentially. Internal production or technological imports had to meet this demand. Both were seen as risky by the authorities. But railways also had massive social and geographic consequences. They enabled greater social mobility, broke down local markets and favoured towns and cities. Like early internet development, vast speculative bubbles burst at great cost to investors. Where internet and IT companies recovered and resulted in the formation of dangerous, powerful global monopolies, railway investment, especially in Russia, remained short-term and corrupt. The resulting railway infrastructure bore signs of get-rich quick schemes rather than serious structural planning. Shoddily constructed single-track lines on poor quality track beds meant use of the lines quickly peaked and, in the worst cases, only a limited number of relatively light trains could run each day. Nonetheless, construction boomed in waves, one around the 1860s and'70s the next in the 1890s and early twentieth century. The line from St Petersburg to Moscow was not completed until 1851. By 1870 Russia had as much railway track as France, but, of course, spread out in a vastly larger space. From 1866 to the end of the century the network grew from 5,000k to 53,200k. The ambitious project for the Trans-Siberian line from Moscow to Vladivostock was inaugurated in 1891 and fully opened in 1904. From 1897 it had been necessary to transfer to a boat across Lake Baikal in the summer, and sledges in the winter. During one exceptionally cold spell temporary tracks were laid across the ice. Thanks to an extraordinary feat of engineering a series of twisting tunnels was constructed, in part by prison labour, to take the tracks around the southern shore of the lake. The entire route was 9,200k but, for the time being, it was mostly single track and could only take twenty-four pairs of trains (a pair means one in each direction) per day.

Railways also had strategic importance, the finishing date of 1904 for the Trans Siberian being a pointer since the rush to completion was largely created by the approaching war with Japan. Armaments were the other great driver of economic and technical development. In 1881, western Europe was in the middle of a military revolution. The groundwork went back to Napoleon and the establishment of tax, recruitment and logistics bureaucracies capable of supporting conscripted armies of over a million. Technical changes, notably the development of ever more powerful explosives, nullified traditional defence methods such as heavily protected fortresses with thick, resistant walls, and called for new techniques. Automatic weapons, such as various kinds of machine gun, and the development of rifling (which spun projectiles making them more predictable and precise in flight) plus strong steel construction, meant larger, more accurate guns and artillery. By the early twentieth-century the range of artillery was approaching 30k for the largest weapons, many of which were deployed on 'Dreadnoughts', very heavily armed and armoured battleships of unprecedented sized. By 1900, Russia's largest factory was the Putilov complex in St Petersburg which specialized in naval construction. Numbers of employees varied but 20,000 workers was normal. Many of Russia's largest factories in the latter half of the nineteenth century were military-related. This includes textiles, the dominant industry in the Moscow region, as military uniforms were an output staple. While some military needs could be met by purchases from allies, full independence required as much good-quality domestic production as possible. The arms race was heating up after 1880 and there was an increasingly desperate game of 'devil take the hindmost' developing which the autocracy could not lose. Its fundamental paradox was tightening around it. Its instincts were still to fight change in order to preserve itself, but without change it would be destroyed.

The quickening of Russian society, based on extended numbers of educated men and increasingly women, spread into many spheres including intellectual and cultural ones. Cultural life expanded, its themes became more complex and the debate about Russian identity extended further in the arts. Science was less and less in the hands of gentleman amateurs and became increasingly professional, and even commercial, though, as elsewhere, it also retreated from the natural world into the closed environment of the laboratory. Russian society was producing an extremely rich cultural life despite stifling censorship, political conservatism and even reaction and a complete absence of legal independent political activity. Three key indicators from the mid-century on embody the new spirit. Thick journals proliferated. Theatre and, especially, opera explored Russian historical themes and identity. The Academy of Sciences broke extensive barriers and many of its members worked at the frontiers of knowledge. In a number of areas Russia was no longer following but in the forefront of European cultural and scientific advance.

The decades from 1850 to 1914 were the golden age of Russian thick journals. Their equivalents also flourished in Britain, France, the United States and other 'advanced' countries but nowhere did they have the breadth, intensity and importance they came to command in Russia. We encountered the early predecessors in the 1780s as the Russian public sphere struggled for its first breath. Many leading intellectuals were editors or publishers and this remained the case in and after the middle of the nineteenth century. They became the sites of first publication of what became literary classics by Tolstoy, Dostoevsky and many other writers. Novels were serialized, stories published in their entirety. In addition, philosophy, religion, science and social analysis filled their pages. Criticism was prevalent in all these fields and thunderous arguments often raged. Each journal had its own orientation – liberal, nationalist, Slavophile, westernizer and by the early twentieth century each emerging political tendency – Socialist Revolutionary, social democratic, liberal, conservative – had its own journal. Even the Ministry of Enlightenment, the official title of the education ministry, published one from 1834 to 1917. Even more surprisingly, one of the forerunners, which was part newspaper part cultural review and was published daily from 1831, *The Northern Bee* (*Severnaia pchela*), was published in St Petersburg (1825–64) in conjunction with the Okhrana (Secret Police) through links with its head, Count Benckendorf who praised it for its 'loyalty to the throne and purity of morals'.[25] The journals were testimony to the great richness and variety of Russian thought. Every month each issue was packed with ideas, information, argument, illustrations, discussions, belles-lettres and criticism of the latest trends and productions in literature, music, the fine arts and science. By and large they were not commercial propositions. Many of them depended on a wealthy patron or the enthusiasm of the editorial team. They spawned many generations of great editors from Novikov onwards which even continued after the 1917 revolution, embracing figures like Alexander Tvardovsky who edited the journal *Novyi mir* (*New World)* from 1950–54 and 1956–70. They were very varied in their longevity. Dostoevsky and his brother Mikhail set up the journal *Epokha* (*The Epoch*). The first issue came out in March 1864 but, despite publishing the early chapters of Dostoevsky's *Notes from Underground* and other of his works, as well as items by Leskov and Turgenev, the last issue came out in February 1865 after the double blow of money problems and the death of Mikhail. Others were more successful. The liberal journal *Russkaia mysl'* (*Russian Thought*) flourished from 1880 to 1918, after which it was published abroad until 1927 and even revived in Paris from 1947 to the present.

Otechestvennie zapiski (*Notes from the Fatherland*) flourished from 1820 to 1884 and *Istoricheskii vestnik* (*The Historical Messenger*) from 1882 to 1917.[26] Circulation figures varied from less than a thousand for niche journals up to and beyond 10,000 for the firmly established ones. *Russkaia mysl'* had 14,000 subscribers at its peak.[27] The financial situation of many of them was precarious and they had to negotiate a highly intrusive censorship. To make matters worse, censorship operated *after* publication, meaning that if something offended the censors it would lead to the confiscation of the entire print run of an issue, which could deal a fatal blow to a journal's fragile finances. It is to the immense credit of all involved that such intimidatory tactics did not prevent the journals from being lively, topical, innovative and controversial, though they were thoroughly policed. Direct political discussion, as opposed to debating principles and abstract propositions, was fraught with difficulties. Nothing testifies better to the vitality, growth and boldness of the intelligentsia and its associates than the thriving culture of the thick journals.[28]

Second only to the reputation of its great writers a brilliant explosion of music and opera also lit up Russia from around 1850 on. The pioneers were Glinka and, following him, the group of five St Petersburg composers who came to be known as 'the mighty handful' (*Moguchaia kuchka*) – Modest Mussorgsky (1839–81), César Cui (1835–1918), Alexander Borodin (1833–87) and Nikolai Rimsky-Korsakov (1844–1908) – who collaborated loosely from 1856 to 1870 under the leadership of Mily Balakirev (1837–1910). From the point of view of our study the importance of these, and later, composers is that, apart from several of them joining the western musical pantheon, they adapted western orchestral conventions and styles but also Russified them by technical adaptations, bringing in new instruments, even using bells, and yet, most important of all, exploring and expressing a distinct Russian identity, not least by adapting Russian folk music. Their characteristic dramatic themes included Russian folk tales (Ruslan and Liudmila, the lost city of Kitezh, the legend of the simple twelfth-century troubadour and *gusli* player Sadko who amassed a fortune); key moments and figures in Russian history (Prince Igor, Boris Godunov, the 1682 rebellion of the Streltsy and Old Believers against incipient westernization) and Eurasian legends (Scheherezade, the Polovtsian Dances, Antar, Tamara). In a series of spectacular operas, concertos, symphonies and, later, ballets the fundamental foundations of Russian identity, in all its nuances and ambiguities, were debated in musical terms. Ironically and revealingly, using an essentially imported medium, the Mighty Handful protested against the suffocation of Russian culture by influences from the west.

The emergence of opera and orchestral music was not only significant for their themes and content but they also indicate a broadening of the cultural élite to provide an expanding market for a very expensive art form. In the mid-century, ballet, opera and music burst out of the aristocratic salon and associated patronage – in the eighteenth century serfs had been trained as performers for chamber theatre, music, ballet and opera performed in aristocratic mansions – into a new public cultural market and audience in the metropolitan cities. Impoverished *intelligenty* and teachers could not afford such things but the growing middle and professional educated classes could and increasingly did form a new audience. Theatre also followed a similar route although, until the modernism of Chekhov in the last quarter of the century, it did not hit heights comparable to music. In both spheres, royal patronage remained important and Imperial theatres increased in influence. Significantly, even at this time, state support was having an important impact on the performing arts. By 1900 the six main theatres in Russia were Imperial, that is state-controlled – the Alexandrinsky, Mariinsky, Mikhailovsky and Maly in Saint Petersburg, Maly and Bolshoi in Moscow – and had an extensive network of schools to develop the talents of young performers.[29] One of the main audiences for theatre in the late nineteenth and early twentieth centuries was students. They were known to go without food in order to save up for tickets which were often available to them at discounted rates.[30]

Finally, Russian intellectuals also began to become of major significance in the development of science. In the field of mathematics Russian scholars, the most pre-eminent being Nikolai Lobachevsky (1792–1856) who developed a non-Euclidean geometry, established a leading role which they inherited from eighteenth-century predecessors such as Euler and Magnitsky, and have retained down to the present. Russian science remained centred on the Academy of Sciences which flourished as never before and expanded in a multitude of directions. It continued to be noted for investigative expeditions especially on the territories of the Russian Empire, including the vast territories in Central Asia acquired in the 1850s, and neighbouring territories and regions including the Arctic, establishing Russia as a leading force in polar exploration and science. As early as 1820, Bellingshausen and Lazarev had led an expedition to the Antarctic. The sky was literally the limit as, in 1839, one of the world's leading astronomical observatories was opened at Pulkovo, near St Petersburg. The leading figures behind it were its first director V.Ia. Struve and his son, O.V. Struve who took over from him. A significant part of the importance of astronomical observation lay in its connections with navigation and many of the sciences developed in Russia had a crucial practical dimension. Geographical and geological expertise promoted industry. In the latter part of the century significant sources of platinum were found in the Urals and, in Fergana in Central Asia, deposits of uranium were detected. The vast reserves of Siberia, including gold, silver, diamonds and coal, were sought out and began to be exploited.

The academy did not confine itself to natural sciences. There was an early and continuing interest in language and linguistics. Academician Ia.K. Grot led the task of standardizing Russian spelling and orthography, establishing norms in his textbook of 1885 which have stood the test of time. They were modified in 1918 by another academician, Aleksandr Shakhmatov, as a result of which certain Russian letters and shapes of letters were changed. There were also linguistic and philological departments in the academy and they shaded into one of the world-leading areas of ethnography. The proximity, diversity and close interaction between the many non-Russian and non-Slavic ethnicities in the empire[31] was not only an intellectual stimulus to study but also a practical one to improve communications and to interact with minorities, in part, of course, to rule over and exploit them and their resources better, but the scholarship went beyond simple orientalist and imperialist norms. There were also close connections with literature and the arts with many leading figures being associates of the Academy such as Goncharov, Dostoevsky, Turgenev, Ostrovskii, A.K. Tolstoi, Tiutchev, Fet and others, a feature which continued into the twentieth century and the Soviet and post-Soviet eras. History was also a major preoccupation. Karamzin's history began to appear from 1818, the same year he became a full academician. As well as writing history the accumulation of source documents and the like was pursued by a number of specialists recruited and led by N.P. Rumiantsev whose collection became the initial core of a museum in 1832 and was then linked to the Imperial Library and named after him in 1862.[32]

As had been the case from the beginning, the academy was proud of its international reputation and sought to consolidate links with leading scientists beyond Russia's borders. Among the illustrious scientists of the late eighteenth and nineteenth centuries who became members were Ampère, Gay-Lussac, T.J. Huxley, Herschel, Goethe, Humboldt, Darwin, Cuvier, Lyle, Liebich and Thomas Malthus. The Academy always had a face towards the outside world and thereby maintained a dimension of pursuing the Petrine westernizing adventure aimed at acquiring material, scientific and military knowledge rather than importing rational and liberal political philosophies. Many scientists were conservative in outlook but it was still impossible to separate the wanted from unwanted consequences of knowledge acquisition. The problem for the autocracy remained, as ever, trying to fit new wine in old wineskins.[33]

There was a multitude of notable figures involved in these and other areas but one of the most extraordinary was the astonishing figure of Sofia Kovalevskaia (1850–91, née Sofia Vasilievna Korvin-Krukovskaia), a mathematical genius from childhood, who is credited with being the first woman to achieve a full doctorate and the first to be appointed to a university chair, extraordinary achievements to fit in her brief forty-one years of life. On account of the prevailing conditions she had to pursue her studies and stellar career abroad where she was celebrated in London, Paris, Berlin, Heidelberg, Göttingen (where she was awarded her doctorate) and Stockholm where she held her professorship and where she died. There is even thought to be a reference to her most significant mathematical contribution – on the theory of spinning solids – in George Eliot's *Middlemarch*. The reference was published many years before Kovalevskaia had made her breakthrough and is perhaps a result of her having discussed the theme she was working on when she attended George Eliot's London salon when she was nineteen.[34] The best Russia was officially able to do for her was the not-insignificant gesture of appointing her as a corresponding member of the Academy of Sciences in 1889, an appointment which necessitated a rule change for it to happen. Although Kovalevskaia spent most of her career outside Russia she lived an intensely Russian life of the period. She was an ardent nihilist, which she understood to mean the testing of all knowledge, customs and practices against the hard rationality of science. She wrote an autobiographical novel entitled *The Nihilist Woman*[35] (*Nigilistka*) and that is exactly what she was, though she was not an exponent of violence for its own sake. As well as smashing through what were concrete platforms rather than glass ceilings with her brilliance, she lived an extraordinary personal life. At the age of nineteen she disputed with Herbert Spencer on the topic of 'Woman's Capacity for Abstract Thought' at one of George Eliot's Sunday salons. One can only speculate what her response might have been to such a provocative topic. She left London to support the Paris Commune with her sister Anna and Anna's common law husband Victor Jaclard, a member of the French National Guard. Anna and her husband were both arrested and only saved from possible execution by intense lobbying by friends and a probably officially connived at escape from French detention. Sofia's radical commitment was not dimmed and she framed everything she did in her nihilist optic. In 1868 she had conducted a marriage of convenience (without it her travels and career would have been next to impossible) with a fellow student who specialized in palaeontology, Vladimir Kovalevsky, who was the first to translate several of Darwin's works into Russian. He was an acquaintance of both Darwin and T.H. Huxley.[36] His own thesis, on the evolution of the large single-toed horse from its more diminutive multi-toed ancestors, which he attributed to the transfer from forest life to the open plain, has been described as 'the most famous evolutionary story of all'.[37] The platonic couple returned to Russia in 1878 with Vladimir hoping to land a chair of palaeontology which never materialized. At some point, possibly in the wake of her father's death, the couple consummated the relationship and a daughter was born in October 1878 (d. 1952).[38] Sadly, unable to get a post and having taken on a position which provided for them for several years but ended up in scandal, bankruptcy and depression, Vladimir, desperate at not being able to support his family, committed suicide in 1883. Although she had left him in 1881, Sofia was devastated and had to be practically force fed for several days. Required to fend for herself, which was not possible in Russian universities, she left once more for the west. Through German contacts she obtained a professorship in mathematics at Stockholm University which she held, adopting an alternative form of her name, as Sonya Kovalevskaia until her untimely death. In 1889 she met and became close to the eminent sociologist and distant relative of her first husband, Maksim Kovalevsky (1851–1916), himself in self-imposed exile because of government harassment in the grim conditions of Alexander III's reign. She rejected a marriage proposal from him, supposedly because she did not want to engage in another formal marriage since it would, she claimed, lead Maksim to take her for granted and seek a mistress.[39] Nonetheless, they spent her last years happily together. In a tragic twist of fate Sofia had reported that she had commented to George Eliot that her characters seemed to die just when they were becoming interesting. According to Kovalevskaia, Eliot's response was that that was exactly what tended to happen in real life. Kovalevskaia's retort was cutting. It was, she said, what appeared to have happened to Eliot herself.[40] Tragically, it was literally true of Kovalevskaia. Just after returning to Stockholm from a holiday in Nice with Maksim, and only five years after she wrote the memoir, Kovalevskaia herself died of pneumonia complications from influenza which she caught during an epidemic.

Kovalevskaia's life draws together many central features of the mid-to-late century intelligentsia. Her network of connections indicated that, despite the expansion, the intelligentsia circle remained a tight one. In London her husband had been tutor to Herzen's daughter as well as being a close acquaintance, associate and disciple of Darwin. Her second husband, Maksim, was admitted to the Academy of Sciences in 1899 as a corresponding member and, in 1914, a full Academician. After 1905 he served as a deputy in the State Duma and was appointed to the State Council, its upper chamber. He was personally acquainted with Marx, Engels, Herbert Spencer and Vladimir Solov'ev. Sofia's sister, Anna, was sheltered by Marx in Highgate when she fled after the Commune. Before that she had turned down a marriage proposal from Dostoevsky in 1864 although, when she and Jaclard returned to Russia, she took up his friendship again, despite the earlier rebuff and the fact that that while Anna remained a utopian socialist, Dostoevsky had moved on from his earlier commitment in the direction of Slavophilism and religious mysticism. Crossing great divides, her daughter became a prominent doctor and translator in the Soviet era. Sophia's personality and achievements were also illustrative of the developing intelligentsia spirit. She was a brilliant scientist but also crossed to the other part of the intelligentsia in being a passionately committed and active revolutionary. She lived her life along highly unconventional lines which reflected her own deeply held and personal convictions. Needless to say she was one of the greatest fighters of the century for women's equality, a trait which most male members of the intelligentsia were happy to acknowledge in theory but did not always carry out in practice. Wives and female family members were more likely to be seen as acolytes of the great men rather than equals or acknowledged superiors.[41] Despite her rebuffs in Russia she was still inspired by science and knowledge as keys to the development and transformation of her country and the true liberation of its oppressed masses.

The case of Kovalevskaia and the other illustrious members of the political, scientific, creative and administrative intelligentsia raises one more puzzle and one caveat. How could such an array of talent burst out in the unpromising environment of repressive government including wide-ranging censorship and a political police; relative economic backwardness; an absence of basic civil and human rights and a vast, exploited peasant population; a confused national identity and perceived external threats. There is no simple answer to this question. One might be tempted to think that the intelligentsia somehow flourished despite the difficult conditions. However, it is more likely that the opposite is true. The very pressures of 'backwardness' in all its nuances were a strong stimulus. Compared to western Europe, Russia lagged behind economically and politically. It lacked rights and it had a completely anachronistic government which began to entrench itself in what, almost inevitably, given the choices of the last three tsars, were its last decades. Even loyal supporters of autocracy could see the need for controlled reform to secure the dynasty. The tsars themselves could not, setting them on a collision course with most of the emerging civil society. Alienating so many, including those who were conservative by temperament, stimulated responses. Even moderate demands – for a constitution, some kind of representation of the élites let alone the middle classes – were considered seditious. For many, revolution was the forced outcome since there was no other channel. The need for change was obvious to many and stimulated restricted and disguised discussion of how and why. Innate loyalty to Russia and the Russian idea was widespread in the educated classes who were outraged to see Russia internationally humiliated, as she had been in the Crimean War and the Berlin Conference of 1878 when she was stripped of critical gains from the latest Russo-Turkish war by the Great Powers, who opposed Russia's geopolitical and cultural encroachment towards its historic goal of restoring Constantinople to the Orthodox world.

Such problems would have been stimulus enough but as we have already seen, the autocracy, though it stifled political change, needed economic modernization to keep up in the developing arms race and all that that implied. To do so it needed educated people and in so doing was sowing dragon's teeth. Educated people would emerge and be more inclined to oppose the status quo, fight for rights and, as had been the case since Radishchev at least, be ashamed of the oppression of the peasants. The autocracy was undermining itself and stimulating a great outburst of political and cultural activity responding to the situation. The great operas of the Mighty Handful and Rimsky-Korsakov, the novels of Dostoevsky and Tolstoy were all imbued, among other things, with questions raised by Russia's dilemmas. Should it follow western paths? Was it self-sufficient and could it ignore the outside world? Should it pursue its own path? What was Russianness in the context of a state with 150 plus ethnic groups? Even radicals wanted Russia to be a strong and prosperous power. Curiously, the dilemmas have never been solved and, as we shall see, stimulated discussions through the revolution and into and beyond the Soviet era. Today, Russia is still, overall less developed than its western comparators though it is more advanced compared to its large eastern comparators such as India and China. But, although this is not to say nothing has changed, far from it, the dilemmas of progress and lack of clearly established rights and a truly representative government have remained the crucible in which the intelligentsia, dissidents and post-Soviet political activists were forged by fire.

And the caveat? It needs to be kept in the forefront of analysis that even in 1900 the intelligentsia, even in its widest definition, only comprised tens of thousands of people in a population of around 100 million. Numerically, they were a drop in the ocean. The radicals were deeply attached to the cause of serving the people but by 1881 had only met failure to connect whether it be through nihilism, populism by propaganda or by terrorism. The would-be recipients of the intelligentsia's self-sacrifice had not stirred. They were little affected by the issue of modernization before 1881. Afterwards it increasingly bore in on them as Europe's Great Agrarian Depression caused adverse market conditions which, thanks to the opening up of local markets into an expanding national and international market for grain, exposed them to falling world grain prices. Even so, this did not stimulate change. A few peasants became small landowners and so on themselves but the peasantry as a whole lived traditional lives based on the village, strip system, redistribution of land and a culture of folk traditions, orthodoxy and vodka. They distrusted the outside, urban-based world, barely distinguishing between the tax collector and the would-be revolutionary saviour. They turned their backs and laid their bets on reproducing the world they knew. This frustrated reformers of all kinds including progressive landlords, the state and the radical intelligentsia. The vast majority of Russians, the peasantry, remained inward looking. The nodes of modernization were mainly in cities and urban settlements. The masses remained unchanged, untouched and unresponsive to the blandishments of their would-be benefactors. At the end of Pushkin's play *Boris Godunov* (1831) and Moussorgsky's opera version (1874) is one of the most famous stage directions of all time – '*narod molchit*', 'the people are silent.' New schemes were afoot to change that.

5

The golden age of the intelligentsia – Apocalypse and the approach of revolution

From the 1881 assassination to the 1905 revolution (1) – Early Russian Marxism i.) Marx, Populism and Peasants

The bomb that killed Alexander also destroyed the revolutionary movement. Energetic repression soon brought about a roundup of members of *Narodnaia voliia*. But arrests and executions were not the worst consequences. The complete immobility of the peasantry, which even had a tendency to sympathize with the victim not the perpetrators, caused its own shock wave among the radical intelligentsia. Propaganda by the deed had, according to a few former exponents, failed as thoroughly as propaganda by the word. The populist movement had been baulked in its two major initiatives. Many leading figures argued the strategies simply needed more time and patience but that was a rare quality among Russian intellectuals. Rather than wait for the cycle of history to turn in their direction, new voices began to be heard. In the forefront was Georgii Plekhanov (1856–1918). He began the process whereby an ever-growing minority of politically committed intellectuals began to turn away from the peasantry and towards the Russian and international working class as the group which would implement the intellectuals' dreams. Naturally, this strengthened a pre-existing tendency among them to study carefully the ideas of Karl Marx (1818–83) who was living out his last years in London at this moment and was, himself, looking more carefully than hitherto at the political economy of Russia.

On the face of it, Marx's ideas did not seem to address the Russian situation. Marx' brilliant, stimulating and penetrating analysis of contemporary society was chiefly focused on how a mature capitalist society would change into a socialist and ultimately communist one. Advanced industrial countries, notably Germany, Britain, France and the United States, were the leading examples. As a large traditional peasant society with an anachronistic state structure, Russia seemed remote from the model Marx and his followers had in mind. And yet, not only did Marxism become most influential in Russia, the Russian experience spread in such a way that the societies in which its ideas came to be applied by governments were not capitalist, industrial societies at all. Russia, China, Vietnam, North Korea and Cuba were, with the partial exception of Cuba, overwhelmingly peasant countries in which capitalism had barely developed. How did this spectacular inversion come about and why did so many Russian intellectuals draw inspiration from Marxism?

Marx' multifaceted theories can be described in a variety of ways. At the basis of his social theory was labour, which he saw ultimately as the human urge to adapt, and even transform, the world in response to fundamental human needs, such as food, shelter, reproduction and creativity. The labour process was the fundamental human creative impulse. It was the foundation of social order and, for Marxists, defined the changing types of human society. Marx and Engels posited that natural human societies at the first stages of development had been classless and shared the goods of the earth and the labour invested in making them useful from the human point of view. However, divisions evolved and different forms of class emerged based on who controlled the labour process, how, and who performed necessary labour. Despotism emerged based on the enslavement of much of the manual labour force, succeeded (to greatly simplify) by feudal society in which, through the concept of ownership of property, landowners controlled the labour of peasants. Slaves were clearly deprived of the rights of free labour and so were peasants, in many cases, through slavery or enserfment (which tied them to a particular patch of land). Under capitalism, money (capital), machinery and land were the sources of production and therefore wealth, and were controlled, (again through the notional convention of ownership), by the bourgeois elite who owned them and could thereby set the terms by which the vast majority of their fellow humans had to work. Compared to slaves and serfs, the controls over the developing class of industrial workers (the proletariat) were less direct and, in liberal ideas, they were considered to be free labour freely entering into contracts with the employer/owners. Class, and ensuing class conflict for control of labour, were, in the Marxist view, the drivers of social change. However, and here began a crucial split of Marxism and liberalism, Marx argued the conditions of the bargain were so skewed in favour of the employer that the idea of free proletarian labour was an illusion. In reality, workers were 'wage slaves'.

So far, these elements of Marxist theory applied to any and all human societies, or so Marxists claimed. In that case they applied as much to Russia as anywhere else. However, we need to move to another crucial dimension of Marx' analysis to find the point at which his interpretation appeared not to suit Russian circumstances. Ironically, it was an aspect which, perhaps more than any other, attracted Russian intellectuals to Marxism in the first place. It was his theory of revolution.

One might say that Marx' theories had two closely linked elements. One was an analysis of class, and especially capitalist, society which, in the eyes of many, has still never been bettered. The second was that the special features of capitalism would lead, not only to the overthrow of unjust and unequal capitalist society itself, but that this would not lead like past overthrows to a new type of class society but to the emergence, for the first time, of a fully free, classless human society. It would, for Marx, be the beginning of true history in which the creative abilities of every person would flourish and oppressive forces would be vanquished. Marx was clear that human history up to the present was actually only its prehistory.

> The bourgeois mode of production is the last antagonistic form of the social process of production – antagonistic not in the sense of individual antagonism

> but of an antagonism that emanates from the individuals' social conditions of existence – but the productive forces developing within bourgeois society create also the material conditions for a solution of this antagonism. The prehistory of human society accordingly closes with this social formation.[1]

This was an astonishing assertion for Marx to make. In the detailed and precise analytical writing of Marx it is a shock to be confronted by what appears to be the most hopeless utopian romanticism. The conditions under which capitalism operated – pursuit of profit, markets, competition, unlimited accumulation of capital (a.k.a. greed) – are precisely those that will introduce a perfect human society based on their antitheses – co-operation and sharing.

How would this apparent miracle be accomplished? Marx altered emphasis on how the revolution might come about and, as discussed below, was open to the idea that the revolutionary process might take different forms in different places. But there were some fundamental features. Class societies had 'contradictions', similar to the antagonisms mentioned in the quote. The main contradiction within capitalism, Marx proposed, was that between the pursuit of profit and the wellbeing of the wider society. In feudal society production had been about subsistence, replicating what had long existed. Feudal societies evolved slowly. Under capitalism, whether agrarian or industrial, the aim of production was profit. Profit, said Marx, was produced by the extraction of 'surplus value' from workers, in simple terms they were paid less than what their output was worth and it was that underpayment which constituted profit.[2] The pursuit of profit was also driven by the need to stay ahead in the headlong competition of the unregulated market. Failure to grow led to stagnation and vulnerability to more successful enterprises. Weaker firms would go bankrupt and be swallowed up by the winners. In Marx phrase – one capitalist strikes down many. Ultimate failure could mean sliding down the social scale from bourgeois (owning the means of production) to proletarian (possessing nothing but the ability to undertake work – that is labour power). But not only could failed capitalists be ruined, the process of accumulating surplus value at an ever-increasing intensity (because of ever-more severe competition) could also impoverish the working class by forcing employers to reduce wages to remain competitive. The contradiction Marx thought he saw was that capitalism could only grow by taking money from the very people it needed to buy its products. It was trying to develop profitable markets through a process which restricted them. The impoverishment of workers would lead them eventually to realize, through the development of an awareness of their social situation (class consciousness), that the problem was not stingy, exploitative employers as individuals but the very system itself. Bourgeois and proletarians alike were servants of increasingly uncontrollable economic forces. Capitalism would be increasingly unstable and its periodic crises would culminate in its complete collapse. As workers awareness of their own situation grew, so they saw that their only recourse was to overthrow the system and ensure that the sources of wealth (the 'means of production' – land, capital, machinery) were in the hands of society so that they could be used to meet the needs of all, not the needs of the few who could afford to pay. In the ringing phrase of the 1848 *Communist Manifesto* the workers would unite because 'you have nothing to lose but your chains!' On the basis of social rather than private control of wealth creation, humanity as a whole, not just the ruling class and lucky intermediates lower down, would prosper. This is what Marx meant by ending the prehistory of humanity.

Russia was far behind in the process of capitalist development which, supposedly, led to its apocalyptic final crisis. Russia had not shaken off strong remnants of feudalism – the autocracy; law as the will of the sovereign; property; the peasant social order (the commune/*obshchina*); peasant agricultural methods (strip cultivation) – all bore witness to its transitional state between decaying feudalism and a struggling, newborn capitalism. Nonetheless, some Russian radicals of the 1860s and 1870s were dazzled by the comprehensiveness of Marx' system. It spoke to the enduring 'religious' substrate of secular Russian thought which preferred concrete, existential ideas to abstractions and maintained a teleological dimension to philosophy, that is humanity was progressing from lower to higher states. It also spoke to the 'whither Russia?' and 'what is Russia?' questions which underlay so much Russian political, literary, historical and artistic output. It also, for many, explained Russia's 'backwardness' and proposed new ways forward.

Many people are surprised to learn that the first language into which the German original of Karl Marx' *Das Kapital* (*Capital* – 1867) was translated was not English or French but Russian (1872). Why should we be surprised? As we have seen the Russian élite was integrating closely with the rest of Europe in terms of high culture, economy and diplomacy. Russian *intelligenty* were enthusiastically hoovering up ideas from the west and maintained close contacts, often through travel, sometimes through exile. It is perhaps more surprising that it was among peasant-oriented populist intellectuals that interest in Marx arose to a significant degree among Russians. The story is a fascinating one, impacting both the Russians involved and Marx.

Marx' model of capitalism fitted agrarian society as much as industrial, but Russian agriculture, especially as far as the mass of Russians were concerned, was still feudal and peasant-based.[3] Marx had had little to say about peasants. When he was thirty, in 1848, he famously referred in *The Communist Manifesto* to 'rural idiocy'. In his writings of 1850 on the rise and dictatorship of Napoleon III he, incorrectly as it happened,[4] attributed Louis Napoleon's success to mass peasant support drowning the progressive votes of the smaller urban working class. He called the peasants' involvement:

> clumsily cunning, knavishly naive, doltishly sublime, a calculated superstition, a pathetic burlesque, a cleverly stupid anachronism, a world-historic piece of buffoonery and an indecipherable hieroglyphic for the understanding of the civilized – this symbol bore the unmistakable physiognomy of the class that represents barbarism within civilization.[5]

Nonetheless, it was among populists that interest in Marx began to develop and it was a populist economist, Nikolai Danielson (1844–1918), who translated *Das Kapital*. One reason for this was that Marx' theory seemed to speak to the question of 'whither Russia?' Like any 'feudal' society the likelihood was that it would transform into a capitalist society. This sparked off a very interesting and creative debate in Russia. Today, it is largely forgotten but it raised a number of interesting and, perhaps, still relevant questions. They fell into two baskets.

The first was exactly how Russia might fit into the model Marx had laid out. For example, capitalism, especially industrial capitalism, had, in Marx' schema, pillaged the world in pursuit of the earliest accumulation of capital – what Marx called 'primitive capital accumulation'. Its pioneer exponents, France and Britain, had roved the world, pillaging, looting and colonizing as they went. The slave trade had become a crucial component of global trade and slave labour – producing sugar, rice and cotton in the Caribbean and the southern states of the United States – not to mention, in Britain's case, the subjection of India and, in Marx own time, the development of the opium trade.[6] The question arose, if it had taken centuries of global looting and exploitation for Britain and France to accumulate the initial pile of capital, how would a notoriously capital-deprived economy like Russia's be able to accumulate its original stash? Many reasons have been given for the sparseness of Russian capital resources. It is beyond our present purpose to pursue this question fully but we might bear in mind that 'backwardness', especially the late survival of serfdom and the peasant subsistence and exchange/barter economy, meant that many economic transactions were not monetized. Peasants had hardly any money and simply 'paid' for their share of the land with labour service before 1861. The problems of adjusting to money relations caused extensive difficulties to the Russian economy that continued into the twentieth century. Serfdom was also a socially polarizing system – there was no large category between serfowners and their allies and peasants. There were merchants, traders, professionals and the intelligentsia (plus clergy and army officers) but no substantial, independent, prosperous middle class who might create capital. In any case, the state dominated such capital investment as there was, leaving less room for independent private capitalists whom the state mistrusted, seeing them as purveyors of westernization and democracy right up until its final moments.[7] To add to the problem, state taxes for the ever-burdensome military soaked up much of whatever money there was in the country.

This was not the only problem in basket one. Danielson and others understood Marx' very well (Marx himself had made complimentary remarks about the quality of his translation) and pondered the implications of the centrality of economic competition for the Russian case. Obviously, already developed countries had an enormous competitive advantage. They were like successful Formula 1 teams. Those with funds and decades of engineering and racing experience were so far ahead in development that newcomers would, in straight competition, find it practically impossible to gain a foothold before being blown away by the big teams. So how could Russia begin to accumulate capital when world markets were dominated by much more powerful countries and companies. But that was not all. In the eyes of Danielson and others Russia had other serious competitive disadvantages. Most obviously its size, the distance between its resources and its harsh climate in winter added heavily to the cost of production in Russia, so how could it overcome these extra costs and compete? This was even more acute since Russia's infrastructure and levels of mass education were far from reaching minimum levels of adequacy. Populists like Danielson were beginning to think that Russian capitalism was near-impossible. This opened up the threat that it might only integrate into the developing world system as a giant colony, dependent on rich foreign investors and providing only cheap labour and basic products – grain, wood, furs plus some gold, silver and diamonds, and, by 1900, oil. It was a disastrous scenario for anyone looking for a more prosperous, independent Russia. Ironically, it also paralleled the nightmare of the brighter advisors of the successive tsars, that falling behind in the growing dynastic arms race would risk Russian disintegration à la Ottoman Empire. Even today Russia remains wary that its enemies seek to break it up.

That was only the first basket of problems. The sole content of basket two was a question that has become much more prominent in the debate of the era and its subsequent historiography. Facing such a bleak prospect, could it be that, especially since the peasantry still had apparently socialist elements underpinning its way of life, Russia might avoid the capitalist stage altogether and, forewarned and forearmed, contemplate a direct transition to socialism? For those who came to develop this idea the ace in Russia's hand was the peasant *obshchina* (commune). To simplify, although there were great regional differences – notably in Poland, Russia's western borders, Finland and the Baltic states – the heartland Russian and Ukrainian peasantry of the European part of the Empire lived under the commune system. The focus of the *obshchina* was the periodic redistribution of land between households as the needs of each changed through births, marriages, deaths, out-migration and other life factors. Some communes only distributed once in a generation, others every five or ten years.[8] Was it possible, some populists thought, that this could be the basis for a direct transition to socialism without the entire society being dragged through the harsh exploitation, violence, poverty and corruption associated with the emergence of capitalism? They argued violently about this issue[9] and continued to do so until 1917 and beyond even though several leading populists in the late 1870s had the bright idea that if they were uncertain about how to interpret Marx' views on this thorny issue they had one totally reliable recourse. They could ask him. So they did.

In a letter of 1877 to a leading populist Marx wrote: 'In order that I might be qualified to estimate the economic development in Russia to-day, I learnt Russian and then for many years studied the official publications and others bearing on this subject.' This, in itself, is a fascinating comment. Marx had, following his own instincts, turned to the case of Russia in his later years and, perhaps if he had lived beyond 1883, would have produced a detailed, focused and, no doubt, penetrating interpretation of Russia's place in the developing world system. His next sentence was equally intriguing: 'I have arrived at this conclusion: If Russia continues to pursue the path she has followed since 1861, she will lose the finest chance ever offered by history to a nation, in order to undergo all the fatal vicissitudes of the capitalist regime.'[10] Sadly, Marx never completed his studies on Russia and did not produce anything substantial detailing his thoughts and arguments. His utterances on it tended to be somewhat Delphic, like the one just quoted. Shortly afterwards, after much hesitation and the production of several draft replies, Marx responded to a letter from another populist leader, Vera Zasulich:

> The analysis presented in *Capital* argues neither for nor against the viability of the Russian *obshchina*, but the particular investigations, which I have conducted on the basis of material drawn by me from primary sources, convinces me that this *obshchina* is the axis of social regeneration in Russia. But in order for it to function as such, it would be necessary, first of all, to eliminate the noxious influence which

> it undergoes from all sides, and consequently, insure normal conditions for its natural development.[11]

It is hard to glean much from this quote beyond Marx giving highly qualified support to populists' assumptions. The *obshchina* might well be an 'axis of social regeneration' of Russia but only if it were soon freed of 'the noxious influence' eroding it. One might speculate that Marx was referring to the encroachment of capitalism in the countryside and possibly to growing peasant social individualism and class differentiation, but Marx did not elucidate. In the 1882 Preface to the Russian edition of the *Communist Manifesto* Marx and Engels still had important reservations but were more explicit about the circumstance under which Russia might avoid capitalism:

> The Communist Manifesto had, as its object, the proclamation of the inevitable impending dissolution of modern bourgeois property. But in Russia we find, face-to-face with the rapidly flowering capitalist swindle and bourgeois property, just beginning to develop, more than half the land owned in common by the peasants. Now the question is: can the Russian *obshchina*, though greatly undermined, yet a form of primeval common ownership of land, pass directly to the higher form of Communist common ownership? Or, on the contrary, must it first pass through the same process of dissolution such as constitutes the historical evolution of the West?
>
> The only answer to that possible today is this: If the Russian Revolution becomes the signal for a proletarian revolution in the West, so that both complement each other, the present Russian common ownership of land may serve as the starting point for a communist development.[12]

Just over a year later Marx died, leaving Engels with somewhat more negative thoughts on the future of the *obshchina* than Marx himself. Possibly Engels was responding to the fact that time was passing and Marx had implied the window for Russia to advance directly to socialism would only stay open for a short while longer. In any case, Engels came down firmly on the negative side. In 1893, writing to Daniel'son, he commented that 'the present capitalistic phase of development in Russia appears … unavoidable'. About the commune, he wrote, 'I am afraid that institution is doomed.'[13] Nonetheless, Daniel'son remained a believer.[14]

The debate had only drawn the attention of a minority of Russian intellectuals but it was of considerable importance because a line can be traced directly from these debates to the renegade populist Plekhanov and on to Lenin and the Bolsheviks. The debate had peaked shortly before the assassination crisis and it even became one of the victims of the crisis, as the government moved firmly to close down radical and terrorist groups. The conjuncture also stimulated a rethink for Plekhanov, and what was only a small handful of fellow thinkers, who were prepared to move on from considering the Russian peasant to be the revolutionary class, to reluctantly accepting that capitalism was inevitably looming in Russia's future and it was time to reset the focus from peasants to proletarians. At this stage, no one could have foreseen the fateful influence that Russian interpretations of Marx would exert, not only over Russia, but over the world in the upcoming century.

From the 1881 assassination to the 1905 revolution (2) – Early Russian Marxism ii.) Plekhanov, Lenin and the dispute with the populists

In one important respect we are giving too much attention to the Marxist and revolutionary wing of the intelligentsia since it was only a small minority even within the intellectual group. However, hindsight tells us to trace the roots of the tendency that was destined to take over the country. It was also a phase through which many young intellectuals passed who moved on to other philosophical and programmatic positions. Also, as radicals do, they dominated political and cultural discourse way beyond their social weight, not unlike extremists today. So we do, indeed, need to understand them, but not make the mistake of thinking they had extensive support in this period. They did not. Throughout the revolutionary period populists, mainly in the form of the Socialist Revolutionary Party after it was formed in 1900, were considerably larger and more influential than the Social Democratic movement including both its Bolshevik and Menshevik wings. Indeed, the two wings never fully split before 1917 because they knew such a development would benefit their SR rivals and consign themselves to oblivion. Throughout 1917 the SRs outvoted all other parties, including the SDs on a national scale. The Constituent Assembly election in November 1917, held shortly after the Bolsheviks had taken control of the government, is very revealing. Even at this point the SRs gained about 40 per cent of the national vote against around 25 per cent for the Bolsheviks. The Mensheviks were virtually eclipsed at this point. Significantly the Bolsheviks won majorities or were the largest parties in key cities, notably Moscow and Petrograd, and in key parts of the armed forces at the front and in the Baltic fleet, assets the Bolsheviks were better able to deploy in their support than the amorphous SR supporters who were spread widely across European Russia, Ukraine and parts of Siberia. It is also significant that once the civil war ended, and the Bolsheviks no longer needed to rally support across a wide spectrum, they turned on the SRs and organized the first political show trial in 1922 at which they put a group of SR leaders still in the country on trial. It is not possible to know exactly how much support the SRs had in the repressive post-civil war conditions, but it is clear that throughout 1917 and probably deep into 1918, they had more supporters than the Bolsheviks. In many ways the commonly asked question of why did the Bolsheviks emerge victorious? should be turned around to ask why did the SRs fail to take power?

In addition to these interconnections, it is also the case that, in many respects and in a much more subtle way, the SDs shared many characteristics with the populists and might well be considered as a particular type of populist themselves in that they embodied the intelligentsia ideal of service of the people as much as the populists. The theoretical differences we are about to discuss – could Russia still avoid capitalism? Were the peasants viable revolutionary material? – and so on should not blind us to the fact that the SDs themselves were deeply influenced by the populist ethos. This was the case with Lenin as much as anyone else. In her memoirs his wife and constant political supporter and chronicler, Nadezhda Krupskaya, commented on how much Lenin respected the founders of populism from the 1860s and 1870s, especially Chernyshevsky who, as already mentioned, had a profound influence on him. Krupskaya also records that Lenin was very acerbic in rebuking colleagues who belittled the great work of the early populists. We will discuss below how Lenin himself could be considered to be a Bakuninist who prioritized the struggle against state and religion almost as much as he fought the orthodox Marxist battles associated with class struggle. In the heat of the October Revolution, again discussed below, Lenin adopted the central policy of the SRs, their plans for land redistribution and the strengthening of the commune. This was in direct contradiction to Bolshevik policy which was to nationalize land and set up collective farms to replace the commune and forms of private ownership. In 1921, Lenin promoted the New Economic Policy which made significant concessions to the peasantry in a way which angered more workerist Bolsheviks, one of whom, Stalin, took it upon himself in 1929 to break with the peasantry, smash its institutions, force them into collective farms and engage in breakneck industrialization policies. Various interpretations of Lenin's life and career have underlined his links with and debt to the ethos, though not the key policies, of populism.[15]

It is also interesting to note, as a preliminary to the discussion below, that the most recent history of populism is based on a much wider definition than previous accounts. In fact, the author's working definition of populism is almost co-terminous with the definition of intelligentsia at the heart of the present study, also a much wider spectrum than in many earlier studies. In both cases the group focused on is defined as those members of the educated class who choose to serve the people in terms of aiding their emancipation from political repression and poverty and also to build a strong country in which the ordinary peasants and workers would play a full part. Consciousness of being an *intelligent* overlaps greatly with being a populist in the general rather than sectarian sense – that is, as a 'servant of the people' rather than upholder of SR positions on, notably, the fate of capitalism in Russia.[16]

Plekhanov and his immediate friends and supporters were all too well aware of the weakness of their movement. One of them, Pavel Aksel'rod, supposedly joked while he and Plekhanov and friends were rowing on Lake Geneva that if their boat sank it would be the end of Russian Marxism. In the 1880s Plekhanov formulated his new ideas. In two related pamphlets – *Socialism and Political Struggle* (1883) and the better-known *Our Differences* (1885) – Plekhanov set out his stall. One summary notes that

> the key propositions are: (i) to retain the concept that the working masses will achieve their own emancipation; (ii) a spontaneous peasant uprising such as that the narodniks had worked for would not take place; (iii) it was necessary to form a party, though details of what this meant were sparse; (iv) industrial workers would be at the heart of the new strategy; (v) ideas of a 'separate path' for Russia, what he calls 'exceptionalism', should be abandoned; (vi) Russia's future lay in following the 'western' model; … (vii) … there was a new epoch … of '*conscious political struggle*'.[17]

The final, italicized, phrase meant class struggle, which would supersede, notably, individual or small group acts of terrorism, not to mention any other form of action which lacked a comprehensive political and economic vision. But it was important to embark on a political offensive rather than 'wait' for the slow machinations of the economic system to reach its prophesied end. The revolutionary offspring needed a midwife to supervise the birth.

In pursuance of these new aims, Plekhanov, Aksel'rod (1850–1928), Vera Zasulich (1851–1919), Lev Deutsch (1855–1941) and others set up a group called Emancipation of Labour (*Osvobozhdenie truda*) in Geneva in 1883. However, it was only in the 1890s that it began to get any traction. It began to win over young radicals like Vladimir Ulianov (1870–1924), who became better known to the world as Lenin. Lenin personally was an example of the autocracy creating its own nemesis. While Lenin might have taken a revolutionary direction anyway, the execution of his elder brother, Alexander, for participation in a plot in 1886 to blow up Alexander III, gave a deep, personal and emotional edge to his hatred of tsarism. Significantly, it was actively shared by most of his sisters and their spouses. His mother, too, was a constant support to him not least financially. This enabled him to neglect the legal profession, for which he qualified with a brilliant external degree from St Petersburg University after he was expelled from his local university in Kazan as the brother of a convicted terrorist. The earliest writings we have from Lenin are, not surprisingly, polemics against the populists, making arguments to support the key points of Plekhanov's new direction. It is worth noting, however, that throughout his career Lenin had great respect for the early populists whom he considered to have heroic status. Lenin probably first encountered radical ideas via the populism of Alexander and, although he became an icon of Marxist orthodoxy, there remained a populist dimension to his thinking. He also replicated some of Marx' old rival Bakunin's visceral hatred and prioritizing of the battle against church and state over the more complex issue of class struggle.

We need to pause for reflection for a moment because at this point there is a danger of getting lost in an ideological minefield. The debates of the 1890s to 1917, and even beyond in legacy groups and the Cold War, have inspired, or better perhaps engendered, literally thousands of studies. While we are not currently engaged in a detailed account of the development of Russian Marxism, we cannot simply pass by. There are a number of aspects of it that we need to keep in mind, along with the already emphasized notion that we are using hindsight to pick them out because of their later importance. This is the other side of the coin of the first new point. Before 1917 these groups, especially the Social Democrats derived from Plekhanov, and including Lenin and later national leaders such as Trotsky and Stalin, were uninfluential, even insignificant. The populists remained the largest radical party and stayed that way even through 1917. Second, while there was clear hostility between populist and Marxist views, the assumption that there was a clearly defined split between the two halves of Social Democracy itself from 1903 onwards, followed by a two-way fight between them, needs to be rethought. There was a third, largely forgotten, group known as the Economists who blurred the division. Third, none of these groups was instrumental in bringing about either the 1905 or 1917 revolutions. Russia was full of revolutionaries but it was not them who brought the political, social, economic and cultural systems to the ground. Their contribution was modest with respect to the outbreak of revolution. However, once the revolutions were underway, they became much more significant. In 1917, of course, one of the smallest and least influential groups before the February Revolution, the Bolsheviks led by Lenin, rocketed themselves into a power they did not relinquish for seventy-four years. Let us take a look at some of these points and then set them aside for a while and look at the wider aspects of the period with the whole intelligentsia in the centre of our focus.

As is too frequently the case elsewhere, Russia's radical intelligentsia spent an inordinate amount of time arguing among themselves. Intellectuals, Russian or otherwise, are people driven by principles. Unlike their bourgeois opponents who, when threatened, are usually able to bury principles and join with ideological opponents in defence of much more influential common interests, such as property, the left is racked by unbridgeable chasms of differences of strategy, tactics and future plans. On occasions, where ruling and dominant social élites fail to congeal around their state in this way, they are all at risk.[18] However, the intelligentsia had no comparable unifying interests and endlessly obsessed over often small points of detail. The result is, from 1895 to 1921, a tower of Babylon of strident, conflicting voices. There are many studies of this cacophony. To switch metaphors, it does not serve our present purpose to get lost in these thickets of debate but we do need to survey their contours. As we have noted before, the conventional way of dealing with debates – looking at one or other of the conflicting sides separately – can overlook the shared underlying discourse where certain themes and issues are the common battleground. Debates are not only specific positions and contests they are usually part of a shared system within which the debates shape themselves. In the Russian case, it still holds true in this period that underlying questions of identity – what is Russia? what is its immediate future? what is its destiny? how can we serve its future and its people be best served? – were shared from revolutionary left to tsarist right. We should also note that the history of the intelligentsia also became a Cold War battleground, especially after 1968 when radical intellectuals re-appeared in relative force, mainly in western Europe and North America but in other parts of the globe as well. In Africa and Latin America, for example, intellectuals like Franz Fanon, Amilcar Cabral, Fidel Castro and Che Guevara inspired and participated in national liberation movements, looking to Marxist and populist ideas, which worried the hegemonic powers and stimulated a wave of studies of their pre-revolutionary Russian predecessors. Many of these were almost polemical in tone and generated more heat than light, adding a second layer of distortion to that already arising from the heavily committed opinions of the primary participants who, of course, were convinced they were right.

It is widely assumed that the difference between the populists and the social-democratic Marxists was that the former were the party for (but not of) the peasants and the social democrats for (but not yet of) urban workers. This is not the case. Even in 1917 the populists garnered as many working-class votes as the Bolsheviks at their peak. In the Putilov works in Petrograd, the biggest factory in Russia, the populists were overwhelmingly larger in number than the Bolsheviks in February. This should not be surprising. In fact, populists had been open to the tiny but developing working class, not least because recruiting them helped to solve one of their key practical problems. How was it possible to reach a barely literate peasantry, spread over a vast space and as distrustful of outsiders as they had been during the 'Going to the

People' episodes of the mid-1870s? Linking up with urban workers was theoretically a promising way of bridging the physical and cultural chasm. Workers in Russia, for decades to come, were largely rural migrants. Wave after wave was recruited as industry expanded. Many of them, up to 1917, retained rural links such as their land allotment, families including wives and children left in the village, remittance of wages to subsidize the rural family and so on. Many, before 1900 especially, were seasonal workers and even if they were permanent workers their factories underwent summer closures to enable workers to go home to assist with the harvest. These practices were dying out in the early twentieth century but two factors meant the working class remained migratory for much of the first half of the twentieth century. The First World War brought new recruits, including a higher proportion of women workers than previously, to meet growing production demands in the arms and metalworking sector and to replace workers called into the military. After 1917 industry collapsed and an unprecedented de-urbanization occurred, Petrograd and Moscow losing at least half of their inhabitants as they returned to the village to try to survive the economic disaster. As a result, the Bolsheviks had almost de-proletarianized Russia, a fact which as we shall see caused problems, but it also meant that as industry recovered in the 1920s and exploded during the First and Second Five Year plans, peasants flooded back in to the cities and factories. Around 1950 Russia became, technically, a majority urban society but even in the Khrushchev and Brezhnev years 'flight from the countryside' was a major social problem. The point is that first, the populists used workers to help approach their brothers, sisters and cousins left in the countryside and second, a clear distinction between rural and urban labourers was slow to emerge. Until after the Second World War, Russian women and men workers had one foot in the village. For decades Russia remained, even remains, a society deeply shaped by its peasant experience and culture.

It should be noted, however, that almost all factions among the social democrats were strongly anti-peasant. They followed the Marxist line mentioned earlier which blamed uneducated, superstitious, reactionary peasants for supporting their own oppression. They had no time for 'innate socialism' in the form of the *obshchina*. The peasantry was, supposedly, shot through with petty-bourgeois rather than socialist principles with the desire for a personal landholding at the top of their agenda. In the eyes of social democrats, peasants wanted to become landowners, not socialist co-operators.

None of these views of the peasants or workers was based on extensive contact with them. Only a handful of the intelligentsia lived alongside either. Rural schoolteachers were an exception and some of them were crucial to populist influence in parts of the countryside. Workers were easier to contact and recruitment in cities and the emergence of organizations like unions and so on did bring some workers in touch with their would-be saviours but most party leaders had very little direct links with actual workers. Much of the ideas about peasant and worker were derived from texts rather than immersion in the peasant and worker worlds.

Part of the sharpness in the debate about peasants was the result of it being tied into a larger question – was capitalism the next item on the agenda for Russia? In standard Marxist opinion Russia was emerging from its own type of feudalism and was entering into the early phases of capitalism. Under capitalism, peasants would disappear as a class. Some would succeed in transforming themselves into landowners but the majority would be forced downwards into the class of agricultural labourers, as opposed to peasants. Their destiny was to lose their land to the upwardly mobile minority and other capitalists and become rural workers who owned no or very little land and lived on wages, not from subsistence agriculture typical of a peasant. Social democratic insistence on discounting the peasants as a revolutionary force in favour of seeing them as a prop for reaction was deeply ingrained. As we have seen, Marx had argued that under certain conditions it might be possible for Russia to avoid the capitalist stage so, in certain respects, the populists were more Marxist than the social democrats. However, as we have seen, by the 1890s Engels was expressing scepticism about the future of the *obshchina* as a building-block of socialism. In his most extensive piece of work, written while in Siberian exile, Lenin took a different tack but ultimately headed towards the same destination. The study, entitled *The Development of Capitalism in Russia* (1899),[19] enumerated in considerable detail aspects of the Russian economy – such as the widening of markets, the turn to cash crops (i.e. crops grown for the market not direct consumption), local specialization such as sugar in parts of Ukraine, apparent class differentiation emerging among the peasants – which added up, in Lenin's view, to evidence of capitalism taking a grip on Russia's economy. However, this was not simply an academic exercise. Like all of Lenin's works this one had an ideological purpose. Lenin was proclaiming that events had overtaken the debate about Russia avoiding capitalism. It had arrived so the debate was over. Populism had lost. The future, Lenin implied, was social democratic.

The second area of development is also one which is widely misunderstood. Lenin's first major work, which is still seen as a revolutionary model today, his take on the old question *What Is to Be Done?* (*Chto delat'?*) (1902), calls for the social democrats to become a party of 'professional revolutionaries'. Later Leninists and warriors in the cause of the Cold War in the west interpreted this to mean a secret élite of underground activists along the lines of *Narodnaia Voliia* in the 1870s. This is partly the case but overlooks the broad context of the time. Until the final two years of the century, intelligentsia political groupings had been organized on an expanded model derived from the mid-century *kruzhki* (circles). They were small. Often all the members were acquainted with one another. The groups were very numerous, literally hundreds in our period. Tsarist law forced them into the underground or exile. But even in exile they did not set up formal organizations with rules, membership and so on. They tended to be formed of a leading, sometimes charismatic, figure who was surrounded by disciples. Often there was a manifesto or equivalent and some formed around the publication of a newspaper. Plekhanov's Emancipation of Labour Group was a typical example. Initially, its members could fit in a rowing boat. His pamphlets *Socialism and Political Struggle* and *Our Differences* were the clarion call for like-minded intellectuals to gather round. Plekhanov's writings and reputation drew supporters from Russia. One such was Lenin who, after visiting Plekhanov and other socialist luminaries in western Europe in 1894, returned to set up the St Petersburg League of Struggle for the Emancipation of the Working Class, itself an amalgamation of twenty or so study circles. It was this that landed Lenin in Siberia for three years as it was betrayed by an informer almost as soon as it met. While Lenin was in exile, a meeting in Minsk declared itself to be the First Congress of the Russian Social Democratic Labour Party (hereafter SDs). Its main task was to formulate a detailed party programme. It was the first, albeit as yet tiny, Russian political party. In the next few years, the other major tendencies also began to take on this more organized form. In 1901 the populists formed themselves into the Socialist Revolutionary Party (hereafter SRs) and in 1903, in the delightful surroundings of Schaffhausen in Switzerland, the liberal intelligentsia formed the Liberation (*Osvobozhdenie*) group which went under several names before settling on the Constitutional Democratic Party (hereafter KDs from their initials in Russian). It was a major step in Russia's modernization and westernization. Other institutions were also emerging. Trade unions had first had an impact around 1895 and 1896 when Russia underwent its first serious strike wave in St Petersburg, in part to assert the right to form unions. By 1900 a number of unions had emerged precariously into the daylight. The economic downturn of 1901 and after gave birth to major general strikes (i.e. ones which embraced workers in a wide variety of trades and industries, not just, for example a leatherworkers' strike) which shook cities like Odessa. The new militancy stimulated one of tsarism's strangest ideas. A police chief in Odessa, named Zubatov, had the bright idea of getting the state itself to organize unions to divide the expression of legitimate grievances from the influence of radical intellectuals, a phenomenon known as 'police socialism'. Clearly, the autocracy was being bested in these areas and the boundaries of repression were being tested as never before.

It was in this context of institutional transformation that Lenin made his appeal. But his examples of 'professional revolutionaries' were not radical assassins and bomb throwers as his critics implied. They were the leaders of the German Social Democratic Party such as Karl Kautsky (1854–1938) and August Bebel (1840–1913) who looked more like respectable pillars of society than revolutionaries. What Lenin was saying was it was time to set up an organized party like the German Social Democrats, the largest Marxist party of its day. The Russian equivalent would need, for the time being, to have special characteristics to protect it from tsarist police harassment, which extended even to western European cities like Paris, Brussels and Berlin.[20] But the time had, nonetheless, arrived when it was necessary to move beyond the circle model and become a regular political party with a fulltime, elected leadership, a programme and a constitution. At its Second Conference, held in 1903 initially in Brussels but forced by police pressure to decamp across The Channel to London, the SDs set about achieving these goals. Unsurprisingly, with such fundamental principles and definitions at stake, the members fell into bitter, uncomradely, wounding and long-lasting arguments between a variety of factions.

The arguments themselves have also been shaped, not only by the polemicists of the time and their later reminiscences but also by the pressures of official Soviet versus Cold War interpretations. Conventionally, the SDs 'split' in 1903 into a Bolshevik faction led by Lenin and composed largely of younger members of the party, and Mensheviks led by Iulii Martov (1873–1923) and the old guard – Plekhanov, Aksel'rod and others.[21] Up to this point Martov and Lenin had been close friends, as had their wives, but the dispute drove the families apart for the rest of their lives. Bolshevik politics had no room for sentiment. The standard view was that the Bolsheviks stood for actively promoting revolution while the opposing faction, the Mensheviks, wanted to 'wait' for capitalism to evolve and only expect a socialist revolution when the capitalist cycle exhausted itself. In fact, this latter position was held only by a small group known as the 'Economists' who were accused by Bolsheviks and Mensheviks alike of giving priority to economic rather than political struggle. Both SD wings shared Plekhanov's view that the time for political struggle had arrived and the task of a Marxist political party was to promote it. The division between the two wings varied. The issue of whether the next step was bourgeois revolution or armed struggle saw each side support one or the other at different times. There were multiple attempts to bring the two wings together, not least because such a small group could ill-afford to divide its meagre resources and membership in the face of the much larger SR party. Arguably, only in, or even after, October 1917 did the split become final. As late as July 1917 Trotsky, a leading Menshevik since 1906, had come over to the Bolsheviks. He did so because he believed, rather like Lenin's final argument with the populists over capitalism, that in February the bourgeois revolution had arrived so there was no point arguing about it any more. The next stage would be proletarian socialist revolution so the issue was redundant. There were many nuances, some of which we will pick up later, but the theory of stages was shared by both factions it was not a solely Menshevik concept.

From the 1881 assassination to the 1905 revolution (3) – Liberals, conservatives, the cultural intelligentsia

These fierce political debates did not much exercise the majority of Russia's men and women intellectuals, even though they would have so much influence not only on the intelligentsia but the entire empire and much of the rest of world. Most Russian intellectuals had more to distract them than dry political polemics. Conventionally the years from around 1890 to 1914 are considered to be a silver Age of Russian literature second only to the Golden Age of Pushkin and others. In terms of overall artistic and cultural achievement the later period could easily be considered to have precedence. Between 1881 and 1917, Russian cultural life was flourishing as never before. It also passed a highly significant watershed around 1881 with Russia becoming a major original contributor to 'world culture' rather than as a net importer and adapter. Consider the following. In a brilliant opening fanfare in the 1860s and 1870s Dostoevsky's *Crime and Punishment* (1866), *The Idiot* (1869), and *The Devils* (1872) and Tolstoy's *War and Peace* (1869) and *Anna Karenina* (1878) became instant global classics. To this day, Russians tend to revere Pushkin and the Golden Age cohort as favourites but Dostoevsky and Tolstoy were the first international household names from Russian literature. From 1880 until the early 1920s Russian culture made a global impact in many areas. Literature continued to be in the forefront. Dostoevsky's masterpiece *The Brothers Karamazov* (1880) was completed two years before his death. Tolstoy turned to religious and moral writings of great international impact such as *The Kingdom of God Is within You* (1894), in which he developed ideas of pacifism and vegetarianism.

His last novel, *Resurrection* (1899), is much underrated but its picture of elites with compromised values and judicial and governmental systems engulfed in corruption speaks powerfully to the global present. To take these two writers alone, their influence was profound. Two of the pillars of twentieth-century ideologies in the capitalist world – Nietzsche and Freud – acknowledged their debt to Dostoevsky with his depiction of 'supermen' in *House of the Dead* and *Crime and Punishment* (that is, people who lived, or tried to, by their own laws rather than convention) and his instinctive discovery of the subconscious mind in *Notes from Underground* and *Brothers Karamazov*. On the other hand, Tolstoy influenced, most notably, Mahatma Gandhi and drew him to his strategy of non-violent resistance which was a key asset in his campaign for freeing India of British rule and, in effect, fatally undermining the British Empire.

Russian culture was assuming an international status it had never enjoyed before. Not all areas shared in this development. For the time being painting and fine arts in general became increasingly influential within Russia. In the 1860s and 1870s, following and preceding similar developments in the west, young Russian artists began to break with the stifling conventions of classic academic art and set up independent movements. The Wanderers (*Peredvizhniki*) extended the range of acceptable themes. Repin's paintings had a radical and populist undertone. His famous works include one of the lowest status and most menial workers in Russia, the *Volga Bargehaulers* (1873) who pulled boats upstream. They had a terrible reputation for being violent dissolute thieves but Repin portrayed the toughness and suffering of a life that reduced them to the level of draught animals. His *Religious Procession in the Kursk Guberniia* (1883) was a visual essay on rural Russia. At the centre a religious tableau is being carried on the shoulders of peasants whose faces exude a weak-minded piety. In front of the tableau is a very fat, self-satisfied priest with a similarly unpleasant and self-important landowner and his lady, the trio making up the real focus of the event rather than the icons and monstrance on the peasants' shoulders. A line of bailiff's with sticks keeps the bulk of the peasantry separate from their betters, and overseers on horseback strike and whip the peasants. The peasants are depicted in their poverty, some including a child having physical disabilities. On the hillock in the background are the ragged stumps of crudely cut trees, a reminder of the rapacious market economy eating into the heart of Russia. Even Repin's government commissions, including one to paint an enormous canvas depicting the tsar presiding over the State Council (1903), which involved Repin in hundreds of individual sittings with leading ministers, grand dukes and even the tsar himself, had a subversive reading. When the canvas was unveiled a leading writer, thinker and critic, V.V. Rozanov (1856–1919) commented that the finished product was lifeless compared to Repin's vibrant canvas of the Cossacks sending a defiant letter to the sultan (1891) but, then, Rozanov realized, that was precisely what Repin was saying. These people were drab and lifeless – *Carthago delenda est* (Carthage must be destroyed) – was the message.

Repin's ravaged trees stood in sharp contrast to the numerous romantic depictions of the Russian forest painted by Ivan Shishkin (1832–98). Many other painters depicted similarly idyllic rural scenes. Historical themes of Russia's past also became widespread, from Repin's brutally realistic painting of Ivan IV and his dead son to Viktor Vasnetsov's (1848–1926) mounted warriors (*Bogatyr* 1898). History and fantasy interacted in the paintings of Nikolai Roerich (1874–1947), who delved back as far as the arrival of the Varangians on the Dnepr (1905), in effect an impressionistic snapshot of the birth of Russia itself. Ivan Bilibin (1876–1942) produced brilliant illustrations to children's and adult editions of Russian folk tales and legends and also produced scenery for operas on these subjects. The industrialist Savva Mamontov (1841–1918) financed a highly productive artistic colony in the village of Abramtsevo near Moscow which provided a secure haven for brilliant artists. It was developed on the estate of the writer K.S. Aksakov (1791–1859) who had specialized in a style of Slavophile realism, simple stories of rural Russian life filled with love for what he wrote about. Incidentally he was connected to land surveying in the 1830s even being named director of a surveying institute. He also fathered a talented family including several prominent slavophile writers. Mamontov turned the estate into a haven for creativity and shaped to form an idealized Russian village.

As we have noted in other fields, conservative slavophile themes and radical populist ones intermingled in much of this art. It evoked a distinctive and deep-rooted Russia but also pointed to the environmental threat posed by industry, the disruption it would entail and the eternal inequalities of Russian society. Western Europe was becoming enchanted by orientalism from the erotic slave-girl fantasies of Edward Leighton, through the 'discovery' of Brittany to the Tahiti of Gauguin and fashions for chinoiserie and Japanese art. For Russia, its own past and its Eurasian inheritance largely substituted for distant exotic locations. As Gauguin and Van Gogh and Monet presented peripheral France and The Netherlands as othered locations, so Russian writers, painters, composers and so on found comparable themes in the Black Sea (including the ocean itself in Aivazovsky's (1817–1900) spectacular seascapes produced from the 1830s to 1900), Caucasus, Siberia, the Caspian and newly acquired (in the 1860s) Central Asian borderlands of the empire. In a sense, this spilled over to Europe in the early twentieth century as a fashion for all things Russian spread, especially to London and Paris where Russia itself became an orientalist other. The *Ballets Russes*, founded in 1909, was a focus but academic and literary interest in Russia dated from this time, the first British university department of Russian appearing in Liverpool in 1912.

Two more aspects of intelligentsia artistic output. First, it was not only in politics that a sense of impending change, even doom, was prevalent. From roughly 1890 to 1914 there was a widespread sense of apocalypse heightened by the ending of a century. It manifested itself in many ways. The painter Mikhail Vrubel' (1856–1910) produced a long series of paintings of demons which were dark and brooding. Themes of death and immortality emerged in the writings of Rozanov and his close friends Zinaida Gippius (1869–1945) and her husband Dmitrii Merezhkovsky (1866–1941) also explored erotic themes and, along with a group who called themselves Mystical Anarchists,[22] they explored the Dionysian/Bacchanalian side of the human mind, in other words the deepest emotions, dreams and ecstatic visions. They had little sympathy with political radicals, who were deemed to be dreary, unimaginative, empirical materialists and positivists, but they were not immune, especially around 1905, to the wave of revolutionary euphoria, expressing their ideas in a collection of essays in French entitled *Le Tsar et la Révolution*.[23] For them a complete revolution was necessary in Russia but it would inevitably have a religious dimension. For Gippius and Merezhkovsky this was because tsarism had a religious dimension to which it owed its power, it was, they said, a theocracy and could only be overthrown by a similarly religiously based but unspecified revolution.[24] In a sense they were correct in that the emergent revolutionary power, Bolshevism, was not a simple revolutionary force re-arranging power and redistributing property but was driven by an urge many compared to a religion to transform human nature in conformity with an ideology that embraced all spheres of human life. Various labels encompassing some or all of the mystical writers have been used. The two most common are to describe many of them as symbolists and also to identify a 'new religious consciousness' taking hold of some of the intelligentsia's greatest minds. A subgroup were referred to as 'Godseekers' and there was a very different left-wing group who were called 'Godbuilders'. Some leading Bolshevik intellectuals belonged to this group. Their two main texts were *Religiia i sotsial'izm* (*Religion and Socialism*) by the writer, critic, playwright and, after 1917, Soviet Minister of Enlightenment (i.e. Education) Anatoly Lunacharsky (1875–1933) in which he argued that socialism was the culmination of humanity's religious search, and the novelist Maxim Gorky's *Ispoved'* (The Confession) which focused on comparing the building of humanist socialism to the now-superseded task of building the kingdom of God on earth. Lenin was highly contemptuous of anything that smelt of religion and told them straight and the movement petered out.

The new religious consciousness in its various forms constituted a small but influential counterweight to the largely traditionally scientific and positivist intelligentsia as a whole. They were the Russian equivalent of the western thinkers and writers who were also rebelling against what they considered overly simplistic, unduly optimistic and distorting ideas of the rationality of human beings. Somewhere between the two were fascinating thinkers who did not fit into any pigeon hole. Vladimir Solov'ev (1853–1900) is often described as 'the first Russian philosopher' a title some accord to Skovoroda (though he was, as we have seen, Ukrainian) but the concept does not fit well on the shoulders of either. They were, indeed, thinkers but hardly system-builders. Their writings comprised existential insights, including the religious and mystical dimension of life remote from the writings even of philosophers like Hegel and Kant, who were practitioners of conventional religion. The central event of Solov'ev's intellectual life was an intense, captivating vision of the Holy Wisdom – Sophia in Greek and Russian – which came to him in the improbable surroundings of the British Museum Reading Room. It haunted him for the rest of his life. He wrote a brilliant essay on love and, at the heart of his mature ideas and the nearest he came to a system, was the argument that the world should be united under the pope, a concept which horrified his Orthodox friends. To this end, in February 1896, he was, controversially, baptized into the small Eastern Catholic Uniate church, a small group which had accepted the mediation between eastern and western Christianity at the Council of Florence (1438), and retained Orthodox ritual but acknowledged the supremacy of the pope. His orthodox admirers deny his conversion happened, though no one disputes his acknowledgement of papal supremacy. For Solov'ev, this was not a betrayal of Orthodoxy. In his view the gathering together of humanity through a process of *sobornost'* would fulfil the separate traditions (he included Jews) not deny them.

Two other visionaries, of a very different kind, moved much closer to science than Solov'ev for whom positivist concepts were constraints on the full expression of human identity and destiny. One of Solov'ev's mentors, who was also a significant influence on both Dostoevsky and Tolstoy, was Nikolai Fedorov (1829–1903), the librarian of the one of Russia's and Europe's largest libraries, the Rumiantsev Library in Moscow which, as we noted, became an Imperial Library and then the Lenin Library in Soviet times and the Russian State Library today. The title of his central work shows his main preoccupation. It revolves around the concept of humanity having a 'common cause' which had occurred to no one but himself. The title of his long manuscript is a kind of summary of his original impulses – *On the Question of Brotherhood or Kinship (Relatedness) and the Causes of the Unbrotherly, Unrelated, That Is Unpeaceful State of the World and The Means of Re-establishing Kinship: Notes from a Non-scientist to Scientists both Spiritual and Secular, to Believers and Unbelievers.*[25] Fedorov was distressed by the disunity of humanity and, like Solov'ev, wanted to bring unity but his vision of how to achieve it was quite different. The title is also a manifesto in itself. Humanity had lost its brotherliness. (Note: Fedorov did not ignore women who had a significant role in his thinking. Maternity was an element in it but not the total. He often used the term 'kinship' or 'relatedness' as a more inclusive option rather than brotherhood.) How could one reach universal peace and overcome dis-relatedness? Here, he thought, lay the mission of science. Its aim should be nothing less than to take up the 'common task' of all humanity – the physical resurrection of the dead. Humanity could unify itself round this great task. He described himself as a non-scientist, though he read widely in the sciences, but appealed to scientists and to members of all the divisive groups to contribute despite their differences. Fedorov thought that scientific knowledge would advance to the point where the bodies of the dead could be reconstituted and the living become immortal.

Setting aside the practicality of this issue, which was remote at the time but has re-emerged since in association with cryogenic ideas (preservation of bodies by deep-freezing to await re-animation), genetic engineering (notably cloning) and transhumanism (technological enhancement of the human body), Fedorov's ideas brought together themes of Russian *sobornost'* (gathering together and communality), religion and rationalism. Perhaps the most remarkable feature is that when he talked about the 'common' task or about 'universal brotherhood' (*vselenskoe bratstvo*) he meant all-inclusive in a way few others had been bold enough to think. He did not simply mean to apply it to those currently inhabiting the planet. He said that morality required the principle to be applied to all past and future generations as well as the present ones. This implied two enormous concepts. One was that the dead should be resurrected. The second that humans should become immortal. It should be noted here that Fedorov was not following the hazy mystical ideas of immortality and the supernatural which we have encountered in the new religious consciousness. It was no idealist, spiritual or imaginary conceit for Fedorov; it was a concrete, material, empirical task.

To achieve it the two main sources of death had to be overcome. One was the bio-chemical process of ageing, the other human vulnerability to natural disaster, disease and accident. Fedorov then made another spectacular leap. The means to reach this goal was not to invoke a supernatural power or to transform consciousness or to rely on visions. For Fedorov it was a scientific and rational enterprise. Not only that, he argued, it was the ultimate scientific task. It was the ultimate purpose of science, what science existed for – achieving resurrection and immortality. Real, full-on science was essential as the means to solve the multitude of material problems Fedorov's project required. Biochemists would have to reverse the decay of human cells. Climate scientists would need to be able to precisely predict and, ultimately, control weather. Geologists would need to be able to control earthquakes. Medical researchers would have to conquer viruses and so on. Fedorov's mind was as broad as the universe. He even pursued issues of detail: if one was to resurrect the dead by gathering up the molecules of the bodies of the dead, how would it be possible to deal with molecules which had transmigrated into other organisms or even into inanimate objects? Fedorov proposed that, in a process sometimes compared to cloning, only a few cells might be sufficient to begin the reconstitution of a human body. Once that was done, then the original personality would have to be re-formed somehow, a task even Fedorov could not see the end of.

Ironically, in yet another extraordinary dimension of his thought, Fedorov was reflecting some of the intellectual foundations of Marxism and pre-figuring aspects of post-1917 Russian communism. Philosophers should not simply interpret the world, they must change it. Humanity was one and indivisible and must be released from the pressures causing division in order to reach universal emancipation. In his personal life, too, Fedorov was a communist in his rejection of property, though in his case the inspiration came from the New Testament not *Das Kapital.* He also foreshadowed some of communism's own fringe thinkers who promoted a promethean, scientific, humanist perfection.

It is hard to trace Fedorov's direct influence on individuals and movements. One can certainly see admiration but not imitation. Tolstoy said, 'I am proud to have lived at the same time as such a remarkable person.'[26] Both remained preoccupied with resurrection, but it turned out very differently in Tolstoy who was concerned with moral, social and spiritual redemption and resurrection, taking the latter word as the title of his last, and somewhat overlooked, great novel *Resurrection* (*Voskresenie*) (1899).

Fedorov remained close in spirit to two other great contemporary admirers, Vladimir Solov'ev and Fyodor Dostoevsky. In a letter Dostoevsky stated that 'he interested me very much .... In essence, I completely agreed with these thoughts. I read them as though they were my own.'[27] Solov'ev was even more fulsome in his praise for Fedorov's project:

> I have read your entire manuscript with hunger and spiritual delight, dedicating a whole night and part of the morning to reading it. The following two days, Saturday and Sunday, I thought a great deal about what I had read. I accept your 'Project' unconditionally and without any discussion .... Since the emergence of Christianity your 'Project' is the first forward step of the human spirit along the path of Christ. I, for my part, can only acknowledge you as my teacher and spiritual father.[28]

Fedorov was certainly a central, influential and, for many, intriguing figure at the heart of the intelligentsia investigation of themes of death and resurrection in the Silver Age and beyond. One can find parallels and similarities, though not direct influences, across a wide range of early twentieth century Russian culture before, and, indeed, after 1917. Immortality, death and rebirth are fundamental elements in Stravinsky's great ballets *The Firebird* (1910) and *Rite of Spring* (1913) which celebrate the annual mystery of nature's rebirth in spring, together with reference to a supposed pagan rite of the sacrifice of a young maiden who dances herself to death. One of the most unusual uses of themes of death and resurrection is associated with the early Soviet-era architect Konstantin Melnikov (1890–1974). It has often been remarked that he was almost unique as a leading architect in designing garages for cars and, in one case, for Moscow's fleet of Leyland buses imported from Britain. One of the roots of that fascination was Melnikov's conception that, after a day of work, motor vehicles came to the garage to die, only to be resurrected again next morning. The famous design for his house in Moscow made his bed the centrepiece. It was designed like a catafalque upon which the sun's rays would fall at dawn and sunset, with its occupant also 'dying' and 'rising' on a daily basis. Ironically, perhaps, it was Melnikov who designed Russia's most famous catafalque, the first sarcophagus in which the embalmed body of Lenin was laid in his mausoleum from where, as the famous slogan puts it, Lenin lives forever.[29] Finally, one can also see strong Fedorovian motifs in the ideas of Russian Cosmists and, in the contemporary world, in those of the Transhumanists.

There were others at the time who also focused on death, including artists and writers in western Europe. In Russia a collection of essays edited was simply entitled *Death* (*Smert'*) in which Vyacheslav Ivanov and others presented metaphysical intuitions of death and immortality. Although not as wide a theme as apocalypse, an associated meditation on death was a significant trend in early-twentieth-century Russian thought.[30]

Fedorov was also acquainted with a third visionary, Konstantin Tsiolkovsky, (1857–1935) who also imagined a scientifically driven human perfection which would lead to the colonization of space. In his memoirs Tsiolkovsky recalls that in the mists of his distant youth he met Fedorov whom he described as a 'wonderful philosopher and modest person'.[31] This encounter would probably have been when Tsiolkovsky was occupied in his studies in the Rumiantsev Library. Like many Russian thinkers Tsiolkovsky is hard to categorise. From boyhood he was deeply focused on the challenge of flight, not just in the earth's atmosphere but beyond, into space. He saw the future of humanity in the task of space colonization, taking in not only the planets but the galaxy. He conceptualized many of the issues involved in space flight. He proposed three-stage rockets fuelled by a mixture of liquid gases, hydrogen and oxygen. He calculated what he considered to be the escape velocity needed to reach space orbit. He theorized airlocks to gain access to the exterior of the space craft when out of the earth's atmosphere. Even more remarkable he achieved all this without formal education and without support for what was a lonely quest. He was home schooled because of hearing impairment after a bout of scarlet fever when he was ten and his later attempts to gain recognition through prize awards or financial backing all failed. He self-funded much of his work, making his living as a school maths teacher in his home province of Kaluga. He published his main ideas in a series of articles in *Nauchnoe obozreniia* (*Scientific Review*) entitled 'Exploration of Outer Space by Means of Rocket Devices'. The first appeared in 1903 followed by others in 1911 and 1914. He also theorized aspects of jet aviation including jet turbine engines and the aerodynamics of wings and was also enthusiastic about the potential of dirigible airships. He also proposed high-speed trains running on a cushion of air and hovercraft. He was disappointed that there was no response to his ideas before 1914 and, during the war years, he gave up his research to focus instead on combatting poverty. He supported the Bolshevik revolution and it was only in his later years that his bold visions were taken up by Soviet scientists and his genius was recognized. He became acquainted with and inspired the chief Soviet rocket designer and head of the space programme, Sergei Korolev (1907–66). He was eventually honoured as part of an iconic monument to the Conquerors of Space at the entrance to the Cosmonauts' Museum adjacent to the Exhibition of National Economic Achievements (VDNKh from its Russian acronym) in Moscow. Of course, as we are becoming accustomed, even someone as involved in the rational scientific quest for knowledge and progress had a philosophical, almost mystical, side. In one of his books, whose title is usually translated as *The Will of the Universe: The Unknown Intelligence*, he proposed colonization of the Milky Way and that human life was a mechanistic working out of the will of a cosmic intelligence. Every Russian thinker, it seems, had a response to the 'cursed questions' (*prokliatye voprosy*) of the meaning and origin of the human spirit.

While Tsiolkovsky's ideas only reached fruition as the technologies capable of implementing them were devised and, even today, his name is not widely known outside Russia, the late nineteenth century saw the emergence of the first Russian scientists to become international household names. On the cusp of this wave of recognition is the chemist Dmitrii Mendeleev (1834–1907). His main achievement was to produce a format for the Periodic Table of Elements which came to be universally accepted and is known, to this day, by every scientist on the planet from high school upwards. Another household name from this period is that of the experimental physiologist Ivan Pavlov (1849–1936). So well-known was he and his work on conditioned reflexes in dogs that his name became a widely used adjective in English – Pavlovian. He was also the first Russian to receive a Nobel Prize which he was awarded in the Physiology category in 1904. Pavlov was a prickly, highly opinionated character who made a number of disparaging remarks about Jews. Pavlov's long life and career remind us of the numerically narrow dimensions of the intelligentsia in that one of his earliest inspirations to abandon religion while he was a seminarian and adopt science was the nihilist literary critic and stereotypical 'person of the sixties', Dmitrii Pisarev (1840–68). Pisarev's ideas had been the object of Dostoevsky's devastating dissection in *Crime and Punishment* in the form of the central character Razumov, whose name derives from the Russian word for 'reason' (*razum*). Although the Bolsheviks adopted Pisarev as one of their own, Pavlov had no time for the Bolshevik experiment and protested against repression and arrests, virtually until his death from pneumonia in 1936. Despite this 'dissident' status Pavlov was admired by Lenin and protected by Bukharin and Stalin and showered with honours and resources. His long life linked the earliest stirrings of the radical intelligentsia to the Stalin purges which passed him by.

Another figure who brought two epochs together was V.I. Vernadsky (1863–1945). He enjoys a stellar reputation in Russia, one of Moscow's main thoroughfares leading to the university district is named after him, but he is much less well-known in the wider world. Unlike Pavlov, who straightforwardly renounced religion and proclaimed himself to be an atheist all his working life, Vernadsky operated in that dimension where science overlapped with the idealist and almost metaphysical dimensions of science. This perhaps makes it less surprising that one of his main contacts, admirers and inspirations outside Russia was the French Jesuit palaeontologist and evolutionary philosopher Pierre Teilhard de Chardin (1881–1955), who was himself marginalized by the western scientific establishment. While their ideas were very different they did share a related central concept. Teilhard called it the 'noosphere' while, although he did not devise it himself, Vernadsky adopted the term 'biosphere' for his version. Many of his ideas came to fruition after 1917 when, like Pavlov, he was given resources to pursue his research. From his early career he developed a wide range of ideas and theories about life sciences as well as extremely important work establishing the foundations of geochemistry. In the words of a fellow Russian scientist 'In his lectures at the University he began to break new ground by stressing the genetic aspect in mineralogy. This genetic approach to mineralogy was fully developed in his books *Essay on Descriptive Mineralogy* (1908, 1910) and *History of Minerals of the Earth's Crust* (1925, 1933)'.[32] He developed ideas about the biosphere and what he called the 'noosphere' – the emergence of consciousness embodied in humans – which have had something of a revival among twentieth- and twenty-first-century ecologists and evolutionists. Vernadsky, like many scientists, viewed his career as a service to humanity and was one of the first to agree to continue to work under post-revolutionary Soviet conditions.

It was not just the cultural élites who were flourishing. Underpinning it was a steady expansion of the urban industrial economy which accelerated to industrial growth rates of 6–8 per cent, albeit from Russia's low base. Railway construction was, once again, a leading sector. In 1890 there were approximately 19,000 miles (30,500 km) of track. By 1905 this had grown to almost 32,000 miles (51,500 km) and over 50,000 miles (80,000 km) by 1917.[33] As ever, while the economic impact was important in, for example, facilitating grain exports from Odessa to Italy and other parts of Europe, the expansion of the system continued to break down not only local markets but local isolation and self-sufficiency, opening ever wider areas to national, and even global, market penetration. They also stimulated spin-off growth in staff employment, maintenance engineering, steel production for rails and rolling stock and practical skills for the complexity of timetabling, accounting, ticketing and a host of other things. They continued to have strategic use, with the Trans-Siberian and Manchurian railways called into service moving troops and supplies to the Far East for the Russo-Japanese war (1904–5) and later, in the west and south to the Caucasus, for the First World War. Armaments – based on metalworking – also boomed especially after 1905 when it was necessary to replace a large portion of the Baltic Fleet, lost at Tsushima in 1905, and keep up in the arms race, especially with a resurgent Germany. From the cultural point of view cultural institutions were consolidated, even expanded. Despite tough censorship, at least until 1905, thick journals proliferated and even those of radical orientation were able to publish. *Russkaia mysl'* (*Russian Thought* liberal 1880–1918); *Mir bozhii* (*God's World* SD 1892–1906); *Russkoe bogatstvo* (*Russia's Wealth* Populist/SR); *Sovremennyi mir* (*The Contemporary World* SD) and even the official *Zhurnal ministerstvo narodnago prosveshenia* (*Journal of the Ministry of Public Education* – or, literally, *Journal of the Ministry of Popular Enlightenment* 1834–1917) were packed with stories, serialized novels, social analysis, chronicles of current events, cultural criticism (some of it still Aesopian), illustrations, art reproductions and the like, testifying to the range and depth of intelligentsia talent. Heavyweight newspapers also proliferated as well as satirical journals, which concealed sharp political barbs behind surface humour, such as *Oskolki* (*Fragments* 1881–1916); *Strekoza* (*Dragonfly* 1875–1908); *Satirikon* (*Satyricon* 1908–14); *Novyi Satirikon* (*New Satyricon* 1913). Around 1905 a group of brilliant fine arts journals emerged – *Mir iskusstva* (*The World of Art 1899–1904); Vesy* (*The Scales/Libra* 1904–1909); *Zolotoe runo* (*The Golden Fleece* 1906–9) and *Appollon'* (*Apollo* 1909–17). Clearly an intellectual class of unprecedented diversity of talent and creative brilliance had emerged.

Although the circulation figures of many of these items were often only a few thousand (or even hundreds for the fine arts journals),[34] they also bore witness to the expansion of a well-educated readership prepared to devour the up to 500-page per month thick journal leviathans as well as the rest of the burgeoning élite press.[35] Precise figures before the 1899 census are hard to come by but we can get an impression of the numbers involved by looking at education, particularly higher and teacher education. From 1860 to 1900 there were about 60,000 Russians, overwhelmingly male, who graduated from university, of which there were seven, excluding Warsaw, in 1881. At that moment they had about 9,344 students with 6,100 more in higher education institutes. From 1900 to 1917 significantly more students graduated than in the previous four decades put together, that is around 85,000. In 1903 there were fifty-five institutes of higher education with a total enrolment of 42,844, about half of whom were in universities. By January 1914 there were almost 72,000 students in the state sector. Other calculations, including private institutions, propose 90,000 higher education students in 1900 and 125,000, of whom 30,000 were women, by the middle of the First World War. Traditional sciences, law and humanities showed least growth over the whole period while technical and medical subjects show the most. These figures are imprecise and unsystematic but they do point unequivocally to extensive growth.[36]

School education, especially at elementary and middle levels, also expanded widely. In 1900 there were 10,000 middle school teachers which rose to 30,000 by 1914. Most were graduates, many were women. Compared to elementary teachers they had a reasonable income and status. In 1900 there were some 60,000 elementary school teachers rising to 72,000 (1906) then 131,500 (1914). Reflecting the population distribution, about 97 per cent of elementary teachers were in rural schools, many having quite a tough life.[37] Increasing numbers brought slight democratization, seen elsewhere, for example among army officers as the traditional superélite was too limited to fulfil the demand for expansion. 'Modernization' was driving education expansion and the children of personal nobles (i.e. people promoted to this level in the Table of Ranks), the middle class and even children of peasant and Cossack background were recruited in increasing numbers and proportion.[38] However, the figures should be kept in perspective in that the population of the Russian Empire in 1914 was around 170 million.

Most of these effects were felt most strongly in the main cities, especially St Petersburg, Moscow and Kyiv together with Warsaw, Riga, Helsinki and others and the outcome was a further divide between rural and urban. The developing metropolises were assimilating into western modes of dress, lifestyles, occupations, culture and expectations. They were almost a separate Russia from the bulk of the small towns and rural hinterlands. At last, some progress had come to the countryside as social differentiation, outmigration and landowner decline slowly changed the shape of ownership and some areas began to achieve small advances in economic growth. The majority of peasants lived above the poverty line but in 1891, crop failure and government incompetence in responding to it brought a deadly famine[39] starting in the lower Volga region and spreading to the Urals and north shore of the Black Sea. The number of dead is thought to be between 300,000 and 500,000. It may have had political consequences. One observer, the Marxist who later became a liberal nationalist, Peter Struve, said that the famine created more Marxists in Russia than *Das Kapital*. The generation which led the revolution in 1917 were young and impressionable around the time of the famine. Lenin was twenty-one. However, the famine was an aberration and it would be wrong to picture the peasantry as a whole to be living in grinding poverty. Some were but others were becoming mildly prosperous and wages remitted by those who had been recruited for industrial work in the city brought a new income stream which helped make village ends meet. Most of the outmigrants were younger women who worked in domestic or retail service and young men who worked in factories, transport, construction, mining and services. They brought a flavour of the wider world to the village and slowly expanded its mental horizons. However, culturally and socially, the peasants lived in a different universe from the educated urban classes although urban workers, on the whole, were as much peasant as urban in many respects.

Russia has never been easy to govern and the growing complexities of the late nineteenth century were not making it any easier. In its last decades the autocracy was ill-served by its advisers. Had there been influential modernizers in the form of Speransky or Miliutin whom the last two tsars trusted it might have been possible to come to terms with these changes. Unfortunately for the autocracy, the most influential adviser, Konstantin Pobedonostsev (1827–1907), took exactly the opposite view. The best survival strategy for the autocracy, he insisted, was to resist imported cultural influences, cleave firmly to traditional Russian Orthodox values and drown dissent in nationalism and religious mysticism. Pobedonostsev, who may not even have been a believer, held the position of Procurator of the Holy Synod from 1880 to 1905. This administrative post was set up to provide state oversight of the church after Peter the Great abolished the Moscow patriarchate in 1721. From this platform Pobedonostsev became chief architect of the autocracy's response to the assassination crisis. This included 'Temporary Regulations'[40] to suspend trial by jury and other of the limited reforms of the 1860s, since the disorder was, in a catastrophic misperception, attributed to the process of reform rather than to the need for more. Pobedonostsev also thought it would be possible to swamp the minority nationalities by pursuing a policy of Russification with two sharp prongs, imposing Russian in schools above the local language and discriminating against those lacking a Russian Orthodox baptismal certificate.[41] To back it up, large cathedrals were built in prominent sites in non-Russian cities like Tallinn (named Reval at that time) to intimidate the local population into thinking the Russian domination was not worth contesting. This also, deliberately or otherwise, roused the slumbering dragon of anti-Semitism. Vicious pogroms broke out in 1881, supposedly to punish the Jews who were wrongly identified as the perpetrators of the assassination. In 1897 a collection of Pobedonostsev's writings was published entitled *Moskovskii sbornik* (literally *Moscow Collection* but best known in translation as *Reflections of a Russian Statesman*).[42] In it, he argued that democracy was 'the great lie of our time'. Its practitioners were hypocrites in that democracy needed selfless, modest people as leaders but instead it attracted the noisiest, most vulgar and dishonest, motivated by lust for power and self-enrichment, to put themselves forward. In full Slavophile mode, Pobedonostsev denounced the human degradation associated with overcrowded industrial cities in the west and rejected the crude materialism which resided at the core of the western soul. Instead, Russia's purity of spirit preserved true humanity from corrosion by unbridled individualism and self-interest. Many of Pobedonostsev's views look less absurd after fascism and in an age of racist neo-populism and the Trump cult but he had severely miscalculated. Democracy also had the advantage of incorporating change. Pobedonostsev's insistence on maximum resistance to it was unsustainable. He gave Alexander III and the young crown prince, Nicholas, whom he tutored, the worst possible advice. He drilled into Nicholas that the essence of his royal duty was that he was ordained by God to preserve the full spectrum of autocratic power and it was his religious duty to pass it on, undiminished, to his successor. When Nicholas succeeded his father in 1894 expectations rose that the clampdown since 1881 might be reduced. Pobedonostsev's hand was clearly visible in the keynote speech of his reign when Nicholas addressed the Assembly of the Nobility in 1895. Hopes for change were dismissed as 'senseless dreams'. Pobedonostsev and his protégé had put the autocracy on a collision course with Russian society. They had the best claim to being Russia's most influential revolutionaries. Russification, in particular, drove people from Sibelius to Stalin into resistance of various kinds. Pobedonostsev's policies were sowing dragon's teeth which would soon reap an unintended harvest.

The intelligentsia after 1905: Reconciliation or radical revolution?

The year 1900 passed without any apocalypse. It was slightly late and turned up in 1905. Russian society from the poorest of peasants to the richest *nouveau riche* industrialist was deeply affected. Peasants were increasingly emboldened to demand more land, workers engaged in strikes to protect their jobs and wages as the industrial economy stalled. The embryonic middle class and much of educated Russia were appalled that

Russia had gone to war with Japan and even more appalled that the war had been conducted disastrously. The main Russian position, at Port Arthur (Dairen), fell in December giving near fatal, for the autocracy, momentum to the growing contempt for the tsar. Naval defeat at Tsushima in May dashed the last card from the war promoters hands and Russia had to conclude a humiliating peace. Politically, it was a hot summer. Peasants encroached on landowners estates. Workers erected barricades in cities. National minorities in Finland, Poland and the Baltic States attempted to gain independence. Caucasus mountain clans, in the Gurian province of Georgia, for example, turned their high, remote valleys into no-go areas for the authorities. The most dangerous development for the autocracy was the collapse of the consensus on how to react. In past crises the landowners and élites had eventually stuck with the tsar to protect their interests. In 1905 more and more of them saw the anachronistic autocratic system as the problem not the saviour.

The autocracy survived by a whisker. Two aspects pulled it through. First, despite numerous mutinies, the military remained loyal and, most of the time, prepared to quell unrest. In his great movie of 1925, intended to be the introduction to a vast panoramic survey of the 1905 revolution to celebrate its tenth anniversary, Sergei Eisenstein (1898–1948) focused on the mutiny on *The Battleship Potemkin* (1925) which became the whole film. It is a celebration of the popular spirit of 1905 depicted in narodnik terms – people, good; authorities bad. But, intentionally or not, his parable precisely pinpoints why 1905 failed. In the final scene the Potemkin sails towards the rest of the fleet. The fact that the other crews refused to fire on them and, instead, let them through the cordon is presented as a great victory. Sadly, it was also the essence of defeat. Those crews did not join them. This type of outcome occurred time and again in 1905. There were hundreds of mutinies but all, like that of the *Potemkin,* remained isolated.

The second survival feature was a new strategy and a new strategist. At last, Pobedonostsev was sacked (October 1905). The new aspiring architect of tsarist survival was Sergei Witte, a railroad man with a father in the same industry. Witte believed, not unlike many Marxists at the other end of the political spectrum, that the peasantry was fundamentally loyal and conservative. For Witte this meant that the way out of the crisis was to set up an electoral system in which the supposedly loyal peasant majority would vote in overwhelmingly large numbers for conservatives and drown the small minority of liberals and socialists in a tsunami of votes. Nicholas may have been especially open to this idea after an extraordinary event in 1904. The church had been viewing most of the developments we have been looking at in this chapter with increasing dismay and wanted to turn back the tide. One plank of their counter-strategy was the canonization of a hermit, Serafim of Sarov (1754–1833) in 1903. According to Witte, Pobedonostsev told him the empress herself had requested it.[43] The focus of the event was a vast procession to his hermitage where the tsar and tsarina were surrounded by hundreds of thousands of pious peasants. It was the embodiment of Witte's strategy and it was not difficult to persuade Nicholas that the people loved him.

As it turned out they didn't, or at least they loved their land more. To implement his strategy Witte drew up the October Manifesto, a vaguely worded bundle of promises that there might be some form of partially elected parliament.[44] It was enough to buy off crucial elements of the opposition. The landowners and part of the industrial élite saw an opportunity to work within such a system and control the dangerous inflexibility of the autocracy. It was the first part of a turning point which went so well that, after having been afraid to use troops to quell unrest in early October in case they embarked on a major mutiny, when the workers of Moscow tried to instigate an armed uprising in December the government was able to quell it with Cossacks and artillery. This was the overture to years of repression in which the autocracy was able to resume its authority even though the peasants spectacularly failed to play their allotted role of loyal executioners of liberal, narodnik and social-democratic hopes. Those were precisely the parties which they voted for. But in the end it didn't matter, except to Witte who was sacked. In his place the governor of Saratov, Peter Stolypin (1862–1911), who had a reputation as a firm repressor of dissent in his province/ guberniia, replaced him as would-be saviour of tsarism. Through 1906 and 1907 he repeated his Saratov strategy on a national scale and the revolution was crushed.

What part did the intelligentsia play in the revolution? At least as far as causing it was concerned they followed the example of Gilbert and Sullivan's House of Lords in *Iolanthe* – they did nothing in particular and did it very well. However, once the revolution was up and running, they tried to ride the wave and guide it. Tkachev had been correct. The tsar and Pobedonostsev had done far more than any revolutionary to create the revolutionary situation, but once it existed the members of the political intelligentsia were prepared to act decisively, though, of course, in different ways according to their political foundation of nationalist, liberal, populist, social-democratic or even, for a few, anarchist principles. Revolutionary euphoria also spread to many members of the artistic intelligentsia.

The intelligentsia had not been passive before 1905. Strikes had, as we have noted, begun in 1895–6 in St Petersburg when women cigarette makers had not only sparked a serious strike across their own and other factories but had also re-started the strike when the employers failed to implement the deal they had initially agreed. Discontent grew slowly but steadily and students themselves took action and St Petersburg University was closed by the authorities to prevent it from being used as an oasis of free speech in a still tightly controlled and censored society. However, the impact of the intelligentsia on events remained small. Strikes were caused by worker grievances not as a result of reading political manifestos and following intelligentsia leaders. If anything, it was the other way round. The tough conditions radicalized workers and they then turned to outside leaders, like Stalin who was a very active union organizer, strike leader and propagandist in the Caucasus region at this point. There, as elsewhere, it was crudely exploitative capitalist employers and international companies that provoked strikes, not union organizers. In fact, the farcical police-socialist unions, which began in Odessa and spread to many cities including the capital, may have had more influence in promoting strikes than the revolutionary parties themselves, though the latter were quick to seize on the openings presented by the official unions for them to surreptitiously contact workers. More spectacular, but probably no more effective though that is a difficult quality to quantify, was a revival of *Narodnaia Voliia* (People's Will) type terrorism. For a number of years before and after 1905 the SR party, like *Sinn Fein* in Ireland, had a relatively open, given tsarist conditions, conventional political wing and a small, highly secret, terrorist wing. The terrorist wing assassinated official figures who symbolized tsarist oppression – senior police leaders, Ministers of Education, a Minister of the Interior. Their attempts after 1905 to assassinate Stolypin failed though he was shot to death in a Kyiv theatre in 1911. But the motives of the assassin, Dmitrii Bogrov, one of numerous double-agents active at the time, have never been satisfactorily clarified. In any case, no matter how illustrious the victim, such acts of horror did not threaten the system. They were little more than pinpricks. Many revolutionaries, including Lenin, believed such acts were counter-productive. Only solid, organized, mass action, he argued, would bring about a revolution though, in December 1905, he did support a workers' armed uprising in a working-class district of Moscow as a catalyst for a mass revolution. The armed uprising was, however, a blood-soaked failure.

Lenin's activities in 1905 are, in some respects, puzzling. Many intellectuals, including conservatives like Rozanov, were intoxicated, so they said later, with thoughts of change and extended freedom. Liberals conducted political agitation in the form of banquets, modelled on the tactics of French liberals in 1848.[45] Political meetings were illegal. Banquets were not. Set up a banquet, conclude it with political speeches and disperse before the authorities had time to act. In 1904, the brilliant young poet, Alexander Blok (1880–1921), gave a memorable talk to the leaders of the SR party in which he depicted the deprivation of ordinary people. In 1905 he walked the streets of the capital entranced by the public protests, but without really participating.[46] For many writers normally considered apolitical, like Blok, or even reactionary, like Rozanov a diffuse attraction to the 'mystique of revolution' could take hold of them. Fringe groups like the mystical anarchists showed it in a very idiosyncratic way. Many political activists thrust themselves into the thick of events in more conventional ways. Trotsky, for example, returned from exile in Brussels and London in October 1905. He immediately threw himself into organizational and street politics, giving energetic speeches and evoking revolutionary sentiments in his working-class audiences. After it was set up in the October 1905 crisis Trotsky was heavily involved in the St Petersburg Soviet and ended the year as its substitute chair after its main chair, Khrustalev-Nosar, was arrested and exiled. Trotsky soon followed him. Others were less keen to get involved directly, perhaps fearing they would be victims of backlash. Plekhanov remained resolutely in exile. Lenin acted somewhere in between Trotsky and Plekhanov. He did not return to Russia until the revolution was already in retreat after the October manifesto. Once he arrived he quickly went into hiding, taking advantage of the new autonomous status of Finland where the authorities had no interest in pursuing enemies of the tsar, whose empire the Finns were extricating themselves from. He made frequent short trips to St Petersburg and Moscow, making the occasional speech to workers, but largely remained within the confines of the tiny group of party leaders. To this end he attended party congresses and conferences in Stockholm, Copenhagen, London and Stuttgart, being frequently seen mounting a conference podium but rarely in the streets or at the head of strike processions. In December 1907, in a perilous journey over sea ice to a remote Finnish island, he was able to catch a ferry to Sweden without attracting the attention of Russian police agents who still checked the major ports. He did not return to Russia until April 1917. Thus the political and artistic intelligentsia participated in the events of 1905 in a variety of ways, including the production of searing political cartoons and satire.

Much more significant is, how did they react to the failure to overthrow tsarism? What does it tell us about the nature of the intelligentsia in the early twentieth century?

The events of 1905 are often underestimated and downgraded to, in Lenin's phrase, a 'dress rehearsal'. It was only from the perspective of 1917 and after that such a thing could be said. For most of the intelligentsia it was an unmitigated disaster. It was no rehearsal it was the opening night, the complete run and the forced closure of the show that all Russian history from the 1860s seemed to have been moving towards. A national-historical moment had come – and gone in a totally dispiriting defeat. Repression was rampant. Where promises of reform had been extracted by the force of the revolution, by 1906 the emphasis was on the authorities retracting as much as possible. In one way this is scarcely surprising. The tsar had fought bitterly against change and, although Pobedonostsev was removed from his post, Nicholas remained imbued with his lugubrious penumbra. The tsar had only signed the October Manifesto under extreme duress. Its drafter, Sergei Witte, told him it was the only way out of the crisis, since the generals had no confidence the army would continue to obey if asked to engage in mass repression. Even then, his uncle, Grand Duke Sergei, had to threaten to commit suicide to make Nicholas sign. As the tsar and his entourage regained their nerve they retracted concessions one by one. In December 1905 guards troops and artillery battered the Moscow workers' rising into submission. In 1906 and 1907 the democratically elected First and Second Dumas were disbanded rapidly until, on 3 June 1907, Stolypin changed the electoral system to effectively put the power of the Duma, such as it was, into the hands of right-wing property owners, which is where it remained until 1917. Urban uprisings, as in Kronstadt in July 1906, were repressed by artillery. Death squads roamed the countryside hanging hundreds, probably thousands, of peasant 'agitators' after tokenistic military trials. Radical parties and leaders went back into exile. Trade unions were again subject to major harassment. Antisemitic pogroms were encouraged by some local authorities and a Jew, Menahem Mendel Beilis, was put on trial in Kyiv on a trumped up charge of ritual murder in 1913. In April 1912, 270 striking goldfield workers were shot dead in Siberia. In 1914, barricades re-appeared in the streets of St Petersburg. The 1905 revolution appeared to have failed comprehensively and the revolutionary scale had been re-set to zero. It seemed it would all have to re-start from the beginning.

It was the radical political intelligentsia which was hit hardest. They and their predecessors had invested most in overthrowing the autocracy and it appeared to have all come to nothing. Most of them recognized the need to come up with new strategies. In his pamphlet *Itogi i perspektivii* (*Results and Prospects*) Trotsky modified the Marxist theory of stages to say that the phase of bourgeois democratic revolution, which was, he argued, still next on the Russian agenda, could blend rapidly and seamlessly into the stage of socialist revolution. Somewhat misleadingly he attached the name 'permanent revolution' to this new interpretation.

Lenin, by contrast, moved decisively away from his December 1905 dalliance with a workers' armed uprising and, recognizing the obvious fact that the peasants were the overwhelming majority, concluded the next step would be a democratic dictatorship of the workers and peasants. In this scenario the petit-bourgeois peasantry would act under the hegemonic leadership of the proletariat (workers) in order to establish a revolutionary government that would overthrow the monarchy, landowners and capitalists and also introduce democratic institutions. It would not, however, be immediately ready for a transformation to socialism as, in Lenin's view, the peasantry had to be released from their toxic addiction to individual private property-holding. Much of this was still present ten years later in Lenin's programme unveiled at the Finland Station in April 1917. Many Mensheviks developed ideas reminiscent of the small Economist grouping, that Russia was totally unsuited for a socialist revolution and would have to accept a period of capitalist development to increase the strength and power of the working class.

The Social Democrats had moved into an almost surreal phase of existence in which ever-deeper and more bitter factionalisms occurred within a series of attempts, brought about by pressure from allied parties abroad like the German Social Democrats, to reunify the fragments. Party membership seems to have fallen from 150,000 at its 1905 peak, to something like 10,000 by 1909. The party crisis was acute in the extreme. It was not just the socialist parties that were in turmoil. The liberals, who, in Russian conditions of an ancient regime, should still be considered on the revolutionary side of the spectrum, were also divided and the pressures of adapting to Duma politics were causing battles over how to respond, ranging from complete boycott to trying to form a government. Socialists and liberals both threw up new variants on their fundamental principles in the form of individuals with very new approaches. Among socialists, Alexander Bogdanov (1873–1928) led the charge while Peter Struve (1870–1944) stirred things up among liberals.

Bogdanov, like Fedorov in this one characteristic, established his principles and took them to absolute conclusions. This may also be one of his few 'Russian' characteristics as he was not engaged in arguments about Russia's future path, or its special features or any aspect of its identity. Bogdanov started out from ultra-rationalist and scientific principles, becoming a doctor in order to develop them and use his talents in the service of the people in the old populist tradition. He was a materialist of such ferocity that he denounced Lenin, whom he rivalled for influence in the party, as an idealist, in philosophical terms.[47] Bogdanov had no place for Russia or any other country in his outlook except as artificial and ever-changing products of historical chance. As any Marxist should, but perhaps few achieve, the only thing that mattered was class. Bogdanov's mission was to liberate the exploited workers. But he also gave his sharp focus a highly scientific matrix. His materialism was monist, heavily influenced by contemporary German thinkers such as Ernst Mach and Richard Avenarius. Nothing escaped from its material nature. Human thought was an as yet unknown but definite outcome of nothing but matter. There was no mind, spirit, soul or psyche, no supernatural or spiritual world that was not a function of matter.

Many thinkers shared, and continued to share, Bogdanov's materialism but few have followed him to the limits, apart from, for example, Pavlov and the later American psychologist B.F. Skinner, who both argued that human activity was an advanced form of conditioning of reflexes and was rooted in chemical not conscious processes.[48] Will and free choice were illusory. In his everyday life, Bogdanov appeared to live much like everyone else, choosing to follow his intellectual path, falling in love, having psychological highs and lows just like other determinists from Calvin onwards. In particular, Bogdanov pointed to the importance of class consciousness in the revolutionary process, in itself a perhaps unexpected priority for someone as scientifically deterministic as he was. In his mind one of the key weaknesses of the proletariat was that it did not live under circumstances in which it could freely develop a culture appropriate to its values. Why not? Because all the means of cultural formation were in the hands of bourgeois and capitalist controllers who established the hegemonic power of their own values. Such values varied from loyalty and fealty to the monarch in feudal society to key values of individualism, competition and material acquisition (to the point of greed) in the case of capitalism. Cultural hegemony was complete when society in general considered the values of the dominant class to be 'common sense' and in conformity with 'human nature' and so on. This posed a massive problem for proletarian revolution. Where bourgeois capitalism had had centuries, at least from the Renaissance and Reformation, to erode feudal values before they came to power in the French Revolution and after, the proletariat had not been able to establish its own values. The dominant class was always throwing substantial spanners – nationalism; religion; race; imperialism; antisemitism (and today even gender and identity politics sometimes play this role from a Bogdanovite perspective) – in the works to disrupt the smooth formation of working-class values of solidarity, collectivism, equality, rationality and altruism. It followed that it was imperative for the proletariat to find ways to form its own culture, without which it would not be able to exercise leadership in society, or even conduct a successful revolution. Bogdanov gave priority to two projects. One was to set up a Proletarian University which taught on the basis of the working-class and Marxist view of the world. The second project was to nurture the development of a Proletarian Encyclopaedia. For Bogdanov, Diderot's late-eighteenth-century encyclopaedia had worked as a compendium of accumulating bourgeois knowledge and values. The proletariat needed its own equivalent. Neither project developed far before 1917. Bogdanov did work with his associates Lunacharsky and Gorky, whose villa on the isle of Capri in the Bay of Naples, was the meeting point, to hold a party school for a small number of working-class activists able to leave Russia surreptitiously. Although there is a famous photo of Bogdanov and Lenin playing chess on Capri in apparent comradely harmony, Lenin and Bogdanov had a bitter falling out. Lenin returned to Paris to set up a rival party school to combat Bogdanov's malign influence.[49]

Bogdanov's criticisms had so stung Lenin that not only did he spend much of 1908 writing a refutation, he was so emotionally involved, so carried away in a sustained fury, that he resorted to childish name calling which was extraordinarily out of place in what was intended as a philosophical discourse, albeit a polemical one. His sister managed to persuade him to tone it down but even now parts of it read like the diary of a child with anger management issues rather than a philosophical treatise. Only 'an inmate of a lunatic asylum', Lenin wrote, or 'a charlatan or utter blockhead' could disagree with him. For Lenin, the German philosophers who inspired Bogdanov, Avenarius, Mach and their followers wrote 'gibberish' and 'sheer nonsense'. Bogdanov was 'a jester'.[50] Bogdanov's position in the party became untenable and he drifted to the sidelines but he continued to have influence as a guiding light in the Proletarian Cultural Educational Association set up by himself and his brother-in-law Lunacharsky in 1917. He also wrote pioneering science fiction novels depicting the socialist future as he envisaged it. He was also a more outspoken advocate of gender equality than most leading male Bolsheviks. He maintained his medical and scientific dimension and began pioneering efforts at blood transfusion, dying tragically in a failed experiment on himself which, according to some, was concealed suicide brought on by disillusion at the way the revolution was failing to realize his hopes and aspirations.

The Liberals also had a disrupter-in-chief in the form of Peter Struve. In his student days and early adulthood Struve was a Marxist. Not only that, he was one of the group of nine delegates and two or three observers who gathered in Minsk in 1898 to set up the Russian Social Democratic Labour Party. He helped draft the party programme and authored a phrase that resonated with Lenin stating that the further east you go in Europe, the weaker the bourgeoisie and therefore the greater the historical responsibility that falls to the proletariat. However, soon after that Struve set out on a path that took him further and further to the right. In 1902 a collection of essays was published entitled *From Marxism to Idealism* (*Ot markiszma do idealizmu*). Several other prominent independent Marxists took part. A main point of difference separating them from Marxism was a growing dislike of collectivism and a corresponding turn to individualism as the necessary guarantor of freedom and independence. The contributors were on different journeys. Struve's led him to patriotism by 1909. Berdyaev continued to consider himself a revolutionary of the spirit for the rest of his life, influencing emerging French philosophies, notably existentialism, from his post-1922 enforced Parisian exile. Bulgakov was ordained as a priest in the Orthodox church. To some extent they were part of the 'new religious consciousness' but in a more restrained and conventional fashion than the likes of the Dionysian mystical anarchists and the eros-oriented ideas of Gippius, Rozanov and Merezhkovsky. Struve, himself, was not even particularly religious beyond recognition of, and occasional church attendance at, Christmas and Easter.[51] Other leading liberals turned to philosophical idealism as a retreat from the, as they saw it, sombre and philistine colourlessness and lovelessness of the materialist interpretation of life. A new critique of the radical intelligentsia's basic assumptions – Darwinism, atheism, social revolution and materialism – was beginning to form within the intelligentsia itself. It had barely begun to appear by 1905 and, after the chaos of that moment, re-emerged stronger and more determined in the wake of those tumultuous events.

The central focus came in February 1909 when a slim volume of essays entitled *Landmarks* (*Vekhi*) was published in St Petersburg. Its seven distinguished contributors thought they were simply adding a modest contribution to the post-1905 analysis of, in the terms of the classic Russian question, 'Who is to blame?' The main shared value was expressed in the Preface. It was that the individual personality should be seen as the source of all creativity and every individual should be recognized as having absolute value.

> Their common platform is the recognition of the theoretical and practical primacy of the spiritual life over the external forms of community. They mean by this that

> the inner life of the personality (individual) is the sole creative force of human existence, and that this inner life, and not the self-sufficient principles of the political sphere, is the only solid basis on which a society can be built. From this point of view the contributors see the Russian intelligentsia's ideology, which rests entirely on the opposite principle – recognition of the unconditional primacy of social forms – as inherently erroneous in that it contradicts the nature of the human spirit, and in practice futile because it does not lead to the goal which the intelligentsia has set for itself – the liberation of the people.[52]

The statement reflected an idea common to most members of the liberal KD party with which most of the contributors sympathized, and also touched a fundamental Judaeo-Christian premise arising from the religious orientation of many, but not all, contributors. The authors were surprised when it proved quite a sensation. It went through five editions (though most were rather small at 5,000 copies) in a year and was responded to by all levels of the educated classes from right-wing priests to the radical left parties. The SRs and KDs put out essay collections of their own, refuting its fundamental premises even though the *Vekhi* authors considered themselves to be Constitutional Democrats. Lenin was enraged by it and gave a public meeting to oppose it among the émigré community in Paris where he was living at that time. He also wrote an article about it. Almost all of the intelligentsia assessments of *Vekhi* were strongly hostile. Embarrassingly for the authors, it was the far right which was most sympathetic. The most prominent example was the non-violent anti-Semitic Ukrainian priest Antonii Khrapovitsky, a founder member of his local chapter of the proto-fascist Union of Russian People in Zhytomyr in 1902 and member of the State Council from 1906, who welcomed it as a sign that, at last, the intelligentsia was coming to its senses. What had provoked such an outcry?

Three factors stand out. *Vekhi* contained an incendiary statement, a particularly incendiary article and it appeared at a moment of deep depression for the revolutionary intelligentsia as it came to terms with the scale of its defeat in 1905. The phrase was written by the inspirer and editor of the collection the brilliant historian Mikhail Gershenzon (1869–1925) who asserted that it was only 'the bayonets and prisons of the autocracy which protected the intelligentsia from the people's wrath'.[53] There was some truth in what he said. For many peasants and workers the educated intelligentsia was part of the élite, a branch of the oppressing apparatus. However, it was a missile fired at the heart of the intelligentsia's self-perception. Revolutionary intellectuals were sacrificing their lives and careers to the cause of liberating the masses. Gershenzon was attacking the fundamental foundation on which most of the intelligentsia, in all its diversity, had constructed itself – the notion of service of the people, the *narod*. No member of the intelligentsia had ever uttered such a blasphemy. It sounded like the utterance of spokesman of the autocracy and some critics compared it to Pobedonostsev's views. Even some of the other contributors to *Vekhi* considered it too provocative. Gershenzon added an explanatory note to the second edition but, even so, it was removed from later editions.

The incendiary article was written by Peter Struve who had become a prominent publicist and leading figure in the intelligentsia at this time, a kind of public intellectual who embodied a set of values which were anathema to most of the intelligentsia. His article in *Vekhi* entitled 'Intelligentsia and Revolution' encouraged the intelligentsia to abandon its revolutionary dreams and address what he saw as the gulf separating it from mainstream society. If the intelligentsia wanted to help Russia, the way forward was to overcome the practical sloppiness he and other contributors saw as typical of the intellectuals and instead take up practical work in which they would excel. They could do more for the country by being good at their jobs rather than wasting time and energy on political agitation. Struve also wrote a very controversial article published in 1909 in which he went even further. It called on the intelligentsia to join in Russia's mission to restore Christianity in Constantinople/Istanbul (known as the city of the tsar – Tsargrad – in Russian).[54] The intelligentsia was outraged. Struve was telling them to become hard-working servants of tsarist imperialism and agents of the worst kind of pompous patriotism.

The intelligentsia was in no mood for such an inflammatory attack on its amour-propre. The main feature of the flood of responses was that, apart from the occasional, usually right-wing and even reactionary voice supporting them noted above, the overwhelming majority were hostile. The debate was very illustrative of the intelligentsia at the time. It covered issues such as who could claim to be a member of the intelligentsia. Several *Vekhi* authors and their critics agreed that the intelligentsia was a special group defined by its self-sacrifice and devotion to the cause. It was a 'monastic order', according to one author (Bulgakov), a chivalric guild according to another (Frank). Contributors on both sides agreed that to be a member of the intelligentsia was an earned privilege not a right to which all highly educated and cultured Russians could lay claim. However, there were others, like Izgoev who included the whole student body in his critique, showing the traditional qualitative definition was cracking as the educated élite expanded rapidly. Other criticisms levelled by the *Vekhi* authors included the charge that the intelligentsia not only did not respect existing law, it did not even respect the importance of law and the rule of law as the basis of a civilized, democratic and just society. Some of these criticisms were unjustified. The attack on the student youth particularly so. As we have already noted, many students lived in harsh conditions of poverty to realize their dreams of education and were prone to disillusionment, depression and suicide.[55] Other claims were also unfair but many had struck home. Not that the rest of the intelligentsia was prepared to concede an inch. Hardly anyone stood in a mediatory position. Remarkably, the torrent of materials in the essay collections produced by the main political groups, reviews in thick journals, speeches at public meetings from Penza to Paris, articles in newspapers all defended the revolutionary tradition and dug a deep trench between the intelligentsia and the autocracy. No accommodation between the two was possible for liberals, populists, social democrats socialists of all kinds and anarchists and even of many non-political artists and writers. It would be to misread *Vekhi* as a whole to say it wanted compromise with the autocracy. Struve was alone in being that explicit, but it was clear there was no appetite for any such accommodation with tsarism despite, or possibly because of, the great setback of 1905. It is a powerful reminder not to map political assumptions from one culture directly on to those of another. Liberal leaders in

Russia, like Paul Miliukov (1859–1943), admired western liberals, adopted western liberal ideas, dressed like western liberals and so on but that did not make them identical. Liberalism in western Europe had become, by and large, conservative and reformist, whereas, given the situation in Russia, it was still revolutionary. All significant Russian political parties from Kadets to Bolsheviks had the replacement of the autocratic state by a constitutional and democratic one as the first demand in their party programmes.[56]

Embourgeoisement?

From his vantage point in Paris, Lenin, in his response to *Vekhi*, identified it as a sign of the embourgeoisement of the intelligentsia. Like its French and German predecessors, Russian liberalism was sliding out of its formative revolutionary chrysalis and beginning to spread its wings as a middle-class butterfly. It was, for Lenin, a sign that the liberals were on the march from the revolutionary camp into that of compromise with the autocracy. The loud denials from liberal spokespeople were dismissed as either deception or self-delusion. The liberals were beginning to put their own class interests to the fore. Lenin, like other members of the intelligentsia, claimed to be hostile to the class to which he so clearly belonged, but he would not accept anything good about the intelligentsia. Even Tolstoy, for all his stylistic brilliance, was, for Lenin, the voice of a declining, quasi-feudal landowning class, 'the landlord obsessed with Christ'.[57] Lenin refused to accept a special role for intellectuals in the party. Workers, he claimed, were all that mattered. Intelligentsia influences were, in his eyes, an obstacle not an asset. So his scorn over the *Vekhi* debate is fully in line with his long-term views. However, did he have a point? Was the intelligentsia absorbing itself piece by piece in the society and, especially, governmental system, from which it claimed to be alienated by definition?

On the eve of the First World War the social and cultural foundations of the intelligentsia were very different from the time a hundred years earlier when Napoleon had been defeated. The knowledge base had expanded exponentially as the economy diversified into a variety of large industries which needed technical, managerial and financial skills on an unprecedented scale. Healthcare became a greater priority, not least in crudely constructed city sectors to house the influx of mainly unskilled workers from the countryside. Poor urban conditions spread diseases of typhus and cholera which refused to confine themselves to the impoverished suburbs and threatened all city inhabitants. More and more doctors, nurses and paramedics (feld'shers) were being trained. Russia needed more and more qualified people for an expanding, modern, urbanized sector. As we have seen the institutions supporting this – schools, colleges, universities – were becoming mass institutions, themselves demanding reserves of highly skilled teachers. Demand for lawyers expanded as capitalist market contracts became the basis of trade. Censorship had burst at the seams in 1905 and the cultural explosion, of 'high' and 'popular' culture, proceeded apace. The proliferation of literary and artistic genres, of journals, of newspapers of publishing houses embodied an unprecedented diversity from the elegance and innovation of Karsavina, Nijinskii and the *Ballets Russes* founded in 1908, to the gutter press of cheap, sensationalist titillation based on racism, imperialism, sexism, smut, horror – real, imagined or exaggerated – and the evocation of dread.

Stalwart institutions of the scientific intelligentsia, notably the Academy of Sciences, were flourishing as never before. The new economic demands and industrial growth provided new stimuli to research and created more funding opportunities. In addition to the world-famous scientists like Mendeleev and Pavlov there was a great expansion of brilliant but less well-known figures. Its expertise in linguistics, ethnography, exploration and so on continued unabated. The Academy had expanded to forty-five full members and twenty-two associates in 1918. In broader fields Russian scientists, technologists and engineers made innovations, some of them world firsts, in parachute technology (the first backpack parachutes), the 'Go Anywhere' (*Vzezdekhod*) tracked vehicle, the first four-engined aircraft and other aviation advances by Igor Sikorskii (who left Russia in 1919 and became a household name in the United States for his fixed wing and helicopter inventions), gas masks, the concept of television (and invention of the word in 1900 by Konstantin Persky at the 1900 World's Fair in Paris), the first diesel-powered ship (a tanker in 1903), ice-breaking ships (though the first ice-breakers were built in Britain to Russian designs) and chromatography (Mikhail Tsvet 1900). There was a proliferation of technology clubs like the Russian Technical Society and the Electrotechnical Society to which Persky belonged. As this very selective list shows, industrial and military innovations were dominant.[58]

In many respects science and technology seem outside the scope of the intelligentsia but many scientists were drawn to their subjects not just by an abstract desire to extend the 'frontiers of knowledge' but also to be of service to humanity. In the words of the doyen of western historians of Russian and Soviet science, Loren Graham,

> scientists and government officials in Russia have always considered science to be closer to politics than have their counterparts in the United States. The tsarist government feared that Russian scientists who studied in Western Europe would bring home not only scientific knowledge but also Western political theories in conflict with those of the supporters of the Romanov autocracy. For their part, Russian scientists usually considered themselves part of the intelligentsia, with all the oppositional implications that this term conveys. Like the government censors, Russian scientists often made no clear distinction between science and politics. By the late nineteenth century many Russian scientists believed that rational scientific knowledge automatically led to criticism of state politics and the state-supported form of the Russian Orthodox faith. Out of this inter-mixing of science and politics arose many clashes, such as the refusal of tsarist censors to publish Ivan Sechenov's work on physiological reflexes on the grounds that it supported atheism.[59]

Handily for the tsarist authorities they had, from 1889, a member of the royal family able to supervise the activities of the Academy of Sciences in the form of Grand Prince Konstantin Konstanovich Romanov who was a noted poet. In the words of the official history of the academy 'he led the Academy unscathed through the tricky conditions of the early twentieth century'.[60] His role was, no doubt, re-assuring to a dynasty, suspicious of all innovation and especially of those linking to the west.

Similarly, artistic leadership remained under the influence of imperial control of, notably, the Imperial (i.e. State) Theatres whose repertoire was closely watched by the authorities.[61] Reassurance was provided elsewhere, the Sarov pilgrimage, the apparent victory over the revolution and also in one of the most interesting intelligentsia-technical phenomena of the time, the colour photography of the pioneer in the field S. Prokhudin-Gorsky. He was commissioned by the autocracy to make a photographic record of the Empire. He took wonderful, lyrical photographs of diverse landscapes, of individuals, couples, families and groups in elaborate traditional ethnic costumes. There were sanitized pictures of small factories and workshops and peasants in the fields and in their villages. There was no trace of real poverty, oppression, squalor or conflict in any of them. They were an essay in a tranquil, traditional, harmonious Russian family with its foster children and vast network of cousins.

Art also contributed to the slightly less re-assuring commemoration of the tercentenary of the Romanov dynasty in 1913 where numerous events were put on. A major theme was the close link between tsar and people and the events were infused with the classic Slavophile values of Russia as a united family clustering round the tsar, the image produced by Prokhudin-Gorsky and others. The tsars advisers, nonetheless, dissuaded him from extensive travel but he did venture to Kostroma, the home town of Ivan Susanin, the legendary peasant who had given his *Life for the Tsar* as the title of Glinka's opera put it. The legend, accompanied by multiple performances of the opera and other promotional efforts, made the legend a key element in the commemoration with the obvious aim of re-inforcing the mutual love of tsar and people. But while it was possible to generate synthetic popular enthusiasm by providing occasional free food and other tokenistic giveaways, reaction in general seems to have remained indifferent. It was, however, enough to fan the flame of Nicholas's self-delusion that the affection was real. He said 'My people love me'[62] and was even bullish enough to suggest the moment had come to dismantle even more of the hated concessions made in 1905 and return to his vision of undiluted autocratic rule.

This reaction, in a sense, pointed to the weakness of the view that tsarism was liberalizing and that a fusion of autocracy and bourgeois market capitalism was evolving. If anything it showed the opposite. The celebrations brought friction between Nicholas and even the tame, right-leaning Duma. A symbol of this was provided by one of several large, set-piece pieces of pageantry marking the anniversary. Many meetings for domestic and foreign dignitaries had shown off Russia's power and newly acquired wealth as industry progressed, passing on a message of Russian power. One of the meetings was focused on bringing together leaders from within the empire in a vast gathering in the Cathedral of Our Lady of Kazan on Nevsky Prospekt, the main thoroughfare of the capital. In the seating arrangements the elected Duma members were allocated seats behind the tsarist-appointed officials of the Senate and State Council. The Chair of the Duma, Mikhail Rodzianko, was furious. Rodzianko was no radical. Quite the reverse, he was a guards officer with deeply conservative opinions, not those of his Decembrist and radical predecessors. His vehement protests worked and the Duma members were seated at the front. Rodzianko's insistence was timely because, flushed with enthusiasm for the supposed renewed relationship with the masses, Nicholas's bubbling over-confidence, stoked by warm encouragement from Tsarina Alexandra, made him feel the time was ripe to retract the biggest 1905 concession of all and disband the Duma and replace it with a consultative assembly based on the Zemsky Sobor (National Gathering) which had last met in the seventeenth century. Such was the tsar's vision in the early twentieth century.

In many ways, parts of the intelligentsia were developing bourgeois characteristics of property accumulation, advancement of professions, financial power and so on but this did not mean, as 'optimists' had once argued and have begun to argue again in contemporary Russia, that a new harmony was building between autocracy and intelligentsia as promoted by Peter Struve. Rather they indicated that, as the bourgeois elements of Russia grew, they would be drawn into ever-increasing clashes with the regime over their right to self-expression, economic independence and political participation. Russia in 1913 was not facing a choice between peaceful transition to constitutional monarchy and liberal capitalism on one hand and radical revolution on the other. There was a three-way choice – radical revolution, bourgeois revolution or a proto-fascist, orthodox Christian, anti-Semitic military-based tsarism as hoped for by Nicholas. The outbreak of war initially postponed further evolution of these tendencies in a welter of patriotism but very quickly, by summer of 1915, the conflict between them reignited. A fuse was lit which led to an explosion that even overshadowed the effects of world war.

Part Three

The intelligentsia transformed: cultural revolution

6

The intelligentsia in the soviet revolution

The revolutionary cataclysm

The revolutionary explosion blew away the autocracy, the bourgeoisie and the traditional intelligentsia. Astoundingly, as the smoke began to settle in 1921 it was representatives of one of the most marginal factions of the radical intelligentsia who sat on top of the ruins. This is an extraordinary story in itself.[1]

The narrative we are following, the transformation of the intelligentsia, is equally surprising, dramatic, in many ways tragic and always absorbing. As ever, its evolution was shaped but not determined by the general swirl of events. There was no guarantee that an intelligentsia faction of any sort would emerge on top after the completely ruinous turmoil of world war, revolutionary social upheaval and cataclysmic civil war. But the Bolsheviks did. They (and the ensuing global communist movement) are often conceptualized as forces having a kind of superagency over history, the ability to manipulate it and finesse it into the shape they wanted, a feature often termed 'Machiavellian'. The converse, that Bolshevism itself was a product of history, is less widely considered and even denied by those who consider it to be a kind of alien force projected into a situation in which it had no roots. This is prominent among a certain nationalist tendency in Russia today who consider it to be 'German' and even 'Jewish' in origin. In the cold war west Bolshevism (and local communisms) were thought of as a 'Machiavellian' super conspiracy controlled from a central point, initially labelled 'Stalin'. Even today there is a tendency to oversimplify Russian-connected events and attribute them to a mysteriously all-powerful 'Putin'. Simple answers to complex problems. However, communist movements, like any other social phenomenon, were as much products of history as its agents. Bolshevism, as we have seen, evolved in very distinctively Russian conditions.

This is not the place to fully analyse how they managed to come to power but we do need to sketch the outcome of the three-way struggle. The liberals in the Duma started the ball rolling. In August 1915, worried by military defeats and increasing social unrest, they formed the Progressive Bloc which called for serious representation of the Duma in government and for the introduction of certain basic civil rights. Their approach was summarily dismissed by the tsar who, instead, took on the role of Commander-in-Chief of the army, effectively turning Tsarist Russia into what he had dreamed of, a military dictatorship for what turned out to be its last seventeenth months of existence. In this brief but decisive period the civilian government and the suspended Duma lost even the meagre powers they had enjoyed. The new authorities shored up the failing military effort quite successfully, so much so that they were able to mount a briefly victorious offensive in 1916. However, as the civilian ministers had feared in the August 1915 crisis, the generals were not at all sensitive to the social havoc their policies inflicted on their own home front. Military expenditure, paid for by recklessly printing money, caused a tide of inflation which seriously unsettled all levels of urban society for the next half decade. It burned away the savings of the middle class and took prices out of reach of the working class. In late winter of 1916–17 social unrest was increasing as food stocks fell in the northern cities, especially Petrograd (the wartime name of St Petersburg – changed to make it sound less German and more Russian). The elites worried that social collapse would destroy the war effort, open the country to German invasion and take their privileged status down in the ensuing chaos. Almost the whole of the political class supported pressurizing the autocracy in a crisis which had been rumbling since late January in Petrograd and began to turn critical on 27th of February. They demanded Duma involvement in government and the removal of the tsar, who abdicated on 2 March 1917.

No one had thought through what would happen next. Many of the army generals, who were decisive in forcing the abdication, thought they were simply replacing the incompetent Nicholas with his more efficient brother Mikhail, since the direct heir to the throne, Tsarevich Alexis, was too young and too ill with haemophilia to take over. But Mikhail refused and the rebellion fell into confusion. A deal had already been struck between Duma members representing the élite and Soviet leaders representing the working people. A Provisional Government of Duma delegates was accepted but the Duma itself disbanded, at first informally and later formally, leaving the new, liberal, authorities suspended in a vacuum of dubious legitimacy. Their ambition to continue the war for imperialist goals clashed with popular opinion and that of the soldiers themselves who, through their army committees, made it clear that they would only fight for defence of country, not imperial aggrandisement such as the acquisition of Constaninople/Istanbul/Tsargrad. The government also disappointed in its second major task, calling a Constituent Assembly to devise a new form of government. The liberal-oriented government were slow to set one up because they knew they could not win a democratic election since their largely middle class and professional supporters were so few in the face of the 90 per cent of the population who were peasants and workers. Their reforms and lack of energy in stopping a growing revolution of peasants and workers alarmed the army leaders and the traditional right. Running out of patience in late August, the Commander-in-Chief, the hard-line General Kornilov (1870–1918), attempted a coup which turned out to be ill-organized and quickly rendered harmless.

However, it was a game-changer. It thrust the Petrograd Soviet into the forefront. The left throughout the country, which comprised some 75 per cent or more of the population, registered its disgust with not only the right's attempts to restore the traditional authority of landowners and factory owners, but also with the Provisional Government itself which was widely believed to have been complicit in Kornilov's plot. The prime minister of the moment, Alexander Kerensky (1881–1970), had released arms to the Petrograd Soviet but had not gained its trust. In October, nationwide elections of delegates to an All-Russian Congress of Soviets resulted in the overwhelming majority of delegates being voted in on a programme of supporting the replacement of the lame-duck Provisional Government with Soviet power and the rapid convocation of a Constituent Assembly. The Congress gathered in Petrograd on 24/25 October and, following skirmishes in the streets of the city which had started on 18 October, the Soviet controlled the city, arrested the ministers and, via the Congress, declared Soviet power.

Up to this point the Bolsheviks had had little influence. They had even been partially dispersed and driven underground by the Provisional Government in July. But they enjoyed a meteoric rise from around the time of Kornilov. It had two foundations. The first was the entanglement of the other main socialist groups – the SRs and the Menshevik right – in supporting Kerensky, who was himself a socialist. They shared his desire to prevent a civil war in Russia, whose only beneficiaries would have been Germany and its allies. Doctrinally, some of them believed a socialist revolution in Russia at that time would be premature and either fail or be grossly deformed. By remaining in the centre they lost contact with increasing swathes of their worker, peasant and soldier supporters who moved en masse to support all power to the soviets. Only one party wholeheartedly backed the mass movement at this point – the Bolsheviks, who rapidly hoovered up the support of dissatisfied Mensheviks and SRs. Lenin, energetically supported by Trotsky who had only joined the Bolsheviks in July, argued powerfully for an armed uprising, even against the opposition of his leading assistants Kamenev and Zinoviev. Overcoming dissent in the leadership Lenin pursued his plan, though the party actually did little to implement it. But when the October Revolution broke out only the Bolsheviks were prepared to support it even though it meant abandoning long-held policies, for example over land which they wanted to nationalize (put in state hands), and supporting the peasants' desire to take it over themselves instead. Consequently, they were in a strong position when the moment came to declare soviet power and name a government. Most of the leaders of the Menshevik and SR right in the Congress committed political suicide by walking out. This left power in the hands of the Bolsheviks so that the Congress voted a government initially including only Bolsheviks though a few SRs from the left of the party soon joined them. In effect, the Bolsheviks had engineered a coup within the Congress to take advantage of a drive for soviet power which they had supported but not exerted much influence on. Lenin and Trotsky, together with the rehabilitated Kamenev and Zinoviev and other party leaders like Stalin, had been catapulted from marginality to government in the space of about two months. They had become the government of the largest country by land area on the planet. An extraordinary outcome by any standard.

However, what did being in power mean? What did they govern over? One commentator had brilliantly argued that the Bolsheviks had not seized power, they had found it lying in the street and picked it up. In truth, by October, state power had eroded to next to nothing. Even the army was teetering out of the control of the officers and generals, most of whom were, not unreasonably, considered to be Kornilovites by their men. The remnants disintegrated even faster after October. That raises the key question, how did the Bolsheviks hold on to what power there was against their multitude of enemies and how did they build it up?

Again, the foundations of their success can be summarized. First, the country polarized as the counter-revolutionary forces, mainly the army generals, landowners and imperialists, were augmented by increasing numbers of liberals and even some socialists including the venerable figure of George Plekhanov himself. A stark choice was emerging. Either support the Whites, as the right became known, and restoration of land and factory owners, or the Reds, the left, and support the revolutionary settlement, especially the redistribution of all estates to the peasantry. The Bolsheviks' critics on the left had little option but to support them under these circumstances. The Red forces, though the majority called themselves Bolshevik, were a coalition with a variety of outlooks who were unaware of the deeper dimensions of the Bolshevik project. They supported the programme promoted by the masses from the beginning – Peace, Bread, Land and All Power to the Soviets. It was Lenin's brilliant insight to see that, from early in 1917, no other position was possible for a socialist, although he blew hot and cold on whether the radical revolution was around the corner or had been delayed indefinitely. The horrendously destructive civil war, which cost some 10 million lives, mostly from ensuing diseases rather than fighting, probably saved the Bolsheviks. Their power crumbled in spring 1918, when the civil war abated for a few months before picking up, with renewed energy, in the summer. This was because the White threat re-ignited and, despite significant opposition to the Bolsheviks for their dictatorial mentality and heavy-handed conduct of the war and the economy, it was impossible for their left-wing critics to oppose them without the severe risk of handing the country back to the old ruling class in the form of the Whites.

As Kerensky and the centre had predicted, civil war seemed to serve German and Austrian interests and they were beneficiaries of a disastrous peace treaty from Russia's point of view, signed at Brest-Litovsk in March 1918 at Lenin's insistence and over Trotsky's reluctance this time. The Central Powers occupied vast grain-producing lands, mostly in Ukraine. Although, as the Central Powers collapsed by the end of the year, the provisions of the treaty did not last long, but they did have the fateful consequence of separating Ky'iv and Ukraine from Great Russia, essentially for the first time in their history. The civil war raged for two more years, the decisive defeat of the Whites coming in 1919, but 1920 saw pockets of resistance remaining, plus an opportunistic advance by Poland against Russia and Ukraine to take advantage of their weakness. The Polish initiative failed, as did the Soviet counter-offensive, leaving the situation much as it was before the war began. The years 1920 and 1921, significantly, also saw the last flare-ups of the popular movement which opposed Bolshevism from the left, demanding more real power for the soviets, rather than the growing central government and party apparatus, and a better deal for peasants, against whom a limited war of forced expropriation of their grain, needed to feed the cities and the army, had been fought since 1918. Serious uprisings in Tambov, West Siberia and the 1917 stronghold of Bolshevism, the Kronstadt naval base near Petrograd, were brutally suppressed. Lenin, not for the first time, was bitterly opposed to compromise with opponents. Nonetheless, by the time of the Tenth Party Congress and the suppression of the Kronstadt rebellion in March 1921, the Bolsheviks were in unopposed control of a Russia, which had lost Finland,

Poland and the Baltic States to independence, but otherwise had reconstituted much of the imperial Russian space including the Caucasus, Caspian, Central Asian, Siberian and, crucially, Ukrainian regions.

The process had been unimaginably destructive. A reduction or reversal of economic growth is often referred to hyperbolically as a collapse. In Russia's case the economy had really collapsed. In addition to the 10 million dead, on top of the 3.3 million military and civilians lost in the World War, industrial production fell to around one-fifth of its prewar level. Russia had, for the time being, de-industrialized. Transport problems, epidemics of influenza, typhus and cholera and loss of the vast Ukrainian bread-basket to the Central Powers and then to the right-wing nationalists favoured by the occupiers, created a demographic catastrophe.[2] Urban populations, many fed meagre rations collected by arbitrary force by expropriation squads sent out to the villages, reduced spectacularly in number. The population of Moscow, which was restored as the national capital in February 1918 as it was more defendable than the exposed Petrograd which lay on a vulnerable border, lost nearly half of its 1.8 million population. Further north, and therefore further away from the wheat growing areas, Petrograd was hit hardest since it and its hinterland could not feed themselves without supplies from overseas or from surplus producing parts of Russia. By August 1920, Petrograd had lost two-thirds of its peak population of 2.5 million. Both were cut off by enemy blockade, occupation and disruption of the rail network. The lucky ones were able to escape the city despite roadblocks intended to keep the industrial workforce in and prevent all illegal trade, including unauthorized food smuggling. How did Russia survive such a cataclysm? As much as anything it was the resilience and self-sufficiency of the peasant economy which pulled the country through. Many of those fleeing the cities went back to their home village and re-absorbed into their family. Traditional methods had not completely given way to market specialization so peasants retained many of their skills in arable farming, animal husbandry and market-gardening and were able to look after themselves much better than the cities. They had the basic skills and materials needed to keep going despite the depredations of the food requisitioning squads. Conditions were tough and shortages widespread. In 1921–2 the social disruption was added to by climatic difficulties – drought – which undermined the crops in the Volga region and brought about 2 million deaths and launched hundreds of thousands of refugees on a search for food to survive. Epidemics and hunger in the period, according to Blum, caused about 7 to 8 million deaths.[3]

Effectively, although the Bolsheviks ruled, they were sitting on a pile of ruins.

The immediate impact of the revolution on the intelligentsia

The intelligentsia was one of the groups which suffered most from the civil war, especially the cultural intelligentsia. They were more vulnerable to the conditions than other classes in that they did not have any significant reserves of wealth and property to use in the barter economy of the most desperate moments, nor did many of them have rural contacts enabling them to flee to safer areas. Nor did they have factory jobs which the Bolsheviks tried to preserve. Sources of income – commissions, patronage, publishers, museums, galleries and so on – were drying up and the great inflation continued to burn up resources. A system of government food rations emerged in 1918–20 which, of course, reflected government priorities. Skilled manual labourers got high rations, unemployed intellectuals, little or nothing. Scientists and engineers fared a little better as they were seen as necessary by the government. Universities and research institutes continued as best they could. A minority of university scientists began to be drawn into the task of contributing to plans for the reconstruction of the devastated country. However, the flower of the intelligentsia was suffering very badly in these years. The novelist Maxim Gorky, who had the ear of Lenin despite having produced penetrating criticism of Bolshevik policies in 1917, and the playwright and critic-turned Minister for Enlightenment (Education) Anatoly Lunacharsky were very worried by this threat. They looked for ways to protect intellectuals whose loss, they argued, would impoverish Russian society. Gorky persuaded Lenin to agree to the setting up of an extremely ambitious plan to translate the classics of world literature and thought into Russian. It would provide a fragile lifeline to intellectuals contracted to edit and translate. Gorky also pleaded for rations to be given to literally starving writers and artists. The publishing commissions handed out, and the rations for fortunate individuals were not yet completely limited to left-wing intellectuals. This was largely because Gorky and Lunacharsky were heavily influenced by Nietzsche for whom the 'superior' achievers of society were its key personnel who embodied a society's cultural health and creativity which needed a degree of diversity to flourish. For those not favoured by getting official support, the outlook was especially bleak. The material conditions under which the intelligentsia lived are unimaginable. Hunger, cold and disease were their constant companions. In the years from 1917 to 1922 there was a unique mixture of material shortages, cultural depression, the excitement of a new Russia being born and the emergence of a deeply controlling government that gave the period a distinctive imprint. How did the intelligentsia find a way through these extraordinary conditions, the worst it had ever encountered?

Different sections of the intelligentsia underwent a great variety of experiences ranging from those who began to flourish in the new circumstances to those who were arrested, exiled and even executed. We can approach this diversity by looking at each of what were the main divisions in the intelligentsia at this time in the sense that some *intelligenty* actively supported the revolution surrounding them, others actively fought against it and the majority more or less neutrally accepted the revolution as a fait accompli and tried to survive as best they could.

i.) Supporters of October

Lenin and his associates had big plans, not just for Russia but for the whole of humanity. They followed Marx' notion that the proletarian revolution would be the beginning of human history in that, for the first time, every person would be a liberated and equal member of the community. History would be made by everyone, not an exploitative class which arrogated power and cultural control to itself and suppressed the natural creativity of the vast majority. They were not, however, so naïve as to think that this could be done without an epoch of transition of unpredictable length. They also knew that there was no blueprint for transition. They were in uncharted waters and had no agreed plan for the voyage into the unknown. There were plenty of plans and in the formative years a succession of battles were fought between groups within the movement who had different ideas on which of those plans should be implemented. But Lenin was not only undeterred by the immensity of the task and the lack of an agreed plan, the Bolsheviks also embarked on their voyage in a destroyed, disorganized, sick and starving country facing the hostility of the most powerful nations on the planet. Given the odds, it is not surprising that when the Soviet government equalled the 1871 Paris Commune's period in power – seventy-three days – Lenin danced a jig of delight in the snow in the courtyard outside his office in Petrograd. Every day more was a victory for the fragile revolutionary state in those early years.

Unlikely though it will seem to some, Bolshevism, for all its gritty, even bloody, realism in power, was built on dreams. Lenin referred to dreams on a number of occasions, such as near the end of his breakout pamphlet *What Is to Be Done?* in 1902. Lenin stated 'We must dream' about the revolutionary scenario which will unfold in the future. A number of scholars have written fine books about Bolshevik dreams, which was the title of one of the pioneering volumes.[4] From its first moments of existence the Bolshevik authorities developed their dreams and did their utmost to persuade the population to share them. The dreams were not confined to exhortatory pamphlets and uplifting stories, they were embodied in some of the most hard-nosed and, frankly, tedious documents of the period such as the 1918 Constitution of the Russian republic and in the 1919 Party Programme and associated explanatory quasi-catechism the *ABC of Communism*. The Constitution would make an excellent model for anyone inclined to develop the principles of liberal democracy beyond civil and voting rights. Its framers identified various weaknesses in traditional liberal democracy. First of all those elected to soviets were delegates; that is, they were expected to carry out the wishes of their electors, rather than, as in most parliamentary systems, representatives who make decisions on behalf of their electors. This was backed up by provisions for recall of delegates and by-elections to replace them or allow them to win over the majority again. Some liberal democracies had provision for recall but it was a rare occurrence. However, the most radical innovation was to not only recognize rights but to allow them to be enjoyed. What did this mean? Rights were not only guaranteed but the means to exercise them was provided by the state. For example, the bourgeois right to press freedom was no use to groups excluded from access to newspapers and so on by capitalist owners who controlled what was in their papers. Under the Soviet Constitution groups were given free access to state presses and, crucially in the shortages of the early Soviet years, to an allocation of printing paper. More complex rights, notably the equality of women, were approached in a similar manner. Bourgeois rights had not extended to women in most parliamentary democracies prior to 1914. The Soviet Constitution not only proclaimed the equality of women but it identified childcare and household responsibilities as obstacles to achieving it. So free state childcare, laundries and canteens were to break the tyranny of the triple burden (childcare, housework and paid labour) holding women back. Along with radical provisions in the 1919 Party Programme, the new authorities were mapping out the parameters of the world's first welfare state. Education was to be universal and free at all levels. Medical care was also provided. State rations (*paek*) were a primitive form of social security and so on. Ultimately, according to the *ABC of Communism*, producers would deposit what they had made in a state warehouse and the population would withdraw from it whatever they needed. 'Products are not exchanged one for another; they are neither bought nor sold. They are simply stored in the communal warehouses, and are subsequently delivered to those who need them. In such conditions, money will no longer be required.'[5]

The Party Programme went far beyond even these provisions promising a socialist-inspired free exchange of products. Overcoming the class system for the first time in history would eliminate crime since everyone would have the same access to goods and money would be a thing of the past.

The utopianism of Bolshevism shines through these idealistic proposals whose implementation was thwarted by numerous obstacles. First, the civil war did not allow any governmental functions to be conducted in a relaxed, unpertubed and calmly innovative manner. Reality imposed short-term emergency measures one after another. In April 1918, when he thought the civil war was over, Lenin turned to inequality and, in his own word, dictatorship, as the guiding principles of transition to socialism and economic reconstruction. Former managers were to be welcomed back and given salaries much larger than those of workers. Discipline was to replace democracy in economic institutions and society. 'We must learn to combine the "public meeting" democracy of the working people – turbulent, surging, overflowing its banks like a spring flood – with *iron* discipline while at work, with *unquestioning obedience* to the will of a single person, the Soviet leader, while at work.'[6] There were no resources available to fund such vast programmes and by making such a move Lenin was making productionism – maximizing economic output – the number one goal of the state and party. The Soviet Union essentially remained in this position for the rest of its life, trying to create the economic abundance which was the prerequisite of socialism. As such it tended to give ironic solace to defeated opponents, like the Economists and some Mensheviks, who had objected to the Bolshevik approach on the grounds that Russia was not ready for a socialist revolution. However, it was not much of a consolation to know that, looking out from obscurity, prison or exile, their analysis had been correct. Lenin and others had believed, as Marx himself had suggested, that a revolution in western Europe would enable a Russian revolution to survive but such a revolution did not materialize and Russian communism was left isolated. Instead of following the system outlined in theory, the situation led Bolshevism to become more and more authoritarian so that, instead of a theoretical new democracy, by 1921 Russia had become a one-party state, negating the essence of the constitution and party programme.

Another problem was that it was relatively easy to proclaim rights and democratic initiatives but in many cases it was not clear what they implied in practice. 'Socialist education' was easy to say, but what form would it take? All kinds of innovative schemes clashed with one another. Some party leaders wanted to link education and production very closely and to build the curriculum from the basis of labour as the foundation of human society and individuality. It would not only embrace practical and vocational elements of education but also provide a grounding for theoretical sciences, socially analytical subjects and the creative arts and literature. The party leaders decided against such a radical restructuring of education in 1918[7] but, in any case, there were no resources to implement it. Teachers had been trained in the imperial past, and textbooks had been written before the revolution and before the war. There was no way a whole new teaching profession and teaching materials could be created in the conditions of the time. The curriculum was not much different from that of tsarist times though religious studies and practices were excluded and study of Marxist ideology brought in, though many of the teachers of it were neither Marxists nor party members and the materials used were whatever was available. Until well into the 1920s, teaching resources included items by those such as the German Socialist Party leader Karl Kautsky, who was branded as a 'renegade' in a pamphlet by Lenin in 1919 after Kautsky denounced the Leninist approach to revolution, but whose work *The Economic Doctrines of Karl Marx* was the standard textbook in early Soviet Russia.

It was not just Bolsheviks who were drawn into the battle for the future. Clearly there was a world being created here and it is not surprising that many members of the intelligentsia wanted to take part in the process. After all, their history since 1860 had been the search for a force to implement their ideas. Now the state itself was committed to building a fundamentally new type of society. This was an intoxicating prospect. *Intelligenty* of many persuasions felt they had a part to play in the process and did so.

The best known and most spectacular involvement came in the visual arts. The twin demands of propaganda and defining a new way of life were irresistible to a large number of artists who had revolutionary, though rarely Bolshevik, sympathies. There was also the practical dimension. Traditional sources of income had contracted severely and even disappeared. The art market, galleries, journals, publishers and private patrons had either ceased to function or commanded such tiny resources that they could no longer offer support. The state had become the only significant patron and it was willing to pay for propaganda posters and other artistic output. Schools and other organizations with educational responsibilities like the Proletarian Cultural-Educational Association (known as Proletkul't for short) and trade unions had some employment opportunities for adult art classes and cultural lectures, music classes, guidance in creative writing plus some commissions for publicity material and the like which helped keep the wolf from the intelligentsia door in the ferocious conditions of famine and disease. The result was an outburst of brilliantly innovative art. Vladimir Mayakovsky (1893–1930) contributed powerful poetry as well as a series of propaganda images in the form and style of folk tales known as *lubki*, a kind of primitive carved and drawn folk comic derived in part from the story images of saints' lives around the borders of traditional icons. In a radically different approach Lazar (El) Lissitzky (1890–1941) produced abstract images of blocs, lines of varying lengths and interpenetrating geometric shapes with a few words, such as his most famous poster 'Beat the Whites with the Red Wedge' of 1919. Artistically Lissitzky had been close to Marc Chagall (1887–1985) and followed him to Vitebsk when Chagall was appointed as Commissar for Art in the region. Chagall decorated the streets of the city for the anniversary of October with items in his own whimsical surrealist but never fully abstract style. Shortly after, another great artist of the time, Kasimir Malevich (1879–1935), came to Vitebsk to bully Chagall into following his Suprematist style.

Chagall remained true to his own instincts and eventually left Vitebsk and lived most of the rest of his life in the south of France. Lissitzky was drawn into Malevich's school and the famous poster was fully within the Suprematist canon of geometric abstraction. While these works have been lauded ever since for their brilliance and originality, they failed to meet the basic criterion for propaganda – a simple message expressed unambiguously. In his memoirs Chagall mentioned that his approach to commemorating the October Revolution in Vitebsk was met with mixed reactions:

> My multicolored animals swung all over the town, swollen with revolution. The workers marched up singing the Internationale. When I saw them smile, I knew they understood me. The leaders, the Communists, seemed less gratified. Why is the cow green and why is the horse flying through the sky, why? What's the connection with Marx and Lenin?[8]

The problem was even greater with Malevich and El Lissitzky. Lenin himself was impatient with avant garde art. Other artists produced much more easily comprehensible posters. Dmitrii Moor (1883–1946) was in the forefront. He produced simple memorable images. One of the most famous was a recruiting poster for the Red Army based on the famous British Kitchener 'Your Country Needs You' poster of 1914.[9] Another shows a stark image of a starving peasant, arms outstretched, desperately asking for help.

The early propaganda industry took innovative forms. Railway carriages and river steamers were adapted as mobile propaganda centres taking the party message to the provinces. New techniques such as photography and documentary film were used extensively. The propaganda trains and ships usually had facilities for showing newsreels and other film material. All these endeavours provided employment – survival – for artists, lecturers, technicians and so on who took part.

Support was by no means confined to the artistic intelligentsia. Writers, performers, scientists and others also were active in support though numbers were lower than in the visual arts. Gorky maintained a critical attitude to the revolution, fearing in particular it was destroying the intelligentsia itself, the flower of Russian society in Gorky's view, and burying it in waves of nihilistic popular violence. Unlike many other revolutionaries, he did not trust the masses and, considering himself to be a man of the people, felt he knew them better than the more middle- and upper-class intellectuals who led the political parties, including the Bolsheviks. He had spent much of his career trying to educate the working masses out of their traditional attitudes and directed his novels towards them, becoming the best-selling writer of the day. From the turn of the century his works were eagerly read by workers in libraries and reading clubs. He supported the Bolsheviks in 1917 but was increasingly appalled by the authoritarianism of Lenin and the post-October emergence of what he considered tyranny, based on a reckless gamble for the support of the untamed masses. His approach has been reflected in many, usually hostile, accounts of the revolution which see any positive potential having been quickly undermined by hooliganism and looting, what he called 'Asiatic savagery'. He continued with his attempts to protect as many prominent figures as he could, writing numerous petitions to Lenin and others asking for proceedings against such people to be dropped in the national interest. Russia, Gorky argued, needed their talents. However, he concluded he was fighting a losing battle against increasing dictatorship and abandonment of the ideals of 1917 and left Russia in autumn 1921, ostensibly to return to Capri for health reasons but also because of disillusionment with the path the revolution was taking.

In many ways it is hard to call Gorky a supporter but he did believe in the abstract notion of revolution but, like many other radicals, he did not support the obliteration of democracy and the attack on civil society mounted by the Bolsheviks, especially as the civil war wound down. In this one of the other great supporters of October, Aleksandr Blok followed a similar path. In his brilliant poem *The Twelve* Blok portrayed a rough and ready group of Red Guards – 'each like a jailbird on the run' – enforcing the curfew in Petrograd around December 1917. The twelve are presented smoking, swearing, talking coarsely about women and even shooting to death the ex-girl friend of one of them after she had changed sides and joined a criminal who was breaking curfew. Extraordinarily, out of nowhere, at the very end of the moderately long poem, the ghostly figure of Jesus Christ emerges from the mist carrying a red flag. In its final couplets the twelve are converted into the apostles of a new religion. In addition to showing once more that religious sensibilities and imagery could penetrate deeply into many areas of Russian culture the poem expressed Blok's populist rather than Bolshevik views. In opposition to Gorky, Blok portrayed a crude, violent and fallible working class but one which would ultimately triumph as Christianity had developed through the rough and ready human material of the fishermen, tax collectors and others called to be the first apostles. It was an affirmation of the masses and the revolutionary spirit of the time. According to Prince D.S. Mirsky, who lectured in Russian Literature at King's College, London in the 1920s, Alexander Blok was the greatest Russian poet of modern times, accepting 'the revolution as an expression of the mystical and craving soul of Russia' and creating in *The Twelve* 'a sublime symphony made out of realistic dirt.'[10] The poem had been written in a body-wracking continuous fit of inspiration over thirty-six hours. Unfortunately, Blok's health declined in the dreadful conditions of civil war Petrograd and his revolutionary enthusiasm also drained away as Bolshevik violence and dictatorship expanded. He died in disillusionment in 1920, leaving later Soviet critics and educators with the dilemma of explaining why one of the unquestionably greatest masterpieces of the revolution culminated in a powerful Christian symbol.

Other writers reflected Blok and Gorky's views of the crudity of the human material on which the revolution was, from the intelligentsia point of view, basing itself. Some followed Gorky in arguing it was the death of the revolution, some, like Isaac Babel (1894–1940), pointed to the revolutionary potential of even rougher, violent, anti-semitic troops in *The Red Cavalry*, a book of civil war stories including graphic depictions of atrocities by both sides. The book itself did not come out until 1926 but was preceded by publication in 1920 of parts of the diary he had written while with Budyenni's cavalry. The book was met with criticism from high places. Budennyi, the commander of the Red Cavalry and a revolutionary legend in his own right, was outraged at a depiction apparently besmirching his heroes of Red victory. Stalin commented that Babel had not understood what he was writing about and even Victor Shklovsky said he had given skewed testimony. In 1928, Gorky came to his defence in an article in *Pravda* saying that by portraying them so realistically Babel had brought out their true heroism.[11]

Apart from a hard core of active Bolsheviks like Bukharin, Preobrazhensky and Lenin himself intelligentsia support for the revolution was conditional, ambiguous, short-lived and, especially for artists, linked to very personal views on what the revolution should be. A much wider range of *intelligenty*, probably the majority, were neither active supporters nor active opponents of Bolshevism but wanted to hang on to as much of their lives as possible in the dramatically new circumstances. They wanted mainly to just get along with the new authorities. Most were glad to see an end to autocracy and many, like Blok, sympathized with the plight of the masses but they were now forced into overwhelming, existence-threatening conditions. Their own survival became a priority. How they reacted is the subject of the next section.

ii.) Acceptance of October

Like many educated Russians of the time Theo Got'e faced an extreme, daily struggle for survival in the period from early 1918 to 1920 which he recorded in his diary. He was forced into extraordinary shifts just to stay alive. His wife, living on the family country estate, reported in summer 1918 that 'I am not eating any potatoes at all. I am on a diet of mushrooms, beans and kasha [a kind of porridge] which I have found on the estate. There is nowhere to buy meat; there are almost no eggs – only enough for Volodia, and I occasionally make fried eggs; the cows give little – they have stopped milking three of them. My spirits are low, like everyone else's.'[12] He even had the extraordinary experience of making a perilous journey to intercede for his brother who was being held by the Cheka in another town. In August 1918, he was informed by a friend of his brother's plight and the circumstances of his arrest. Many prisoners in Novgorod and elsewhere were being transferred out of Cheka control to be processed for release 'But then' his informant wrote, 'the events in Petrograd struck', that is the assassination of Uritskii and the shooting of Lenin on 30 August. As a result 'all the cases were hastily recalled to the Extraordinary Commission [that is, the Cheka] and on the following morning six persons were shot.' He needed to get a railway pass for his journey to Novgorod. 'The passes for business trips were issued by a comrade-worker whose rudeness was unmatched by anything I had heard or seen. And since our office had not seen fit to put a number on the certificate given to me, they didn't give me the pass at all, and I lost another day' a particularly insupportable delay given his mission was to save his brother who could have been executed at any moment. The ride to Novgorod was slow and uncomfortable in a grossly overcrowded train. Surprisingly, Got'e tells us, its rigours were endured by the passengers not in the 'nasty and unpleasant way' he expected but in a spirit of being 'mutually well-disposed, meek and courteous,' together with 'a hint of mockery at the state of things'. Such were the oddities and inconsistencies of early Soviet Russia that 'My task in Novgorod,' he wrote, was 'to liberate my brother; I achieved that quickly and, moreover, without great effort'.[13] It was almost easier for him to get his brother released, simply by vouching for his political reliability, than it had been to get his train pass. The fact that his mission succeeded, apparently without the involvement of bribes or interventions from above, is almost as surprising as his account of the journey. It shows how arbitrary arrests were and the fine line between life and death. Had Got'e arrived a few days later it is likely his brother would already have been executed. Got'e also showed extraordinary courage. Had things turned bad he might, like numerous others, have been arrested as an associate of a state criminal.

The intelligentsia were especially vulnerable to the cataclysm as most of them lacked the resources of the propertied classes and did not enjoy the political favouritism of the working class. They were also tied in to the city and did not have rural family to fall back on. They were forced into desperate measures in order to survive. Many did not. A few lucky ones were able to find a few precarious protective structures like Gorky's publishing project which could mean the difference between life and death. Got'e was helped by having a marketable skill tragically in great demand at that time. He was a much-needed doctor but still faced the dangers outlined above.

For non-party intellectuals – that is, the great majority – a number of other lifelines existed. Schoolteaching, from remote villages to urban metropolises, helped preserve tens of thousands of women and men and their families.[14] Conditions were tough and schools were under pressure to teach the new ideas despite a complete absence of teaching materials and of training for the teachers. Heating schools was a big problem especially in Petrograd and the North around 1919 and food supplies, officially revolving around a meagre state ration for many teachers and pupils, had to be supplemented by allotments or purchase and barter with peasant producers which was a risky operation since it was theoretically illegal as well as vital for survival. At the highest levels universities and research institutes, including those of the Academy of Sciences, were desperately short of every kind of basic resource. Lectures were given in near-freezing, even subzero, temperatures in the lecture halls. Coats and fur hats were necessary, even inside buildings, during the colder months. Food was also in short supply and mortality rates, especially among older professors, rose rapidly. Naturally enough, many students were dissuaded from pursuing their studies and numbers fell, despite efforts by the state and party to recruit 'non-traditional' students of working-class and peasant background via special accelerated courses in newly established 'Workers' Faculties' (*Rabfaky*). They attracted some very enthusiastic candidates prepared to endure the harshest of conditions in return for eventual entrance to university. The conditions in élite institutions were little better. Ailing professors fought off the cold to conduct such experiments as they could in labs deprived of almost everything. The chemical engineer Ioffe tells of working in Moscow university labs where the temperature was –8°C.[15]

As if the practical shortages were not enough, the non-party intelligentsia was under ubiquitous political scrutiny. Many academics had been supporters of the liberal Kadet Party and were firmly westernizing in terms of supporting parliamentary democracy. There was also a populist spirit of serving the people and the country which softened their opposition to a Bolshevism, which very few academics had supported. Waves of arrests riffled through their ranks, clawing in the neutral as well as actively anti-Bolshevik *intelligenty*. Some, like Ivan Pavlov who made some anti-semitic and anti-Bolshevik comments, were protected by their international status and a curious but enduring respect for high-achieving intellectuals in many spheres on the part of the Bolshevik leaders. Nonetheless, as became the case throughout Soviet history, the arbitrariness and extent of arrests were counterproductive. Many of those arrested were no kind of threat. Take the extraordinary example of Mikhail Novikov, the Rector of Moscow University. Novikov was arrested for supposed complicity in anti-soviet activities in 1919. While in prison in Moscow he encountered directly the desire to learn of many of his fellow inmates from the lower classes who pestered him with questions. He held impromptu seminars in the jail itself. His case was sorted out fairly quickly. Novikov benefitted from the baffling Bolshevik tendency to, in the blink of an eye, entrust responsible tasks to those who had moments before been considered enemies. Novikov was released in order to participate in a very important commission with a remit of assessing Russia's resources and economic potential versus disadvantages. The commission, initially set up by the Academy of Sciences in 1915, was known as the Commission for the Study of Natural Productive Forces (*Kommissiia po izucheniiu estestvennykh proizvoditel'nykh sil* – KEPS was its Russian acronym). It brought together experts, more or less regardless of political opinion, prepared to work to get the collapsed economy back on its feet and propose priorities for government policy to support.

Of course, Novikov's case, and the increasing number of similar ones, indicate that, in some ways like tsarism, the new Soviet authorities were forced to recruit beyond their immediate circle to find experts for a wide variety of essential tasks. In the forefront were those skilled in military science, needed to strengthen the Red Army, and economic managers who could restore the output of ruined factories. Lenin turned to such people early in the revolution, in March/April 1918. It was a very unpopular policy with the party but Lenin was prepared to, in effect, roll out a red carpet for any such people prepared to work uncritically for the new regime. They were paid much more than regular workers, despite the egalitarian tendencies of the early Soviet years. Although most beneficiaries were business people this policy also provided a safe haven for many members of the intelligentsia. Engineers, in particular, were needed to repair war damage to key infrastructure including the railway system, bridges, river and canal locks not to mention machinery of all kinds and residential and industrial buildings. In the words of a perceptive English eyewitness of the time, and later children's writer, Arthur Ransome, 'In circumstances in which it seemed that Russian civilisation would disappear altogether, starving and ragged engineers were planning the future electrification of Russian industry and rationalisation of Russia's industrial geography.'[16]

Indeed, Ransome caught something of the spirit of the moment among many intellectuals, especially the younger ones. In his reminiscences of the period, Nicholas Berdyaev, one of the *Vekhi* writers, recalled moments of intellectual ferment despite the grimness of everyday life. He was able to set up a Free Academy of Spiritual Culture in 1919. Weekly meetings brought figures from clashing ideologies to fight out their ideas. Like Belinsky confronting Turgenev, they were more concerned about the existence of God than the next meal. Unlikely pockets of artistic creativity could be found in small corners such as bookshops and surviving art galleries. Incidentally, cinema, theatres, museums and art galleries all had free admission under the new regime.

But for many others, unable to find a protective space or obtain a sufficient ration of food and firewood, the outlook was considerably darker. Perhaps the bleakest account can be found in Evgenii Zamiatin's (1884–1937) story *The Cave* which describes a starving, freezing intelligentsia couple in Petrograd in winter 1919 having to sacrifice all their furniture and books to the 'stove-god' around which their survival revolves. The city has become a wilderness of cliff faces (housing blocks) in which the inhabitants live in apartments-turned caves, while mammoths of hunger roam the streets outside. Civilized values break down, the unscrupulous find it easier to survive. In a central moment in the story the husband steals a few logs from a neighbour. His conscience is tormented even though it was a necessary act to keep his wife alive. The dilemma penetrates to his deepest self:

> And on a line drawn by his hardly audible jerky breath-two Martin Martinyches had come to a deadly stand: the old one, with Scryabin and all, who knew: I mustn't; and the new one, the cave one, who knew: I must. The cave one, grinding his teeth, brought the other one down, stifled him-and Martin Martinych, breaking his nails, opened the door, shoved his hand into the stack of wood, one log, a fourth, a fifth one – under his coat, behind his belt, into the pail-slammed the door and sped upstairs-in enormous, animal-like jumps.[17]

In the end she demands the lethal dose of morphine they have kept back in order to end it all.

Although it is fiction, Zamiatin is writing in the Russian realist tradition and was depicting events which were all too common in reality. Isolated intellectuals tried to survive as best they could. Many headed for the provinces or the countryside but there was little guarantee they would find salvation there. Some went to the south, not least to escape the harsher climate of the north, but armed conflict, ethnic rivalries and peasant hostility often worked against them. Some succeeded and simply dropped off the radar and lived quiet, provincial, local lives like the great symbolist poet Maximilian Voloshin (1877–1932). Before 1917 he had been a well-known figure not only in Russia's capitals but in Paris and elsewhere in western Europe. As a pacificist he had opposed the war and during the revolution he claimed to stand above the struggle, a true neutral. Amusingly, his bushy grey hair and extravagant beard caused a soldier in a busy square in Moscow to mistake him for Karl Marx and go up to him praising him for his Marxism 'which we study in our political literacy classes'. 'Study, study young man', Voloshin replied.[18] In 1917 he retired to the house built by his mother in Koktebel', Crimea, where he protected Red refugees from the dominant Whites, and White refugees from the dominant Reds once the tables had turned. He has been credited with saving the life of the Jewish poet Osip Mandel'shtam when he was in the hands of anti-semitic Whites. Through the twenties he worked with the local Soviet authorities offering his house as a free retreat for writers and bequeathing it in 1932 to the Writers' Union after his death following a stroke. His wife continued to manage the house and preserve his work and reputation.

iii.) Active opposition to October and flight from Soviet Russia

The *intelligenty* who 'accepted' the revolution often remained hostile to much of what the Bolsheviks were doing but, especially during the civil war, they did not take active steps to oppose them. The number who did was actually quite small. In the immediate aftermath of the October revolution opponents could be found across the whole political spectrum including within the Soviet camp. Unsurprisingly, nationalist and Slavophile intellectuals as well as liberals were horrified. Leading figures in the soviets, including the SR and Menshevik establishment – Chkheidze, Tseretelli, Chernov, Kerensky – bitterly opposed Soviet power. Even radical Mensheviks, like Lenin's former close friend Martov, and Sukhanov, who were in favour of soviet power, did not trust the Bolsheviks. Poignantly, Plekhanov himself denounced the Bolsheviks' actions. He became the figurehead of a short-lived attempt to reverse October via a Committee for the Salvation of the Motherland and the Revolution (*Komitet Spaseniia Rodiny i Revoliutsii*) which merged into even looser organizations for the defence of the Constituent Assembly which was elected in November with a non-Bolshevik majority. When it met in January 1918 it was dispersed on Lenin's orders within a few hours. That was not quite the end of it. A group of elected delegates eventually formed a 'Committee of Members of the Constituent Assembly' (*Komuch* from its Russian acronym) which started with five members rising to about ninety. It was initially formed in June 1918 in Samara, under the protection of the White forces in Siberia. Later it moved to Ufa in the Urals and, on 18 November 1918, it was disbanded by the White military government.[19] These weak, ephemeral groups were, for a while, the only centre of anti-Bolshevik intelligentsia hopes for democracy.

The intelligentsia opponents of the Bolsheviks were alarmed by several aspects of what they feared would follow. The most immediate was the risk of dividing the country and starting a civil war which would benefit only the Germans and their allies. The devastating Treaty of Brest-Litovsk in March 1918 appeared to bear that expectation out. The brief peace which followed was, unexpectedly, transformed in June 1918 into a renewed civil war of proportions unimaginable even to those who had predicted it. As we have noted, cities emptied, factories closed down, infrastructure decayed and was destroyed. Secondly, they feared the Bolsheviks would not adhere to democratic norms and would deny basic rights of free expression and so on. The growth and consolidation of a one-party state by 1921 and the trial and expulsion of remaining SR leaders in 1922, not to mention the depredations of the Cheka, were more than enough to convince left-wing opponents of the Bolsheviks that their expectations had been terribly borne out in practice. There was, however, a third, more penetrating, issue arising from the disputes we have seen among socialist intellectuals from the 1870s on. Was Russia ready for revolution? Plekhanov in particular had remained insistent until his untimely death, on 30 May 1918, that Russia was not ready for the transformation to socialism. By the end of the civil war it had even de-proletarianized further and had an urban working class of only around 10 per cent of the population which Marxist critics of Bolshevism believed was a pitifully sparse foundation on which to construct the magnificence of a socialist society.

Echoing the response of Marx to the populists, Lenin and Trotsky in 1917 professed to believe that international, even 'world', revolution was approaching and would help Russia overcome its deficits in the task of socialist construction. However, as early as April and May 1918 Lenin was advocating an as-yet-temporary version of 'socialism in one country'.[20] By the end of the civil war the revolutionary moment in western Europe had all but ended and the isolation of Russia as the only socialist and anti-capitalist state was obviously going to last indefinitely. Again the critics appeared to have proved themselves correct. Even so, they were unable to make much practical impact. By spring and early summer 1918 many of them had decided to try to compete with the Bolsheviks within the soviets. It was soon apparent that any advances they might make would be met by Bolshevik 'dirty tricks' of arresting opponents, denying supplies to factories which supported them, closing down newspapers and so on. However, despite such tactics being used against them, as the civil war deepened, many of them reluctantly decided they had to work alongside the Bolsheviks to defeat the Whites as a priority. Once that was done they hoped democratic opposition would be possible. But it wasn't. The Bolsheviks tightened their dictatorship in 1921 and the only options for opponents were emigration, internal exile (i.e abandoning politics and keeping ones head down), arrest or assimilation into Bolshevik ranks. For all that they may have been 'correct' in their predictions they were unable to form any effective organizations or persuade any significant part of wider society – worker or peasant – to follow them. This is not least because they had made one other prediction which was spectacularly wrong. They expected that, as a result of Bolshevik actions being premature from the theoretical Marxist viewpoint and catastrophic on the world and civil war front, Bolshevik rule would soon collapse. Indeed, had it not been for the civil war forcing polarization and bringing them reluctant supporters as the only force able to defend the revolutionary settlement of land and capital expropriation, the Bolsheviks might well not have survived 1918. But they did and by 1921 there was no force in Russia or beyond which could or would challenge their nonetheless still shaky power. The new state was still weak and ill-organized but its internal and external enemies were either weaker still or preoccupied with their own disastrous and, in many cases, potentially revolutionary situations. The Bolsheviks had been 'wrong' on so many major points but their assets and the working out of broader events had conspired to keep them in power.

Apart from the Committee of Salvation and supporters of Komuch a handful of *intelligenty* found themselves standing alongside the Whites, with whom they had little in common. This was especially true of several distinguished figures who gathered around Denikin and his Volunteer Army in Rostov and later Sevastopol'. Two of the *Vekhi* group, Struve and Bulgakov, were part of Denikin's administration. Struve returned to Moscow in early 1918 and, together with other, largely Kadet liberals, including G.N. Trubetskoi, N. Avksentiev, N. Astrov, N.S. Arsen'ev and others, worked underground for the 'Right-Centre' organization and its shadowy successors. Struve made his way to Finland and then Paris where he represented Denikin at the peace talks. Other liberals, notably Miliukov, used Paris as a base to argue at the Versailles conference for active measures of intervention against the Bolsheviks. Paris became the political headquarters of the White movement. While in Moscow, Struve had helped produce what is often seen as a successor to *Vekhi* a collection of essays entitled, quoting the opening of psalm 130, *Iz glubiny* (*Out of the depths* or *De Profundis*).

The book itself had a curious history illustrative of the 1918–19 moment. It was produced as a book but, at the last minute, the authorities realized what it contained and prevented it from being distributed. Some quick-thinking printer, it is said, pilfered a handful of copies before the rest were taken for pulping. According to some accounts only two copies survived.[21] Whatever the number, it was a bibliographical rarity until a reprint was made in Paris in 1967 from the personal copy smuggled out by one of the authors, Nicholas Berdyaev. What did it contain? Five of the original seven authors of *Vekhi* were among the eleven contributors, almost all of whom were Kadets.[22] Largely the essays were a series of literary-philosophical and religious denunciations of the Bolsheviks. Most of the contributions were philosophical, such as Bulgakov's article claiming Dostoevsky's devils had now come and were suffocating the Russian soul. There was even less engagement with social issues than in *Vekhi*. In the words of the introduction: 'The contributors are united in the opinion that the positive principles of social life are rooted in the depths of religious consciousness and that tearing these links apart is a misfortune and a crime.'[23] Even if it had been allowed to circulate it seems unlikely that there was much of an audience at the time for its high-level abstract religious thought. People were starving, not worrying about demonic possession. It was an extraordinary example of how, at times, intellectuals can retreat to a brilliantly constructed ivory tower of irrelevance.

As the civil war continued some of the intellectuals on both sides were busy reconsidering their opinions. Many, like Blok, who had welcomed the revolution were being progressively disillusioned by its ever-more dictatorial and repressive aspect. It appeared to be abandoning the principles on which it had been built. Though little affected by intellectuals, the general conjuncture of events, as the Bolsheviks secured their predominance, showed a similar process of fighting for the principles of 1917 was affecting others. Most symbolic of all, the Kronstadt rebellion of 1921 was based on a desire to restore genuine soviet power in place of one-party dictatorship. Among the Whites, a small minority was coming to the conclusion that the White cause had got it wrong. It was the Whites who depended for their existence on handouts and resources from foreign powers while, by 1920, the Bolsheviks had fought off all comers on their own resources. Which side, some White officers reflected, really represented a strong, independent Russia? A group of them produced a collection of essays along these lines entitled *Smena vekh* (*Change of Landmarks*) which argued for reconciliation with the Soviet Government. They also convinced themselves that the Soviet system was 'normalizing', by which they meant dropping its utopian dreams and coming to terms with *realpolitik*. A powerful, traditional Russian state was, they believed, emerging. The Soviet authorities began to sponsor some of these groups. One of the leading figures, Iu.N. Potekhin (1888–1937), became an advisor to the Foreign Ministry in the 1920s while the leading light in the movement, N.V. Ustrialov (1890–1937), worked on the Soviet payroll for the Chinese Eastern Railway administration in Harbin, China.

By and large, intellectuals had been left to survive the dreadful conditions in their own way. The new authorities had not taken any special steps against them. They had been damaged as a group by the state takeover of publishing and of cultural institutions, including theatre, cinema, museums and galleries. The art market had collapsed and the state was sole patron. As a result many *intelligenty* had died from disease and hunger. Some had been victims of the oppression. The noted case of the poet Nikolai Gumilev being a prominent example. Equally, some intellectuals had taken advantage of the conditions like Mayakovsky, El Lissitsky, Moor, Tatlin, Malevich and others who were commissioned by the new authorities. Universities and the Academy of Sciences up to 1921/2 were deeply undermined by lack of resources but policies such as rapid preparation of workers and peasants for higher education were not intended as an attack on universities as such. The end of the civil war and the restoration of the market and private trade, under constraints, led to optimism that a form of 'normality' was re-emerging. For a while, even private publishing was possible. It seemed the worst might be over. However, the intelligentsia would never return to its pre-October condition. In its traditional sense it was now dead. Its spirit lived on in individuals and scattered groups within and beyond the Russian border but it would never regain its former political and social significance. Though it was not noted at the time, the economic easing was accompanied by heightened ideological firmness. Few had so far realized that Bolshevism was not a simple political movement taking power for a class and representing its interests. It had, as we have seen, a utopian element of transforming human nature. The intelligentsia and culture had been on the back burner while economic and military survival topped the government's to do list. Now the economy, despite the terrible famine of 1921/2, was stabilizing and enemy forces had been ejected from the country, the true business of the Bolsheviks came to the fore. Revolutionary transformation was now the top priority, way ahead of any others. In this context the intelligentsia would feel the full force of transition. An independent radical intelligentsia which questioned the state in a developing civil society was not about to re-emerge. It was imperative for the Bolsheviks to enlist intellectual power to take the next step in realizing their hopes and dreams. But the last thing this intelligentsia was expected to embody was critical social analysis. The new religion demanded only useful believers. It began by tolerating those whom it hoped to win over, but the intelligentsia it wanted to construct was very different from the one that had engaged in the heroic struggle for freedom in tsarist times.

7

The intelligentsia and the Soviet cultural revolution: From Proletkul't to the new Soviet person

By 1921 the traditional intelligentsia – the people-serving, 'mind, honour and conscience' of Russia – had been scattered to the four winds. The revolution for which they had yearned had come and they had been among its casualties. The ideas remained to inspire but the group had been fragmented. Or had it? Its spirit lived on in unexpected corners of the new Russia and even the new rulers retained a share.

It was a supreme irony that the destruction wrought on the intelligentsia had not come from its assumed enemies on the right or, for those of a Gorkyesque persuasion, from the masses, but from one of its own factions. It was not the feared 'dark people', the supposedly barbaric masses, who had risen up and cut their throats. On the contrary, many workers and peasants had shown a thirst for knowledge and turned to the intelligentsia to supply it. It was one of their own radical factions which had dismissively swept them away. In that sense October was also an intelligentsia triumph. For the first time in history an intelligentsia group had taken over a major country and was determined to use its position to further an intellectual plan. It was not driven by the immediate interests of any social group but by a philosophically derived view of the future interests of the proletariat and of the whole of humanity in a classless society, the nature of which very few, including its Bolshevik clergy, had any firm idea. In Reformation Germany and Switzerland sects had taken over cities and tried to turn them into provinces of the kingdom of God as perceived by their prophetic leaders. But here was a country covering one-sixth of the world's land area trying to implement a secular version of salvation. Perhaps the most overlooked feature of Bolshevism and communism is its ambition to forge a new humanity by mobilizing people to the cause. While productionism and Marxist theory provided the new authorities with fundamental policies in the economic and political sphere the underlying drive was to enlist support in a quite different and decisive field – cultural revolution. This did not simply mean passing on the glories of high culture to the masses, or even teaching them literacy, though this was an essential starting point. It meant totally transforming existing ways of life and giving birth to a perfected human individual. Though the traditional intelligentsia had been savagely and almost unintentionally uprooted by 1921, this key project of human perfectibility had the intelligentsia hallmark all over it. Who was to carry out cultural revolution if not the bearers of culture themselves?

The destruction of the intelligentsia had brought to the fore a project requiring their essential, not only participation, but leadership. The Bolshevik project was one intelligentsia scheme which had, it appeared, driven out all others. But it desperately needed its own believers in order to survive. As we have noted, it was frequently said that in Russia even atheism became a religion. In many respects communism was a new, secular, authoritarian theocracy; a humanist, evangelizing fundamentalist caliphate built on the work of true believers. It was driven by its principles to both mobilize support, and energetically condemn heresy. Soviet power became noted for both.

The pursuit of cultural revolution was, from the outset, beset by a multitude of problems, though two were perhaps most defining of the new government's actions. The idea of cultural revolution, like the Marxist notion of future communist society or the Christian concept of heaven, was vague and undefined. It raised more questions than it answered. What exactly did the goal look like? What were the characteristics of the liberated person? There was also the fundamental challenge facing all visionaries. Having a vision of the end of the process was all very well but what were the immediate steps towards it? What did one need to do today? Tomorrow? The days after? The devil was certainly in the detail and the Bolsheviks had little notion of it.

The second problem, completely intertwined with the first and possibly mutually cancelling, was the near absence of believers. The civil war years showed many shortages but the most important shortage of all for the Bolshevik leaders was Bolsheviks. The new government was taking on responsibilities over and above any previous government in the modern world. In addition to the traditional functions of government, defence plus law and order, the Bolsheviks were trying to control the economy, replace the market, expand education, provide welfare services and supervise all aspects of society including the party itself. There was a massive demand for people who understood what was going on from a Bolshevik perspective. A classic example is provided by the problem of law. What would the new government's attitude be to law? It was unthinkable that it would continue with tsarist law. Obviously, in an ideal situation, it would promulgate its own laws, judiciary and law enforcement, which it eventually did, but initially there was no such body of law, nor were there law schools to train lawyers, nor were there established courts to implement it. The short-term solution, defined in the first constitution in 1918, was that judges, drawn from the working classes, would decide cases according to Soviet law, where it had come into existence, but, in areas not yet covered by written law, the judges should exercise their 'socialist conscience', i.e. decide according to what they would expect a socialist law to say if it had existed. Clearly, this called for many thousands of socialist Solomons to be presiding over the new courts. But, even if there could be such people, where would they be found? Who would train them? How would they perfect their socialist conscience? It is not our task to unpick these problems in detail[1] but to note that the system put a heavy demand on believers to take control in the name of the party.

The party itself grew. In February 1917 it may well have had only 10,000 active members rising to about 250,000 around October, although the Party Secretary Sverdlov claimed about 400,000. During the civil war numbers fluctuated but reached about 732,000 by the end, rising to a million in the mid-twenties. The party from 1919 on was busy trying to raise the level of socialist consciousness not only in society but even within the party itself. The very fact of being in power attracted some of the wrong people to it, people interested in the fruits of office not service of the cause. They became known as careerists and there were attempts to stop the party becoming 'bureaucratized', meaning its operatives considered themselves responsible to their superiors, not to those whom they supposedly served. These twin evils weakened the party from the outset and it began to set up mechanisms to weed them out. The first review of party cards, quickly known as 'purges' as they were supposedly cleansing operations, occurred in 1919. Members were expelled for not fulfilling the duties of a communist which, echoing the traditional intelligentsia code, called on them to selflessly serve the interests of the people, not themselves. Rather like the critical contradiction we noted in tsarism – that in order to maintain its economic power and military strength it needed education, but education engendered people unprepared to put up with the restraints of tsarism – so Bolshevism found its nemesis in 'bureaucratization'. Lenin and subsequent party leaders did not question what later came to be called 'the leading role of the party' in society. It was there to supervise and guide society towards the shining peaks of communism. However, this engendered a controlling bureaucracy which stifled social initiative. Although 'bureaucratization' was energetically criticized from early on by Lenin and, especially, Trotsky, who weaponized it in his failed battle with Stalin, neither admitted that its main roots lay in the Leninist tactic of using state power to generate 'revolution from above'. It was very difficult, probably impossible, to reconcile this idea with meaningful democracy, civic freedoms and human rights. At the very least it required a plethora of believers. The vast majority of Russians were not believers. From the beginning the state apparatus swelled uncontrollably. Its desire for personnel was insatiable. The first purges showed that. The members expelled from the party seem to have been re-admitted over the next few months and years. The party could not do without them even though they were seriously compromised. The more the party bureaucracy was compromised, the more cynical the rest of society became about it and the less inclined they were to be converted to the project. Millions did become believers in the early decades, especially young people,[2] but tens of millions did not.

By 1921, the party had evolved Control Commissions at all levels to raise standards and weed out corruption and self-serving. Interestingly, the Commissions were appointed with a stipulation that only those who had been in the party before February 1917 could be members of the National Commission. Different generations – membership before October and after October – were also defined as ways to objectify party commitment. Only pre-February members, it was implied, could really be trusted. Since they were very few, not least because a minority had become disillusioned with the anti-democratic and dictatorial direction of Soviet rule and left the party, the crucial shortage was again highlighted. To overcome it the 1919 Party Programme was intended as a teaching tool to raise the level of consciousness of the party members themselves. A basic manual of party doctrine, *The ABC of Communism,* was produced to accompany it for use in party reading groups in factories and other party sections. The first task of Bolshevism was to educate the Bolsheviks. Lack of them was creating crucial weaknesses across the whole system and spawned from the beginning a network of institutions, like the party generations, to instill, or substitute for, the required level of socialist consciousness.[3]

The seriousness and centrality of the issue are underlined by the last writings of Lenin himself. In two short articles, one critiquing Sukhanov's view of the revolution and the other entitled 'On Cooperation', Lenin summarized the situation of the revolution shortly before his death. Sukhanov had taken the classic Menshevik position that Russia was unprepared for a socialist revolution because of its low economic and educational level. Lenin's retort was that who says the preparations have to be made that way round? We have, he argued, shown such assumptions to be wrong because we have taken power and held on to it. So we have the key prerequisite for building socialism – state power. Can that not be used to overcome the obstacles of backwardness? Lenin was advocating productionism as a crucial component of socialist transformation. In 'On Cooperation' he said we have power, we have economic control so all we now need is to combine the principle of co-operation with that of cultural revolution:

> Our opponents told us repeatedly that we were rash in undertaking to implant socialism in an insufficiently cultured country. But they were misled by our having started from the opposite end to that prescribed by theory (the theory of pedants of all kinds), because in our country the political and social revolution preceded the cultural revolution, that very cultural revolution which nevertheless now confronts us. This cultural revolution would now suffice to make our country a completely socialist country.[4]

It is obvious that for Lenin cultural revolution was of the utmost importance. It was the key to the future. What was less clear was, as mentioned earlier, what did it mean and how would it be implemented? The complications in resolving these questions had begun even before October though, like many aspects of Bolshevik policy for government, the likelihood of them ever being in power was so slight they had made little provision for it beyond broad principles.

The development of Bolshevik cultural policy

i.) The battle over Proletkul't (The Proletarian Cultural Educational Association)

In mid-August 1917 a notice was placed in the left-wing Petrograd press inviting anyone interested to the inaugural meeting of a group which took the title of The Proletarian Cultural-Educational Association, quickly abbreviated to Proletkul't. Precise details of the meeting are unclear. It was one moment in a great swirl of events, meetings and organizations. But from this modest start one of the most original and exciting experiments in mass education began. It was radically different from the earlier very worthy activities of various institutions in the preceding decades which had provided worker education. They included, notably, Sofia Panina's People's House project for young women, the Bestuzhev Courses in Moscow and numerous small worker literacy circles, at one of which Lenin had met his wife and life companion Nadezhda Krupskaya. Earlier groups had aimed at making accepted canons of education and skills available to those excluded by poverty and social position. Proletkul't, by contrast, wanted to develop a set of cultural values appropriate to the working class to serve as an ideological and intellectual platform for what its founders saw as the approaching proletarian era. If it were to rule, it needed a set of its own values to do so. Its leading inspiration was Alexander Bogdanov. We have already noted that one of the few Bolsheviks who had paid serious attention to issues of cultural revolution as a critical aspect of revolutionary strategy was Bogdanov. He had been expelled from the party for his pains, not least because he was also perceived by Lenin as a serious rival as well as a heretic. But his ideas continued to develop and to be influential in parts of the party. Like any good intelligentsia group, its initial steps were to issue a self-definition in the form of a manifesto and set up a journal in which to publish it. Bogdanov and the leaders thought of Proletkul't groups as 'laboratories of proletarian culture'. The point was to set up pure, uninfluenced (as far as possible) creative spaces in which workers themselves could develop their own values. Bogdanov had been one of the most workerist Bolsheviks, even influencing Lenin in that direction in 1904 during their period of close friendship. In line with Marx' comment that the liberation of the workers should be the task of the workers themselves, Bogdanov wanted to minimize intelligentsia guidance and hold those deemed bourgeois and aristocratic at arm's length though, after some debate, peasants were admitted to the organization though, in practice, it did not have many branches in the countryside.[5]

However, this drive for class purity was rather disingenuous on Bogdanov's part. He already believed he knew the foundational values of proletarian culture. Labour was the bedrock of human social interaction and everything developed from the need for humans to engage in socially necessary labour – grow food, build homes and so on – in order to survive. Work was an essentially co-operative rather than competitive activity and best results came from working together in teams. The labour process was being constantly improved by reflection and thinking about better ways to work, so reason was more important than tradition. Science was the source of progress, not superstition, the supernatural and the religious. Bogdanov saw co-operation, collectivism and scientific reason and philosophical materialism as essential components to replace the dominant values of individualism, competition, religion and philosophical idealism. So it was not so much developing fundamental 'proletarian' values as working out how to implement them in everyday practice through the labour process, the creative arts, personal relations, child-rearing, science, education and so on. Bogdanov's priorities were very practical and aspects of life such as emotion, intuition, belief, the 'spirit' or 'mind' were seen as material functions. Like most Bolsheviks (and many intellectuals in general at that time) the implications of the existence of a subconscious part of the mind were not really drawn out.

Like the wider problem for the Bolsheviks, Proletkul't's ambitious programme fell foul of the shortage of convinced, 'conscious' believers and was forced to get help from 'bourgeois' cultural 'specialists' to help train workers in the skills of creative writing, painting and so on. Despite protests from hardliners in the organization who feared such people would pollute the purity of proletarian values, leading non-proletarian cultural figures like the writers and poets Briusov, Belyi and Khodasevich[6] took part in Proletkul't workshops. Though resources were even more sparse, science was also included and the quest to devise a 'proletarian science' was begun. During the revolutionary war Proletkul't developed steadily but unspectacularly. By 1920 it had 1,400 groups and a regular journal, *Proletarskaia kul'tura* (*Proletarian Culture*), in which its ideas were thrashed out, plus numerous other journals and publications. It claimed 80,000 members with half a million workers 'grouped around it'.[7] Leading Bolshevik educationalists, notably Luncharsky and Lenin's partner Nadezhda Krupskaya, who was commissar for adult education, contributed to the ongoing discussion. It also set up links with a number of trade unions. Through the Civil War Proletkul't had quietly and unabrasively cultivated its patch. It spread to many Soviet-held towns and developed in a slow but steady and unspectacular fashion. For tactical reasons arising from him being *persona non grata* with Lenin, Bogdanov had remained in the background, almost invisible. But this was not enough to avert Lenin's wrath, which burst like a summer storm from a clear sky in late 1920, culminating in a decree drafted personally by Lenin which ended Proletkul't's autonomy.[8]

Why was Lenin so hostile to Proletkul't? The official charge laid at its door was that it had supported futurist attempts to obliterate 'bourgeois' and other existing forms of culture. Futurists, who were strong in Italy as well as Russia, said it was necessary to create a cultural *tabula rasa* to enable new cultures to develop. The movement was influenced by Nietzsche's call for a 'revaluation of all values' in the light of the rise of science and rationality and the 'death of God'. A small number of Russian writers and artists were influenced by it. The proletarian poet Mikhail Gerasimov (1889–1939) welcomed the news, fortunately exaggerated, that Amiens cathedral had been destroyed by the fighting in Northern France and in one of his poems said that it was necessary to 'burn Raphael', i.e. wipe away the Renaissance and, by implication, all art forms bequeathed by former generations. The poet and party propagandist Vladimir Mayakovsky was one of a number of voices raised in support of ending subsidies to the Bolshoi Theatre and abandoning its existing repertoire of opera and ballet. However, Bogdanov, and especially Lunacharsky who broke out in tears when he heard the Kremlin had been severely damaged in revolutionary fighting in October 1917 (also, fortunately, fake news), had never called for anything so drastic. They had, at, for example, the Capri party school, tried to wean their students away from previous culture but had, nonetheless, at the students' request, made cultural tours of Rome. In the crisis of 1920 the organization passed official motions defending the importance of past cultures – what it called the 'treasure house of culture' – and the importance of studying them, not least because of the part played by workers in, for example, constructing great buildings.

Defence of Proletkul't values was not sufficient to ward off the blow. In part, this is because there are solid grounds to think that Proletkul't's ideas were not the main problem. True, Lenin was exasperated by Proletkul't's experimental approach and he had little sympathy for its basic aim of creating a new proletarian culture. He was scathing that there could ever be such a thing as proletarian science or proletarian mathematics. For Lenin, science existed on its own basis which was mainly independent of class. He considered the idea that there was such a thing as 'proletarian' science as ridiculous. Like most of the intelligentsia, Lenin's aesthetic and personal life and cultural tastes were largely conventional. He did not like avant garde art of any sort and preferred figurative sculpture, painting and so on. Gorky, in his encomium for Lenin, said he once interrupted Lenin who was lost in rapture:

> Listening to Beethoven's sonatas played by Isai Dobrowein at the home of Y. P. Peshkova in Moscow one evening, Lenin remarked: "I know of nothing better than the Appassionata and could listen to it every day. What astonishing, superhuman music! It always makes me proud, perhaps naively so, to think that people can work such miracles!"

Revealingly, Gorky added that it also softened Lenin's political hardness:

> Wrinkling up his eyes, he smiled rather sadly, adding: "But I can't listen to music very often, it affects my nerves. I want to say sweet, silly things and pat the heads of people who, living in a filthy hell, can create such beauty. One can't pat anyone on the head nowadays, they might bite your hand off. They ought to be beaten on the head, beaten mercilessly, although ideally we are against doing any violence to people. Hm-what a hellishly difficult job!"[9]

From his custom of wearing a suit to his repulsion at the notion of sexual experimentation and free love, such as his fellow Bolshevik Alexandra Kollontai's advocacy of casual sex, his lifestyle was more petit-bourgeois than Bohemian. He loved chess, sulking when Bogdanov beat him in a game on Capri.[10] He read literary classics, loved realist writers such as Balzac and Gorky. His radical edge came in his critiques of the content of culture. He was especially sharp in attacking anything that he thought smelled of religion. This led him to give, for example, a somewhat simplified assessment of Tolstoy as a mystical and guilt-ridden representative of a fading class of landowners.

> On the one hand, we have the great artist, the genius who has not only drawn incomparable pictures of Russian life but has made first-class contributions to world literature. On the other hand we have the landlord obsessed with Christ. On the one hand, the remarkably powerful, forthright and sincere protest against social falsehood and hypocrisy; and on the other, the "Tolstoyan", i.e., the jaded, hysterical sniveller called the Russian intellectual, who publicly beats his breast and wails: "I am a bad wicked man, but I am practising moral self-perfection; I don't eat meat any more, I now eat rice cutlets." On the one hand, merciless criticism of capitalist exploitation, exposure of government outrages, the farcical courts and the state administration, and unmasking of the profound contradictions between the growth of wealth and achievements of civilisation and the growth of poverty, degradation and misery among the working masses. On the other, the crackpot preaching of submission, "resist not evil" with violence. On the one hand, the most sober realism, the tearing away of all and sundry masks; on the other, the preaching of one of the most odious things on earth, namely, religion, the striving to replace officially appointed priests by priests who will serve from moral conviction, i. e., to cultivate the most refined and, therefore, particularly disgusting clericalism.[11]

As a result Lenin's notion of 'cultural revolution' and of proletarian culture was very different from that of Bogdanov. When his close associate in the leadership, Nikolai Bukharin, tried to defend what he considered the exciting experimental approach of Proletkul't, Lenin immediately shut him down with simple formulae brooking little contention: '(1) proletarian culture=communism (2) it is carried out by the RCP [Russian Communist Party] (3) the proletarian class=RCP=Soviet power. We are all agreed on this aren't we?'[12] In one of his last articles, 'On Cooperation' he made it clear that he had no truck with Proletkul't's more fancy notions. Teaching basic literacy and numeracy and breaking the peasants of the habit of trading in 'the Asiatic manner' (presumably meaning by barter, haggling, exchange and on a small scale) and spreading knowledge of book-keeping and more 'modern' market aids were the necessary first step. Once again, the demands of productionism trumped socialist construction. Indeed, Lenin had been even more forthright in 1919 when the first party purges were being conducted. There had been a time for dreamers in the movement but that moment had passed. It was now time to apply practical knowledge and acquire practical skills. Quiet, modest, competent and hard-working individuals of any ideological persuasion who would work with the revolution were more valuable than poor-quality communists. Ironically, though in transformed circumstances, Lenin was echoing *Vekhi*'s call for the intelligentsia to abandon grand schemes and simply apply themselves to simple, valuable, practical, everyday tasks.

ii) Towards a cultural dictatorship 1920–22

However, as the Bukharin equation implied, the issues of party control and Soviet power also had an important role in Lenin's objections to Proletkul't. The assault on it came at the moment when, as the civil war wound down, old oppositions that emerged from within the left and the popular movement were being put down – movements like the Workers' Opposition; the Trade Union Opposition; the west Siberian and Tambov uprisings and, most heart-wrenching of all, the uprising in Kronstadt among sailors who had been the bedrock of Bolshevism in 1917 and wanted to return to original revolutionary principles of soviet rather than Communist Party power. Party discipline, rather than being relaxed as the white threat vanished, was being increased to give the centre greater leverage in imposing its own plans and principles. It is no coincidence that Proletkul't was having its wings clipped at the same time as the trade unions. There had been a now naïve-looking effort to suggest a separation of spheres. The party should lead on political control, the trade unions on economic control and Proletkul't on cultural revolution. The Lenin-led actions against both in 1920 and the crucial Tenth Party Congress in March 1921 banished such illusions for good and strengthened centralism in the party to complete the main foundations of dictatorship. In cultural terms, the new direction meant that, far from being a moment of cultural and ideological relaxation, the adoption of a more market-oriented economic path was accompanied by a major tightening of control and narrowing of the spectrum of the permissible. Before 1920, cultural issues were low priority in the face of economic collapse and white counter-revolution. As the external threats receded the business of building communism, albeit still via productionism, took centre stage. The fact that it was an attack on Proletkul't's independence rather than any inclination to futurism is born out by the fact that once it had been absorbed into the Ministry of Education and set up alongside other propaganda and educational organizations – like The Main Administration for Political Education (*Glavpolitprosvet* founded on 12 November 1920) and the Central Committee Department for Agitation and Propaganda (*Agitprop otdel'* April 1920) – it was allowed to continue but in a constrained way. Its experimental laboratory dimension was abandoned and it became a more conventional worker education operation teaching literacy and spreading cultural knowledge and skills – creative writing, dramatics, music – to working women and men who were drawn to them. There were still significant attempts to produce 'proletarian' music (exemplified by Arseny Avraamov's (1886–1944) Symphony for Factory Sirens of 1922), poetry (a poem produced collectively by 200 factory workers contributing a line or so each) and sports (including games without any scoring of points or goals). However, these had become eccentric side shows when they were undertaken in the early 1920s.

The year 1920/1 was a significant turning point in government and party-driven cultural policy. Although, as just mentioned, it was low priority, many key policies were introduced in the years of civil war. We have already mentioned schools but, and this intersected with education, one of the earliest decrees was the separation of church and state, the former having been deeply entwined in the schools. All major cultural assets were nationalized, including major collections such as the Russian Museum and Tret'iakov and Hermitage Galleries which were transferred from various jurisdictions, the Tret'iakov for example was under the administration of the city of Moscow, and transferred to direct state administration. Major works in private hands were also confiscated and added to the state collections. Major theatres like the Bolshoi already belonged to the state but all concert halls and commercial theatres were also taken under state authority as were all cinemas. For a while, access to performances and film showings was free. Since private trade was banned the cultural economy, from art sales to bookshops, more or less collapsed leaving the state as the only significant patron of the arts, with dire consequences for anyone without an alternative source of income and, therefore, survival. Private publishing, including not only book publishing but also remaining *tolstyi zhurnalyi*, and the daily press were also taken over or shut down, bit by bit. This caused bitter arguments within the Bolsheviks and their allies and opponents on the left who fought for the fundamental principle of an independent free press, as the Bolsheviks as a whole had done prior to October. When the first step in press control was taken, only two days into the revolution when the Second All-Russian Congress of Soviets passed a Decree on Suppression of Hostile Newspapers, Trotsky was quick to explain. Under bourgeois conditions a free press was a good thing, he argued, but under proletarian conditions it became a weapon in the hands of the counter-revolution. Press freedom for all was, he said, part of the party's minimum programme. It was now time to move on to the maximum programme. This was not the only sphere in which what was considered by almost everyone to be Bolshevik policy turned out only to be a 'minimum' which concealed a 'maximum' which, in crucial issues even including the most evocative ones of 'Bread', 'Peace', 'Land' and 'All Power to the Soviets', turned out to be masks concealing their opposites. Despite constitutional guarantees of not only press freedom but also sponsored access to publishing facilities, only the state and its sub-organs – trade unions, soviets, the Cheka and so on – had the right to publish. But even here an overarching censorship emerged to supervise all publishing including newspapers, official publications and literature and artistic production. The main censorship, which initially focused on the new megapublisher, Gosizdat (State Publisher), spread its wings and was accompanied by sister institutions dealing with fine art, theatre performances (a seat had to be reserved at all performances in case a censor should turn up) and, eventually, music in 1922.

One of the initial cultural interventions was a Decree on Monuments of spring 1918 (1 April) calling for the removal of tsarist symbols which lacked 'historical or cultural significance' and defining which historical figures were, henceforth, worthy of being memorialized in the upcoming Mayday celebrations. Lenin personally signed a final list of approved subjects on 2 August 1918. Naturally, the list was led by socialist luminaries Marx and Engels but also was fairly eclectic including a broad range of Russian revolutionaries of various schools from Lavrov to Plekhanov, not to mention Marx' great opponent, Bakunin. Andrei Rublev, Grigorii Skovoroda, Tolstoy, Dostoevsky, Lomonosov, Novikov and Vrubel' also made the cut. Non-Russians included Spartacus, Brutus, Robespierre, Gracchus Babeuf (a pioneer communist executed in Vendôme, France, in 1797), Saint-Simon, Robert Owen and, one of only three composers, Chopin. Incidentally, very quickly after the publication of the list, on 15 August, the Moscow Association of Sculptors distributed commissions to produce an assigned sculpture from the list to sixty-six of their number, another example of a state commission providing a little sustenance for hard-pressed *intelligenty,* even though the majority of the commissions were not completed.

Perhaps surprisingly two sets institutions, for the time being, avoided the worst of the intellectual carnage. They were the universities and the toughest of all survivors, the Academy of Sciences. They could not escape the ravages of economic collapse and shortage of research materials, including paper which was needed for communication, but, as institutions, the Bolsheviks remained 'hands off'. Several factors contributed to this outcome. First and foremost education was in the hands of Lunacharsky and others like Krupskaya who had a respect for learning per se. They were prepared to protect intellectual talent more or less irrespective of political opinion. Pavlov, for example, made anti-Bolshevik and anti-semitic comments but, for the conditions of the time, his work was bountifully supplied with necessary resources.[13] Associated with this, the practice began very early on of demonstrating the high quality of Soviet-era science to the outside world to counter the view, spread by their enemies, that Russia had been taken over by a bunch of Yahoos. Respect for learning was not the only factor and was not, itself, characteristic of all wings of the party, many of whom wanted to dismantle higher education and the Academy as bastions of elitism and privilege. For the time being such aims were not a priority as there was a vital civil war to be won and the issue was just not that important.

The period of revolutionary war was thus rather complex in its effects on the intelligentsia. Most of the organizations of civil society from newspapers to cultural patrons had been blown to the four winds but, where they could find a hidden niche, a wide variety of intellectual activities carried on. Associations like Berdyaev's 'Free

Academy of Spiritual Culture' continued meeting through 1919 and 1920. Poets and writers could write what they liked but it was hard to publish, so they recited in small groups. *Intelligenty* who were of use to the government fared much better. Scientists, engineers and economists were recruited to help lay the foundations of productionism by advising on the rebuilding of the Russian economy. Propaganda artists and writers flourished and created a wave of world-leading avant garde output. There is a deep irony in that the international political and social revolution, so promoted and so needed by the Communists to support their own 'wrong-way-round' revolution, failed to materialize, whereas Russians, notably Kandinsky, were pioneers of one of the most significant cultural/artistic revolutions of the twentieth century, the breakthrough into abstract art forms. The creative intelligentsia proved itself more capable of creating a world revolution than were its seemingly tough and streetwise new government. Perhaps because the attention of the authorities was elsewhere it was a period of wider toleration (by default rather than policy) of ideas and cultural schools than at any time in the Soviet era apart from the final years of perestroika. However, as the military struggle wound down and enemies had been put to flight, the attention of the revolutionary leaders began to turn elsewhere. The only partially completed job of capturing the commanding heights of culture was moving up the 'to-do' list.

Proletkul't autonomy was the first victim but not the last as cultural formations were increasingly targeted in the wider process of tightening political, social and cultural control as the economic loosening of the New Economic Policy emerged, piece by piece. Adopting NEP was a clear defeat and Lenin admitted as much.[14] Partial market relations and co-operative enterprises were permitted in order to re-balance the economy. Major industries and the levers of economic policy remained in state hands. One corollary of this was that, as a Marxist, Lenin understood that societies and their culture were shaped by the economic foundation of society, so making concessions to the market could, it was feared, open up cracks through which undesirables – commercial traders, shopkeepers, the petty-bourgeoisie in general – might wriggle back into Soviet society and begin to exert a cultural and ideological influence in opposition to the party. Economic easing meant greater political vigilance was needed to keep this from happening. It was thought at one time that the NEP era, the Soviet twenties in effect, was one of cultural breadth and toleration. Compared to what came after it was but, compared to the brief period of the revolutionary war, it was not. From 1920 onwards an ever more onerous policy of tightening political and cultural control was developing. In politics it saw the final dissolution of the remnants of the Socialist Revolutionary and Menshevik parties to achieve the absolute completion of the one party state. Measures at the Tenth Party Congress in March 1921 narrowed the already constricted boundaries of inner party freedom by banning factions within and condemning lobbies like the 'Workers' Opposition'. The big guns of the party were turning onto the realms of ideas and culture. The first barrages, in 1920–22, inflicted more heavy blows.

In line with its objectives the Soviet government had begun a process of proletarianization of universities during the civil war, evolving the *rabfaky* (Workers' Faculties) to provide crash courses for university entrance. The number of *rabfak* students began to rise, from 8,682 students in 1918 to 21,279 in 1922.[15] Many of them had come via the crash programmes and even without any qualifications as admissions criteria, along with tuition fees, had been abolished in 1918. The rising numbers were overwhelming all the universities and there was a great fear that academic standards would totally collapse. The conditions were chaotic and many professors were pushed into protests and even a wave of university strikes. This was the signal for the authorities to take a firmer grip on the institutions, which they did by enforcing a decree ending university autonomy in 1921. In many ways, it is quite extraordinary that they had survived longer than the autocracy, business, banking and even the Imperial army and navy, indicating that soft power can sometimes endure longer than hard power. According to the constitution for higher education approved by the Soviet government (*Sovnarkom*) on 2 September 1921, the role and functions of the Soviet university were defined thus:

1. The creation of specialists for all branches of the RSFSR (Russian Republic)
2. The preparation of scientific workers to serve in the scientific and scientific-technical and productive institutions of the Republic and in particular in higher education institutions themselves
3. The diffusion of knowledge among the broad worker and peasant masses whose interests should be in the forefront of all higher education institutions.[16]

Universities were becoming, first and foremost, engine rooms of productionism and were seen for their utility value in spreading higher skills required for economic and social development and contributing to all aspects of cultural revolution.

In an extraordinary consequence of the upheavals of the moment, one of the most remarkable, unfortunate and tragic moments in the history of the intelligentsia played itself out. The Cheka was charged with, along with other authorities, compiling a list of unwanted professors who were, from the party point of view, obstructing the objectives of cultural transformation and were deemed to be too immersed in 'counter-revolutionary' values to be reformed. In effect, a purge of senior professors was undertaken but where party purges led to lost jobs and responsibilities, the Cheka was ordered to supervise the expulsion from the country of the unwanted professors. The bulk of them were forced to take a ship from St Petersburg to Stettin in Germany (today Szczecin in Poland) while others were sent from Odessa to Istanbul or by train from Moscow to Riga in Latvia. Almost 300 were expelled usually with their wives and families. There is no simple criterion by which they were chosen as many more, of very similar views, were not included in the round-up. For example, several of the core authors of *Vekhi* and the suppressed *Iz glubiny* were included, namely Berdyaev, Frank and Bulgakov, who had made his way back to Moscow after being with the Whites in Crimea. Struve had left directly from Sebastopol' to Istanbul by choice. Perhaps surprisingly the editor of *Vekhi*, Mikhail Gershenzon, was not expelled. Quite a number of the expellees were philosophers with a religious or idealist orientation like V. Il'in, Karsavin, Lossky, Stepun, Sergei Trubetskoi, but the mystical anarchist, Vyacheslav Ivanov, was not on the list.[17] An official announcement in *Pravda*, the Communist Party newspaper on 31 August 1922, said that the 'most active counter-revolutionary elements of the professoriate, doctors, agronomists, writers are being exiled, some to Northern Russia, some abroad'. The list, the communique continued, 'contained hardly any names of highly significant scholars'. It made a point of emphasizing that 'Soviet power highly esteems those representatives of the old intelligentsia who, like the majority of specialists, are prepared to work loyally with the Soviet authorities' but would not tolerate any attempt at secret struggle against the worker-peasant state and in favour of restoration of the bourgeois-landowner regime.[18] Elsewhere, Trotsky described exile as suitable for those 'with whom we cannot make peace' because, he implied, of their ongoing intransigence.[19] It was at this time that the concept of the 'fellow traveller' (*poputchik* from the Russian for a travelling companion) began to gain traction. Official policy was to tolerate those who were not active opponents in the hope that they could be won over to actively support the construction of socialism. It was a major theme of cultural policy in the 1920s and even beyond.

Although many of those expelled were professors in major universities like Moscow, Petrograd, Kazan and Kiev, the number of university teachers was rising rapidly. Taking Moscow as benchmark the number of professors in the Physics and Mathematics faculty rose from 28 to 109, including the universities first female professor the distinguished palaeontologist and later Academician, M.A.Pavlova. Since those removed or exiled were mostly senior figures the average age of the professoriate fell as the numbers increased. In addition to those expelled many major luminaries of the pre-revolutionary Silver Age had left of their own accord. Rachmaninov left in 1917 to be followed by Prokofiev in 1918. In 1919 Vladimir Nabokov left but the greatest exodus came in 1920–22. Among those who left were Bunin, Merezhkovsky, Gippius, Bal'mont, Belyi, Ehrenburg, Kandinsky, Shaliapin, Tsvetaeva, Shklovsky, Chagall and Khodasevich, vastly enriching the cultural quality of the émigration. Significant clusters of émigrés were forming in Sofia, Prague, Belgrade, Berlin, Paris, New York, San Francisco and Harbin. They took the spirit of the old intelligentsia with them as their younger successors began to be moulded to modified values of practical utility, and positivity towards the Communist project of constructing socialism and, ultimately, transforming human nature.

iii) Cultural policy wars in the NEP era (1922–8) – Building a Soviet intelligentsia

It is not the case that the NEP era was one of cultural toleration. Soviet cultural policy shows successive narrowings of 'toleration' from the period of the revolutionary war, the tightening of control in 1920–22 and the gradual extension of party interference in the cultural sphere during NEP. There were no steps back in this process which ended with the cultural upheaval of 1928–32 which, in fact, was followed by a limited retreat.

By 1922 the traditional intelligentsia was in ruins and many luminaries had left, or been forced out of, Russia. The party had set up a range of supervisory institutions in the cultural sphere including censorship across the board, The Main Administration for Political Education (*Glavpolitprosvet*), the Commissariat of Enlightenment, i.e. the Ministry of Education which also had cultural responsibilities for museums, theatres and cinemas and the Agitation and Propaganda Department (*Agitpropotdel'*) of the Central Committee which held the ultimate authority in matters of ideology and became increasingly involved in cultural questions as the 1920s continued. The policies which evolved were formed through the interaction of multiple pressures and priorities. Ultimately, the goal of all policy was cultural revolution, the utopian transformation of humanity into a socialist mould with leading values of co-operation, collectivism, shared labour and freedom for all in a society in which coercion would no longer be necessary. That was, at best, a very distant prospect, at worst, completely unrealizable, but the construction of a 'new Soviet person' embodying the basic values of socialist commitment and collective achievement was beginning to be focused on. However, a second aspect was that it was still the case that there was no useful, agreed definition of cultural revolution and there was a multi-sided, often bitter, fight within the party and immediately around it over definitions and priorities. Cultural exchanges in the twenties inevitably became entangled in the well-known broader struggles between those holding clashing, incompatible views of how the revolution as a whole should be developed. It should be noted that part of cultural revolution involved transformation of everyday life but, since the present focus is on the intelligentsia this is largely beyond our concern, although it should be noted that it involved everyone having an element of the *intelligent* in their personality. This was in response to the Marxist idea that future communist society would overcome the division of labour in general and the split between mental and physical labour in particular. The basic foundation for this was literacy and campaigns to make the whole country literate began in the 1920s. Thirdly, the immediate issue was productionism, doing everything to develop national wealth in order to create the 'abundance of products' without which socialism and communism would be impossible. The cultural policy of productionism was already giving high priority to areas associated with production like science and engineering, plus attracting non-party specialists with technical knowledge into working in the Soviet economy. Economists were required as planners; teachers of all subjects, including literature and history, were needed in schools to develop 'conscious' individuals who understood the world around them; and committed evangelists had to spread the word of the goals and objectives of the party with a view to 'winning over' the country to the party's goals. In order to achieve these aims a group of party cultural entrepreneurs emerged who ran cultural associations (including the defanged Proletkul't), wrote propaganda, edited journals and ran the various censorship bureaucracies. These were the key parameters within which a new Soviet intelligentsia was emerging. In the short term the main focus was on mental labour in the cause of productionism but that was only a first step.

Such was the background of NEP culture. There was some toleration but less than before though more than came later because the general direction, including the twenties, was towards ever more extensive cultural control in the interests of promoting cultural revolution and of imposing a particular, as yet unclear, vision of what that meant.

Nonetheless, within the narrower parameters of control, a vibrant radical culture was able to thrive. It had, and still has, global significance for its originality, energy and commitment to revolution in a variety of definitions. The new energy embraced visual arts and literature but also new fields related to the job description of the post-1917 intelligentsia which embraced preparing a new way of life for all. This stimulated radical artists, architects and designers to imagine buildings in the new idiom and also practical objects of everyday use such as work clothes, communal reading rooms and even cups, plates bowls and other household objects including furniture. Creative artists believed they were being invited to shape a new, in some sense socialist, way of life.

It is not our purpose to chronicle the brilliant output of the Soviet 1920s but we can linger briefly over some of the high points and then turn to the underlying pressures which were narrowing the scope of what was acceptable to the authorities who, even by 1922, had full control over the cultural field, in that the state and its approved adjuncts, such as trade unions, were the sole funders of public art and controlled all the media – print, radio, cinema, galleries, places of performance and so on. In these conditions, including hangovers from pre-revolutionary traditions in which writers like Tolstoy and Gorky had mass readerships among literate workers and many peasants, literature and the arts developed mass audiences especially in the great metropolises of Soviet Russia – Kyiv, Petrograd (renamed Leningrad from 1924) and Moscow, the ancient capital which the Bolsheviks turned into their own capital on 12 March 1918. While this was done for supposedly practical reasons of security against invasion, it could not but evoke the view that, as in the original Muscovite period, Russia was turning in on itself and concentrating on its own problems and development in relative isolation. The west was no longer a model. Instead, Bolshevik Russia was immersed in the fantasy of a new Muscovite 'Third Rome'; that is, it would become the model for the west.

One impact of the changes was that literature and poetry began to lodge themselves in popular culture. Large numbers of novels, including world classics, circulated but there were also the beginnings of an unprecedented adoption of writers, and especially poets, as 'celebrities' and even icons. The greatest performers in this arena were the young, super-confident poets Vladimir Mayakovsky (1893–1930) and Sergei Yesenin (1895–1925). They were very different people and had very different styles and poetic concerns. It is tempting to see Mayakovsky as the poet of the emerging Soviet working class and Yesenin as the poet of the peasant ally. Mayakovsky had associated himself with the party from early on and wrote of the pride of a communist and of the mass power of the workers to build a new world. He, as we noted, also contributed directly to the propaganda apparatus with cartoon posters promoting clear party messages expressed in an artistic style which was a modern version of traditional woodcuts (*lubok*) and even of the stories of saints lives and biblical scenes depicted on the borders of icons. Yesenin was even younger, still in his twenties. His poetry built on the extensive populist tradition, evoking nostalgia for the Russian village and rural way of life which he portrayed in all its grimness and difficulties as well as its community and humanity. He deeply disliked cities and, after a tour, pronounced repulsion at the United States with its crassness and materialism. Both were very subjective but Mayakovsky's 'I' tended to be part of a mass where Yesenin was more sentimental and investigated feelings of love and sexual attraction, which were major elements in his own life, not least in him having four children by three different wives, plus a whirlwind romance and twelve-month marriage to the famed American dancer Isadora Duncan. Mayakovsky, too, was famous for his liaisons with women, especially the author and socialite Lily Brik (1891–1978), the 'It Girl' of Russia's roaring twenties. Mayakovsky and Yesenin were rock stars of 1920s culture who pioneered mass poetry readings which, in Mayakovsky's case, had begun before the war and included that most typical of all rock star accomplishments, a wild national tour in 1913 broken up by the authorities. Yesenin had another rock star hallmark, a devoted fan base of young women. The last of his sadly few years were also marked by increasingly riotous behaviour and drunkenness which, according to Mayakovsky, got him mentioned more in police ledgers than poetry magazines.[20] His behaviour and his poetry came to symbolize the wild elements of the spirit of the village and the *narod* and, as such, he was not just a reversion to populist themes but a destroyer of the romantic view of the notion of a 'platonic' peasant á la Tolstoy's Karataev, the fount of wisdom. Ironically, perhaps, Yesenin's final marriage in 1925 was to Sophia Andreevna Tolstaya, one of Tolstoy's granddaughters.

Yesenin and Mayakovsky appeared to be the crest of a wave of new, post-revolutionary mass culture. Of the two, Mayakovsky was the more avant garde. He was deeply imbued with futurism, a movement which the party held at arm's length because it rejected the culture of the past and associated itself exclusively with the new, with forward movement, speed, a new world. Much of this coincided with the communist vision but tended to lead to assertive independence which the party did not approve of. It also led to experimenting with verse forms. Mayakovsky wrote so-called concrete poems in which words and phrases were laid out on the page in patterns rather than conventional lines. However, he somewhat reined in his pre-1917 flirtation with futurism and his later work was not so experimental that it did not communicate widely and he remained an accepted, popular, iconic influence and symbol of Soviet culture throughout the Soviet era. Yesenin, on the other hand, used conventional verse forms and did not engage in formal or thematic experimentation but his whole life was performance of the wilder, more destructive, instincts of the *narod* and, as such it was already attracting criticism from the party. The final, one might almost say inevitable, piece of the drama was his tragic suicide in December 1925 in one of Leningrad's most select hotels, a final celebrity trope. He was given a lavish state funeral.

Very few cultural figures achieved the star status of the two poets and certainly no politician came close, although the cult of Lenin's personality created it posthumously for the ultimate icon of the revolution. Popular cultural heroes included the famous clowns Bim and Bom whose act began in 1891. They gained popular acclaim by satirizing the authorities in the early revolutionary years. One of their best-known jokes involved Bim appearing on stage with framed portraits of Trotsky and Lenin and being asked by Bom what he was planning on doing with them. 'I'll hang one, and put the other against the wall' was the reply. This was not the way to garner official approval. The frequently told story of them, their sad fate as the first cultural figures executed by the Cheka in 1920, has been told many times. Happily the story is not true. An incident at the Moscow Circus during the civil war, when Chekists in the audience objected to the act and intervened, even shooting in the air, has been the source of a classic *kliukva* (cranberry) – an old Russian term for false information about their country peddled by ill-informed foreigners. Neither clown was harmed and the main figure, Igor Radunsky (1872–1955) who was Bim to a series of other clowns who played Bom, continued to perform until the late 1940s. However,

> The Bim-Bom incident is often inaccurately reported in Western accounts with the book *KGB* (1990) by Christopher Andrew and Oleg Gordievsky describing Bim-Bom as an individual rather than a duo. Orlando Figes, in his *A People's Tragedy: A History of the Russian Revolution* (1997) repeats this mistake and then states that Bim-Bom was shot in the back, with several hundreds of people attending his funeral! Peter Julicher in his *"Enemies of the People" Under The Soviets* (2015) repeats the story about the shooting of the clown. Adam Ulam in his *The Bolsheviks: the intellectual and political history of the triumph of communism in Russia* (2009) states that whilst Bom escaped shooting, several of the audience were shot.[21]

This is a salutary lesson in how even the best can get caught in a minefield of inaccuracy since Russian history is so polluted by rumour and distorted information from both sides during the Cold War. However, the point for us is that, with Bim and Bom becoming popular cultural heroes, official cultural norms still had a long way to go to reach the hearts and minds of the people in the way that dissident role models, from Bim to Yesenin did.

Many of the other leading figures in Russian culture of the 1920s were held at arm's length by the authorities, even Gorky, by far the best-selling living author of the time, and one of the most genuinely supportive of the 1917 revolution. The problem was, he did not see the Bolsheviks as the legitimate arbiters of that revolution. He was prepared, however, to mute his criticisms, especially during the revolutionary war, because he did not want to give aid and comfort to the counter-revolutionaries. Other writers went further in their criticisms. One of the most extraordinary cases is that of Evgenii Zamiatin (1884–1937) who became, in a sense, one of the Soviet era's first dissidents. After his acute observations of life in Petrograd in *The Cave* he turned his burning insight into the essence of the Bolshevik project itself in *The Church of God* (1922). In only two pages he wrote a parable of a medieval monarch who built an amazing church 'to make the heavens blaze and the devils wilt'. However, its construction had been financed by murder, extortion and robbery and at its grand opening, when the world came to admire it, a great stench arose from under the foundations, from the bodies of the buried victims. Long before the rule of Stalin, Zamiatin was suggesting that Bolshevism was fatally undermined by its ruthless methods and belief that the ends justified the means. He also wrote a longer science fiction piece entitled *We* investigating the nature of a 'perfect' future human society. It was one of the first anti-Utopias which, according to some sources, influenced the iconic works *Brave New World* by Aldous Huxley and George Orwell's *1984*. It was another parable about the Bolshevik project. Zamiatin expressed deep scepticism about what it would be like to live in a society in which everything was supposedly for the best. Life would run along a path of perfection mapped out by the state and enforced by its Guardians. But for Zamiatin one precious feature would be missing, there would be no freedom. Human freedom, in Zamiatin's view, was the most essential of all. In an unfree society there would be no value to human acts. Life would be a pre-packaged commodity. Rawness of emotions, love, fear, pride in success, anguish at failure would not exist. Abolishing suffering would abolish humanity itself. Zamiatin was expressing a preference for the messiness of reality over the supposed perfection of the future, a notion which was entirely the opposite of Bolshevik aspiration and echoed Dostoevsky's objections to the possibility of a rationally organized society. Zamiatin was a classic *intelligent* by formation. He was the son of a priest who rejected Christianity early in life and joined the Bolsheviks for whom he fought against tsarism in the 1905 revolution. He was an engineer by profession and, during the world war, spent almost two years in England supervising the construction of a warship for the Russian navy being built in Newcastle-upon-Tyne.[22] His English experience is the basis of his novel *The Islanders*. He regretted missing the February revolution as he did not return to Petrograd until later in 1917. He accepted the October Revolution but was soon critical of the growing coerciveness of the Soviet state, hence his stories and parables about its negative characteristics. He was soon categorized as a bourgeois intellectual and despite his friendship with Gorky and other less critical writers he was considered an 'internal émigré' according to Trotsky. *We* was refused publication. It was smuggled abroad and published in English in 1924 and in Russian by an émigré publisher in Prague in 1927 with many copies finding their way into Soviet Russia, with consequences for Zamiatin considered below.

In many ways literature was the most contentious area but the early 1920s saw extraordinary creativity in many other fields of expression. Theatre, the performing arts and cinema attracted world attention because of the work of brilliant innovators. Theatre broke new ground in terms of elaboration of sets, design of costumes and breaking with classical naturalistic styles of performance appropriate to Chekov and his foreign contemporaries like Ibsen, Strindberg, Oscar Wilde. Theatre packaged together a range of artefacts beyond the play itself which fused the leading artistic schools of the time. Avant garde music, poetry, clothing design, posters, programmes and the sets themselves were works of art in their own right. Like many aspects of the 1920s, the origins lay in the pre-war years. Indeed, one of the most extraordinary of the avant garde productions opened, to a very hostile reception, in 1913 when the sensational and still highly controversial production of the opera *Victory over the Sun* brought together a constellation of futurist talents in a way no other art form could. It combined experimental music by Mikhail Matyushin (1861–1934), a 'nonsense' language called zaum invented by the poet and librettist Alexei Kruchenykh (1886–1968) and set design by Konstantin Malevich (1879–1935) whose first 'Black Square' adorned the stage. El Lissitzky (1890–1941) designed a poster for a Soviet era revival. Continuity of inspiration can be seen in a well-known post-revolutionary example of artistic fusion, Meyerhold's 1922 production of the Belgian farce *The Magnanimous Cuckold*, with a constructivist set by Lyubov Popova (1889–1924) which drew in the whole auditorium via film projections.

The seminal theatrical figure – impresario, playwright, director, critic – Vladimir Nemirovich-Danchenko (1858–1943) – had already linked up with Konstantin Stanislavsky (1863–1938) who pioneered a new way of acting and training actors through greater incorporation of physical gestures, body language, to expand the techniques and range of emotional expression. Together they had founded the Moscow

Art Theatre in 1898. Stanislavsky, in turn, became Meyerhold's patron and shortly before his death in 1938, stated Meyerhold (1874–1940) was his only successor.

The chain continued on into the emerging art of cinema, reminding us that even after 1917 the creative intelligentsia was still a fairly small family, many of whom were personally acquainted. The leading figure here, Sergei Eisenstein, was a great admirer of Meyerhold. Eisenstein is widely credited with first using the now-universal filmic technique of montage, a form of editing which creates meaning by juxtaposition of images. Eisenstein, like Meyerhold and Stanislavsky, accepted the Bolshevik revolution in its early years and he produced powerful propaganda films, most notably *The Battleship Potemkin* (1926) and *October* (1927). The latter incorporated the Bolshevik myth of the October revolution depicting wildly supportive crowds uniting behind the charismatic figure of Lenin. So powerful was it that the much exaggerated depiction of a supposed 'storming' of the Winter Palace has become embedded in many histories of October and footage and stills from the film are often presented as newsreel of the non-existent event. His filming of the toppling of the statue of Tsar Alexander III in the opening scene[23] is widely held to have influenced the wave of toppling statues in more recent times, notably those of the founder of the Cheka, Feliks Dzherzhinskii, in Liubianka Square in Moscow (23 August 1991), of Saddam Hussein in Baghdad (9 April 2003)[24] and of racist figures in the United States by Black Lives Matter (2020–21) and of slave-trader Edward Colston in Bristol (7 June 2020).[25] *The Battleship Potemkin* was initially supposed to be only an episode in an epic to commemorate the twentieth anniversary of the 1905 revolution but it became the whole film. Lenin had famously stated that, for communists, film was the most important of all the arts, by which he probably meant was the best propaganda medium on account of its realism and that it was, itself, a new medium which would, it was hoped, impress its mass audience as a new, revolutionary form of communication. There were many other cinematic innovators including the brilliant pioneer of newsreel, Dziga Vertov (1896–1954), who screened footage of the civil war under the brand name of *Kino glaz* (Cinema Eye) alluding to his view of the camera as an eye picking up unadorned reality.[26] Esfir Shub (1894–1959) was one of the first major women directors. Her 1927 anniversary film, *The End of the Romanov Dynasty*, was based entirely on compiled footage of the actual events and people depicted. In fact, she was deeply critical of Eisenstein's practice of using historical reconstruction in his celebrated film.[27]

However, the jewel in the artistic crown was painting and the visual arts. The two abstract schools of Suprematism and Constructivism dominated the early Soviet years. Its leading practitioners, Kasimir Malevich (1879–1935) and Vladimir Tatlin (1885–1953), were among the most influential artists of their day. Their paintings were largely based on geometric shapes. Like Kandinsky, Malevich had evolved from fully figurative painting through projection of recognizably human figures presented in a non-natural form, involving cylindrical shapes for Malevich, arriving at a completely non-figurative abstract style. He became famous for a series depicting a white square on a white background or a black square on a black background. Another famous Suprematist image was a propaganda poster urging support for the Reds in the revolutionary war, produced by El Lissitzky depicting a wedge of red, surrounded by white, driving from the upper left and penetrating an almost circle of white surrounded by black on the lower right of the poster with a few red, black and white splinter-like shapes scattered towards the edges. The tableau was completed by the words of the piece's title 'With the red wedge' on the left side and 'beat the whites' on the right. El Lissitzy, like many other artists, was keen to respond to the call for practical application of art in the lives of 'ordinary' people. Clearly this was linked to the traditional intelligentsia urge to serve the *narod*. Lissitzky, in addition to poster art, developed ideas about architecture and its application to everyday life. He was opposed to skyscrapers, considering them inhuman and impractical from the point of view of construction, heating, maintenance and so on, and preferred the idea of horizontal 'skyscrapers', that is long buildings parallel to the ground but raised above it on stilts. None was ever built but one of his designs, for a print shop for the journal *Ogonek*, did become reality in the early 1930s and, though it is in a damaged and altered state and not subjected to any heritage protection order, can still be seen at 17, Pervyi Samotechnyi Pereulok in Moscow.

Architecture was the point at which avant garde art met the revolution in many other cases. In particular, Constructivism, with its leading figure Vladimir Tatlin, saw the artistic task to be one of designing the material base for the socialist future. In Tatlin's case this ranged from the super-imaginative proposal for a monument and skyscraper headquarters for the Comintern (The Third Socialist International), which would have three interlocking structures one which revolved daily, one monthly and one annually, down to the furniture for village reading rooms and clothing for the new workers. The Comintern Tower, intended to rival and outdo the Eiffel Tower, was completely unconstructable at the time but it did demonstrate revolutionary aspirations and imagination. Many other projects of the time were of similar character, boldly revolutionary in architectural and political terms but largely unconstructable, not unlike the Bolshevik revolution itself. Someone who actually did get a number of avant garde buildings realized was Konstantin Melnikov, whose work included, in addition to the somewhat unromantic project of a bus garage, mentioned earlier, also built his own house, six workers' clubs, three more garages and the renovated Sukharev Market and temporary pavilions for Soviet exhibitions abroad. He also designed the first sarcophagus to display the preserved body of Lenin after his death in 1924 but the commission for the permanent granite structure which adorns Red Square today was in the hands of Alexei Shchusev. It was very appropriate that Melnikov should have designed the sarcophagus because, in an odd fit with the rising scientific materialism of communism, Melnikov linked many of his works to mysteries of death, resurrection and eternity which had more resonance with mystical tendencies of the Silver Age than the productionism of hard-faced commissars. The sarcophagus for Lenin, like the bed in Melnikov's house mentioned earlier, focused light through glass and crystal onto the visible face.[28] So far, unlike the buses and the occupants of Melnikov's house, Lenin has not enjoyed resurrection, though it is an eventuality which forms the foundation of many Soviet and post-Soviet era jokes and some famous slogans, notably Mayakovsky's 'Lenin lived! Lenin Lives! Lenin will Live Forever'.

Architecture is, of course, an important intersection between artistic creativity and practical skills from engineering to bricklaying, all of which contribute to the end product. Within the framework of productionism, engineers, managers, planners and those with many other practical and technical skills were vital and Soviet Russia was desperately short, not only of such people who were favourable to the Bolshevik project but to those with no matter what philosophy and outlook. As we have seen, from April 1918 Lenin had turned to the highly divisive policy of attracting skilled people in key fields of science, engineering, economics and more in order to rebuild Russia. The emigration of a sizeable proportion of the practical intelligentsia – engineers, professionals like lawyers and teachers, managers – had handicapped the efforts to rebuild Russia. There were some in the party who said, in effect, good riddance because they were ideological enemies and would be replaced by reliable supporters of socialism. In terms which emerged later in the Chinese revolution, the party was caught before the dilemma of 'Red' and 'Expert', the politically committed versus the technically competent. In time, communism could educate its own experts within the framework of accepted ideology but, given the acute shortage of the 'Red' element, even educating party educators was partly conducted by 'spetsy' (specialists) and, even later in the decade, a third of teachers of party ideology in the crucial *rabfaky* were not party members.[29]

There appeared to be a shortcut that might, for the time being, alleviate the desperate shortage of 'experts'. If qualified émigrés could be encouraged to return they could help out with reconstruction. As we noted earlier, the notion of coming to terms with the Bolsheviks was occurring to a few White officers in Kolchak's capital, Omsk in 1919.[30] A collection of essays entitled *Smena vekh* (*Changing Landmarks*) (1921) picked up Struve's theme from the original *Vekhi* but turned it upside down. It was, the *smenavekhovtsy* said, the moment for nationalists to reconcile with the left-wing Bolshevik state. There were a number of reasons. Clearly, the White cause was foundering by the end of 1919 but, for a nationalist, it was especially alienating to see that the Whites were increasingly dependent on foreigners for support as their own cause was met with indifference and hostility, while the Reds were much more successful at mobilizing the Russian population for their own defence. As former supporters of autocracy, the democratic deficit in Bolshevism did not worry them unduly. There was also a crucial piece of wishful thinking especially following the adoption of the New Economic Policy in 1921. The change of direction included the return of significant elements of the market. For the *smenavekhovtsy* this meant that the utopian dreams of the Bolsheviks were being replaced by hard-headed 'reality' leading to increasingly pragmatic decisions taking the new state along a path of 'normalization'. In other words, it would lose its socialist shell and become a pragmatic authoritarianism. The Soviet authorities, or at least some of them, saw this tendency could be nurtured and exploited to persuade like-minded nationalists to return from western Europe. There was also a push factor at work on the émigrés. Western European countries were themselves wracked by postwar crises of inflation and unemployment which made conditions very harsh for the incomers. In addition to language and cultural barriers the economies of the host countries could not sustain the influx. The major destinations – Prague, Belgrade, Sofia and, especially, Paris and Berlin – underwent severe economic cycles. Unemployable Russians drifted from one to the other as the cost of living fluctuated. Some found niches as writers, tutors and so on but many were unemployed and impoverished as any remnants of personal wealth were eroded by currency collapse. Some accounts claim that, for example, senior army officers were sleeping rough under bridges which crossed the Seine in Paris. A state-sponsored journal, *Nakanune* (*On the Eve*), was published jointly in Moscow and Berlin to demonstrate it was not only safe but also desirable for them to return. The combination of economic hardship, creeping normalization in Russia, feelings of isolation in the host communities and homesickness for their beloved Russia led to tens of thousands to do so.[31]

Such policies of class conciliation gave 1920s Russia an unusual degree of diversity. Former 'enemies', real and imagined, were being enrolled in the task of national reconstruction, initially the productionist prerequisite, before moving to the more specific task of transition to socialism and communism. Important tasks were undertaken by former Mensheviks, SRs, Liberals, Nationalists and even priests. The economic hub of the country, *Vesenkha* (The Supreme Council of the National Economy), was staffed by just such an eclectic range. One of the most extraordinary figures, who turned up daily in his priestly robes, was Father Pavel Florensky. In addition to his theological and religious expertise in icons, among other things, he was a keen scientist and polymath who was employed in *Vesenkha* to use his brilliant mathematical talent to help develop forms of planning for the economy.[32] Like many of those involved. Florensky was, in many respects, a classical pre-revolutionary intelligent, fiercely intellectual, deeply original in his philosophical and theological views, immensely absorbed in the science of nature from astronomy to botany and a highly original mathematician. The generic term 'fellow travellers' emerged at the time and the idea was, from the party perspective, that not all non-Bolsheviks were irreconcileably hostile. Bolshevik leaders were sufficiently confident in the truth of their ideas that they thought it was only a matter of time before their seductive power would win over anyone with an open mind. Lenin, in particular, based future strategy on successfully winning over what he recognized was an unprepared, unBolshevik mass, not only of peasants but of many workers, hence his prioritization of cultural revolution we encountered earlier to turn them from being 'unconscious' into 'conscious' constructors of the socialist future. In 1925, a journal that survived to the end of the Soviet era, *Novyi mir* (*New World*), was set up with a brief to engage in dialogue with fellow travellers. Incidentally, it also showed that the tradition of thick journals had also jumped over the revolutionary divide. A number of new, Soviet journals, reflecting different nuances of party and literary-artistic groups, echoed their pre-revolutionary predecessors though the Soviet journals were much thinner physically and carefully supervised politically by a censorship that was much more intrusive than that of the tsars.

iv.) Darkening horizons

The year 1925 was actually a rather inauspicious time for a journal like *Novyi mir* to appear. The spring and summer of class conciliation were turning to the autumn of class struggle. The skies were darkening as disputes around key questions became more ferocious. Dangerously, cultural issues got tied into the increasingly bitter battles within the party over who and what policies would succeed Lenin, who had died in January 1924. Debates deepened only months after his demise.

Despite having established a one-party state and introducing measures, like the Ban on Factions in 1921, to enhance control of the party by its higher echelons, it was riven with differences throughout the 1920s and, though on a lower intensity, even into the thirties and beyond. The main fault line related to strategy for the transition to socialism. There was no blueprint and Soviet Russia was the first state to engage in it, each step being unprecedented. In simplified terms the poles around which the fundamental debates occurred were about the pace of transition. Should it be fast or slow? Nikolai Bukharin (1888–1938) defended what he believed was the line chosen by Lenin of continuing NEP, not coercing the peasantry and using any support and expertise available including that of *spetsy* who were not socialist in outlook. His proposal that the revolution should move forward 'at the pace of a peasant pony' was not well received by militants who wanted something more exciting, more heroic. After all they had taken on the world during the revolutionary wars and had been victorious. Constituting the left of the party, with Trotsky as its key spokesman, the militants wanted a faster pace of change, especially in terms of building up industry to not only promote the economy but also to create more workers. In effect they wanted to construct the economic and social prerequisites that should have brought them to power in the first place, an absolutely extraordinary situation rooted in the pre-revolutionary debates between Bolsheviks, Mensheviks and Economists. Along with this they wanted a sharper class war and encouraged a more rapid 'proletarianization' in the party and state and in the upper echelons of society. Only a powerful proletariat and a weak peasantry would, they believed, create a stable platform for socialist construction.

Culture, far from being peripheral in this fight, was at its core. After all, cultural revolution, in its broad definition, was the process by which the revolution would lodge itself in the minds and hearts of the population. Institutions were easier to change but only 'winning over' the population and 'raising consciousness' was thought to create a firm foundation for the revolution in that it was not just about creating a strong proletariat, it also had to be a 'conscious' one. It was still a struggle with three main dimensions. The party wanted to exert greater control over intellectual life and culture in general, but had no blueprint on how to do it or what it might mean. Second, there was still no agreement on what principles and practices should be followed to best construct the socialist future once control had been achieved. Third, the disputes around the first two intertwined with internecine struggles within the cultural community for the hegemony of particular individuals or schools.

Following the 1921/2 initiatives to end university autonomy and expel the 300 or so *intelligenty* with their families, the party's next significant interventions came in debates, ostensibly about literature but with implications for culture in the broad sense. Counter-intuitively, perhaps, the intervention came about more because the party was sucked into disputes between artistic groups rather than by its own momentum. There was no shortage of often bitter fights within the creative intelligentsia. The mid-20s cultural scene contained an alphabet soup of acronyms and abbreviations of writers and artists organizations and journals. Most confusing of all was the proliferation of groups identifying as proletarian. In addition to the rump of Proletkul't, which soldiered on as an adult education and literacy provider rather than a laboratory for the preparation of the new culture, and its old foes in the proletarian education department of the Ministry of Enlightenment (which was Nadezhda Krupskaya's main institutional base as Commissar for Adult Education) several other groups had sprung up claiming to be the guardians of the one true faith. There was an association of proletarian artists (AKhRR The Association of Artists of Revolutionary Russia) and, what became the most militant and noisy, the All-Union Association of Proletarian Writers (hereafter VAPP from its Russian acronym). The party became concerned because it had, as we have noted, set up a delicate balancing act of eliminating what were considered incorrigibly bourgeois or otherwise counter-revolutionary individuals, groups and institutions but, given the absence of large numbers of Bolshevik intellectuals, tolerating a swathe of intellectuals, from poets to engineers, who, the party leaders thought, could be won over to the socialist and communist cause. The self-consciously 'left' VAPP was not happy with the compromise and threatened to turn the planned seduction of susceptible *intelligenty* into mass rape. Its journal, appropriately and militarily entitled *Na literaturnom postu* (*On Literary Guard*), screamed intolerance and radical advance from every issue. In their view, the party had been brave enough to eliminate the bourgeoisie from all of its other positions, why hesitate in the face of culture?

Why indeed? Cultural policy remained an anomaly. Ironically, the universities and the Academy of Sciences were the most resilient of Russia's pre-revolutionary institutions and survived longer than the levers of 'power' such as the High Command and the military, the judiciary, the police, the state itself not to mention banks, factory owners, the gentry, the aristocracy and so on. The twenties was also a golden age of the peasantry, which had, in essence, beaten off the Bolshevik assault during the revolutionary war and, unknowingly, awaited its terrible fate. But intelligentsia survival, for the moment, came from other sources. The Bolshevik leaders, though they would rarely admit it, included many *intelligenty* in the classic mode of educated 'servants of the people' including Lenin, with his populist intellectual substructure,[33] Trotsky the radical *litterateur* and polemicist, Kamenev the lawyer and so on. The Bolshevik project was itself an intelligentsia product with distinctively Russian characteristics. As a result the party leaders differed in many respects over culture but Lenin, Bukharin, Zinoviev, Kamenev and Trotsky were united over the policy of respecting fellow travellers. Lenin, who died in January 1924, kept to his view that there was no such thing as a purely proletarian culture and that, in the first instance, 'bourgeois' culture should be taught to the workers and peasants to raise their cultural level. To achieve this, specialists from non-working-class backgrounds were still essential in filling in for the small numbers of party intellectuals and in building up new cadres of cultural, scientific and managerial workers. Cultural revolution was, Lenin had insisted in one of his last articles, the essential next step in beginning the construction of socialism. Up to the last Lenin's position was one of using the full power of the 'proletarian' state to nurture 'bourgeois' culture in the masses. Perhaps unexpectedly since his interventions in the cultural field had been infrequent, Lenin's friend and wingman Grigorii Zinoviev joined the debate, supporting the idea that there was no single intelligentsia but an intelligentsia layer in every social class and sub-class which articulated the consciousness of that particular group. Bukharin, in a number of speeches and articles, energetically defended the fellow travellers and specialists as necessary and very welcome co-workers. Trotsky, more surprisingly as his positions usually coincided with the party left whereas Bukharin was the most gifted spokesperson of the party right, fully shared his rival's position on the issue. His book *Literature and Revolution* (1923), essentially a collection of essays on writers pointing out what is socialist and non-socialist about them from his own point of view, also ends with a paeon of praise to the massive expansion of the capabilities of every human being which the achievement of communism and abolition of repressive class forces will release, concluding with the striking assertion that: 'The average human type will rise to the heights of an Aristotle, a Goethe, or a Marx. And above this ridge new peaks will rise.'[34]

Party intervention came in two stages. In May 1924 the Press section of the Central Committee organized a debate intended to bring order to the chaotic struggles in the field of literature and, by implication, culture in general. The main battle was between supporters of the fellow-traveller line and those who wanted rapid, even immediate, transition to proletarian culture. The champions of each cause were A.K. Voronsky, editor of the journal *Krasnaia nov'* (*Red Virgin Soil*), and I. Vardin, editor of *Na literaturnom postu* (*On Literary Guard*). Voronsky (1884–1937) was formed in the classic intelligentsia mould, son of a priest, subversive seminary student and, from 1904, full-time Bolshevik activist and political prisoner with a special interest in establishing workers' newspapers. After 1917 he worked with Gorky on his various literary projects and, in 1921, took on the editorship of *Red Virgin Soil* which consciously followed the traditional model of a thick journal, though it had less pages and a narrower remit than its classic nineteenth-century predecessors. Vardin (1890–1941) followed a similar path but from the Georgian provinces, joining the party in 1906 becoming an energetic activist on the left wing of the party. Both of them had links with Trotsky. Voronsky's pitch was that there should not be just one line in art and literature. The social complexity of the era – especially the closeness of the workers to the peasantry and the need for the skills of non-proletarians – meant that, for the time being at least, all those who accepted the October Revolution (broadly defined as those who did not actively oppose it) were welcome. Vardin counter-argued that the policy of toleration had been in place since 1921 and, so far, no significant movement towards the party had been seen. Here he differed from Trotsky who had said it might take decades or longer to build a new culture. Instead, Vardin continued, hostile forces in the capitalist world had begun regrouping and it was necessary to strengthen ideological unity, not encourage half-hearted collaborators who did not share the goals of the party. The correct path, he said, was to establish his journal and the group which published it (RAPP – the Russian Association of Proletarian Writers) as the official party representatives in culture and charge them with supervision of the literary field including fellow travellers. A decisive intervention in favour of maintaining the status quo came from A.Ia. Iakovlev (1896–1939) who was an important Central Committee apparatchik (administrator) who had been involved in setting up the CC's cultural apparatus and had experience in *Glavpolitprosvet* (Main Political Education Department) and the Agitprop Department, the two main propaganda and political education organs of the party, as well as going on to work in key institutions like the Worker-Peasant Inspectorate and the Central Party Control Commission. Both sides claimed the mantle of Lenin but Iakovlev had actually been personally close to him and had been used as his mouthpiece to float Lenin's ideas, for example on Proletkul't, under his own name but with Lenin's approval, in order to test the waters without committing Lenin himself. He was in no doubt where Lenin stood on the issue. The On Guardists threatened to drive talent away from the party, not towards it and 'Comrade Lenin had always fought against this path and it is our duty not to distort the Leninist line.'[35] Vardin was not slow to dig out quotations from Lenin and accounts of eyewitnesses to testify to Lenin's constant urging to keep a close watch on the activities of the ever-cunning bourgeoisie. Only four months after Lenin's death he was already being used as a talisman in the increasingly bitter debates of the moment. In this case, Iakovlev got to draft the resolution agreed by the meeting which affirmed full support for the toleration of fellow travellers.

This did not even cause the On Guardists to pause for breath. Their belief that the revolution was under threat drove them forward. In February 1925, at the First All-Union Conference of what now called itself VAPP (All-Union Association of Proletarian Writers) continued its aggressive tone and posture and even turned on Trotsky, accusing him of being a Menshevik who underestimated the power and potential of the Russian working class. This was a shocking attack on someone to whom the proletarians had been close in many other policy fields but may have been a cowardly tactical move, as Trotsky's ship was sinking fast at this time. In June 1925 the Central Committee was constrained to produce a resolution, drafted by Bukharin this time, asserting the leading role of the party in the field of culture (further confirmation of a significant expansion of its claim to complete supervision of society), the goal of proletarian hegemony and the need, for the time being, to collaborate with non-proletarian groups. The resolution defended the line of toleration, though it left enough of a chink of light for the proletarians to claim victory as well. Who was correct? Actually neither. The long-term winner from the squabble was, unsurprisingly, the authority of the party. Even the 1924 resolution called for 'more systematic supervision' of party agents and agencies involved in 'belles-lettres'.[36] The Central Committee resolution was even more forthright charging itself with the task of 'weeding out anti-proletarian and anti-revolutionary elements', 'fighting against' new forms of bourgeois ideology and 'supervising literature as a whole'. Without doubt, all of the organizations were to defer to party authority. The ground for diversity was diminishing and the mechanisms to limit it further were in place.[37]

The juggernaut of party hegemony began to gain pace in the cultural area as in the key areas of political line and economic policy and structures. Fellow travellers began to feel more and more insecure. The next few years, far from building on the brilliance of the first years of the decade, many *intelligenty* began to fear that the horizons were darkening, a sure sign that storms were approaching. On 28 December 1925, in a Leningrad hotel room, Sergei Yesenin fulfilled his rock star lifestyle in the classic way with a tragically early death, even more sadly at his own hand. He had negotiated the rock singer nemesis of dying at twenty-seven but only just. He was thirty when he died. His action, and the motives behind it, aroused a controversy which still continues. His last years were marked by depression, drunkenness, brushes with the law and a loneliness which was not relieved by a relationship that produced a son in May 1924 and a final marriage to Sophia Tolstaya just three months before his suicide. Even though no one close to him at the time suggested it and he left a farewell poem written the previous day, unsurprisingly, in the rumour and conspiracy hot bed of late and post-Soviet Russia, fantasy theories of murder by the authorities gained traction based on the flimsiest of evidence. In reality, there are suggestions the authorities were worried about Yesenin's decline and wanted to help him through his troubles since he was widely regarded as the finest poet of the day. It would be a loss to Soviet culture were anything to happen to him.[38] He was given a secular memorial service in Leningrad and a state funeral in Moscow.

However, within two years the authorities were attacking his legacy and his works were being withdrawn from libraries. In a 1927 article Bukharin criticized him as a bad influence on young people because of the melancholy, dispiriting and discouraging tone of much of his poetry. There had been a wave of suicides following his death, particularly among his young female fans, one of whom killed herself at his grave in 1926. The episode became known as the *Yeseninshchina,* a verbal form derived from a name used in Russia to denote a period of disaster. Together with growing problems of drunkenness, promiscuity and violence, especially among the young, the party was deeply concerned that the morale of young workers was declining rather than rising as it should have been.[39]

By 1927, Bukharin was himself beginning to feel pressure. Efforts from right and left among party leaders to defend the fellow-traveller line had resulted in temporary respite at best. In 1927 Trotsky and his group were broken and he was expelled from the party. His cultural wingman Voronsky was also sacked from his editorship of *Red Virgin Soil.* Oddly, as the party left sank, the proletarian faction continued an apparently inexorable ascent. The rising tide of proletarian chauvinism, that is the belief that the workers could act independently and did not need support from other classes, extended beyond the literary field to reach technical *spetsy*. In 1928 a group of engineer specialists were put on trial for supposedly sabotaging the work of the coal mines in the city of Shakhty. They were in part being scapegoated for fatal accidents and production delays but the trial was, from our perspective, also an unmistakable signal of a change of policy towards *spetsy* in general.

Across the board non-party figures were being removed from important posts and even arrests had begun. Father Pavel Florensky, for example, was removed from *Vesenkha* and exiled to Nizhnyi Novgorod. However, in the relatively lenient atmosphere of the moment, after representations by Maria Andreeva, Gorky's wife, he was able to return to Moscow, but not his post, until his arrest in 1933, after which he was swallowed up by the gulag and executed in 1939. Another example of the, as yet, less vindictive times was the case of Evgenii Zamiatin. Although he was an Old Bolshevik he had, as noted above, been out of step with the growing dictatorial tendencies of the revolution. In September 1929 he resigned from the Writers' Union and in 1931 took the unprecedented step of writing to Stalin for permission to leave because he had no literary future in the Russia of that time. With Gorky's intervention, Zamiatin received a passport and left Russia, never to return.

Also in 1929, the tolerant and artistically pretentious Anatoly Lunacharsky was eased out of the key position of Commissar of Enlightenment/Education. In its various departments – including liquidation of illiteracy; fine arts; proletarian culture; supervision of cultural censorship by Glavlit and Glavrepertkom (Theatre Censorship Commission) – his ministry had held a protective umbrella over many of the artists and avant garde cultural tendencies of the time. His successor, Andrei Bubnov, opened the door to unrestrained proletarianization and a utilitarian, productionist agenda in which education was linked ever more closely with the immediate needs of the economy. Bubnov had been an active party militant since 1905/6 and had allied himself with the left from 1917 until around 1923 when he switched his allegiance to Stalin. By this time he was actively involved in the Central Committee Agitprop Department and then became head of political education in the army and editor of the army newspaper *Krasnaia Zvezda* (*Red Star*). He was in a completely different mould from that of the urbane, cosmopolitan litterateur Lunacharsky. But he was very much in the mould of the rising forces in culture and party. It is tempting to call this force Stalinist but that can hide crucial aspects and conjure up clichéd responses. It is as true to say that Stalin emerged in the image of the new forces as it is to say the new forces were in the image of Stalin. Despite supporting the chief protector of *spetsy*, Bukharin, and opposing Trotsky (who had, confusingly, combined a left line of high tempo revolutionary transition with support of *spetsy*), Stalin had been a consistent proletarian chauvinist. During the revolutionary war he had unsuccessfully resisted the help of a military specialist sent to assist him in his duties at the front line.[40] He maintained his criticism of specialists through the twenties, though he rarely spoke about the issue, nor did he say much about cultural life. Recent research has brought out his intellectual dimension more clearly than the cold war and Trotskyist clichés of a bureaucratic mediocrity.[41] The rise of Stalin highlighted the paradox that, having come to power through associating with the moderate line of NEP and opposing Trotsky, once in power a leftist line was unleashed across the board. The implications in terms of society, economy, foreign policy and politics have been well-rehearsed elsewhere[42] but for our domain of culture the story is illuminating. Proletarian cultural activists had been straining at the leash throughout the NEP period. Their strength had grown despite opposition from the highest party authorities. In 1928/9 a wave of unrestrained proletarianization swamped all cultural fields.

v.) Assault of the 'proletarians'

The change of direction has often been described as 'cultural revolution'.[43] To be precise, it was a new turn in an ongoing process of cultural revolution which had begun before the October revolution and continued throughout the Soviet period as the goals of winning over the fellow travellers, raising consciousness, creating a cultured workforce and building a wider skill and knowledge base to serve productionism, were pursued. The new phase was certainly distinctive but grew organically from the preceding decade or so. It represented a turn to 'the left' – that is towards a speedier and more energetic and direct pursuit of revolutionary goals without reliance on compromise with non-proletarian elements. In culture, it included an outburst of utopianism, a more active assault on religion, a break with fellow travellers, an attempt to control the curriculum of universities and the activities of the Academy of Sciences and a massive expansion of higher education. Like the other components of this radical turn – collectivization of agriculture and a raised tempo of industrial growth based on (itself utopian in many ways) planning – the drive was provided by 'voluntarism', the application of will and exhortation to achieve 'impossible' goals. The slogan that emerged around 1927 expressed this perfectly: 'There is no fortress the Bolsheviks cannot storm.' The phenomenon could appear in unlikely places. According to E.H. Carr a geologist, who repeatedly opposed an order to drill for oil where he knew there could not be any, was eventually told by a party official 'It is clear you are no Bolshevik!' For four years 'impossible' became the norm. By sheer strength of will and application of human physical effort, Soviet Russia would break the forces holding it back from its revolutionary destiny. The economic targets of the First Five-Year Plan were quickly found to be unattainable. The response was to increase them. Inevitable failure to reach them was greeted as an historic success and the plan was pulled after only four and a half years and declared to have 'by and large' fulfilled its objectives. The accompanying attack on the traditional peasant way of life through forced collectivization was equally rooted in fantasy and was also stopped, or at least slowed down prematurely. In both cases chaos had reigned, threatening the stability of the system itself, before the tempo was reduced. The same pattern was repeated in the cultural field. A massive wave of proletarianization swept all before it, until it too was halted from above because of the damage it was doing and replaced by a partial reversal of its main foundations.

It has frequently been pointed out, quite accurately, that these polices had immense human and material costs with millions of deaths, streams of exiles and a controversial famine that followed. What is less frequently mentioned is that all three were profound game changers. The principles on which the three dimensions of revolution were based were modified extensively during implementation but there was no reversion to the status quo ante. By 1932, Russia of the 1920s and major remnants of pre-revolutionary Russia had been ruthlessly swept away, with the peasantry in first place. After having achieved a quasi-golden age in the '20s, when their commune ruled in rural society, they held all the land and landowners had been liquidated as a group. By 1932 the peasants had become, or were about to become, collective farmers; an unprecedentedly large working class living in rapidly expanding cities was emerging fast; a new practically oriented, vocational, scientific, technical, managerial and educational/propagandist intelligentsia was becoming a key element in the new system. This 'new class' was also non-political, in that space for its traditional philosophical and political arguments had been replaced by a necessary loyalty – sometimes real, often simulated – to Stalin and the Communist Party. Religion was also effectively removed from Russian public life. Sleepy, agrarian, Orthodox, village-oriented traditional Russia had been smashed to smithereens and a Russia of cities, factories, science and reason was developing irresistibly. It was being done in the name of socialist construction but, according to the ideologists of the time, it was not yet socialism. That lay in the future. It was still very much within the productionist ethos. What's more, the main parameters which emerged in these tumultuous four years or so and the compromises arrived at, remained fundamental to the Soviet system until 1985. The Five-Year Plan and the economic system of control associated with it became the centrepieces of society and almost all other institutions orbited around them, including the party itself which adopted the roles of plan manager and booster. There was an official teleology – each plan would build on the one before and register a new step towards socialism – but over time the destination lost sharpness and the journey became everything. While we need to bear these wider perspectives in mind, our present task is to look at the ominous moment of transition and then look at the characteristics of the Soviet cultural settlement and the fate of the intelligentsia.

One of the most strikingly original, though frequently impractical, areas in which the new radical idealism was applied was architecture. Expanding cities needed to be built and, as the pressures of the moment dictated, they needed to fulfil the party's prescriptions for the future socialist way of life. Bourgeois individualism was set aside and buildings supposedly facilitating collective rather than individual values were needed. Already, in the 1920s, apartments in newly constructed blocks would not have much of a kitchen, if any at all. Instead, one kitchen provided for several apartments. In addition, each group of buildings was supposed to have a cafeteria (*stolovaia*) and shared laundry facilities. Ideally, there should also have been a crèche, as society 'freed' parents of childcare and relieved women of housework, shopping and food preparation. In practice such developments tended to be very unpopular because the specification was only implemented against a background of tight financing of projects. In other words, they were often an excuse for building cheaply. Even so, some residents preferred the interactions with neighbours in such communal apartments (*kommunal'ki*) to the relative isolation and possible loneliness of 'bourgeois' privacy. Variants of the *kommunal'ka* became standard in housing developments in the 1930s and during postwar reconstruction. Other architectural plans attempted to provide spaces for the development of socialism. Marx himself had talked about socialism abolishing the distinction between town and country and it had been incorporated in party policy, though it was hard to see exactly what it meant. One spectacular idea was the construction of cities on a linear rather than circular pattern. Cities would snake through the countryside only a couple of buildings wide, every one with a view out towards the countryside. A transport hub, an internal metro or tram system, would convey people and goods along the length of the city. There could also be extensions that crossed the main hub in a sort of enormous rack pattern. All the usual elements of a city, such as workplaces, residences, commercial enterprises, schools, hospitals and so on, would be incorporated in the linear pattern. The concept appears to have originated in late-nineteenth-century Spain and Madrid which had a suburb, named Ciudad Lineal (Linear City), constructed around 1900, following the ideas of the urban philosopher Arturo Soria who wanted to build a form of city to serve its inhabitants rather than the capitalist city which served its owners first. The Soviet architect Nikolai Miliutin saw the potential for using the model to develop the socialist city, in which social distinctions were minimized and work, education, public services and leisure were all brought into proximity with one another. No fully realized linear city was constructed but the concept was widely influential in the development of Stalingrad (now Volgograd) and Magnitogorsk, the two largest urban-industrial projects of the First Five-Year Plan period.[44] There was a variant in Magnitogorsk. Its German architect, Ernest May, proposed five-storey apartment blocks, equidistant from one another, to achieve socialist equality.

It is often overlooked that the First Five Year Plan period was one of significant collaboration on numerous industrial and other projects between the USSR and western countries. Ford collaborated extensively in the development of the 'Soviet Detroit'.[45] The British armaments company and battleship constructor Metro-Vickers contracted engineers to work on electrification projects, though that ended badly with them being put on trial for 'wrecking' in 1933 and deported. In architecture, many foreign architects joined competitions for new buildings. Le Corbusier designed two for Moscow. Walter Gropius put forward designs in competitions, the most significant being for a monumental Palace of Soviets. In the end, a Russian design was chosen for a massive skyscraper, which would have been the tallest in the world at the time, topped by a giant statue of Lenin. In the spirit of the moment the site for its construction was designated as the one on which the late-nineteenth-century Cathedral of Christ the Saviour stood. In 1931 it was dynamited out of existence, the site cleared and, in 1937, construction began, only to be halted by the war when the preliminary steel work was dismantled and incorporated into defensive works and bridges around the city. After the war, the reconstruction of Moscow and its famous 'Seven Sisters' skyscrapers was envisaged with the completed Palace of Soviets as the central point, overshadowing the Kremlin itself.[46] However, construction was never re-started and in 1958 the site became a giant open-air swimming pool. After the fall of the Soviet system the cathedral was rebuilt (1995–2000).

If the rebuilding of the cathedral announced unequivocally the return of the Orthodox church to the centre of Russian life, its destruction in 1931 underlined a new Bolshevik ferocity in the face of religion. For all that he got top marks in school for Religious Knowledge, Lenin had a deep loathing of it which, as we have seen, made him highly critical of those close to him who wanted to present socialism as the culmination of world religions. Early attacks on the church brought about its separation from the state, confiscated its land and buildings, excluded it from education and attempted to shame it into handing over sacred objects. The number of clergy killed during the revolutionary struggle is not known with any accuracy but was probably in the hundreds and, maybe, over a thousand but no solid evidence has been presented to back up the higher figure. But there was one important restraint on anti-religious activity. The party programme of 1919 emphasized that believers should not be coerced into abandoning their beliefs. To do so, it was said, would only serve to entrench their views more deeply. Bolshevik anti-religious policy was based on childishly simple principles. Religion was nothing but ignorance, irrationality, superstition and clerical deception for personal gain. It was the ideological wing of the ruling class, used to damp down opposition and rebellion with promises of happiness in the hereafter for those who were compliant. Science and reason were considered to be the antithesis of religion, which would wither as science and medicine progressed. In the atmosphere of NEP, a group in the Orthodox church, which split away from the main body, was known as the Living Church. It differed from the original version in accepting the revolution as an attempt to establish social justice in forms acceptable to Christianity. It received less hostile treatment from the authorities but barely caught on among the faithful. However, any thought of conciliation and restraint was cast aside during the upheaval of 1928–32. Up to that point, like other cultural fields, the party struggle for atheism was divided between 'moderates', led by the journalist Yemelian Yaroslavsky, and proletarian radicals. Yaroslavsky argued that experience had shown earlier, naïve views about religion had proven incorrect and it had proved to be a more complex phenomenon. The proletarian left simply saw that as an excuse for inaction and called for an increased tempo. In 1929 the organization changed its name from All-Union League of the Godless to the more aggressive sounding League of Militant Godless (*Soiuz Voinstviushchikh Bezbozhnikov*). The pace was ramped up and pressure on all religions increased, culminating in the dynamiting of the Christ the Saviour Cathedral. The same picture of chaos and resistance played out as in other spheres and the assault was reversed, though the religious field had one unusual feature. Yaroslavsky, who had sided with Stalin and the party centre throughout, remained in charge. The church was never entirely closed down but the number of churches fell from some 5,000 to 500 by 1941, after which a number of churches were re-opened.

It was in this short period that the full force of sovietization finally hit the universities and the Academy of Sciences. It was, of course, amazing that they had retained so much of their pre-revolutionary character for so long. The universities had been diluted by the forced intrusion of rapidly educated *rabfak* (Workers' Faculty) students which, the older professors continually complained, had driven down academic standards. But, despite the statute of 1921 restricting their autonomy, a great deal had survived. The Academy of Sciences was still largely self-governing in 1928. Partly, as we noted, this relative toleration was because the Bolshevik leadership dealing with them were themselves educated *intelligenty* with a respect for learning beyond the rigid confines of class and party ideology. The new attack originated with a different group with a more doctrinaire mindset. The proletarian leftists had no time for 'bourgeois survivals' of any kind and were prepared to sweep them away without any fear of the consequences. With universities it was not so much a reconfiguration as a massive expansion, and new shaping of what already existed. Perhaps counter-intuitively, the early Stalin years saw the largest expansion of higher education in human history. Capitalism itself was also re-constructing itself on a base of mental labour – scientific innovation; engineering know-how and a wide range of managerial skills. Modern production depended on it even more than on the skilled and unskilled manual labour of the first generations of the industrial revolution. The objective of productionism directed Soviet development down the same channel but, having the full weight of state and party behind it, the expansion of higher education greatly outstripped pre-Second World War capitalism. The following table encapsulates the changes in universities:

The total number of university students rose from 159,800 in 1927/8 to 469,800 in the academic year 1932/3, that is almost tripling from a high base in six years. The numbers in VTUZy increased fivefold in the same period (see Table 2). The latter had a higher proportion of students of working-class origin, reaching almost two-thirds by 1932, while universities were evenly split between working class and students of 'bourgeois' origin.[47] It is also clear from the figures that the expansion was driven by utilitarian – productionist imperatives of prioritizing science, technology and engineering though humanities, arts and social subjects (economics, geography)

Table 2 Enrollment in higher education 1927–32.

Total enrolment of students in higher education with working-class percentages 1927/8–1932/3		
	Total in all VUZy and VTUZy	Working class %
1927/8	159,800	25.4
1928/9	166,800	30.3
1929/30	191,100	35.2
1930/31	272,100	46.4
1931/2	394,000	51.4
1932/3	469,800	50.3

(Kneen, Peter 'Higher Education and Cultural Revolution in the USSR' SIPS Discussion Paper No. 5 Birmingham 1976.) A VUZ is a regular university; a VTUZ is a technical university

retained a strong foothold. Like many aspects of the second revolution of these years, university policy combined some admirable aspects – such as social diversity opening study to working-class people and uncovering practical, productive talents which would help build the wealth and military strength of the country – with ill-though-out and disruptive elements such as the tempo of change which created chaos here as it had in the other dimensions of the new revolution. If student numbers are tripled and quintupled where do the professors come from to teach them? The lecture rooms, the textbooks, the libraries, the laboratories and so on? Like other elements there was an air of pulling oneself out of the swamp by ones own bootstraps. And as with other areas the process was slowed down before too much damage was done and a slower phase of consolidation followed. But also, like other areas, it was a game-changer. The old tsarist university with its autonomy, community of scholars and focus on the highest academic standards had given way to universities being incorporated into the state planning system and tasked with producing target numbers of specified graduates with a bias towards production rather than pure scholarship for the expansion of human knowledge. And how did standards survive? Very badly, as vast numbers of inadequately educated graduates were pushed out of the educational sausage-machine. A probably apocryphal story encapsulates the problem. Supposedly, too few engineers were passing their exams and the question of what to do about it was put to Stalin. 'Lower the passmark!' was his instantaneous reply. If true, this might make Stalin a candidate for the role of patron saint of exam candidates but few people would want to entrust themselves to an aircraft designed by a substandard engineer. Poor quality was a besetting problem of Soviet industrial output throughout the period.

Party attention also turned to the Academy of Sciences and it, too, had its surviving autonomy seriously reduced and had its activities directed more towards production and science. Sergei Ol'denburg (1863–1934) was forced to resign as Permanent Secretary (effectively Chief Executive) of the Academy and was replaced by the historian of French socialism and party member Vyacheslav Vol'gin (1879–1962). Ol'denburg's survival in post from 1904 to 1929 is extraordinary. He was from the highest aristocratic levels of tsarist society, a member of the Kadet party leadership and, from 1912 a member of the State Council. He had, in the extraordinary circumstances of late tsarism, also been a revolutionary conspirator associated with Alexander Ulyanov whose younger brother, Lenin, he had also met in the 1880s. His academic field was orientalism specializing in India, in Sanskrit and in Buddhism. In other words he was a typical late-tsarist-era liberal academician. He owed his continuation to another encounter with Lenin during which he made a case for the Academy to contribute to Russia's recovery and to minimize interference to enable it to do so as efficiently as it could. While Vol'gin was a respectable scholar, the broader administration of the Academy was tied in more tightly to the party and state. Perhaps foolishly the Academy had voted against three communist candidates for membership in January 1929. The patience of the authorities was broken and shortly afterwards the Academy was purged. A total of 128 out of 960 full-time members and 520 out of 630 associates and part-time staff were dismissed. However, the Academy still retained some independence and prestige and was not, in any other way, 'proletarianized' in the crude ways creating chaos almost everywhere else.

If the Academy had held the radicals at arm's length, elsewhere the proletarians continued to be rampant into 1930. Collectivization was storming through the villages, industries were being willed out of the ground and proletarian norms were dominant in culture. Old Russian remnants – the peasantry; the church; the universities; the 'bourgeois' elements of the intelligentsia – had been flung into the grinder never to emerge in their former shape. Party rule had strengthened in all areas. The state was getting to grips with its unprecedentedly vast responsibilities. At the heart of all this the proletarian factions seemed to have conquered. But the situation was reversed in a single stroke. On 2 March 1930 readers of *Pravda* were confronted with a relatively short but extremely sharp article published in Stalin's name. Its ominous title was 'Dizzy with Success'. Who were the people in whom success had gone to their heads? None other than the militants unleashed two years earlier. The main focus of the article was on the collectivization drive. The militant detachments swarming over the country in response to the leadership's appeal to collectivize agriculture and to 'Eliminate Kulaks as a Class', as a key slogan put it, now had the leadership turn on them. It is not our present task to follow all the nuances and implications of this bombshell but its effects spread way beyond the countryside. Stalin's argument was that, in 'certain areas' or 'a number of places' (Turkmenistan was mentioned specifically), militants had got out of hand and – surprise of surprises – had actually *forced* peasants into collective farms. Of course, this was exactly what they had been expected to do and they had done so, not in 'certain areas' but practically everywhere. Ironically, given that the party had launched radicalization around the slogan that 'There is no Fortress the Bolsheviks Cannot Storm', the militants were accused of groundless overconfidence and the belief 'We can do anything'. They were also accused of needless provocation of the peasants. Interestingly, removing church bells was quoted as an example, phrases echoing among the militant godless as well showing the interconnectedness of these policy initiatives. The final denunciation of excesses applied not only to the countryside but across the board. Stalin denounced the leftists and re-asserted a middle position of neither lagging behind nor getting too far ahead:

> I say nothing of those 'revolutionaries' – save the mark! – who *begin* the work of organising artels by removing the bells from the churches. Just imagine! Removing the church bells – how r-r-revolutionary!
> How could there have arisen in our midst such blockheaded exercises in "socialisation," such ludicrous attempts to overleap oneself, ...
> They could have arisen only as a result of the blockheaded belief of a section of our Party: "We can achieve anything!", "There's nothing we can't do!"
> They could have arisen only because some of our comrades have become dizzy with success and for the moment have lost clearness of mind and sobriety of vision.
> To correct the line of our work in the sphere of collective-farm development, *we must put an end to these sentiments. That is now one of the immediate tasks of the Party.*
> The art of leadership is a serious matter. One must not lag behind the movement, because to do so is to lose contact with the masses. But neither must one run too far ahead, because to run too far ahead is to lose the masses and to isolate oneself. He who wants to lead a movement and, at the same time, keep in touch with the vast masses, must wage a fight on two fronts – against those who lag behind and against those who run too far ahead.[48]

The article overlooked the national crisis but allowed peasants everywhere to read it in such a way as to identify their area as one of those 'certain places'. Militants in the villages had their authority cut from beneath their feet and were often beaten up, even killed, by peasants who were now led to believe the militants had overstepped the mark and were responsible for the rural chaos. The timing of the article, in early March, was linked to the need to minimize the chaos to allow the spring sowing to take place. Disruption to that would cause national starvation and the collapse of the drive to industrialize. However, 'Dizzy with Success' was a watershed for all of the radical drives, including in culture. They did not immediately stop but they did slow down and the authority of the local campaign leaders evaporated quickly. In the countryside the rate of collectivization fell after March. It took until early 1932 for the industrial plan to be wound up and replaced by a more moderate speed of development. On 4 February 1931 Stalin had made another key intervention when, in a famous speech to industrial managers, he urged that the tempo of development should not be reduced, because the Soviet Union only had ten years to prepare its defences against renewed assault from traditional invaders.[49] On one hand, this was the last play in the tactic of facing failure by ramping up the 'tempo' of whatever process was failing. On the other, Bolshevik u-turns were often cloaked with assertions that the opposite was taking place, which is what happened here. Stalin's speech was a prelude to reducing the tempo.

Where did these broader developments leave the cultural proletarians? In a word, they ceased to be all-conquering and became vulnerable, like the militants in the village. Like their rural counterparts they had made many enemies by riding roughshod over those who disagreed with them, failing to show respect for any opponent, indeed, treating them with contempt. Now it was payback. The apparently all-conquering RAPP went into a final series of its interminable internal wranglings but far from achieving its aim of becoming the party's cultural leader of choice, on 21 April 1932, along with all other cultural and literary groups, it was disbanded to make way for the emerging Soviet Writers' Union and corresponding bodies for other cultural fields. Its leading figure, Leopold Averbakh (1903–37), lost all authority and was deserted by most of his supposed friends and allies. Gorky, true to his habit of defending people irrespective of the coincidence of their views with his own, protected him until his own illness and death in 1935–6, and the fall of another patron, the NKVD chief, Iagoda, left Averbakh completely isolated, opening the way for his arrest and execution in 1937. He was only thirty-four, a perfect example of the relative youth of many of the brash militants, whose moment of glory was going very sour indeed. The left turn of 1928–32 was not so much a triumphant victory but rather it was the end of the first phase of the assault on traditional culture and the intelligentsia. Its acolytes, like Averbakh, rapidly became victims. 'Proletarian' adventurism was reined in. The juggernaut of cultural aggression not only slowed down, it partly reversed. A new stability emerged which was to last almost until the end of the Soviet era.

8

Soviet intelligentsia, Soviet culture, Russian culture 1932–53

The cultural battlefield – 1932–91: Overview

As the intelligentsia, along with the rest of Soviet society, stumbled into the 1930s they entered into a rare, maybe unique, cultural bifurcation. Official party efforts to establish a new culture were beginning to have an effect but the old culture did not entirely die out. As the decade progressed and direct government control and repression began to build, culminating in the savage and unprecedented period of the Great Purge (1936–8/9), many members of the intelligentsia began to inhabit two cultural spheres. The party-sponsored public sphere was populated by those who, to a large degree, bought into the party's core values while a private sphere, difficult for the historian to access and difficult to assess in terms of extent, remained a repository for more traditional values which had to be largely concealed from official scrutiny. There were an infinite number of shades between the two. Research into memoirs, letters and so-called ego documents in general shows that official goals did elicit support especially among younger, urban dwellers. Often this was associated with the romantic dream, associated with productionism, of building a new world based on the needs and values of ordinary working-class people.[1] At the other extreme there were many, often older, citizens who rejected the official culture lock, stock and barrel. In the wider society religion was a touchstone for affiliation. Many people continued to identify with it and even some party officials resorted to it for family events like christening new born babies.

The official culture never achieved full legitimacy and universal acceptance, even though it had to be nominally acknowledged by almost everyone in order for them to thrive, as best they could, in often atrocious circumstances. As the decades of high Soviet influence rolled on the relationship of the public and private cultures changed in relation to one another. During the war years, aspects of Soviet socialist culture were modified by limited rapprochement with older 'anti-Soviet' values associated with religion, nationalism and a very mild 'thaw' in cultural links with the world of imperialism. After the war, by means of the 'Zhdanovshchina', attempts were made to re-instate Soviet values and resume the process of constructing socialism by means of productionism. Public culture reverted to its key purposes of being prescriptive – that is, depicting behaviours and attitudes appropriate to a revolutionary socialist society – and mobilizing – that is spreading those values among the population at all levels from party members themselves and through the intelligentsia and working people, raising their consciousness, converting them into what the authorities saw as liberated socialists, new people, models of the new humanity.

The denunciation of aspects of Stalin's governance by his successor Khrushchev in 1956 rocked the cultural system to its foundations. In order to signify his ideological rectitude as a communist despite the denunciation, Khrushchev engaged in a massive drive against religion and, despite another limited 'thaw', ideological pressure towards socialist cultural construction was maintained. However, it seems that less and less Russians and non-Russian Soviet citizens were listening. The suppressed private culture took on a new life of discussions in private homes, ever more bold circulation of unofficial copies of restricted or banned works (*samizdat'* – self-publishing) and a broader spectrum of officially sanctioned publications. By the time Brezhnev established his leadership the public culture was losing the battle and a resurgence of more traditional values, fuelled not least by inevitable contacts with the rest of the world through films, TV, scholarly exchanges, tourism, international exhibitions, stimulated a more sophisticated and less official culture. Brezhnev's death in 1982 followed shortly after the death of the last of the traditional ideologists, Mikhail Suslov (1902–82), Second Secretary of the party and in effect the chief party ideologist who had been running the country on behalf of the ailing Brezhnev. Suslov's death heralded the beginning of the end for Soviet ideology. In the perestroika period the old official culture was repudiated step-by-step by Gorbachev and, in a dramatic series of retreats in the final two years, the party abandoned the cornerstones of Marxist-Leninist ideology in favour of what Gorbachev called 'humane democratic socialism'. In an amazing, but overshadowed final gathering in July/August 1991, a few weeks before the ultimate collapse of the system it underpinned, the party declared itself open to all positive elements of human ideas and culture, not only failing to give special pre-eminence to the Marxist-Leninist tradition, but not even mentioning Marx or Lenin. Soviet history itself was being exposed to deep critical scrutiny. Astonishingly, the public culture of Soviet values had collapsed. The Leninist model of a revolution from above, followed by a period of 'winning over' the working people to the values of the new system and promoting productionism to create the prerequisites that should have, in Marx's view, preceded the seizure of power, had crashed in ruins. Some continued to believe, blaming Stalin for the disaster and proposing Trotsky or Bukharin as alternatives who could have created a better outcome. Mensheviks could only feel vindicated that the revolution was, as they had argued at the time, 'premature' in that the foundations on which socialism could be constructed were not in place and the whole edifice had been built on sand, with the inevitable outcome.

Whatever one's interpretation, it was clear that, against all the odds, the apparently vanquished values had survived better. A renewed private culture of traditional values emerged from the long tunnel through which it had been journeying. But it was not simply a reversion to the past. There were scars everywhere and the emerging post-Soviet culture was an unprecedented amalgam which included some hangovers from the Soviet system itself alongside new and updated elements of traditional culture. In the new Russia, tendencies towards a broad, western-style liberal democracy had no more traction than had been the case in 1917 and were defeated. A new authoritarianism presided over an initially chaotic but also, in many ways, vibrant civil society. An amalgam of unlimited private acquisition (the great winners in this enterprise being so-called oligarchs whose wealth appeared boundless), a re-animated Orthodox church (whose Patriarch somewhat inappropriately sported a Rolex watch), an economic boom driven by speculation and by oil and gas exports in a market of rising prices, an explosion of mass consumerism and western supermarkets, created a 'New Russia' and a tribe of 'New Russians'. Did the intelligentsia survive this transition? The question was asked in Russia itself. The answer is not clear. To respond we must trace these process from 1932 to the present in greater detail.

A 'great retreat'?

After the emergency brakes had been applied in 1931–2 yet more unthinkable processes began. As apparent leaders of the radical left like Averbakh were put under suspicion, then arrest and, in his case, eventual execution, their former victims re-emerged. A striking example was the rehabilitation of the eminent historian of the French revolutionary and Napoleonic era Evgenii Tarlé (1874–1955). Before the revolution Tarlé had established himself as a distinguished Marxist historian. By 1927 he had been inducted into the Academy of Sciences but from 1929 to 1931, like other historians, he fell under suspicion and was accused of belonging to an organization devoted to overthrowing the Soviet government. He was arrested and exiled to the remote Central Asian city of Almaty, capital of Kazakhstan. In 1934 he was allowed to return and in 1937 re-instated into the Academy, even though he still had critics but they were rendered powerless because Stalin admired his work.[2]

The unprecedented reverse flow affected many other areas. The more extreme experimental and avant garde forms of art as well as experimental forms of living to replace the family, for example, were modified, even abandoned, in favour of traditional family values; embellished neoclassical models in architecture rather than linear cities and towering monuments; neoclassical and realist rather than abstract artistic forms; poetry of the classical nineteenth-century kind and a reduction of tempo not only in the assault on religion but also in the process to achieve revolutionary transformation in general. There was also a new emphasis on Soviet patriotism as an updated form of nationalism. The chaotic but vibrant and stimulating conflicts of schools, cultural strategies and socio-political initiatives of the 1920s were being replaced by a new stability and new, relatively unchallengeable, orthodoxies. According to the émigré Russian historian Nicholas Timasheff, all this amounted to a 'great retreat' from socialism to a more traditional form of Russian statism and nationalism.[3] While acknowledging the changes, more recent analysts have tended to distance themselves from Timasheff's thesis, pointing out as a central criticism, that at no point did the party or Stalin suggest the pursuit of socialism was being abandoned.[4] More accurately, Terry Martin pointed out that the new measures represented a 'consolidation rather than repudiation' of socialist goals.[5] However, the situation to which Tarlé returned was very different from the one he left. The cultural 'free market' of the 1920s (restricted though it was even then) was being replaced by the incorporation of culture into the administrative-command, centrally planned model of society. Obviously 'culture' was not a commodity like coal and direct instructions on production could not be the same but, nonetheless, writers, artists, scientists, engineers and the full range of the intelligentsia were being incorporated into the Soviet system. In 1932 Stalin described writers (and by implication a wide range of intellectuals) as 'engineers of the soul'.[6] They were expected to step up in their specialized tasks of raising consciousness, without which the socialist project would fail, and also develop its prescriptive and mobilizing dimensions.

As we have already noted, cultural factions in the 1920s were competing to become the official voice of the party and establish their values as the foundations for socialist cultural construction. The dissolution of all those that remained in a decree of 23 April 1932, including RAPP, came as a great shock. The reason given was that the 'narrowness of RAPP' had 'obstructed the growth of proletarian literature' by 'excluding many writers sympathetic to socialist construction'.[7] It was also targeted at the avant garde, who were considered to be useless to the cause because they could not be understood by ordinary people. Ironically the date of the decree is that of Shakespeare's birthday and St George's Day as the party leadership set out to slay dragons of its own. The task of the creative intelligentsia was now to facilitate the emergence of proletarian writers and artists from factories, workshops and collective farms. The authorities were not going to judge between schools; they were going to take formal control and impose their own one-size-fits-all solution from above. The first step, which had begun already in the 1920s, was the extraordinary one of organizing the cultural professions into single nationwide unions for each cultural sector.

The result was that, at one level, the Soviet government took great care to nurture its intellectual capital. In a unique process all the major intellectual professions had their own associations (*soiuzy*). In addition to the Union of Writers, 1932 saw the establishment of Unions of Architects and Composers. Other fields underwent comparable but different and asynchronous restructuring. The radical phase of cultural revolution had impacted lawyers to the extent that it was proclaimed that law would die out and be replaced by administration and only in 1936 did the government reverse direction and set up a constitution, which would be the basis of Soviet legality, and revive a declining legal profession and stimulate law teaching and training in the moribund law faculties of Soviet universities.[8] Only in 1965 was a fully fledged Union of Soviet Cinematographers set up although the industry had been unified under the Soiuzkino conglomerate bureaucracy in 1932 and underwent a number of changes subsequently. Prior to that, film had been organized on a regional basis.[9] This was not unusual before and after the 1932 watershed. Soviet cultural policy encouraged smaller nationalities and ethnicities to develop their own national traditions and languages so that cultures could be 'national in form' as long as they were 'socialist in content'.[10] The major unions, such as the Union of Writers, spawned a network of associations at the level of the fifteen constituent republics of the USSR and even at that of certain Autonomous Regions, such was the concern to work through rather than against local tradition. The Union of Artists were all regional and local and only in 1957 was the patchwork of local unions of artists amalgamated into a single entity. It should also be noted that the sciences were also subject to some re-organization at this time. This focused especially on the Academy of Sciences to which we will return below.

The precise responsibilities of the unions varied but most of them became the unique portals through which individuals had to pass in order to access public life. Even then there were regulatory and censorship hurdles. Membership of an artistic union only allowed a person to attempt to produce a film, publish poetry or display a painting at an authorized exhibition. It did not guarantee acceptance. Nonetheless, the stronger unions did provide privileges for members. These might even include stipends which were independent of actual artistic output. There were also chains of 'Houses' (*Domy*) like the House of Writers, House of Architects, House of Cinema and so on, a tradition going back to pre-revolutionary private clubs, but taking on greater significance in the 1930s and after. The Houses might provide a decent meal in the canteen/restaurant, privileged access to goods in short supply including luxury foodstuffs like caviar and vodka. They were also points of access to imported professional magazines, films, books which were kept from the general public. The point of such access was to enable Soviet intellectuals to know their enemies and to keep up with technical and stylistic innovations around the world. Rewards were substantial for those who were enthusiasts for the regime's goals of prescription, mobilization and consciousness raising in the battle to win over doubters and promote the construction of socialism. It would be going too far to say they were bound by golden chains since, in the realm of shortages, very few enjoyed anything particularly 'golden', but some very substantial perks did begin to accrue. One of the most interesting developments was, as Moscow was being rebuilt in the neoclassical style, apartment buildings set aside for the exclusive housing of special categories of administrators and intellectuals. The House of Government Officials and the House of Writers became much sought-after desirable residences.[11] In 1934 work began on an even more fascinating development, the construction in the countryside outside Moscow, of a residential village for writers which was called Peredel'kino. Leading writers including Boris Pasternak, Kornei Chukovsky and Yevgeny Yevtushenko had homes there as, at present, does the controversial painter, architect and sculptor Zurab Tsereteli.[12]

There is no such thing as a free apartment. Privileges and perks came with the gilded chains. The restructuring of institutions promoted centralization of supervision and the emergence of a single aesthetic code – socialist realism. The Union of Writers was the template adapted for many of the others and the impact of its founding conference was felt across all creative fields. It was at this assembly that Stalin described writers as 'engineers of the soul', indicating he was still thinking in terms of creating a new consciousness, a new human nature. That new human came to be known in a widely used phrase as 'The New Soviet Person' who would embody socialist characteristics. The latter applied to everyone in Soviet society but the new aesthetic was primarily an issue for the creative intelligentsia. It was, so to speak, the set of rules by which they were to pursue their duty of being crucial assistants in the construction of the new Soviet personality. The dual aspects of raising consciousness – being prescriptive in terms of defining, demonstrating and describing what socialist society and people should be and, second, mobilizing the population to achieve it – remained as before.

The difference was that there were no more independent factions to compete over a variety of ways to attain these goals. The party had spoken.

Nonetheless, socialist realism was not totally inflexible and writers, artists, architects and others found ways of accommodating a variety of styles within the canon. There were a number of principles on which the new doctrine was based. The pre-eminent British authority[13] selected class (*klassovost'*), party (*partiinost'*) and populism (*narodnost'*).[14] In this formulation they distantly echo Uvarov's trinity of tsarist values from 1829 (autocracy, orthodoxy, nationality – also *narodnost'* in the original). The survival across over a century of the centrality of the term *narod* in Tsarist and Soviet contexts indicated broader cultural continuity, though the terms had different nuances for each. What the terms meant in 1934, when they were incorporated into the statutes of the Union of Writers and recommended to the other artistic unions, which were further behind in the process of organizing themselves, including artists, architects, composers, was that writing should be based on class principles, in particular showing the proletarian perspective on issues; that it should be informed by the authority of the party; and that it should be accessible to the ordinary person. It is defined as follows in the statutes accepted by the First Congress of the Union of Writers:

> Socialist realism, being the main method of Soviet fiction and literary criticism, requires from the artist a truthful, historically concrete depiction of reality in its revolutionary development. Moreover, the truthfulness and historical concreteness of the artistic depiction of reality should be combined with the task of ideological adjustment and education in the spirit of socialism.[15]

Great stress was put on the 'concrete historicality' of the depiction and of the historical movement forward towards the socialist and communist goal. In other words, it was the writer and artist's duty to show how the process of building socialism was rooted in real material, historical processes as depicted by Marx and was not simply a figment of the imagination. The process was also intended to defend fellow travellers from the earnest depredations of more fanatical party-oriented groups. The patron saint of the process was Maxim Gorky, who abandoned his self-imposed exile in Sorrento and returned definitively to live out the rest of his days in Moscow. He presided over the conference and defended a relatively tolerant approach. The conference was indeed a rather broad church. Only a small minority of its 2,000 delegates were party members and a third or more of those who addressed the conference were members of national minorities. Very few women took part but some had prominent roles. It is no coincidence that it was during Gorky's final illness and eventual death on 18 June 1936 that the situation deteriorated.

These official terms and definitions accepted at the congress were, unavoidably, broad and unspecific and it is no surprise that they were already being tightened up in January 1936 through the setting up of the State Committee for Artistic Affairs attached to the Council of People's Commissars. In particular, issue was taken with the continued existence of remnants of the abstract avant garde. The artists and writers involved were accused of 'formalism', namely prioritizing the form and style of a work over its content. Such approaches were considered to be showy, empty and self-indulgent and therefore useless to the proletarian cause. But these developments also showed how difficult it was to control such a diverse and individualistic kind of people as writers and artists. However, the overall situation in the Soviet Union was darkening rapidly. The first show trials had begun and the vortex of the Great Purge was beginning to spin and suck Russian life into a black hole.[16]

Intelligentsia life in the 1930s

How did the intelligentsia respond to the radically new circumstances? In a brilliant essay from the 1960s, the Ukrainian dissident writer Valentyn Moroz (1936–2019) described the state's efforts at control as the attempted construction of 'a giant refrigerator for the human mind'. The effect, he contended, was that:

> Fear was in the air, and, at a single thought of it, thinking became paralyzed. The goal was reached: people were afraid to think; the human brain stopped producing *independent* criteria and standards and considered it normal to receive them ready-made.[17]

Hard though it is to qualify comments by a great figure who was formed in those very times, it has to be noted that Moroz's description does not have room for himself. He, and, as we shall see, many others clearly had developed independent thinking even before the 'thaw' of 1956 (which is also hard to fit into his brilliant metaphor). In those years of the intellectual freezer there were areas which eluded being frozen. Intellectual life, especially for the creative categories, certainly became schizophrenic to an unprecedented degree. In any society, there is a tendency towards public role-play, entangling discourse and parameters of acceptable expression, which draws people away from the honest, direct expression of their ideas and values which often come out only in private circles. However, the gap between the publicly accepted and the private was, for most of those involved, almost pathological in Soviet times and, in the worst moments, dangerous. Some creatives were more at home in the public sphere and, for a variety of reasons, were prepared to assist with socialist construction, while many others found it completely alienating. For scientists, engineers, professionals and, in many cases, teachers, the burden was less heavy in that conducting experiments, building roads or aircraft, planning economic growth and production, or teaching French, while they shared the universal political pressures of the time, could simply get on with their jobs. They had no need to pay more than lip service to official ideology. For all categories of the intelligentsia (and much of society in general) these were, of course, treacherous times. However, they were not uniform times. Situations varied for different individuals, different places and different moments. The Stalin era and after, often thought of as simple and 'totalitarian' in terms of control, was, in reality, very complex.

At one level, that of the public and official spheres, the 1930s was a decade of explosive growth, unprecedented social and economic transformation from an agrarian to an industrial economy and a period of official heroes and massive official construction projects. Railway lines, enormous canals, giant dams to produce hydroelectricity, the Moscow Metro, super-cities built from scratch like Magnitogorsk and Novosibirsk were the focus illustrating the official line of impending breakthrough from preparatory productionism to fledgling socialism.

For the first time in its history the intelligentsia, in the developing Soviet sense, was becoming a vital pillar of society. A major reason for this was that, in a way which had barely been foreseen, modern societies were being built on mental rather than physical labour, on practical discoveries in science and engineering and on responding to ever-more complex challenges of management and logistics of ever-larger enterprises and infrastructure networks, from telephones to railways. Lurking in the shadowy background, as in all industrial societies, was the military and its needs. Complex arms races made scientific and technological advance a necessity for national survival. The challenge of logistics in supplying weapons, ammunition, food, accommodation to armies of millions required massive managerial and technical support.

We have seen that the development of economic possibilities and technical needs had driven the development of the intelligentsia in Russia. The interwar decades put unprecedented demands on the new intelligentsia and, undoubtedly, knowledge, skills and culture, the stocks-in-trade of the intelligentsia, underwent great advances in many areas in the Stalin years. The new knowledge requirement grew exponentially. The intellectual sinews needed for such an advance included architects to design factories, schools, universities, domestic accommodation, cultural facilities like sports stadia, cinemas and *Dom kultury* (Houses of Culture); electricians to develop power supplies and adapt them to factories, domestic and leisure purposes; geologists to seek out raw materials and identify sites for new construction including dams, railways and so on. New fields like aviation needed mathematics as well as brand new areas of practical engineering to support avionics and flight, not to mention the complexities of navigation and many other specialities from pilots to accident investigators. Bridge-building, roads, electricity transmission systems all made demands. In the military sphere weapons development – tanks, fighters, bombers – called on new skills and new types of bombs, shell, bullets and so on. Pure science underpinned much of this. The laws of physics governed flight, chemistry assisted in the construction of new substances from lighter materials for building aircraft, to new explosive compounds. Psychological and biological knowledge supported more efficient use of labour and laid out frameworks for human endurance in accomplishing extreme tasks and working in hostile environments. As well as practical scientific skills the new conditions demanded more medical personnel at all levels, lawyers to negotiate and adjudicate contracts of all kinds, humanities specialists to provide the teachers to produce the rounded, cultured, civilized New Soviet Person. Social analysts were few and far between, but developed later to investigate what was happening in the new, tumultuous, ever-moving society. Languages, history and literature faculties also expanded to meet cultural needs and the practical necessities of understanding processes within the country and in the wider world and helping to engage with other countries and other cultures. The list could go on forever but the point is that, even under Stalin – or one might say especially under Stalin – education was a crucial necessity for Soviet economic and social development and the ever-vital need to defend the nation's complicated and extensive borders. Practically all of these needs were met from within. Traditionally, from the time of Muscovy, as we have noted many times, foreigners were encouraged to come to Russia to fill in its gaps in knowledge and expertise. The early thirties were no different. Western engineers and capitalist companies were recruited to build car factories and assist in other projects. Later, during the war, Lend-Lease made an important contribution to getting the Soviet Army mobile on American jeeps and trucks, supplying communications devices such as radios plus some combat aircraft and other weapons. But as in peacetime, most of the heavy lifting in innovation and production was done by Russia itself with T-34 and KV tanks, Katiusha anti-tank rockets, fighter and bomber aircraft and so on which were developed through the 1930s. The vast majority of this innovation was the result of uncovering human potential within the USSR itself. At no time in its past had its human knowledge and skill base expanded as rapidly as it did in the late 1920s and 1930s.

One way to get the measure of this is to look at the figures for numbers of schools, pupils, higher education institutions and students. If there were 159,800 higher education students in 1927/8 and 469,800 by 1932/3, ten years later there were about 30 percent more at 619,000 compared to 112,000 in 1913/14. Many of these were at technical and vocational colleges specializing in engineers and constructors of various kinds. The number of schools (and, of course, teacher-training institutions) also increased massively. In 1914/15 there were 105,524 schools and 7,896,249 students. Corresponding figures for 1930/31 were 152,813 with 17,614,537 pupils and in 1938/9, 171,579 schools with nearly twice as many pupils at 31,517,375. Of these, 635,591 in 1914/15 and 9,028,156 in 1938/9 were in secondary schools. It should also be noted that the complexity of this growth is even greater since education was provided as much as possible in the native languages of the Soviet Union's many nationalities. In 1943 textbooks, books and newspapers were published in 150 languages.[18]

The emergence of a mass education system also brought an end to a number of the stopgap practices of the 1920s. *Rabfaky* were closed as there was no need for special measures such as accelerated promotion for those of working class or peasant origin (*vydvizhenie*), now education was universal and quotas for working class and peasant entrants to higher education were dropped. This had the effect of starting a system whereby children of administrators took up 43 percent of higher education places and the working class fell back to 32 percent and the peasantry rose to 23 percent.[19] The system was now producing its own experts and the need for *spetsy* was declining fast. The leftist, anti-specialist policies of the late 1920s (often known as *spetseedstvo* – eating specialists) were no longer necessary and the privileges of specialists were replaced by differential salaries between various professions and specializations.

It is hard to disagree with the conclusions of Moshe Lewin that the mass processes of education and associated exponential expansion of the administrative/command planning bureaucracy were beyond the party's control. A number of official enquiries at the time into a variety of ministries came up with similar conclusions. Chaos and disorganization were everywhere. Bullying by local and regional bosses kept the system going. Lewin points out that

> A leading jurist, seemed quite astonished by the discovery of what every official already knew; that government departments were engaged in fierce in-fighting, a real "class warfare" in which, he commented, the parties behaved like enemies and competitors. But he could only sigh. … … had he said more, he would have been open to accusations of counter-revolution. The leadership clearly did not understand what was happening.[20]

It was a different story at the apex of the research and educational pyramid. Despite the encroachments of the party and some crude but unsuccessful attempts to 'proletarianize' it, the Academy of Sciences maintained more independence than any other surviving pre-revolutionary institution, though it was undergoing reforms. In 1934, in order to bring it closer to the planning apparatus and to make it easier for the government to supervise, many of its departments were moved from Leningrad to the capital. It was expanded in areas deemed important to the productionist agenda. Science and technology, with a slant towards uncovering the Soviet Union's exploitable resources, was a main concern. Mathematics became more important than ever and maintained and even extended Russia's lead over the rest of the world. It was emphasized not so much for its own sake, but as the vital underpinning of physics and engineering as well as the developing science of cybernetics. In the mid-1930s a technical science (*tekhnicheskaia nauka*) division was set up so that by 1938 the Academy sections comprised: Physical-mathematical; Technical; Chemical; Biological; Geological and Geographic Sciences; Economics and Law; History and Philosophy; and Literature and Languages. It was also setting up branches around the country in the union republics and major regions of the Russian federation.[21] It also played a major role in shaping the education system at all levels including universities and teacher training as well as pioneering 'permanent education', or lifelong learning as it is known today.[22]

Despite attempts to increase party control the Academy retained a degree of independence, not least because the party had few major scientists and intellectuals in its ranks other than those attached to the Academy, universities and creative and professional unions. The vast majority of such sympathizers tended to be fellow travellers, often with a populist streak, rather than full-on Marxist believers. Despite being essential to help the government fulfil its productionist agenda. The Academy also played a key role in enhancing the defence capability of the USSR and in putting its industries on a war footing as the crisis approached. This meant there was a degree of toleration, even in the late 1930s, which allowed the Academy to follow its own instincts in its professional areas which belied the more extreme interpretations of the totalitarian nature of Soviet society at this time. The Academy was something of a shelter, though by no means a complete one, against the ravages of repression. On the basis laid down in the 1930s, the Academy became a partially independent institution which looked to the continuance of the great nineteenth-century tradition of Russian science and scholarship rather than to dialectical materialism for its inspiration.[23]

It repaid the state for its massive investments with an extremely impressive set of achievements including nine Nobel Prizes in the Soviet era. Leading academicians became household names in the Soviet Union and had formidable reputations in the outside world, though the names of those who worked on secret defence projects were not known until later. Nonetheless, in the later Soviet decades there were massive achievements. Leading figures included I.M. Vinogradov (1891–1983) and many of his students in Mathematics. Mstislav Keldysh (1911–78) and Mikhail Lavrent'ev (1900–80) pioneered aspects of maths and Lev Kantorovich (1912–86) received a Nobel Prize for mathematical economics. S.A. Lebedev (1902–74) and his associates produced the first early Soviet computers around 1950. Astronomy and astrophysics were a continuing strength and V.A. Ambartsumian (1908–86) was an inspirational figure in the area and the fact his career began at the Pulkovo Observatory symbolized the continuity of pre- and post-revolutionary traditions in the Academy. Igor Tamm (1895–1971) and Andrei Sakharov (1921–89) laid the foundations for thermonuclear operations under the leadership of Igor Kurchatov (1903–60). S.I. Vavilov (1891–1951) became well known for research on bioluminescence and radiation as did his brother N.I. Vavilov (1887–1943) for establishing basic principles of crop rotation and genetics which, eventually, survived the assault of Trofim Lysenko (1898–1976) who, against all orthodoxy, maintained that characteristics acquired by an organism in one generation could be passed on through the genes, a heresy which attracted Stalin and Khrushchev because it suggested that hybrid crops could provide a quick expansion of output with little input and that, for humans, socialist-inspired 'improvements' in the psyche could also perhaps be embedded in genes. Followers of Pavlov made advances in the study of brain physiology and emotions. V.I. Vernadsky (1863–1945) continued his work in the field of geochemistry and the biosphere. In 1917 he had been involved in, and became founding president of, the Ukrainian Academy of Sciences until 1921. He continued to work almost until his death, at which time he was researching nuclear power and had located vast uranium reserves in the country. This reminds us that many of the most important discoveries came in the sphere of what one might call the military-industrial complex. Aviation breakthroughs were made by S.V. Iliushin (1894–1977), A.V. Iakovlev (1906–89) and A.N. Tupolev (1888–1972) who developed jet aircraft and whose names were given to aviation construction enterprises. The main inspiration for Soviet rocketry and space vehicles was S.P. Korolev (1907–66) who remained anonymous for security reasons and was known only as 'The Chief Designer' until his name was published in his obituaries. There were many others. But what is clear is that the Academy was continuing in the centre of Russian cultural and intellectual life and that the nation's skill and knowledge range expanded rapidly throughout the period. The list also shows continuity between tsarist and Soviet times, a feature embodied in the appearance of a number of academicians such as Vernadsky and Otto Shmidt, whose long beards made them look every inch the successors of their mid-nineteenth-century predecessors. Like many of them the academicians were motivated by a combination of love of their subject, personal and careerist ambition and a desire/necessity to serve the Russian people, or at least the Russian Soviet state. Finally, it is remarkable how male-dominated the academy remained. Very few women broke through into the scientific élite in the Soviet era.[24]

Like the Academy itself, the Soviet public sphere in the 1930s, despite its serious constrictions and eventual brutal repressions, retained an unlikely breadth and dynamism. Parades and official ceremonies for key holidays – notably May Day and 7 November (October Revolution) – reflected the powerful official myth of a country progressing on the road to the construction of a workers' state and society. For the first time a film, *Chapaev*, depicting a maverick guerrilla commander in the civil war being patiently moulded into more effective shape by a quiet spoken, pipe-smoking political commissar, succeeded in being massively popular and putting across the party's values. It was a microcosm of Stalin's tutelage of unruly Russia. Other popular films included spectacles, inspired by the chorus line and dance movies of Busby Berkeley in Hollywood, celebrating a happy, carefree country advancing smoothly to socialism. Official celebrities were promoted. Alexander Stakhanov was feted for his norm-busting workrate in his coal mine. Linking to pre-revolutionary prototypes flyers and explorers became national heroes.

The two came together in one of the great exploits of the decade, the exploration of the frozen north and the Arctic. Heroes of this enterprise included academician Otto Shmidt (1891–1956) who had been a dedicated communist and member of the Soviet cultural bureaucracy since the civil war era and had been chief editor of *Gosizdat*, the State Publishing House. He was, following nineteenth century precedent, a scientific polymath with expertise in mathematics, geophysics and astrophysics. This last led him to a controversial theory of cosmogenesis (star birth) of the planets as a result of the close approach of another star to the sun. His polymathic status as well as his political convictions led to him being editor of *The Great Soviet Encyclopedia* from its origin in 1924 until 1941, an enterprise not nominally linked to, but echoing, Bogdanov's plan for a proletarian encyclopedia, interpreting knowledge from a working-class, Marxist standpoint. In the late 1920s, Shmidt became a keen Arctic explorer and accomplished the first non-stop transit of the North-East Passage in 1932, even though his vessel, the ice-breaker *Sibiryakov*, lost its propellor in the Bering Strait and had to complete the voyage under sail. Earlier Shmidt had been put in charge of operations to open up the Arctic frontier of the USSR to commercial traffic. He became world famous not least because of his involvement in spectacular Arctic rescues on two occasions. On the first in 1933, his research ship the SS *Cheliushkin*, with a hundred people on board including women and children, became trapped in the sea ice and had to be evacuated as it was crushed and sank. By constructing shelters, conserving the food supplies and building a crude runway, almost all involved returned safely in a series of flights by various aircraft. On the second occasion, in 1937, he was involved in rescuing scientists from a research base in the Artic which found itself on a melting ice floe which had broken away from the main mass of Arctic ice. He was awarded many prizes including three Orders of Lenin, two Red Banners of Labour and a Red Star for his work in helping evacuate the Academy in the early stages of the war. However, he was removed from other key posts at the same time, possibly because of his German predecessors. He had become, and remains, a major celebrity of the 1930s and he was, in the words of one account, the subject of many newspaper articles and cinema newsreels and girls' hung pictures cut from magazines in their rooms.[25]

Cultural and intellectual continuity is detectable in a number of ways in considering the scientific heroes of the 1930s. The co-ordinator of the 1937 rescue operation was the pioneer aviator Nikolai Kamanin (1902–82). The boat had sunk in February. No help was available from American Arctic resources since their flights had been grounded after a series of accidents. Initial rescue attempts had failed and, in March, Kamanin was called in to lead a group of seven rescue planes. Between 2 and 13 April everyone was evacuated and Kamanin returned on the last flight with the last ship's officer and eight sled dogs. The following day he and six other pilots became the country's first recipients of the order of Heroes of the Soviet Union and were feted around the world. In the USSR they, like other role models of the time, were seen as forerunners of the New Soviet Person, showing characteristics of courage, self-sacrifice, service, skill, intelligence and loyalty to country and party.[26] Kamanin went on to show the same qualities during the war, in which his son enlisted at age fourteen as a fighter pilot and survived the war only to die of meningitis in 1947. Kamanin became a key member of the space progamme in the 1950s and was in charge of cosmonaut training. Another link between the aviators of the thirties and space was the development of high altitude balloons which explored the outer reaches of the earth's atmosphere. Those involved also became national heroes and role models. The two programmes were also linked by tragedy. One of the first high altitude flights reached 22,500 metres but ended in tragedy when the balloon lost buoyancy through lingering too long at the apex of its flight, resulting in the gases cooling and the balloon and gondola crashed to the ground. The three victims, including the initiator of the programme Pavel Fedoseenko (1898–1934), were hailed as heroes and given a ceremonial joint burial in the Kremlin Wall, an event not repeated until the 1971 Soiuz 11 tragedy when three cosmonauts were similarly praised and buried after their space capsule depressurized on re-entry (29 June 1971).

Perhaps the only area to match science and exploration in the 1930s in terms of widespread prestige was literature. It is, perhaps, the best-known and most studied area of 1930s Soviet culture and it is not necessary to rehearse the full story.[26] Instead, the focus is on aspects of literature and visual cultures which are relevant to our theme. It was an area in which the party continued to have ongoing problems in that even those writers deemed relatively sympathetic were very critical of their situation and the restraints on freedom. The party had very few writers of quality on whom it could call. Literature was still an important area and many writers from the party enthusiasts to out-and-out sceptics remained prominent. We will look briefly at a sample from a variety of categories.

In many respects Demian Bednyi (1883–1945), peasant by background and upbringing, party enthusiast and self-taught poet, was an ideal 'Soviet writer', but, despite that, his career showed that unwavering support for the party and for Stalin was not enough to keep a writer out of trouble. In the literary sphere Stalin's preferences were particularly marked and he criticized Bednyi on the perhaps surprising grounds that he was too disrespectful of Russia's Christian and tsarist past. Stalin wanted to develop Russian nationalism in a Soviet direction, not reject it out of hand. In addition, quite correctly, Stalin considered his verses to be poor poetry. Consequently, Bednyi was in the penumbra of acceptance, thriving in the 1920s but held at arm's length in the 1930s.

The stress added to his drinking and alleged tendencies to debauchery. By comparison, Gorky's successor at the head of the Union of Writers, Konstantin Fadeev, a better writer, smarter politician and more long-lasting enthusiast, appeared to be the real deal. Like Bednyi, he was no slouch when it came to fawning on Stalin and he maintained a position of leadership in the Stalin years. Nonetheless, when Khrushchev's criticism of Stalin began to develop, Fadeev went into depression. He was deemed by the rising authorities to be responsible for the poor state of Soviet literature and was denounced by another Stalin admirer, his friend of many years, Mikhail Sholokhov. In a shock re-evaluation of his whole career in a suicide note in May 1956, Fadeev proclaimed a curse on both the new and old political leaders including accusing Stalin of behaviour appropriate to a satrap. In many ways, Sholokhov (1905–84) was the most valuable to the party. His work followed socialist realist principles but was also stylistically elegant and thematically engaging. In 1965 he was awarded the Nobel Prize for Literature. Added to his Stalin Prize of 1941 and his Lenin Prize of 1960, he did seem to be the party's man for all seasons. His career seems to belie many of the clichés associated with the era. On numerous occasions he was able to send critical comments directly, not only to Stalin, but also to later leaders. Even more surprising his complaints were acted upon. They included pointing out the truth about the disasters of collectivization, getting two OGPU officers convicted for using torture in 1933. He came out on top in a tussle with police chief Yezhov involving Sholokhov being bugged in his home village and in a Moscow hotel room he shared with Yezhov's wife, which resulted in Yezhov attacking her when he heard the recording. Sholokhov retained official favour in the Khrushchev era but lost any support he might have had among many writers of that era when he declared the sentences passed on Andrei Sinyavsky and Yulii Daniel in the early Brezhnev years were not harsh enough. Perhaps because it was doubted by many outside Russia in the Cold War years that a supposed party toady could also produce great literature, completely unsubstantiated claims that he had stolen the text of his first major novel, *And Quiet Flows the Don*, from the pocket of a dead white officer were repeated on a number of occasions, despite objective analysis including close computer and expert stylistic studies confirming Sholokhov's authorship.

As we have already seen in the case of Zamiatin, writing to Stalin was something a number of writers did, with varying consequences. Almost all other major writers who did so were less attached to the goals of the party than Fadeev and Sholokhov. Boris Pasternak (1890–1960), unlike Sholokhov, was forced to refuse his Nobel Prize in 1958, awarded for his brilliant novel *Doctor Zhivago*, a love story of survival through the turmoil of the revolutionary years from 1905 to the 1930s which enraged the party by being largely apolitical and mildly critical of the Reds as well as the Whites in the civil war. Pasternak engaged in many struggles to get his work published. The first edition came out in Italy in 1957. The CIA produced a pirate edition in Russian shortly after to be smuggled copy by copy into the USSR. Today the novel is part of the Russian school curriculum read by every schoolchild. Writers like Pasternak, Zamiatin and Mikhail Bulgakov (1891–1940) were all sceptical about soviet power and the socialist project and did not hide their views. Even so, some of their work was published. The works that made Bulgakov's name were written in the 1920s and, in two plays, *Day of the Turbins* and *Beg (Flight)* and a novel *Belaia gvardia (The*

White Guard) he lyrically and sympathetically portrayed the pathos of the defeated, retreating Whites in South Russia as the civil war drew to its close. It portrayed them as feeling human beings who loved their country, not the message Soviet propagandists wanted to convey. Why were they permitted? Simply because Stalin admired them and attended performances of *Beg* and wrote to Bulgakov about it. In the 1930s Bulgakov still communicated directly with Stalin on occasions but his main battle, to get his play *Molière* performed, ended in failure. It was both caught up in arguments among theatre producers themselves and the author, which led to a six-year battle at the end of which it was staged at the Moscow Arts Theatre but was banned by the censorship after its first seven performances.

Bulgakov wrote about his experiences and reactions in his, at the time, completely unpublishable novel *The Master and Margarita* which intertwines stories of the devil dropping in on Moscow in the mid-1930s and episodes from the trial and passion of Christ. He completed it shortly before his death and read the finished product to his friends, telling them he was going to take it to the publishers the very next day. More realistically, in a note to his wife on 15 June 1938, he wrote "'What's going to happen to it?' you ask. I don't know. You will probably put it away in your desk or in the cupboard with all the other rejected plays .... we don't know the future."[27] There is no more powerful symbol of the survival of the private sphere, even, or perhaps especially, in the bleak moment of the late 1930s. There was always an area of private discussion at home and writing 'for the desk drawer', as the emerging expression put it, that the authorities found very hard to penetrate. The private sphere was the absolutely crucial ark on which unofficial, unapproved ideas and works were conveyed through the dark years of cultural oppression.

Retreat into the private sphere was obviously more difficult for the scientific and technical intelligentsia, as least as far as their professional interests and ideas were concerned, since they needed access to labs and other resources. This did not prevent them discussing politics and culture and many other issues in private but they also found some very unexpected 'protected' space in which to operate. This was what Solzhenitsyn later described and termed the first circle of the gulag hell, the sharashka.[28] Sharashkas were special camps and the one described by Solzhenitsyn, based on his own experiences in one in 1948–9, the Marfino sharashka, housed in a former seminary on the edge of Moscow, was a community of scientists sentenced to imprisonment for political offences. Nonetheless, they worked on top secret telephone communications, including the production of a secure scrambler telephone and identifying recorded voices for the MGB (Ministry of State Security, the current acronym for the political police). In an astonishing irony the Marfino sharashka was later converted into a free research institute. In a key scene in his novel *The First Circle*, Solzhenitsyn describes the inmates enacting a mock show trial of Prince Igor, the hero of an ancient Russian epic poem. The prosecutor character, Lev Rubin, is based on one of Solzhenitsyn's co-prisoners, the communist and dissident Lev Kopelev, with another character, Gleb Nerzhin, based on Solzhenitsyn himself. The unfortunate Prince, not to mention one of the 'Mighty Handful', Borodin, who had written an opera about him and the anonymous author of the original epic poem were condemned for crimes against the state. This imagined episode brilliantly connects twelfth-century Rus', the classic intelligentsia of the 1860s and the Soviet era, embodying the ongoing and complex interaction of ideas and values and transpositions across centuries. A final irony is that the massive Moscow telecommunications tower was constructed near the site of the sharashka.

Sharashkas were not a postwar development. One of the most extraordinary involved several of Russia's brilliant aircraft, jet engine and rocket designers including Korolev and Tupolev.[29] As prisoners they worked in a sharashka on vital aircraft developments including the iconic Tu-2 bomber used extensively in the Second World War.[30] Tupolev was arrested on 21 October 1937 on charges of wrecking and spying and eventually was sent to a sharashka in 1939 where he remained until July 1941. In a number of cases it appears that sharashkas seamlessly turned into free research and design institutes leading one of Tupolev's fellow prisoners, the genius rocket designer Korolev, to joke that the guards keeping him in prison were turned overnight into security guards protecting him and the institute.[31] Korolev had been arrested on 27 June 1938 and, after being tortured in the Lubianka, spent five months in the remote, frozen wilderness of Kolyma during which he petitioned for his release including writing to Stalin. In late 1939 he was returned to Moscow for retrial and sentence reduction as a result of which he rejoined his mentor Tupolev in his sharashka. He remained there for five years at the end of which, in 1945 he was promoted to general and assigned to evaluating and building on the elements of Nazi rocketry which had fallen into Soviet hands.[32]

Of course, the majority of gulag inmates, intelligentsia or non-intelligentsia, were in the tougher, lower circles and many were either executed or died. The purges have yet to be fully explained, if that is even possible since in many ways one of its striking features is its irrationality. Many contributory factors have been suggested. They include paranoia at the top, including personally in Stalin; the snowball effect of vague orders tumbling through a still ramshackle state system, in which the executors of a command were over-eager to please their superiors, not least as a form of self-defence; a conscious if totally misguided effort to strengthen the country in the face of impending Nazi attack by eliminating the inner enemy, the 'fifth column' in the terminology of the time; creating forced labour to push through projects that free labour could not be attracted to and many others. What is sometimes overlooked is an aspect brought into clear focus by the sharashkas – the imbecility, inefficiency and completely unnecessary nature of the process. If it had any rational objectives, and that is questionable, they were undermined not enhanced by a totally counterproductive process. Fortunately it is not our present task to analyse the phenomenon but to examine its effects on the intelligentsia and cultural sphere. Nowhere, can its unnecessary and counterproductive core be better illustrated? Successive waves of arrests, executions and deaths in custody cut swathes through intellectuals and non-intellectuals alike, most of whom wanted no more than to get on with their lives and, in many cases, serve the nation and even the communist cause as best they could. The impact made scientific work much more difficult. The masses of deaths deprived the Soviet Union of some of its best qualified and most skilled people, including a multitude of officers purged in an army about to face the biggest challenge of any predecessor in history. The Academy of Sciences was ravaged, a process chronicled by the contributors to a volume edited by V.A. Kumanev, entitled *A Tragic Fate: Repression of Scholars of the Soviet Academy of Sciences*.[33] The roll call of executed writers and creative intellectuals is beyond all reason. Victims came from all corners of the cultural spectrum from proletarians to Soviet sceptics and included many immensely gifted people: Averbach, Mandelstam, Pilnyak, Kliuev, Klytchkov, Babel, Meyerhold, Voronsky, Kirshon and thousands of others. Even in this selection the randomness of the process is clear. Averbakh had headed the leading 'proletarian' association, until his fall. Voronsky (1884–1937) had fought against him but was caught out because, in addition, he had been a supporter of Trotsky. Babel (1894–1940) had chronicled the complexities of the civil war like Bulgakov, Fadeev, Leonov and Sholokhov but had, perhaps, been too graphic in his account of atrocities performed by the Red Cavalry whose commander, Budennyi, was riding high alongside Stalin as a Marshal of the Soviet Union from 1935 to 1954. Mandel'stam (1891–1938) wrote an incautious poem about Stalin, although all he was interested in, like most of the rest, was simply to be left alone to write his poetry. He had himself famously said that 'Only in Russia is poetry respected, it gets people killed. Is there anywhere else where poetry is so common a motive for murder?' Meyerhold (1874–1940) also made incautious public statements criticizing current cultural policy, notably an attack on 'formalism'.[34] By no stretch of the imagination did any of them constitute a threat to the Soviet Union. Like Russia before it, the Soviet Union seemed to have an infinite capacity for inflicting unnecessary suffering on itself. Unprecedented levels of absurdity and surrealism had taken over crucial parts of the country.

After Britain's appeasement of Hitler at Munich in 1938 it looked ever more likely that the Soviet Union would have to face the full force of Nazi expansion. It was also facing a possible nightmare-inducing two-front war, as Japanese advances in Manchuria and major fighting had taken place between Japan and the USSR in 1938 and 1939. For whatever reason the purges wound down in 1938 and 1939 though they never went away until Stalin died, as Meyerhold's tragic fate in 1940 showed. However, as the inevitability of war appeared to be growing and Soviet-sponsored collective security was spurned by Britain, the government began to change tack. The card of nationalism, updated to what is more accurately termed Soviet patriotism – a blend of pride in Russia's past, with a focus on the people and important individuals rather than glorifying tsars and saints, brought up to date with pride in the revolution and the 'people's' achievements of the thirties in science, engineering, social welfare, education and construction – began to share the motivational limelight with older exhortations to work for socialism and the party. Many intellectuals – scientists, engineers and creative artists – threw in their lot with the government and contributed to the war effort, whether it be in a sharashka, a research institute or a publishing or printing house. Veterans of early revolutionary art were still around. El Lissitsky, for example, had long abandoned the abstractions of the Red Wedge and was involved in official projects to decorate Soviet pavilions at international exhibitions, including a statue of Stalin. He also designed striking propaganda posters in the approved style. Shortly before his death from tuberculosis he produced one making a powerful appeal to the working class, represented in the resolute faces of a man and a woman against a machine-shop background, to 'Give Us More Tanks' (*Davaite pobolshe tankov*). Very soon the Soviet

Union was to need every one it could get as it faced the greatest military challenge not only in Russian history but in world history. The upcoming conflict would shake not only the intelligentsia but the Soviet state and society to the core.

Wartime and after

In the well-known words of one of Pasternak's characters in *Doctor Zhivago*, the war came as 'a purifying storm, a stream of fresh air, a whiff of deliverance'. A friend of Pasternak reported that he had remarked that war was 'a breeze coming into unventilated premises'.[35] Pasternak himself, already too old to fight, engaged in fire-watching duties when in the Writers' House in Lavrushinskii Pereulok in Moscow and the Home Guard when in his country cottage at Peredelkino. In human terms the war was, of course, the deepest circle of hell, costing some 27 million Russian lives and massively outweighing even the terrible toll of famine and purges in terms of victims. Pasternak's extraordinary comment referred not to the comparative suffering but to the totally altered atmosphere. Only the war and only victory mattered, at no matter what cost. Dreams of utopian social engineering were in the background. The country, the party and the government came together more closely than before. Even so, secret police were still active. Arrests and executions on charges of dereliction of duty went right to the top of the army command, including several generals one of whom, Dmitrii Pavlov, had commanded the Western Front. Heavily armed units waited behind front lines to intercept any deserters and armed cordons surrounded cities, especially Moscow, to prevent uncontrolled flight by the inhabitants as the fascist forces approached. Despite all this, Pasternak and other intellectuals believed that war would bring change and change could only be improvement. On the first point they were right. On the second they were not. Some easing of cultural control occurred during the war but the ensuing Cold War made the intellectual world even more bleak than ever.

In two areas cultural policy was modified. The battle against religion, especially Christianity, was moved to a much lower priority. Churches, theological academies and seminaries began to be re-opened, at first in small numbers,[36] and the church had a presence in public life including raising funding for the military during the war. It raised voluntary funds for fighting units. The second area was nationalism. Soviet patriotism had been heavily invested in during the thirties but in the war years the minor theme – comprising inspiring individuals and events from the pre-revolutionary past – was given much more prominence, the war itself being named 'The Great Patriotic War'. Generals like Kutuzov, Bagration and Benningsen, who had fought off Napoleon were held up as exemplars, as was Saint Alexander Nevsky, Grand Prince of Vladimir and Kyiv, who defeated a force of German invaders, the Teutonic Knights, in the thirteenth century. In 1938, even before the war actually broke out, Sergei Eisenstein made a brilliant film about him with a musical score by Prokofiev. Kutuzov was the subject of a biopic, directed by Vladimir Petrov which was shown in 1943 in Moscow. The titles prominently displayed the name of the rehabilitated Academician Tarlé as historical consultant. There were also a few more links with the western allies which were opened up. A small number of British and American journals and some films were allowed to circulate in Moscow and a few other major cities.[37]

The war made immense demands on the intelligentsia. The whole of society was thrown into turmoil. All parts of the intelligentsia, the scientific, technical and managerial/organizational and vocational wing as well as the full spectrum of the creative intelligentsia, pitched into the struggle, even critical figures like Pasternak were drawn to do their part. It is hard to find any ethnic Russians who, unlike in 1914, thought defeat would be a better outcome than victory. Of course, the vicious racism and aggression of the Nazis were a much more intense version of imperialism than that embodied in the Kaiser. Such support as there was for the enemy was limited to extremists from some of the national minorities, especially Ukraine where there was a strong indigenous strain of anti-semitism which the Nazis could have, but failed, to build on, and the Baltic states where enforced incorporation into the USSR was followed by vicious purges of the national élites and also Finland, against which a short war had been fought as a result of which the Soviet Union ripped a large area of territory from Finland in order to make Leningrad and North Russia more defensible in the approaching war. It did, however, throw Finland even more enthusiastically into alliance with the Nazis. Within the creative and scientific intelligentsia, support for the Soviet cause fused with nationalism and humanism to create an almost unanimous response. Figures as different as the visionary scientist Vernadsky and Trotsky, Stalin's arch enemy who was assassinated in Mexico in 1940 by a Kremlin agent, supported the defence of the Soviet Union. Incidentally, Vernadsky was Ukrainian and Trotsky Jewish-Ukrainian. In this spirit, the intelligentsia went forth to play a number of important roles in the great system of national defence.

The war drew on intellectual labour and expanded its scope in a multitude of directions. Most obviously, intellectuals were closely involved in the development and production of armaments. Advances in aeronautics in the 1930s, including the record-breaking exploits, in terms of duration, altitude, speed and so on, of pilots known as 'Stalin's Falcons' had laid the groundwork for the development and equipment of a vital air force. Although a dreadful toll of actual aircraft were destroyed, mostly on the ground, in early German attacks in 1941, the know-how and rapidly expanding production capacity enabled the Soviet Union to start producing on a mass-scale so that by 1943 it was outproducing Germany in terms of fighters and bombers. The quality was also good. When Churchill sent a few British Hurricane fighter aircraft to the USSR as a gesture of support and as a peace-offering when the promised second front was postponed in 1942, Stalin told Wendell Willkie, an American diplomatic visitor at one of their meetings in Moscow, that Soviet pilots preferred their own planes, finding the controls easier to manage.[38] The Tupolev 2 (Tu-2), designed in the Tupolev sharashka, became not only iconic but a vital weapon in turning the tide of the war. It is poignant and highly significant that the other major bomber of the war, the Petlyakov 2 (Pe-2), was also designed in a Moscow sharashka in which its chief designer, Petlyakov, had been imprisoned since 1937. It is said that, when the bomber was chosen to take part in the May Day Parade of 1940, Petylakov and his team watched the fly-past from the sharashka roof. Illustrative stories could be told about other iconic weapons from the T-34 and KV tanks to the postwar AK-47 Kalashnikov automatic rifle.

Weapons production was only one aspect of the intelligentsia war effort. Military science itself had flourished in Soviet times and one of the leading theoreticians of warfare was Mikhail Tukhachevsky who had supervised the writing of the military manual of the Red Army in 1936 before he was sucked into the deadly network of the purges. In 1937 he was accused of spying and executed. Tukhachevsky was a leading advocate of blitzkrieg. Partially developed with the involvement of the German army during the Weimar period of post-Locarno Treaty co-operative Soviet-German relations, blitzkrieg was a response to the static stalemate of the lengthy frontlines of the First World War. Building on limited experience of tanks in the war's later stages, Tukhachevsky argued for the overwhelming concentration of force of all available kinds, especially tanks and attack aircraft, in concentrated sectors to break through front lines and roll them up from behind in a classic *kesselschlacter* (*kotel' bitva* cauldron battle). However, in Soviet military doctrine, blitzkrieg was only an optional, tactical component of a wider military philosophy of 'deep battle' which took into account not only the concentrated point of contact assumed by classic blitzkrieg, but the combination of offensive forces over front lines up to eighty kilometres and to a depth of twenty to thirty kilometres. The works of Georgii Isserson (1898–1976), including *The Fundamentals of the Deep Operation* (1933) which has yet to be declassified by the military censorship,[39] outlined and developed the idea and his lectures on it at the military academy influenced a number of Soviet generals during the Second World War. Soviet military science has been of the utmost importance since its origin. However, modern military science, apart from German, is not widely recognized in the broader community.

Many of those involved in the scientific and vocational intelligentsia war effort were people who owed their education to the widening access to, and broadening provision of, technical education in the early Soviet years. Their design and engineering skills, like those of many others in many sectors, had to be backed up with logistics, managerial ability and entrepreneurial and accounting skills. Without the cultural revolution, the country would not have been able to tap into so many qualified people, even if it had not seriously damaged itself by the barbaric absurdity of the purges. While many of the designers and so on were communists, many of those who made important contributions were not, but the majority, whether party or non-party, were imbued with the old instinct of the populist intelligentsia to serve the people in Russia's hour of need.

The career of Vladimir Vernadsky is a case in point. Before the October Revolution[40] he had been an active liberal, member of the Constitutional Democratic movement from its origin and a minister in the Provisional Government. Nonetheless, he turned his talents seamlessly into working with the new Soviet authorities, within the framework of the Academy of Sciences (of which he was a member from 1912 and founding director of the Ukrainian sister-branch in Kyiv from 1918 to 1921). His scientific credentials were wide but, in his main role as a mineralogist, he specialized in uncovering exploitable resources. At the time of his death in 1943 at the age of eighty-one, he was energetically promoting the use of nuclear power and weapons and actively engaged in uncovering some of the largest reserves of uranium-based products anywhere in the world. His career reminds us that the Academy of Sciences remained fundamental to the war effort with, for example, Academician Abram Ioffe (1880–1960), the world-renowned physicist and student of Wilhelm Roentgen the German inventor of the X-ray, and the Leningrad Physico-technical Institute, playing an absolutely vital role in the development of a Soviet radar system from the mid-1930s on, as well as laying the foundations, at that time, of its radiation and electromagnetic research, which later provided a base for the Soviet nuclear energy and weapons programme.

However, it was not only the scientific-vocational intelligentsia which became involved in new areas. The war also brought forth new types and fields of activity for the creative intelligentsia who, like their scientific brothers and sisters and like members of their own classification such as Pasternak, were eager to throw themselves into the task of national defence. Obviously, the main arenas of activity for creative intellectuals was to describe, report and evaluate the experience of war and to encourage the defence effort. To call this propaganda is to oversimplify and to distort their activity but much of it was in the context of the propaganda effort. We have, for example, already mentioned Eisenstein's 1938 film about Alexander Nevsky. He also produced a multi-part film devoted to the life of Ivan IV (Ivan the Terrible), focusing on his role of taking the Mongol stronghold of Kazan' but presenting a multi-layered image of Ivan, a tsar who broods and plots against his enemy within from the inner sanctum of the Kremlin and forcefully drives Russia from the feudal age to the threshold of the modern. For some, the presentation seemed too close to the more immediate reality of the current occupant of the Kremlin who had, in fact, commissioned the film from Eisenstein.[41]

The same could be said for what is probably the other best-known work of wartime – Shostakovich's Seventh (Leningrad) Symphony. To describe it as propaganda would be deeply insulting. Shostakovich (1906–75) had had serious run-ins with the authorities in the thirties and his opera, *Lady Macbeth of Mtsensk*, based on a story by Nikolai Leskov, which had been published in Dostoevsky's thick journal *Epokha* in 1869, another example of continuity in intelligentsia culture reaching back to its roots. The opera was deeply disapproved of by Stalin himself. On 26 January 1936, Stalin, along with Molotov, Zhdanov and Mikoyan, attended a performance after which, on 28 January, an article appeared in *Pravda* heavily criticizing it for making a heroine out of an adulteress and murderer and for a musical style which was too complicated and 'was not reminiscent of the music of classical opera, had nothing in common with the sound of a symphony, with simple, widely accessible musical language'. It was said to be 'reactionary', 'anti-populist and formalist'.[42] Shostakovich had a threatening cloud hanging over him, but he was not arrested or charged and continued writing, though his music was not performed. The war found him in his home city of Leningrad, where he was trapped by the siege enforced by German and Finnish forces. Like many others in the grim conditions, which may have caused a million deaths, Shostakovich carried on as best he could and wrote his memorable symphony dedicated to the courageous defenders and inhabitants of the city. Even more remarkable, on 9 August 1942, it was performed and broadcast by radio to the nation from within the heart of the city, a truly astounding act of defiance to the attackers. Loudspeakers were set up to project the sound to the German front line. Today its majestic tones still ring out daily at the Piskaryevskoe Memorial Cemetery in the suburbs of St Petersburg, a site where almost half a million soldiers, sailors and civilians are buried in 183 mass graves, more than the entire British or American death toll in the Second World War.

Nothing better encapsulates the relationship between intelligentsia, people, party and state than the Leningrad performance. The première itself was performed on 5 March by the Bolshoi Theatre Orchestra, which had been evacuated to Kuibyshev (now Samara) on the Volga in accordance with government policy to preserve the best of Russia's cultural assets from German invasion and occupation. The date itself was chosen for symbolic purposes. It was the day Hitler had declared would be the moment of the victory party when he would host a gala celebration dinner in the Astoria Hotel in Leningrad to celebrate conquering the city. Tickets to the event are still extant. Shostakovich and copies of his symphony had also been evacuated from Leningrad and the score had been sent to the west via Teheran. The first foreign performance was conducted by Sir Henry Wood in London on 22 June. The challenge of performing it in its home city was enormous. There had been no concerts for many months and orchestras had been disbanded. Many musicians were among those who had died. The designated conductor, Karl Eliasberg, went from door to door to renew contact with his musicians. He noted how thin they were from starvation but that for many, the project gave them a new purpose and they garnered what little strength they had. The first rehearsal only lasted some fifteen minutes until the musicians, especially the brass section, were exhausted. Three members died in the period of preparation. All were incentivized by additional rations, voluntarily donated by music-lovers. The performance was only the second time they ran through the whole piece, the first being the dress rehearsal on 6 August. It was by no means great from the musical point of view, not least because only thirty or so musicians could be mustered of the 100 needed for a full performance, but as an act of defiance it was extraordinary. It was broadcast to the country and arrangements were made to play it through loudspeakers over the German front line, where it dispirited many soldiers who realized the inhabitants of the city were far from broken, despite everything. A military operation, Operation Squall, was conducted to silence the German guns so that they did not drown out the sound of the music. One soldier commented that the army's instruments had also been played alongside those of the musicians. Intelligentsia, people, party and state had come together in a national act of defiance which had nothing to do with socialist construction but everything to do with national pride. In conditions of astounding hardship, so many people willingly gave their ebbing strength to send a message of unique power.[43]

After the performance, apart from a 'banquet' with civic and party leaders, the government did not react and Shostakovich did not fully return to the limelight until after the Khrushchev era thaw when he received prizes and became president of the Union of Composers and was an international celebrity. Having been put at risk by the authorities, some critics argue that he became too close to them afterwards. In 1960 he joined the Communist Party. By that time this was more a bureaucratic convenience than a political commitment. In any case, it would be a travesty to classify the Leningrad Symphony as propaganda. It was a cry of defiance from the depth of the Russian soul.

The symphony exemplified the war effort of intelligentsia and people. Their commitment went far beyond simple politics into the deep reflexes of national defence which had been part of the Russian mentalité from the beginning of our period, a reflex which lived through tsarism, victories and defeats, global conflicts, barbaric dictatorship and authoritarianism. Many other aspects of the intelligentsia contribution to the war come into the same category. As we have already seen El Lissitsky had remained a 'propagandist' from *The Red Wedge* to *Give Us Tanks* but the causes were not simple partisanship. The war saw a high tide of war propaganda of a classic kind. The painter Alexander Deineka (1899–1969) painted a savage picture, entitled *Fallen Ace,* which portrayed a blond haired Teutonic German flier plunging headfirst to earth, with an unopened parachute strapped to him and his burning aircraft in the background. He is mercilessly shown at a point where his head is about to impact a sharp protrusion from an anti-tank barrier.[44] Deineka had been born into a family of railwaymen and went on to prove himself to be one of the finest artists within the socialist realist code. He retained a personal style, which abjured photographic realism, but was based on unnatural, but easily identifiable, figurative images, not unlike the sublimely elongated figures of the great icon painters, depicting workers, sportswomen, heroes of 1930s labour, rural dwellers and, in 1944, a tableau of female warriors destroying a Spartan army legion. There was also a populist element in that his subjects were all anonymous 'normal people' from the masses and without leaders. They portrayed positivity – joy, celebration, happiness, victory – and did not dwell on anything negative. He was a graduate of VKhUTEMAS and, before the 'proletarian' militants tried to dominate, he had been drawn to scenes of working life and leisure from the beginning of his career. He gathered a group of artists who shared his love of portraying women and men in their workplaces which was called *Obshchestva stankistov* (Society of Machine Tool Operators). Despite his near-figurative style and humble subject matter, in the 1940s he was subjected to criticism for being a formalist. However, the mid-fifties thaw saw him rehabilitated and presented as a leading Soviet artist, showered with praise, awards and positions in his last years. His war art was remarkable, linking the harsh realities with legendary battles, but always portrayed in a bloodless, heroic light.

The war also boosted other forms of artistic and literary representation of war, such as war correspondents, as well as more innovatory areas such as photography and documentary film in addition to the historical feature films we have already encountered. The USSR had become a major photographic innovator, with Alexander Rodchenko (1891–1956) an acknowledged master of the art. He was the son of a self-taught working-class artist and as such had a predilection for simple, everyday subjects and styles. He was, like Deineka, a member of the leftist *Oktiabr'* group of artists founded in 1930. In 1932 the ultraproletarians denounced him for formalism and he abandoned photography for two years, only resuming after the 1934 dissolution of all the squabbling groups and the proclamation of the norms of socialist realism. He excelled in several artistic fields but photography is the one for which he is best remembered, most notably for a photomontage poster of a woman in a headscarf calling on her fellow citizens to read books on every kind of topic. His work was very influential within and outside Russia. He gave up photography in 1942 but continued to organize wartime exhibitions in the field and to encourage and inspire many hundreds of Soviet war photographers. The range and depth of Soviet war photography have not been fully recognized within, let alone beyond, Russia's borders. There are iconic, arguably staged, images of, for example, the meeting of Soviet and American forces on the Elbe in Germany in 1945 and the image of Soviet soldiers precariously placing the Red Flag on top of the Reichstag Building in Berlin. But there are a multitude more which evoke the horror, scale, humanity and complexity of the war on the Eastern Front.[45]

Another interesting and innovatory art group, entitled the Grekov Studio had been set up in 1944, in the Red Army itself, supposedly at the instigation of the army chief, Voroshilov. It encouraged amateur painters from all ranks of the service to depict what they saw during their military lives. The Studio was in a tradition of attempts to raise the cultural and artistic levels of the masses, an instinct which had been at the heart of Proletkul't. In the late 1920s, newspapers, notably the party newspaper *Pravda*, recruited 'rural correspondents' from the village.[46] Later, during the war, the encouragement of ordinary people to express themselves artistically led to the emergence of many poets from among the people.[47] A photo from the Valerii Faminsky (1914–93) collection at the *New York Times* both exemplifies the immediacy of the war photographer's art and depicts a soldier-artist.[48]

Faminsky, who, ironically, had been turned down for military service because of poor eyesight, was only one of a host of war photographers who provided an unprecedentedly immediate reflection of the war. In many ways it was more direct and intimate than newsreel, which required more preparation and pre-location and was not immediately available in a multitude of locations. Dziga Vertov (1896–1954) had pioneered not only Soviet newsreel but was also very influential in the West. He had begun with film of the revolutionary war in 1919 and made some iconic documentaries in the 1920s. Although he is seen as a realist by his admirers, his films were deemed to contravene the 1934 prescription for socialist realism and his film-making career ended in 1937. Nonetheless, many other newsreel film-makers followed in his footsteps covering the full range of war-time experience.[49] However, it was a writer-turned traditional kind of war correspondent who became one of the best-known recorders of the war from the Soviet side. Vassili Grossman (1905–64) was born into a left-wing Jewish family in Berdichev, Western Ukraine and, unusually for a future writer, studied Chemical Engineering at Moscow State University. In the late 1920s and through the 1930s Grossman produced stories acceptable to the authorities with one being published in *Pravda*. Others appeared in the prestigious *Ogonek*, *Literaturnaia gazeta* and in 1937 he was accepted in to the Union of Soviet Writers. Even so, he and his family were caught up in the repressions of the 1930s and he and close relatives were accused of being associated with Trotsky. His wife Olga's former husband and best friend of Grossman, Boris Guber, was arrested, tried and shot in 1937. Grossman's wife was arrested because of her association with Guber. Bravely, Grossman wrote to President Kalinin and the NKVD arguing that Olga had been separated from Guber for many years and was his, Grossman's, wife now. In one of the myriad inexplicable outcomes in those absurd days, Olga was released. It was not the first time Grossman had petitioned the authorities. The line between those who were themselves arrested for doing so and those who were successful had, like the repressions themselves, no real rational basis. However, it was his war reporting that brought him widest acclaim. He was present at, and produced brilliant accounts of, major battles – Moscow, Stalingrad, Kursk, Berlin – and, items for which he became especially renowned, harrowing accounts of the liberation of Treblinka and other Nazi extermination camps. However, while this was going on, he became more and more critical of the system and began to think heretical thoughts which he later incorporated in brilliant novels, notably *Life and Fate*, *Stalingrad* and *Forever Flowing* which we will encounter below.[50]

Intelligentsia and culture after the war

As victory became inevitable as Operation Bagration (named after Russia's Napoleonic era general), rolled up the last, vicious Nazi resistance and approached Berlin via Warsaw, Prague, Sofia Bucharest, Belgrade, Prague and Vienna, thoughts began to turn towards the postwar world. There is an immense literature on the events which led from the East-West alliance which had brought victory, to the dark, bitter and universally damaging Cold War that emerged in 1947. It is beyond our scope to investigate this issue but we do need to note that, in the eyes of many, Stalin did not have any clear plans. Indeed, he appears to have favoured continuation of the condominium of the world, shared with United States and Great Britan, and encapsulated in the plans for the United Nations which would institutionalize that condominium, with the addition of France and China, in its Security Council. Associated with this, it has been argued that Stalin was all too aware of the risks and limitations of imposing Russian-backed communism on Germany and other countries. Soviet policy seems to have favoured 'universalism', effectively a sharing of influence by all the great powers across the whole continent. The United States favoured 'spheres of influence' whereby, as with the *cordon sanitaire* (literally 'health-protection line') of 1919, Russian communist influence would be contained into a zone as far east as possible and excluded from all of western Europe.[51] Whatever the truth, from our point of view Soviet cultural policy hesitated in 1945 into 1946 and only in 1947 did the cultural authorities gear up for a new imposition of orthodoxy. For a while links with the west were preserved and limited cultural interchange began. In 1945, for example, the Moscow Dynamo football team made a short tour of the UK. In Moscow in 1946, the British author J.B. Priestley and his wife Jane, who had been invited by the official Society for Cultural Relations with Foreign Countries, found a vibrant cultural scene: 'Seats for the theatre, opera, ballet, concerts are relatively cheap, as are books and anything else to do with knowledge and the arts … (F)or less than the price of an ice-cream … you can see theatrical productions of a perfection that not all the money in America can buy.'[52] He gave lectures which attracted crowds he said could only be compared to those at a football match back home in terms of enthusiasm and size.[53] He concluded with words that echo down to the present, urging Stalin to 'throw the country wide open and take a chance', because 'Soviet Russia has far more friends and fewer enemies than she imagines.'[54]

Unfortunately, events were moving in the opposite direction. As the Cold War intensified, so the Soviet government responded by increasing cultural control and increasing the tempo of socialist construction in the cultural sphere by warning about the dangers of fellow travellers. In a seminal speech in 1947, the Minster for Culture

Andrei Zhdanov (1896–1948), who had been a leading party speaker at the 1934 First Congress of the Union of Writers, laid down new, more constricted guidelines. The speech took the form of an attack on two individuals, two literary journals and an organization plus an assertion of what should and should not be considered to be Soviet literature. The two individuals were the writer Mikhail Zoshchenko (1894–1958) and the poet Anna Akhmatova (1899–1966). Zhdanov criticized both of them at great length. Zoshchenko's short story, 'The Adventures of a Monkey,' was a children's story initially but republished in *Zvezda*. It recounted the experiences of a monkey that escaped from a zoo in Odessa when bombs damaged its cage. The monkey wanders through the streets, jumping a food queue to steal a carrot, being chased by dogs, encountering people who want to sell it, make a pet of it or simply capture it. Eventually it concludes city life is not all it was cracked up to be and it would be better off back in its cage. The story is light-hearted and amusing but Zhdanov was not prepared to see the joke. He accused Zoshchenko of sitting out the war in the comfort of Alma-Ata (Almaty today) and making fun of those who had fought for victory with their labour or blood. Anna Akhmatova, now acknowledged universally as one of Russia's greatest poets, was accused of combining religious and sexual themes, being, in Zhdanov's words, caught between the 'boudoir and the chapel' and being 'part nun, part whore'. The heart of Zhdanov's critique was that both of them, and the journal editors, had overlooked politics:

> What is the cause of these errors and failings?
>
>> It is that the editors of the said journals, our Soviet men of letters, and the leaders of our ideological front in Leningrad, … ….. consider politics to be the business of the government …..When it comes to men of letters, engaging in politics is no business of theirs. If a person has done a good, artistic, fine piece of writing, his work should be published even though it contains vicious elements liable to confuse and poison the minds of our young people. We demand that our comrades, both practising writers and those in positions of literary leadership, should be guided by that without which the Soviet order cannot live, that is to say, by politics, so that our young people may be brought up not in the spirit of do-nothing and don't-care, but in an optimistic revolutionary spirit.

His comments also illuminate a number of other features. The frequent accusation of 'formalism', prizing literature for its style and verbal magic rather than its content, its 'message', is also a theme, but that theme leads on to another. Zhdanov, rightly, sees the positions as being deep-rooted in earlier literary disputes. He quotes Gorky who 'once said that the ten years from 1907 to 1917 might well be called the most shameful, the most barren decade in the history of Russian intellectuals; in this decade, after the 1905 Revolution, a great many of the intellectuals spurned the revolution and slid down into a morass of pornography and reactionary mysticism.' Numerous writers, including Merezhkovsky, Zinaida Gippius, mystical anarchists like Vyacheslav Ivanov are mentioned. Like them, Akhmatova, Zhdanov continued, preached 'Art for Art's sake', 'Beauty for Beauty's sake', and had no wish to know anything about the people and the people's needs and interests, or about social life.

This was a 'bourgeois-aristocratic trend in literature'. Zhdanov traced the Soviet tradition back to a long line of critics and writers including Belinsky, Chernyshevsky and, surprisingly, Plekhanov who represented healthy realist tendencies:

> We know that Leninism embodies all the finest traditions of the Russian nineteenth-century revolutionary democrats and that our Soviet culture derives from and is nourished by the critically assimilated cultural heritage of the past.
>
> ....Art cannot cut itself off from the fate of the people. Remember Belinsky's famous *Letter to Gogol*, in which the great critic, with all his native passion, castigated Gogol for his attempt to betray the cause of the people and go over to the side of the Tsar. ... ... Chernyshevsky, who comes nearest of all the utopian socialists to scientific socialism and whose works were, as Lenin pointed out, 'indicative of the spirit of the class struggle', taught us that the task of art was, besides affording a knowledge of life, to teach people how to assess correctly varying social phenomena ... ... Marxist literary criticism, which carries on the great traditions of Belinsky, Chernyshevsky and Dobrolyubov, has always supported realistic art with a social stand. Plekhanov did a great deal to show up the idealistic and unscientific concept of art and literature and to defend the basic tenets of our great Russian revolutionary democrats, who taught us to regard literature as a means of serving the people.[55]

Note the purely populist final phrase. Zhdanov also criticized the Leningrad literary journals *Zvezda* (*Star*) and *Leningrad* for allowing the publication of unsuitable works and, a touch which in some ways shows how little had changed underneath, for setting 'personal interests, the interests of friendship, above those of the political education of the Soviet people or these authors' political tendencies. It is said that many ideologically harmful and from a literary point of view weak productions are allowed to be published because the editor does not like to hurt the author's feelings.' However, Zhdanov's criticism also was expressed fully in the terms of the time:

> The Leningraders in charge of *Zvezda* must indeed be lacking in vigilance if a "work" of this sort [Zoshchenko's story] is offered to the journal's Soviet readers, if it is found possible to publish works steeped in the venom of bestial enmity towards the Soviet order. Only the scum of the literary world could write such "works", and only the blind, the apolitical could allow them to appear.[56]

It is also worth noting that Leningrad and Leningraders are mentioned ninety-six times in the speech on literature and it is identified as a nest of non-party Formalists clustered around the institution that came under attack, the Leningrad branch of the Writers' Union. As well as indicating that the traditional spirit of Russian literature was still relatively strong in Leningrad it may also be that the campaign was intertwined with wider attacks on the party in Leningrad. Zhdanov himself had been in the city organizing its defences. Political analysts have argued[57] that the emerging 'Leningrad Affair', which peaked in 1948–9 and resulted in six executions[58] in 1950 including that of the mayor and some 200 sent to prison, was a factional attack on Zhdanov and his supporters to pre-empt him as a likely successor to Stalin. Zhdanov's sudden death from a heart attack on 31 August 1948 left his supporters vulnerable and their enemies moved in. However, Zhdanov's literary critique also attacks Leningrad and it is hard not to see it as part of the rising criticism of the party authorities there. It is a question that has yet to be fully explored.

Incidentally, sanctions against all those criticized in Zhdanov's campaign were relatively mild. Zoshchenko was deprived of his pension until after Stalin's death and he and Akhmatova were banned from publishing their works. In earlier Soviet times Akhmatova's husband, the Christian and poet Nikolai Gumilev (1886–1921), had been executed in 1921 for supposedly joining an anti-soviet conspiracy and their son, Lev Gumilev (1912–92), an unorthodox orientalist, ethnographer and historian had been imprisoned in the purge era. Interestingly, Lev is now quoted favourably by President Putin.[59] Zhdanov argued that publishing such unacceptable work showed there was insufficient healthy material to sustain two journals, so *Leningrad* was closed down until such time as they had a better supply of approved items in which case 'Should so many appear that there is no room for them in one journal, a second and even a third may be started; it all depends on the intellectual and artistic quality of the works produced by our Leningrad writers.'[60]

Zhdanov followed up his comments about literature with similar remarks about music and philosophy. In the speech on music (January 1948) Zhdanov does not directly criticize individuals but focuses on the mutually self-congratulatory nature of the Union of Composers which, he complains, cuts it off from the life of ordinary people. The leading figures are named – Shostakovich, Prokofiev, Myaskovsky, Khachaturyan, Popov, Kabalevsky and Shebalin – but the critique is not directly personalized. Once again, the exemplars of good practice included the great composers of the nineteenth century notably 'Glinka, Tchaikovsky, Rimsky-Korsakov, Dargomyzhsky, Mussorgsky, who considered the basis for development of their creative power to be the ability to express in their works the spirit and character of the people.' In a stinging rebuke to contemporary Soviet music Zhdanov emphasized that

> Half-forgotten by us seem to be the clear statements about the popular roots of music by the "Mighty Handful" and subsequently too by V.V. Stasov, the great music scholar, when he associated himself with them. Half-forgotten is Glinka's "The people create the music – we, the artists, merely arrange." … … But Mussorgsky set the Gopak to music, and Glinka used the Komarinsky[61] for one of his best works. It has, in fact, to be admitted that Glinka, the land-owner, Serov, the civil servant, and Stasov, the nobleman, were more democratic than you.[62]

Zhdanov's strictures on philosophy focused on a textbook by G. Alexandrov who was accused of not focusing sufficiently on scientific materialism and minimizing references to the 'big three' scientific breakthroughs which were the forerunners of dialectical materialism and, therefore, also of Soviet science and philosophy as indicated by Engels, for whom 'the way was prepared for the dialectical method by the advances of natural science. The dialectical method was prepared for by the discovery of the cellular structure of organisms, by the theory of the conservation and transformation of energy, by the theory of Darwin'[63] once again claiming Soviet thought is rooted in a long tradition going back to the early and mid-nineteenth century.

Finally and briefly we should note that the campaign shows that, despite the authorities best efforts, cultural life still retained some semblance of independence and continuity with the multi-faceted past rather than simply reflecting the more homogenous, single-school aspirations of the party.[64] Zhdanov himself commented that: 'We know that Leninism embodies all the finest traditions of the Russian nineteenth-century revolutionary democrats and that our Soviet culture derives from and is nourished by the critically assimilated cultural heritage of the past.'[65] Contrary to the opinion of certain cold warriors and Russian critics of Bolshevism like Alexander Solzhenitsyn, that Bolshevism was a non-Russian import with west European, German and Jewish rather than Russian roots, socialist realism, and Bolshevik ideology, in general, were deeply rooted in the Russian intelligentsia tradition. Far from being non-Russian, Bolshevism was a phenomenon which is more plausibly considered to be deeply Russian, something that could only emerge in the autocratic circumstances of tsarist Russia, a blend of Bakuninism, populism, Russian Marxism and unavoidably conspiratorial tactics enforced by autocratic conditions in a situation of economic backwardness. Bolshevism gained power in 1917 and became one faction of the pre-revolutionary tradition which was trying to stifle the rest. But the evidence, even of the 'zhdanovshchina', is that many other tendencies rooted in other branches of pre-revolutionary and early revolutionary culture were still maintaining a flickering, fragile but real existence. As Bolshevik influence declined in the later decades of the twentieth century, so the suppressed tendencies began to gain strength.

The final years of the Stalin era were dominated by the lengthening shadow of the Cold War. A series of still largely unexplained policy zigzags characterized the era.[66] The Soviet Union was the first major power to recognize the new state of Israel. The larger-than-life figure of Golda Meir, later to be a formidable Prime Minister of Israel, was the Israeli ambassador in Moscow and built links with the Jewish community at the highest levels, there being many Jews in party, state and military élite circles. However, in December 1948 no less a person than Polina Zhemchuzhina was arrested and imprisoned for associating with Mrs Meir. Zhemchuzhina was the wife of Stalin's close associate Vyacheslav Molotov, whose extraordinary career in the party élite went back to March 1917, when he preceded Lenin as a member of the Central Committee active in Petrograd, through to 1957, when he was transferred to a minor provincial assignment by his victorious rival for the post-Stalin succession, Nikita Khrushchev. There were also dark rumours of antisemitic policies being developed. What had caused such a dramatic U-turn? Zhemchuzhina's arrest may have been part of Stalin's curious machinations to prepare for his succession but apart from that the change was driven by changing perceptions of Israel. Initially, as Jewish terrorists blew up British targets like the King David Hotel in Jerusalem, the British administrative HQ, on 22 July 1946, Zionism appeared from Moscow to be a useful anti-British and anti-imperialist irritant. However, the unexpected and extensive patronage Israel began to receive from the United States caused Moscow's view to change. The United States was using it to undermine the British Empire, which it had long resented as a restraint on American international trade, but also to drive its own imperialist wedge into the oil-rich Middle East, much of which was hostile to the United States. From being an apparently anti-imperialist force, Zionism now appeared to be a stalking-horse for American influence in the Soviet Union's back yard. As far as the Soviet intelligentsia was concerned, it made life difficult for those who had been close to Mrs Meir. The main casualty was the State Jewish Theatre in Moscow and its leading figure Solomon Mikhoels. Mikhoels died in Minsk in January 1948, probably at the hands of the secret police[67] and the theatre was shut down a few months later. A campaign began against 'rootless cosmopolitans'. The term is often seen as a coded term for 'Jewish' but many Jews were not targeted and many of those targeted, especially in the so-called Doctors' Plot in which Kremlin doctors were accused of trying to kill Stalin, were not Jews. Moscow historian Roy Medvedev and his brother Zhores have cast doubt on the antisemitic motive of the campaign and even of the likelihood of it initiating trials.[68] Be that as it may, the cultural atmosphere in Moscow was subdued and foreboding, as was the case in Leningrad under the influence of Zhdanov's attack and the Leningrad Affair.

The overarching influence behind this was not so much racism, which was prevalent in Russian society but had always been rejected fiercely by the authorities including Stalin, but rather the Cold War, which was spawning excessive distrust between the former allies and a frenzied arms race. Together with the massive demands of postwar reconstruction of ruined housing and infrastructure, the Soviet Union needed its technical intelligentsia more than ever. Engineers, architects, surveyors and many others were drawn into repairing roads, bridges, railways, power stations and grids, factories, mines, port facilities, superdams like the DneproGes, a show project which had been sacrificed in the face of German advances, all had to be rebuilt. Ironically, perhaps, the Dnepr dam turbine generators were acquired from the US company General Electric.

However, it was not hydroelectricity but nuclear power which made the greatest demands. The Academy of Sciences worked as a priority on developing nuclear weapons to counteract the American monopoly and succeeded with a rapidity which exceeded the expectations of western intelligence. The first Soviet atom bomb was tested on 29 August 1949 at the Semipalatinsk site in Kazakhstan. In November 1955 the first Hydrogen bomb was tested. Although the Soviets had considerable success in spying on US atomic research, there is no doubt that Soviet scientists, led by Mikhail Tamm, Mstislav Keldysh, Igor Kurchatov, Vitaly Ginsburg and Andrei Sakharov, did most of the work themselves. Some of the leading academicians worked in privileged conditions of relatively comfortable residences and better access to scarce goods, food and foreign cultural artefacts like films, academic journals and newspapers which were not readily available to the general population. Soviet scientists were also ordered to prioritize rocketry which had fallen behind when Stalin had de-prioritized it at the beginning of the war. That was reversed on 13 May 1946 when a decree from Stalin made it a priority once more. Stimulated by a group of German V-2 scientists, kept under guard in sharashka-like conditions at a facility near Moscow, Korolev moved ahead rapidly with the project. The rapid development of guided ballistic missiles was the foundation of the even more ambitious Soviet space project.

The twin developments of nuclear weapons and missile delivery systems and space rockets gave rise to a number of special communities surrounding the laboratories working on them. Communities like Dubna, near Moscow, and Arzamas-16 near Nizhnyi Novgorod and the area round the main rocket research institute TsNiimash (The Central Institute for Research into Machine Building) became scientific communities. They were far removed from the armaments 'yards' of the early Kremlin days but differed in scale rather than essence, reflecting a continuing Russian tradition for concentration of effort and of close state supervision, exercised in the modern cases, by Lavrentii Beria and Dmitrii Ustinov who were both energetic managers of these projects.[69] Several of these, with the addition of Star City, the cosmonaut training base on the outskirts of Moscow, became 'closed' cities requiring special permits to enter and were under the direct supervision of either the Defence Ministry or agencies like Sovatom and Sovcosmos (today Rosatom or Roscosmos) in charge of nuclear and space research respectively. The German 'sharashka' on Gorodomlya Island rejoices today in the name of Solnechnye (Sunny). In another nod towards continuity, Arzamas-16 reverted to its original name of Sarov in 1995, which conjurs up references to the holy recluse St Serafim who had lived there, a curious association for a facility devoted to devising weapons of mass destruction. Today, Star City, Solnechnye, Dubna and Sarov remain closed towns.[70]

Thus, in a variety of ways, the intelligentsia made major contributions to the continuing Soviet objectives of cultural revolution, consciousness raising, productionism and the perennial Russian concern for national defence and border security. However, this by no means meant that those involved were committed communists. Many were but many were not. The wartime thaw and the Zhdanovshchina demonstrated, in their different ways, that, despite determined efforts by the party to exert control, many heterodox intellectual currents still flowed. The spirit of the engineers and scientists involved in reconstruction and weapons development often showed, alongside simple professional pride, a sense of national duty and even elements of populist 'serving the people' rather than straightforward support for communism and Stalin.

On 5 March 1953, a sudden convulsion began. Stalin died. No one knew what would come next.

9

Reconstruction or deconstruction – The intelligentsia and the dissolution of the Soviet system

In the early hours of 25 February 1956, the emerging leader of the Communist Party of the Soviet Union, the unexpectedly flamboyant Nikita Khrushchev (1894–1971), read out a long report at a special session of the party's Twentieth Congress. It contained harsh criticism of Stalin. It came just three years after his death. It had been coming. *Pravda's* front page on the second anniversary of Stalin's death had not had a black border to indicate mourning. Stalin's fall was rapid. Khrushchev's speech was not an outright condemnation as that would have undermined the foundations of the Soviet system and Khrushchev himself. His key faults were seen to have been conducting repressions against the party which destroyed many honest, loyal members; establishing a cult of personality to circumvent party control of his actions and, with the same end, using state institutions like the NKVD (political police) against the party. The fundamentals of his policies – collectivization, industrialization, mass purges (the main victims of the show trials such as Trotsky, Bukharin, Zinoviev and Kamenev were not rehabilitated) – were not attacked. His war leadership was still praised, though it was qualified by the accusation (which, like others in the speech, has been shown to be wrong) that he hid himself away in the earliest days of the war in a fit of cowardice and despair. Repressions of minor party figures were condemned. He was accused of a crime no one had seriously thought to attribute to him, the murder of his close associate Sergei Kirov in Leningrad on 1 December 1934. Subsequent research has suggested he was not responsible. However, there was no rehabilitation of intelligentsia victims such as Mandel'stam, Meyerhol'd and a multitude of others. No apologies for sharashkas, no apology for suppressing the work of figures from Eisenstein to Shostakovich though some of their works came out in dribs and drabs and their names were mentioned more frequently. Some were restored to glory. Shostakovich himself was elevated to high status and showered with honours and privileges in the Khrushchev years. The speech had immense ramifications, especially in the recently and superficially communized countries of Eastern Europe which found themselves within the Soviet sphere of influence after the Cold War drew a firm line down the middle of Europe. It had a shock effect within the USSR but did not bring unrest or demonstrations. From our point of view the most important consequence was its impact on a process which became known as The Thaw, from the title of a novel by one of the most loyal but also talented writers of the era, Il'ya Ehrenburg (1891–1967).[1]

It 'was the time of our awakening.'

> Young men and women began to lose their fear of sharing views, knowledge, belief, questions. Every night we gathered in cramped apartments to recite poetry, read "unofficial" prose, and swap stories that, taken together, yielded a realistic picture of what was going on in our country … … To us, the thaw was the time to search for an alternative system of beliefs. Our new beliefs would be truly ours … … Without asking permission from the party or the government, we asserted that writers had a right to write what they wanted; that readers had a right to choose what they read; and that each of us had a right to say what he [*sic*] thought.[2]

Such were the memories of Ludmilla Alexeyeva (1927–2018), an immensely courageous fighter for human rights in Russia, written down thirty years later from her vantage point in the United States. Many sources confirm her picture of the Moscow scene at that time. They depict the emergence of a fragile, microcosmic civil society in the Khrushchev years from 1956 to his removal from office in 1964, a process which, according to Alexeyeva, was brutally ended with the suppression by Soviet tanks of 'socialism with a human face' in Czechoslovakia in August 1968. Others point to the arrest and trial of the writers Andrei Siniavsky (1925–97) and Yurii Daniel (1925–88) three years earlier as the turning point, shortly after Brezhnev came to power. However, as we will see, even after these reverses the process of cultural diversification continued.

It is also the case that the thaw did not begin with Khrushchev's speech. The speech itself was as much a symptom as a cause. Even before it there were signs that the ice was melting. Ehrenburg's novel was published in 1954. According to two later major communist reformers, Mikhail Gorbachev (1931–2022) and an architect of the Prague Spring and Socialism with a Human Face, Zdenek Mlynar (1930–97), who were friends at Moscow University in 1951, there was extensive criticism of Stalin among fellow students at that time.[3] Accounts from other universities also show that there was guarded criticism. It might take Aesopian forms or focus around apparently innocuous questions. A discussion about a new statue, for example, could trigger a debate about aspects of local and national history and national, for example Ukrainian, identity.[4] Such phenomena were very risky and arrests were still common. The mathematics teacher and future author Aleksandr Solzhenitsyn (1918–2008) was sentenced to imprisonment in 1945 for making disparaging remarks about Stalin in a perlustrated letter sent while he was a soldier. He observed the victory celebrations for the end of the war from a cell in the Lubianka, the KGB HQ in central Moscow. He was sentenced to eight years, as a consequence of which he found himself in the Marfino sharashka he fictionalizes in *The First Circle*, together with, as we have already seen, the dissident communist Lev Kopelev (1912–97). The cultural 'turning points' were less sharp than they often appeared and continuities and interconnections, fragile though they often were, were crucial.

Khrushchev's changes in cultural policy and in the atmosphere of cultural awakening noted by Ludmilla Alexeyeva were not especially radical. In essence they amounted, first and foremost, to a pushback against the restrictions imposed by Zhdanov. In the broader sense, the post-Stalin leadership was attempting to blunt, or even end, the Cold War and had engaged in a number of what they considered to be conciliatory gestures over the colonial war in Vietnam, in encouraging the non-aligned movement of countries largely emerging from colonial or imperial subjugation and in proposing agreements with the United States and its allies. Leaning out from Zhdanov's Cold War-induced cultural narrowing of what was acceptable, and to exert greater control over links to the western capitalist world, might be seen as part of the broader strategy. But Khrushchev was not open to extensive innovation in culture, quite the reverse. In a well-known encounter on 1 December 1962 at an exhibition of art in the Manège, just outside the walls of the Kremlin itself on Prospekt Marksa, he proclaimed a truly Leninist attitude to some of the abstract items on display, though his language was less 'cultured' (*kul'turnyi*) than Lenin's. The main exhibition was to commemorate thirty years of the Moscow Artists Union and was put on to demonstrate the breadth of achievement which had survived the trials and tribulations of the intervening decades, especially the *zhdanovshchina*. A total of 100,000 people had visited since its opening before Khrushchev's visit. While viewing it Khrushchev, accompanied by his soon-to-be successor Leonid Brezhnev (1906–82) and the ideological chief Mikhail Suslov (1902–82), completely lost it when he came to a separate but parallel exhibition of abstract art. The items he disliked, he claimed, could have been produced by a donkey swishing its tail on the canvas. In so doing he expressed the views of many over time and space who decried abstract art in similar terms from those who questioned Chagall in Vitebsk in 1919 as to why his cows were flying in the sky to the multitudes who disparaged the art of Mark Rothko, Jackson Pollock and many other artists in western Europe and the United States. The encounter was remarkable in many ways. Khrushchev may not have used the donkey's tail image exactly, though he did say the art on display was fit for donkeys, but, in his earthy, peasant way he decried the art for giving him constipation, for being fit only to hang in urinals and 'accused' the artists of being gay several times. He lashed out at jazz, which, he said, gave him gas and sounded like radio static, and suggested the foxtrot was a simulated sex act. He also claimed, not incorrectly, that his views were shared by many, even in the west, who, as he claimed British Prime Minister Anthony Eden had said, did not understand the art of Picasso and other abstractionists. Khrushchev claimed in the true socialist realist fashion that 'Pictures should arouse us to perform great deeds. They should inspire a person.' However, his sanctions were less severe than had previously been the case. He, rhetorically at least, offered to pay for the artists to emigrate should they so wish and his direst threat to one of the artists standing by his canvas was that he should pull his trousers down and sit on a bunch of nettles. He also said government money should not be spent on such art and that they should be denied any future government commissions. His words illuminate so much of the debate of the time they are worth quoting at length:

> What is this anyway? You think we old fellows don't understand you. And we think we are just wasting money on you. Are you pederasts or normal people? I'll be

> perfectly straightforward with you; we won't spend a kopeck on your art. Just give me a list of those of you who want to go abroad, to the so-called 'free world.' We'll give you foreign passports tomorrow, and you can get out. Your prospects here are nil. What is hung here is simply anti-Soviet. It's amoral. Art should ennoble the individual and arouse him to action. And what have you set out here? Who painted this picture? I want to talk to him. What's the good of a picture like this? To cover urinals with?
>
> The painter, Zheltovskii, comes forward.
>
> N. S. Khrushchev: You're a nice-looking lad, but how could you paint something like this? We should take down your pants and set you down in a clump of nettles until you understand your mistakes. You should be ashamed. Are you a pederast or a normal man? Do you want to go abroad? Go on, then; we'll take you free as far as the border. Live out there in the "free world." Study in the school of capitalism, and then you'll know what's what. But we aren't going to spend a kopeck on this dog shit. We have the right to send you out to cut trees until you've paid back the money the state has spent on you. The people and government have taken a lot of trouble with you, and you pay them back with this shit. They say you like to associate with foreigners. A lot of them are our enemies, don't forget.[5]

Khrushchev also severely criticized the sculptor Ernst Neizvestnyi (1925–2016) who led him away from the main exhibition where his sculpture was displayed, to the upstairs exhibition of abstract art. Neizvestnyi got into a lively discussion with Khrushchev in defence of his and others art. In a gesture that must have impressed Khrushchev, Neizvestnyi ripped open his shirt to show Khrushchev that he had scars from his war service. Khrushchev is quoted as having said at the end of the conversation: 'You're an interesting man – I enjoy people like you – but inside you there are an angel and a devil. If the devil wins, we'll crush you. If the angel wins, we'll do all we can to help you.'[6] In the end the two men shook hands but Khrushchev ordered that he should not be given any more state commissions. There was an intriguing outcome to this encounter. When Khrushchev died in 1971 his family approached Neizvestnyi to sculpt a headstone for his grave. Neizvestnyi based it on black granite intertwined with white marble 'representing the progressive and reactionary impulses that competed for primacy in Khrushchev's soul'.[7] Consciously or unconsciously Neizvestnyi had embodied the same concept that Khrushchev had applied to him. After Khrushchev's momentous visit the crowds continued to pour in to the main exhibition but the abstract side exhibition was closed down immediately.[8]

While the exhibition and the incident are, rightly, shown to illustrate the power of the party and the repressive nature of the Soviet authorities, despite their very different styles at different times, it also shows that culture survived in spite of the great pressure. Subtracting thirty years from 1962 thrusts us right back to the closure of all artistic groupings and the proclamation of socialist realism. The Moscow Artists Union had set the 1956 exhibition up with precisely the old battle in mind, not least because the national federation had fallen into the hands of survivors and successors of the proletarian groups, notably AKhRR, the Association of Revolutionary Russian Artists. The old battle lines were being drawn up. The main exhibition and the abstract exhibition also show that innovation continued, despite being crippled by the pressures, and an art which diverged from the strict principles of socialist realism was developing. But how? Moroz's brilliant metaphor of the freezer fits partially in that a freezer preserves and when thawed out the original content re-emerges but Neizvestnyi himself was perhaps nearer to a more appropriate explanation in his description of his own experiences. Evoking the underground existence of early Christians in Rome, Neizvestnyi described his own path of development in terms of coming through a 'catacomb culture' of self-education.[9]

The restricted but authentic and innovative underground catacomb culture was beginning to come back to the surface. The party did what it could to restrain it. Art exhibitions were circumvented, literary and political manuscripts were confiscated. Solzhenitsyn arranged for the typescript of his great *Gulag Archipelago* to be passed from supporter to supporter to minimize the chances of the KGB (the updated acronym for the Cheka/NKVD) finding it. In 1961, Grossman was told by the ideological chief Suslov that the confiscated manuscript of his great work *Life and Fate* 'would not be published for two or three hundred years', a curious comment which seemed to acknowledge the literary value of the piece at the same time as trying to dishearten the author. Both Grossman and Solzhenitsyn were published writers in the USSR. Grossman retained an idealistic attachment to the socialist and libertarian ideals of 1917, as did Solzhenitsyn, whose short novel *A Day in the Life of Ivan Denisovich* was published along with several short stories including the evocative *Matryona's Home*. Solzhenitsyn was, however, evolving away from 'westernizing' socialism and becoming attached to more conservative and Slavophile ideas.

The vehicle in which many of the heterodox works which verged on unacceptability (to the censorship) were published was the courageous and influential journal *Novyi Mir* (*New World*) edited by the poet Aleksandr Tvardovsky from 1950 to 1954 and again from 1958 to 1970. The journal had been a leading light of the literary world since its founding in 1925. It specialized in publishing 'fellow travellers' (who, remember, according to party policy since the 1920s, were to be tolerated as part of winning them over to the Soviet project) rather than hard-line socialist realist party devotees who gathered around the journal *Oktiabr'* (*October*) and the official newspaper of the Writers' Association *Literaturnaia Gazeta* (*Literary Gazette*). Submerged currents of westerner versus Slavophile, 'liberal' versus 'conservative', continued to swirl and eddy within these settings. They also echoed, in limited form, the *tolstyi zhurnaly* (fat journals) of the pre-revolutionary years.

It may seem odd to think of Communist Party loyalists as 'conservatives', since they were ideologically committed to Marxist revolution. However paradoxical it may seem, official Soviet culture excelled at traditional forms rather than radical or innovative ones. It is likely that Khrushchev's views on abstract art echoed those of the woman and man in the street, not only in the USSR but around the world. By taking the average person as the measure of what is acceptable, the leaders were avoiding many challenging encounters. Indeed, conservatives elsewhere have used an 'anti-elitist' and faux-democratic platform to evade engagement with progressive ideas which might undermine their powers and privileges.[10] Be that as it may, the first associations most people make with Soviet culture and the achievements of its intelligentsia are usually the Bolshoi Ballet, symphony music, Olympic sport, ice hockey, complex weapons and space. Paradoxically, the Soviets put themselves among the finest exponents of 'Victorian', 'bourgeois' culture.

Even accepted artists could be damaged by the Procrustean bed of being forced to be easy to understand. In his outburst at the Manège Khrushchev mentioned that 'Even Shostakovich surprised us once in this connection. At the final concert of the plenary meeting of the Composers' Union we were regaled with a trio which wasn't entirely pleasurable listening.'[11] This was even more interesting in that Shostakovich had been adopted in the Khrushchev era as a jewel in the crown of Soviet culture. His brushes with Stalin and Zhdanov were no longer a shadow over his career but an enhancement of his reputation. In 1960 he joined the Communist Party in order to fulfil Khrushchev's request that he become the General Secretary of the Composers' Union. He was also elected as a delegate to the Supreme Soviet (the Soviet quasi-parliament) in 1962. He had a long roll call of major honours, mostly from the Khrushchev years and after, including Hero of Socialist Labour (1966), Order of Lenin (1946, 1956, 1966), Order of the October Revolution (1971), Order of the Red Banner of Labour (1940), People's Artist of the USSR (1954), Lenin Prize (1958) not to mention the Gold Medal of the British Royal Philharmonic Society in 1966. His motives for getting so close to the party have been controversial but, like many others at the time, joining the party was often a formality needed in order to take on a high-level job in the administrative and social élite, a process weakening the political commitment of the party but drawing in more and more people as membership climbed rapidly towards the 20 million mark. However, Shostakovitch certainly shared some of the party's values in a sympathy, more populist/narodnik than strictly Bolshevik, for the lower classes and patriotism in connection with the Second World War. In 1961 he completed his Twelfth Symphony which he dedicated to Lenin and entitled it 'The Year 1917'. He did use his position to join protests against and petitions to the government to right abuses such as the sentence of exile for vagrancy passed on the young poet Joseph Brodsky, who was released as a result. In this period there were a number of other members of the creative intelligentsia, notably the 'rehabilitated' Anna Akhmatova, the cellist, composer and conductor Mstislav Rostropovich, who were prepared to do the same thing. The boundaries between the officially acceptable and unacceptable were permeable and fluctuating at this time, as they had been, but to a far lesser degree, even in the 1930s as Bulgakov and Pasternak's complaints directly to Stalin showed. Such was Khrushchev's desire to win over the intelligentsia he even made overtures to émigrés, as a result of which Igor Stravinsky made a memorable three-week visit to Moscow in 1962 at the invitation of the Composers' Union. He conducted six concerts and met fellow composers, Shostakovitch of course and Khachaturian, as well as many dignitaries including Khrushchev. Once again vibrant Soviet, Russian, Russian-Jewish and pre-revolutionary elements were intertwining.

One of the jewels in the crown of Soviet era culture was cinema. From the Thaw to the collapse of the USSR film had a very special role to play. At one level great epics of the civil war – like *Beg* (*Flight*), based on Bulgakov's play, which presented a nostalgic view of the Whites – and Great Patriotic War – in the form of the eight-part multi-film *Osvobozhdenie* (*Liberation*) (1970–72) – built up the official themes but a vast range of superb, non-ideological films – from international hits like *The Cranes Are Flying* (1957), through to the disturbing and brilliant works of Andrei Tarkovsky (1932–86) from *Ivan's Childhood (*1962*), Andrei Rublev* (1966 but not shown until 1971) to *Solaris* (1972), *The Mirror* (1975) and *Stalker* (1979). Very few of these films could be confined to a 'socialist realist' category. They were warmly humanistic and interacted with the great themes of Russia's nineteenth century novelists – moral dilemmas, love, loss, the 'cursed questions' of life's meaning – with no reference to the aesthetics of Marxism. Film is an area in which the continuities with the past are stronger than links to socialist transition as required of the 'Soviet artist' in any genre.[12]

The 1960s and 1970s were a time when elite Soviet cultural figures and institutions were regaining more and more independence. Of course, in the final analysis, party power and patronage – since, as Khrushchev had crudely pointed out at the Manège, the state paid for all of their activities – ruled, but figures like Shostakovitch, the young poet Yevgenii Yevtushenko who gave recitations to stadium audiences, and institutions like the Academy of Sciences and the Bolshoi Ballet, carved out niches for themselves which the party was often loathe to disturb. The case of Pasternak was interesting. He was forced to turn down his Nobel Prize for Literature, offered in honour of his great novel of the revolutionary era *Doctor Zhivago* but he continued to live freely in his state-provided dacha at Peredelkino. Sanctions against intellectuals and 'politicals' were relatively restrained compared to the harsh treatments and even execution faced in the 1930s. In his rural tone, Khrushchev at the Manège might threaten transgressors with exit visas, tree felling to pay the state back for its investments or being made to sit in bunches of nettles but sanctions were not the worst. In reality, imprisonment did not disappear but refusal of publication was the most widely used sanction.

The situation took a turn for the worse when Brezhnev replaced Khrushchev. One of the first signals of harsher times was the arrest in 1965 of two writers Yulii Daniel and Andrei Siniavsky on charges of anti-Soviet agitation and propaganda, prompted by them having sent items to be published abroad. The following year they were sentenced to five years and seven years hard labour respectively after which Siniavsky was permitted to emigrate to become a distinguished professor in Paris but Daniel refused to leave and lived out the rest of his life in Kaluga and Moscow. The trial was an international PR disaster, uniting conservative, liberal and radical critics and intellectuals around the world in condemnation of the outrageous act. However, more importantly it sparked off major protests within the USSR including Moscow's first unofficial street protests for decades. It also prompted petitions from many leading cultural figures. Sixty-three members of the Union of Writers petitioned the party Praesidium and twenty-five leading cultural figures sent an open letter to Brezhnev. Among the signatories were Ilya Ehrenburg, Viktor Shklovsky, Academicians Andrei Sakharov, Igor Tamm, Pyotr Kapitsa and the diplomat Ivan Maisky, the writers Konstantin Paustovsky and Viktor Nekrasov plus Shostakovich, the nation's leading actor Innokenty Smoktunovsky, the global star ballerina Maya Plisetskaya. On the other hand, Mikhail Sholokhov, who had been awarded the 1965 Nobel Prize for literature, denounced Daniel and Siniavsky and said their sentences would have been harsher in the past. He, in turn, was denounced by the poet and now activist Lidia Chukovskaya whose life became increasingly taken up with defending intellectuals and freedom of speech. The letter of the 25 was not published but began to circulate in secret. The response to the trial is often seen as the beginning of what became known as the dissident movement in the USSR, though the Russian term for dissident, *inakomysliashchii* 'the one who thinks differently', is much more evocative, almost equating it with Orthodox and other religious notions of a shared faith and heresy. The underground circulation of the Letter of the 25 is also often considered the moment of the birth of the phenomenon of samizdat, unofficial 'self-publishing'. Cultural boundaries are rarely clearcut and there are precedents for protests and petitions as well as for circulation of unofficial publications but there is no doubt the trial projected such things to a higher level. The intelligentsia and public intellectuals had become used to relative security under Khrushchev and, without diminishing the bravery of the signatories, had come to feel more secure than they had been before 1956 and were determined not to let the situation slip backwards. The main theme of the Letter of the 25 was the need to avoid a return to Stalin-era practices: Stalin's 'crimes and wrongdoing distorted the idea of communism to such a degree that our people will never forgive him'. A confrontation between party, state and intelligentsia had begun. Against all the odds, the intelligentsia came out on top.

Those who think differently – From dissidents to re-structuring

The Writers' Trial, as it became known, was not the actual beginning of intelligentsia protest against state and party but it gave a powerful boost. The protestors in this instance were, on the whole, not 'anti-Soviet' but were writers, artists and scientists who were, in Soviet terms, often quite privileged. However, the focused criticisms of 1966 gave way to an increasing wave of dissent and the emergence of a diverse group known in the west as dissidents, and in official Soviet circles as 'those who think differently', *inakomysliashchii*.

Before looking in detail at the Dissident Movement it is worth noting a number of key features. First of all, their moral courage in standing face-to-face in opposition to the state must be saluted and celebrated. Like their nineteenth-century and early Soviet predecessors they faced immense risks. Fortunately, these did not include execution as they had in the purges of 1936–8 but they did face harsh prison sentences, labour camps and internal and external exile. They faced exclusion from their chosen activity such as denial of publication of written items or the right to exhibit ones artistic production. In the early 1970s someone had the bright idea that, since only a madman would not want to build the shining communist future, then anyone who opposed the party must be insane. Dissent officially became a psychological pathology, a mental illness, and required treatment in a psychiatric hospital. As a result, a number of dissidents were forcibly confined to mental health facilities where they might face 'treatments' amounting to torture.[13]

This brings to mind a second key feature, links to pre-revolutionary predecessors and examples. Nicholas I had been complicit in having Chaadaev declared to be a madman but the intellectual links went deeper. As we shall see, as the dissident movement expanded, so it fell into intellectual furrows ploughed before 1917. This, in turn, points to another feature, its intellectual diversity. Socialists, communists,

Zionist Jews, Christians of several denominations, Muslims, liberals, humanists, rationalists, fascists, nationalists of various kinds can all be found within the ranks. The spectrum ranged from far left to far right. Some tendencies, such as authoritarian Russian nationalism, seeped into the ruling élite itself and, although it was not noted at the time, so did social democratic reformism, Czechoslovakia's 1968 'socialism with a human face'. This diversity is also evidence of a fourth important aspect. The diversity is evidence of the failure of the massive agitation and propaganda institutions to 'win over' key elements of the population. If we accept Moroz's refrigerator metaphor, the system had done a good job preserving the tendencies it wanted to snuff out, through mechanisms we will examine below. To illustrate these key points and other attributes, let us look at some leading individuals, ideas, strategies and institutions of the movement.

There were two main tendencies among dissidents and a third which turned out to be more important than it seemed at the time. All the tendencies were linked to major intelligentsia schools of the pre-revolutionary period. One was reminiscent of Slavophile nationalism and orthodoxy, the second echoed westernizing liberal democracy. The third was reformist democratic socialism. The best-known spokespeople of each tendency were, respectively, Alexander Solzhenitsyn, Andrei Sakharov and Roy Medvedev (b.1925). An examination of their main ideas will illuminate the nature of the tendencies to which they subscribed.

It is likely that, in the 1970s and early 1980s, Solzhenitsyn was the best-known dissident inside and outside the Soviet Union. A small but influential number of his works had been published in response to Khrushchev's appeal to writers to talk about the state labour camp (Gulag) and prison system. His main work published in the Soviet Union, in 1961, was a short novel entitled *One Day in the Life of Ivan Denisovich,* which is a brilliant catalogue of conditions inside the camps after the war, just as he experienced them before he was transferred to the Marfino sharashka. It also demonstrated the innocence of the prisoners, (zeks in prison slang), something which many on the outside still doubted. It showed trivial reasons why people might be arrested, for example a former naval officer was convicted because a British officer whom he had known during the war when the two countries were allies had sent a gift in the postwar years. By that time the two countries were Cold War opponents and the gift suggested possible treason. That was enough, in the system of assumed guilt unless proven otherwise, to get ten years. In secret he was working on his extraordinary compilation, entitled *The Gulag Archipelago,* which runs to three volumes of stories and memoirs by and about zeks and their families. It was first published abroad, although portions circulated clandestinely as samizdat, which means self-published and was a term applied to all illegal literature which circulated from hand to hand, mainly among the intelligentsia of the large cities and research centres. He and those close to him were intently watched by the security forces, who tried to get their hands on his manuscripts but failed to find all the copies. Despite this, his great novel about Marfino, *The First Circle,* and his account of the immediate post-Stalin years, *Cancer Ward*, came close to being published thanks to the advocacy of Tvardovsky.[14] However, the authorities were not interested. As far as they were concerned Solzhenitsyn was an embarrassment they could do without. However, Solzhenitsyn had become too well known as an international figure and that, plus the delicate international situation of developing détente, made it impossible for the authorities to put him on trial or confine him to a psychiatric hospital, so they devised a third solution. He was bundled onto an airliner heading for Frankfurt and exiled to Germany and Switzerland. He eventually settled in Vermont in the United States before returning to Russia in 1994 after the collapse of communism.

What were Solzhenitsyn's core ideas? He certainly saw his fictional writings as political acts and was fully aware of the Aesopian strategies used a hundred years earlier. Indeed, he claimed, in Russia writers formed an alternative government. But in addition to his fiction there are also several direct sources in which he expounded his basic values. One of the most revealing, an item which followed a long Russian tradition of petitioning the ruler from medieval times via, as we have noted, Chaadaev, Zamiatin, Bulgakov, Pasternak and many others, was a *Letter to Soviet Leaders*.[15] It was completed on 5 September 1973 and, rather than being published as an open letter, it was sent individually to a number of Soviet leaders in the hope that they might heed its message. In fact, it added to a crisis in Solzhenitsyn's relationship with the authorities precipitated by the first publication, in France, of *Gulag Archipelago* in late 1973, which led to his deportation in February 1974. The *Letter* is a very complex piece of work which contains all of Solzhenitsyn' key themes. Many readers, especially in the west, tended to take parts of it separate from a whole which was often not properly understood at the time. The main pillars of the argument are that the west has become weak and lacking in conviction; the Soviet Union is the dominant force in the world, capable of bullying and deceiving foreign leaders to get its way; the USSR is threatened by two forces, Maoist China and the global impasse caused by the ecological crisis; the inadequacy of progressive ideologies arising from the Renaissance and the Enlightenment and the uselessness of Marxism in the current situation. Solzhenitsyn continues the argument by saying that, for the Russian leaders, the key thing is 'To crack the ideology', which is nothing but a burden, and to cast off global pretensions and expansion which bring no benefit to the Russian and Ukrainian peoples (Solzhenitsyn being careful to separate the two and not conflate them into a single 'Russian' identity) and instead to concentrate on the internal development of the Russian north-east and Siberia for the good of the domestic population. Democracy, Solzhenitsyn thought, was not an immediate possibility as the experience of 1917 had shown how Russia lacked the experience to make it successful and any rush towards it would likely repeat the disasters of that year, contemplation of which had brought Solzhenitsyn to the conclusion that revolutions were no more than blood-soaked catastrophes. Authoritarianism was more likely and, Solzhenitsyn argued, it should be underpinned by a revival of true Orthodoxy of St Sergius of Radonezh and Nil Sorsky, not the church of Patriarch Nikon bureaucratized by Peter the Great. Russia should re-find its Slavophile heritage and its unique destiny and pursue its own identity irrespective of the rest of the world and eschewing all expansionist objectives such as the centuries-long quest to control the Straits. It could then divest itself of its enormous burden of arms expenditure. In place of democracy, Solzhenitsyn speculated that maybe a revival of ancient institutions like the Veche and Duma could be combined with, perhaps surprisingly, free soviets at regional and local level. Ideological control should be abandoned and Marxism released from its established links to government, state and society and left to develop freely in competition with all other ideological and cultural tendencies, if anyone felt it worthwhile to do so. The toleration of ideas would release an explosion of cultural creativity to drive the new, internally focused and environmentally sound opening up of Siberia and other useful national projects to sustain the Russian and Ukrainian peoples.

It is easy to see why this heady mix bamboozled many of his supporters in the west who saw him mainly as a source of embarrassment to the leaders and thereby an asset to western objectives, without taking on board his contempt for western materialism and moral compromise. After his exile this eventually led to a crisis when he was asked to give the graduation address at Harvard (8 June 1978) and thundered at the assembled children of the American and global capitalist élite, calling on them to regain moral courage and abandon excessive materialism. 'We shall have to rise to a new height of vision, to a new level of life where our physical nature will not be cursed as in the Middle Ages, but, even more importantly, our spiritual being will not be trampled upon as in the Modern era.'[16] His unrestrained criticism of what he considered the weakness and moral feebleness of the west, caused by its material comfort, was the beginning of the end of his unrestrained affection from the American and western public. His status as lead dissident for the American right was taken over by Vladimir Bukovsky (1942–2019), a courageous defender of human rights in the USSR who underwent detention in a psychiatric hospital and enforced administration of drugs after reviving unofficial, open public poetry readings and similar activities in Moscow. He was much more reliable in his unfailing support for the American 'hawks' in denouncing western peace movements for falling into 'the Soviet booby-trap', calling for the west to be militarily strong and build up its nuclear arsenal to enable it to force the USSR into compliance with its will.[17] He became their poster-dissident. He died in Cambridge England amid official investigations and criminal charges for having forbidden images of children on his computer which he eventually said had been planted by Russian security agents. The prosecution was not dropped but it was suspended on account of the ill-health which brought about his death. He did not share Solzhenitsyn's Slavophilism and lacked any discernible ideological roots, apart from a deep scepticism about Soviet and post-Soviet Russian governments. He suggested that Russia should be broken up into a number of smaller parts, an idea that rooted itself in Hilary Clinton's foreign policy options when she was Secretary of State.

Ultimately, Solzhenitsyn himself became less and less relevant in his home country as well. After his return in 1994 he had a fifteen-minute fortnightly TV show which was watched eagerly at first by the intelligentsia but support began to dwindle as his notions of spiritual quest, emptiness of material possessions and support for the Orthodox church went deeply against the grain of thinking of younger Russians. It was cancelled in 1995. His later works, including his massive novel cycle on the war, revolution and civil war (1914–22) evoked little interest in Russia or abroad. In his last years before his death he acknowledged support for Vladimir Putin especially in his denunciations of the revolution, of Marxism and of the Stalin era. In many ways, Putin's early governance resembled that envisaged by Solzhenitsyn in his *Letter to Soviet Leaders*.

While Solzhenitsyn's writings were admired his apparently backward-looking but in fact somewhat prophetic ideology was not. Much wider spread and more focused and in tune with western ideas was the large liberal tendency among dissident intellectuals. The centrepiece of their critique of the Soviet Union was the weakness of human rights as defined by the UN Charter – individual freedom, freedom of speech, assembly, organization (including political groups and parties), the rule of law, the right to a fair trial and many others. One of the most energetic organizers on this basis was Aleksandr Yesenin-Volpin (1924–2016), one of Sergei Yesenin's sons, who promoted the simple but devastating tactic of holding the Soviet government to account in terms of its own laws. As well as asserting the right to assemble in public, the movement began to list violations of the law carried out by government and its agencies. The first expression of this new tendency was a demonstration in Pushkin Square in Moscow on 5 December 1965 protesting that the trial of Sinyavsky and Daniel was illegal. Yesenin-Volpin, Bukovsky and others held banners proclaiming 'Respect the Soviet Constitution' and 'We demand an open trial for Sinyavsky and Daniel'. The small gathering of around 200, many, even a majority perhaps, being KGB agents who quickly confiscated the banners and arrested the protestors. Yesenin-Volpin and others were held in prisons and psychiatric hospitals, some for several months. However, a tactic had been launched which the authorities were unable to fully counter.

There was another step forward in 1968, when a demonstration of protest at the Soviet suppression of the Prague Spring was itself quickly suppressed, leading to dozens of arrests. However, the organizers, including Pavel Litvinov (b.1940), the grandson of one of Stalin's foreign ministers, Maxim Litvinov and his English wife, Ivy, decided to set up something more permanent. The outcome was one of the most outstanding publications of the dissidents, the samizdat *Chronicle of Current Events*. Covering the major cities and provinces the compilers of the *Chronicle* produced a devastating picture of a government routinely ignoring its own constitution and laws. It focused on illegal detentions and the use of psychiatric hospitals as centres for detention, abuse, enforced therapies and drug regimes and torture. The editors were careful not to make unsupported allegations and were as scrupulous as they could be in their reporting. The very first issue had been produced to cover an earlier 'Trial of the Four' in 1968, in which the writers Yuri Galanskov (1939–72) and Alexander Ginsburg (1936–2002) were the best-known defendants alongside Alexander Dobrovolsky (1938–2013), a neopagan, Slavophile nationalist and Nazi who testified for the prosecution in exchange for a light sentence, and Vera Lashkova (b.1944), a human rights activist and extensive contributor to the *Chronicle of Current Events*. The first issue was very brief but one of the people mostly closely associated with the *Chronicle*, Natalia Gorbanevskaya (1936–2013), who retained a role typing up later issues and was herself a writer, produced a fuller account in her book *Noon*. The *Chronicle* continued to be published at irregular intervals by an ever-changing and underground group of editors, including Litvinov, who was arrested and condemned to five years hard labour for his part in the Pushkin Square demonstration, and left the USSR for the United States in 1974. Apart from a period of harsh official crackdown from 1972 to 1974, a steady stream of issues came out. The final issue, number 64, which was compiled by June 1983 but not issued until August 1984, ran to over a hundred pages with universal coverage of state malpractice with respect to its own laws. All parts of the USSR were reported and even malpractices in the camps and prisons were included. The *Chronicle* was also a seedbed for other, largely liberal, movements including a Moscow branch of Amnesty International and, after the Helsinki Treaty (1975) incorporated human rights in 'Basket 3' of its provisions, a Helsinki Human Rights Watch, to unofficially hold the Soviet state to account.

Many hundreds of brave people, almost 100 per cent of whom were intellectuals, including many scientists, were involved in these activities and, even when exiled abroad, Litvinov and fellow dissident Valery Chalidze set up a human rights publishing enterprise in New York and published English translations of the *Chronicle* and material from other human rights organizations still in the USSR. However, the outstanding voice belonged to Andrei Sakharov, the academician and nuclear weapons pioneer.

Sakharov's voice had a completely different register from that of Solzhenitsyn. Sakharov based his views on science and reason and had no space for faith and tradition for its own sake. This made his modern tone much more congenial to the western audience than the backward-looking religious matrix of Solzhenitsyn's outlook. He produced a number of summaries of his ideas. The most comprehensive was his 1968 extended essay *Progress, Co-existence and Intellectual Freedom.*[18] Sakharov described it later as his 'turning point' which he had discussed with his fellow nuclear physicist and mentor, Igor Tamm. In Sakharov's words: 'My reading and my discussions with Tamm (and others) had acquainted me with the notions of an open society, convergence and world government (Tamm was sceptical on the last two points).'[19] Much of it was taken up with discussion of the imperative need to restrict the nuclear weapons he had been instrumental in producing. It was also influenced by the ideas of the Prague Spring. His Nobel Prize (for Peace) Lecture (1975) focused on human rights. In between the two, in 1972, he wrote a *Memorandum* intended for the eyes of the Soviet leader at the time, Leonid Brezhnev. In March he had delivered it to the letters department of the Central Committee and waited for a hoped-for reply which did not come, despite him eventually personally lobbying the department to find out what had happened to it. He was told it had been divided into separate parts each of which had been sent to a number of appropriate departments, but there was no response forthcoming. The party office no longer returned Academician Sakharov's phone calls so, in June he added a postscript, removed the appendix on political repression and gave it to foreign correspondents and to samizdat.[20] The *Memorandum* made a number of technical suggestions about how the industrial and agricultural economies might be improved by extending the 1965 de-regulation of factories (the centralized planned economy was not criticized) and expanding private plots for collective farm members. In foreign policy it shared Solzhenitsyn's concern about the threat from China[21] and advocated the development of the massive untapped resources of Siberia. However, the heart of Sakharov's appeal to Brezhnev was to open the country up by active co-operation on the international scale, internal democratization and recognition of human rights and the admission of more foreign publications into the USSR. On cultural issues he argued that complete freedom of conscience and speech should be permitted and the scope of social science and humanities research should be broadened and conducted without recourse to 'any preconceived opinions' by which he meant official ideology. There should be freedom of religion and complete separation of church and state. He added in the postscript that he could only see a convergence of capitalist and socialist systems as the way forward for humanity. He stated bluntly but not inaccurately, that

> The buds of moral regeneration … which sprouted after the curbing of the most extreme manifestations of the Stalinist system of blind terror, encountered no proper understanding on the part of the ruling circles. The basic class, social and ideological features of the regime did not undergo any essential changes. With pain and alarm, I have to note that, after a largely illusory period of liberalism, there is once again an increase in restrictions on ideological freedom, efforts to suppress information which is not controlled by the State, persecution of people for political and ideological reasons, and a deliberate aggravation of the nationalities problem …[22]

At the core of his ideas was an updated version of westernization. In classic westernizer fashion Sakharov claimed 'Our society is infected by apathy, hypocrisy, bourgeois egoism and hidden cruelty. The majority of representatives of its upper stratum … cling tenaciously to their open and concealed privileges and are profoundly indifferent to violations of human rights … to the security and the future of mankind', a situation which can only be retrieved by following the western path of democracy and human rights, reason and science. We can also detect a Gorkyesque distrust of the great mass of the population, almost the 'dark people' who had haunted the fears of liberals and conservatives alike before 1917 returning once again. This interpretation is backed up by a quoted conversation with a Danish pastor named Jorgen Laursen Vig who reported that Sakharov had expressed 'deep anxiety over the "psychology of the masses."'[23] Curiously but not unprecedentedly, it is the conservative Slavophile Solzhenitsyn who sees salvation in the moral uprightness of outstanding ordinary individuals. In the published story *Matryona's House* Matryona, a simple widow, let down by all around her, keeps to the right path. She is, the story concludes, 'the one righteous person without whom the village cannot stand. Nor the city. Nor our whole land.' It has been suggested that Sakaharov's lack of belief in such ordinary people was behind his persistent quest to change Russia by appealing to foreign forces to make such changes happen.[24] Interestingly, for reasons about which we can only speculate, the then head of the KGB, Yuri Andropov, reported to the Central Committee on 7 March 1974 that the appropriate response was to make no public statements about Sakharov for the next five or six months. With the contingency of expelling Sakharov in mind, he also proposed consulting to see if the knowledge of the Soviet nuclear programme which Sakharov possessed still, given his retirement six years earlier, constituted a state secret.[25]

While Solzhenitsyn and Sakharov were the giants of dissidence there were many other schools of thought represented. To the left of them was Roy Medvedev (b.1925) who stood on a platform of what he considered genuine Leninism and socialist democracy as opposed to the faux versions peddled by the official system. In fact, in his famous speech of 1956, Nikita Khrushchev had called for the country to 'completely restore the Leninist principles of Soviet socialist democracy expressed in the Constitution of the Soviet Union'. Medvedev responded enthusiastically. At that time he was a schoolteacher from a strongly committed party family. He and his twin brother Zhores (1925–2018) were named after famous socialist activists – the Indian Comintern leader Manabendra Nath Roy and the assassinated French socialist Jean Jaurès. His father was a regimental political commissar and lecturer at the Lenin Military-Political Academy. He was arrested on 23 August 1938 for having Trotskyist sympathies and died in the Kolyma Gulag in February 1941 an event which, Medvedev said, left an indelible mark in his memory.[26] In this sense Medvedev was linked to the tradition of army *intelligenty* of the first half of the nineteenth century. His brother was also a dissident. He was a biologist and gerontologist who spoke out against the false genetic ideas of Trofim Lysenko, which had resurfaced under Khrushchev's patronage as part of a search for quick solutions to the complex problems of Russian agriculture. He was confined in Kaluga psychiatric hospital in May 1970 but released in the face of widespread international protests. He was deprived of his citizenship while on a scientific project in London where he lived for the rest of his life. Roy was a Komsomol (Young Communist League) activist, served in the army in the final years of the war, took a philosophy degree after and qualified as a secondary school teacher. From 1971 he became an independent scholar. His work placed the blame on Stalin for the degeneration of the revolution, a thesis developed in his extraordinary biography of him entitled *Let History Judge* which circulated in samizdat and was published abroad in 1971.[27] He also wrote *On Socialist Democracy* in 1972 in which he developed his ideas for the regeneration of the Soviet system on what he considered to be true principles of Leninism.[28] His ideas appeared to isolate him from most dissidents, who had little or no time for Marxist or Leninist ideas and simply identified them, as they still do, with Stalinism and the Soviet system. He did, however, influence foreign historians, notably Stephen Cohen (1938–2020) whose early works, on Bukharin for example, made the same distinction between Leninism and Stalinism. Most importantly, however, and hidden from view, his ideas linked to a small number of party reformists, admirers of the Prague Spring, such as Gorbachev and Iakovlev. Unlike most other dissidents, including his brother, Medvedev was not seriously targeted by the security forces and, even though he only published his work abroad or in samizdat, he was allowed to conduct extensive independent research. He was excluded from the party but re-admitted in 1989, with full membership from 1959 acknowledged, and he played a role in perestroika and later supported Putin in his early years in power. Uniquely, from 1971, Medvedev was able to pursue his vocation as an independent scholar, delving in libraries and some archives to illuminate the dark realities of the Stalin era and its damaging legacy. As we now know, he had protectors in the Central Committee who were developing parallel ideas for Soviet renewal.

Not all dissident ideas were liberal or rational in the enlightenment sense. There was a powerful current of conservative Slavophile ideas emerging. One leading figure was Vladimir Osipov (1938–2020) who was associated with the samizdat journal *Veche* (the *Veche* was an early Slavic national gathering). It's ideas were based on traditional nationalism and Slavophile principles of Russia's unique path of development. In its pages the ideas of Khomiakov, Pobedonostsev and other fathers of Slavophilism were revised, debated and applied to the situation of the 1970s. Osipov saw Solzhenitsyn as a kindred spirit but never quite persuaded him to contribute to *Veche* despite extensive common ground. It criticized liberals and socialists as westernizers but it had some very, and again we have to use the word, complex ideas which brought together what might be considered opposites in western thinking. For example, partly following Dostoevsky, Osipov excoriated the west for being undermined by Marxism-Catholicism but also claimed Leninist antecedents for his view of renewal by means of the peasantry.[29] Obviously totally unlike the dyed-in-the-wool militantly atheist Lenin, Osipov saw the Orthodox church as a central focus of Russian identity. It is such compound, and to the outsider contradictory, concepts that set traps for many unwary westerners looking at Russian nationalist ideas, which they all-too-frequently map into western equivalents which are quite different. It is quite difficult for the western mind to understand a position based on support for the Soviet state but not its ideology, not to mention combining of Orthodoxy and Leninism. Osipov was at pains to distance himself and his journal from accusations of anti-semitism and proclaimed support for the right of Jews to a homeland, though his associates also wanted to show support for Palestinian rights. Osipov refused, not least because he opposed terrorism.[30] Less fastidious with respect to Jews, a more right-wing manifesto was published under the title *Slovo natsii* (*A Word to the Nation*) which was, in many ways, reminiscent of fascism (as distinct from Nazism), lauding a strong state, ethnic unity, strong national defence and resurrection of imperial glories. It was also overtly anti-Jewish believing Jews had no place in Russian culture.

Fascinatingly, the samizdat schools did not exist in a separate zone from the official culture. Sakharov and Solzhenitsyn lived and wrote in the official sphere as well as samizdat. The editor of the legal journal *Novyi Mir*, Aleksandr Tvardovsky (1910–71), promoted Solzhenitsyn's cause and, as we have noted, tried to publish items like *Cancer Ward* and *The First Circle*. The nationalist tendency, perhaps even more than the liberals and sparse socialist dissidents, had strong links in the legal sphere. In the 1960s and 1970s a rural school of writers (in Russian the *derevenshchiki* – countrysiders) emerged with ideas close to those of the right. They included Vladimir Soloukhin (1924–97), Vasilii Belov (1932–2012), Valentin Rasputin (1937–2015) and Vassili Shukshin (1929–74), who was also a successful film director. The 'court' artist Ilya Glazunov (1930–2017), who painted many official portraits, also reflected nationalist themes, as did the Young Communist League journal *Molodaia Gvardiia* (*The Young Guard*). Soloukhin and Glazunov lobbied for the preservation of historic monuments. One of Soloukhin's books of stories, *Searching for Icons in Russia* (1968),[31] describes his travels through villages around Moscow looking for decaying treasures in the multitude of village churches forcibly closed, notably in Khrushchev's anti-religious campaign. He also writes warmly of many of the mainly peasant population he meets and even finds a patch of small farms that had never been collectivized. It is also likely that *Slovo natsii* and *Veche* had sympathetic readers in the upper levels of the armed services which greatly helped in protecting the contributors. In a perverse way, the crossing of borders is confirmed by shock actions like the dismissal of the editor of *Molodaia Gvardiia* in 1970 for being too close to the Slavophile nationalists.

The indistinct line between the official and unofficial and the fact that for every dissident activist there were hundreds of readers and passers-on of texts[32] were indicators that, for the third time following the turn of the century and the post-1917 decade, a form of civil society was trying to crawl out from under the weight of an ubiquitous state with waning authority, especially for its ideology. As we have seen, no dissidents believed in it, or at least not in its current rather uncreative and dogmatic form. In many legal publications there would be a Lenin or Marx quote or two at the beginning, a lip-service conclusion showing how the work confirmed the Marxist-Leninist point of view and a central content which often did no such thing. Let us consider the field once led by Tarlé, whose photo was still displayed in the History *kafedra* (department) office in Leningrad in 1971.[33] Perhaps the doyen of historians of Russia was the Moscow University professor P.A. Zaionchkovsky, a specialist in late tsarist governance and the autocratic state. In volume after volume he produced path-breaking archival-based research on his topic which rarely touched a Marxist-Leninist base. Great historians like N.P. Danilov, Vitalii Startsev and others analysed the peasantry and the revolution in original and source-based terms without excessive kow-towing to the ideological authorities. Senior academicians in the Institute of History including its head, P.A. Volobuev, developed what became known as the New Direction in the historiography of modern Russian development.[34] It was a loose group rather than a school but there were a number of new approaches to late tsarism and the revolution of 1917. Rather than the official narrative of capitalism being well-established in pre-revolutionary Russia and the triumph of the Bolsheviks as an inevitable historical development the new approach, which was emerging around the time of the fiftieth anniversary of October in 1967, proposed that late-tsarist Russia was not capitalist but 'multi-structured' (*mnogoukladnyi*) bringing together elements of capitalism and pre-capitalist and even feudal political, social and economic formations. As for 1917, they argued that the Bolshevik triumph was far from inevitable and the course of events included elements of spontaneity and chance rather than iron pre-determination of the outcome.

There was a predecessor to this group, Eduard Burdzhalov (1906–85). From an early age he had been a party activist. He began his studies in the mid-1920s at a Moscow *rabfak* and went on to a variety of roles in agitprop (agitation and propaganda), spending the war as a political officer mainly lecturing in military academies. In other words he was a dedicated party believer. In 1953, a time when orthodoxy was still paramount, he was appointed deputy chief editor of the main historical journal *Voprosy Istorii* (*Problems of History*). His tenure did not last long. In 1957 he was dismissed for throwing doubt on the official (and completely unhistorical) line that the Bolsheviks played a crucial role in the overthrow of the dynasty in the February revolution. In Burdzhalov's presentation they were marginal and divided over what to do. Even in the early 'thaw' this was too much and Burdzhalov was dismissed from his editorship. However, this was not the Stalin era and he did not share the fate of Tarlé in being arrested. He vehemently protested that he was loyal to the party and was able to take up a professorship at Moscow Pedagogical University and continue to publish books though they were somewhat more guarded in the presentation of fresh ideas. Incidentally, his fellow deputy chief editor, Aleksandr Nekrich, also fell foul of the authorities with an Academy of Sciences book published in 50,000 copies which criticized Stalin and the Soviet leadership for not being prepared for Hitler's assault in June 1941.[35] He was also dismissed and expelled from the party. In 1976 he left the Soviet Union and lectured at Harvard. In 1972, the Academy of Sciences held an historical colloquium at which critics of the new tendency were in the minority. The party, and its ideological chief Suslov, was not prepared to tolerate it any longer. In their eyes the new approach was threatening to undermine the entire legitimacy of the revolution and the Soviet system which emerged from it. None of these historians was a dissident. They were all working within and attempting to extend the parameters of the intellectually possible and serve to remind us how far independence of thought had survived and was finding increasing outlets for its expression. The various attempts by Suslov and the ideologists to hold back the tide were looking increasingly reminiscent of the comparable efforts by King Cnut. Cnut was supposedly demonstrating he could not control the tide. Suslov believed he could. He was wrong.

It is widely, but not universally, agreed that the Soviet Union was in a slow-moving crisis in the 1970s and early 1980s, a concept precisely summed up in the Gorbachev era phrase that these were 'years of stagnation' brought about by abandoning the reform path set out by Khrushchev. Economic growth rates were falling, living standards barely rising and, as we have seen, ideological contestation near the point of uncontainability. Some, like Marshall Shulman, argued that it was not so bad and the glass was half full but the half empty people were in the majority. The slowdown encouraged American hawks to ramp up the arms race through vast but probably unachievable programmes like 'Star Wars' which promised a missile defence shield to create invulnerability to incoming nuclear warheads. Many scientists, East and West, pointed out the simple flaws of the concept but it was hoped it had just enough credibility to push the USSR into one more massive turn of the arms race screw, which it would not be able to afford. In reality, weapons production was an area in which the scientific intelligentsia continued to be able to innovate and produce effective weapons.

A leading figure in this respect was Aleksandr Nadiradze (1914–87). He was born in Stalin's home town of Gori in the Caucasus mountains of Georgia. He owed his career to Stalinist era developments in that he was able to attend the Transcaucasus Technological Institute and, in 1936, take up a post at the Moscow Aviation Institute where he worked on components for pioneering Soviet aircraft like the Su-2. In 1941, when he was only twenty-seven, another example of Stalin-era advancement, he became a chief designer at the Moscow Experimental Design Bureau, a weapons-producing establishment. He concentrated on rockets and, in 1949, designed the world's first high-altitude meteorological rocket. In the mid-1960s he and his team won a competition to design the first solid fuel mobile ground-based nuclear weapons and, at the Moscow Institute for Thermal Technology, he continued to develop more mobile nuclear weapons. The best known was the medium range 15Zh45 (SS-20 in its NATO designation) missile with up to four warheads and a range of 5,500 kilometres, which was launched from a road-based vehicle, making it virtually impossible to target its infinitely variable launch sites. The missiles went into service in 1981. In addition to his two Heroes of Soviet Labour and four Orders of Lenin, this crowning achievement earned him election as a full member of the Academy of Sciences in the Department of

Mechanics and Control Systems. The main Russian nuclear missile in the early twenty-first century, the Topol, is the result of work initiated by Nadiradze.

Space technology also continued to develop at a rapid pace. After the American moonshots of 1969 and 1970 the focus turned away from long-distance crewed space voyages to uncrewed probes of Mars and near space and also to the development of a permanent crewed orbiting space station and re-usable space shuttles. After the death of Korolev in 1966 the mantle of head of the space programme fell to Kerim Kerimov (1917–2003) whose name was only made public in the glasnost' years. He was born in Azerbaidzhan, just a week after the October revolution, and cut his teeth taking part in the commissioning of the innovative multiple, lorry-based, anti-tank rocket clusters known officially as Katiusha rockets and unofficially as 'Stalin's organs' since the multiple launchers resembled a group of organ pipes. On Kerimov's watch the space race became more complex and the United States regained the propaganda initiative with the first and only crewed moon landings. Soviet rockets had made the first orbits and soft landings on the moon and continued with fairly successful probes to Mars, Jupiter and Venus but a number of the main projects failed, such as the production of a super-heavy rocket for moon orbit and landing. Also the Buran (Snowstorm) space shuttle made a single flight but was decommissioned as its military paymasters considered it too expensive for its role as a defence against Star Wars. One of its pilots, Viktor Zabolotsky, said it was like using a Kam-Az[36] truck to carry a matchbox. Together with another veteran cosmonaut, Yuri Usachev, Zabolotsky claimed it had shown itself to be superior to the American version in size, payload, potential flight duration, heat protection technology and ability to land automatically, which was the mode used for its only space flight.[37] The setbacks to and failure of the American space shuttle project confirmed the decision and the last prototype was moved to Gorky Park in Moscow in 1995 where it underwent the ignominious fate of being turned into a café. In 2014 it was moved to the space section of the Exhibition of Achievements of the National Economy in another part of Moscow. Nonetheless the space programme continued the military/scientific tradition going back deep into Russian History. Collaboration between the military, the Academy of Sciences and independent institutes followed the tradition of Academician Shmidt, and predecessors back to Bering and beyond. The mixed motives remained. Many projects were military and as a result, before glasnost', were concealed from view but many projects were also scientific and civilian and military – planetary exploration, meteorological, communication, GPS satellites and so on. Much was made of the secrecy and military dimension of the Soviet space programme in the Cold War era but the US programme was also driven by military requirements. The first American GPS (Global Positioning System) satellites were designated to guide nuclear missiles and the exclusively military aspects of the programme, including launches, were rarely publicized, though Soviet concealment was much greater. It was even able to conceal its greatest failures including two explosions of rockets on the launch pad in 1960 and 1980 which, together, cost dozens of lives.

However, the blend of scientific and military interests led to one of the programmes most enduring successes, the design and development of a permanent orbiting space station in which cosmonauts lived for record periods of over a year in a state of weightlessness. In 1986 Kerimov's supervision of the space programme (1966–91) was crowned by the launch of the Mir (Peace) space station which remained in use until 2001. It was an extraordinary success in many areas. It was occupied for twelve of its fifteen years in space with a record of 3,644 days of continuous habitation and the longest single space flight of 437 days achieved by cosmonaut Valeri Poliakov in the mid-1990s, after the collapse of the USSR. It had multiple modules and was used for a long relay of scientific experiments, many of them sponsored by the Academy of Sciences for which it provided a platform for unique scientific experiments designed to assess how space might be exploited for enhancing physical and chemical processes associated with industry and medicine and so on, and to devise and investigate how human beings might adapt to long-term space flights with an ultimate view to interplanetary flight and moon colonization. This last, known as the Zvezda (Star) Lunar Base, was an objective of the Soviet space programme in the 1960s but was abandoned in 1974 on grounds of cost, impracticality and the US moon initiatives taking the propaganda glory. Nonetheless, the technologies involved in the Mir space station were a testament to the continuing brilliance of the Russian and Soviet technical intelligentsia. They independently developed docking techniques, modular design, solar electricity generation, air, water, food and waste management necessary for survival without wearing a space suit, including measuring and counteracting the higher radiation doses undergone outside the earth's atmosphere, external maintenance trips (i.e. spacewalks) and so on. In a curious way, the fact that Mir survived several accidents – including a serious fire which resulted in the permanent sealing off of one of its key, energy-producing modules, and two collisions – was unwanted testimony to its robustness. In 2001 its orbit finally began to decay and, given the high cost of maintaining it in a Russia reeling from the catastrophic economic policies of the Yelt'sin era, the Putin government cancelled its financing, not least because it was committed to the International Space Station from 1998 onwards and could not afford both. Rather than risk a Skylab-type freefall with a risk of debris reaching the earth's surface and causing damage and even death, it was decided to conduct a controlled de-orbit while its systems were still under control, which took place with several engine bursts on 23 March 2001. As hoped, most of the module burned up in the atmosphere, providing spectacular television pictures taken in Fiji, with remnants landing, fortunately harmlessly, in the Pacific.

One of the greatest achievements of the Russian intelligentsia had been destroyed, but the technologies that sustained it lived on and were invaluable in the programme of the International space Station which pooled Russian, American, Canadian, European and Japanese knowhow and money. Many of its modules are Russian and many of the ferry flights originate from the Baikonur cosmodrome, the world's largest spaceport.[38] The knowledge base of Russia had come a long way from the monasteries but, like the Moscow Cannon Yard in 16th c. Moscow, the everlasting imperative of border defence and the endless inquisitiveness of Russian minds combined in a great technological and human achievement.

What does the Brezhnev period mean with respect to our themes? It shows several important aspects. In the forefront, the failure of Soviet ideology in its endless quest to 'win over' the population and the extraordinary survival of the repressed traditions. This is not to say that Soviet society was not deeply affected by censorship and a multitude of forms of cultural and intellectual control, but there were crucial alternative channels. Consider this social media exchange of summer 2021. The Ukrainian website Kluber asked its subscribers what was the stupidest mistake they had made in their lives:

> **GM** – I blindly believed in the Soviet government and the party … … ….
> **IV** – Essentially that is not your fault. It is the work of the most powerful Soviet propaganda machine
> **GM – IV** No. It is my fault. I should have paid more attention to my grandmother and grandfather and when I got older read more of the classics like Dostoevsky and Tolstoy, especially their journalism … … and used my own head [thought for myself – dumat' svoei golovoi][39]

Ludmila Alexeyeva said something similar about her childhood in the 1930s:

> As our mothers spent their time at the universities and Komsomol meetings, the grandmothers gently rocked our cradles, singing the songs from their mothers when the Bolsheviks were just being born.
>
> Whether Comrade Stalin liked it or not, traditional values were being instilled alongside the icons of the new era. And sometimes, as in the case of my instinctive rejection of Pavlik Morozov, old values directly contradicted the new icons.[40]

Older people, literary classics and thinking for oneself were powerful corrosive forces. For the intelligentsia, second-hand book stores were only lightly regulated and many philosophical and intellectual works by unapproved but popular writers, like Nikolai Berdyaev, could be bought and sold at affordable prices. It was also possible for academics to access a wider range of literature in the main libraries, although there was an inner sanctum of restricted books that needed high-level clearance to access. It is interesting that, like Suslov's comment about publishing Grossman's *Life and Fate* in the distant future, there was no instinct to destroy items. Items were kept in order to know what was actually going on. Stalin's own wide reading knew no ideological boundaries as a careful study of his personal library shows.[41]

If the reader will indulge me, a good way to convey the complexity and anomalies of the late Soviet years heading in to perestroika would be via some of my own experiences, which were very revealing for me. It was more than a smart quip to tell my students that, of all the countries I had visited, the Soviet Union was the only one in which I had never met a Marxist. This is doubly odd since I shared a room as a graduate exchange student in Leningrad (academic year 1971–2) with a Soviet postgrad preparing a dissertation to qualify him to be a teacher of the official ideology – dialectical materialism. He told me his title was the influence of Hegel on Lenin's *Philosophical Notebooks*. Since Althusser and others in the west were touching on similar topics at the time I ventured to suggest it was interesting. He simply said 'No' and never mentioned ideology ever again. He was not in the least bit involved. Another student of diamat, as it was known, was studying Lenin and the electrification of the USSR which, it seemed, meant seeking out and underlining all references to electrification in Lenin's work and quoting them. He too was totally uninterested.

While in Leningrad I met an extraordinary young woman named Marina Volyn'skaia-Delgiado who most embodied the spirit of the literary intelligentsia. She had been a university student but had not been able to graduate because she refused to have anything to do with the party and its requirements and refused to join the Komsomol, which immediately cut her off from completing higher education. In her tiny flat at the top of a six-storey building, apart from being a single mother, she read and enjoyed the poetry of the Silver Age and had a circle of like-minded friends who had informal seminars about poetry and current cultural events such as new ballet productions at the Kirov (now Marinsky) Theatre. She lived for the literary and imaginative life and loved her city and its historical and literary associations. She made a meagre living in menial jobs like caretaking. She ridiculed Soviet affectations (like naming the theatre after Kirov) and lived parallel to the system but completely outside it. She was the only person I met who could pull this off. She was an intelligentsia equivalent of Solzhenitsyn's Matryona, the righteous person without whom the world could not stand.

I made many close friends with whom I am still in touch. Through a small group of Austrian students in the hostel I was introduced to Anne Kurepalu and Toomas and Maruta Varrak on a visit to Tallinn, Estonia. Toomas was a political sociologist, a specialist in Swedish Social Democracy, Maruta and Anne were historians who worked in museums. This was a way in which a genuine interest in history, especially national history, could be maintained at the edge of the system. Anne worked at different stages in her life in an Estonian national park called Lahemäa which conserved not only wild life but Estonia's rural historical legacy, including an impressively renovated manor house and a variety of wooden peasant homes, including some moved to the park from other locations. Maruta eventually directed one of the main museums in the city – the Kiek in de Kök a city and military museum in the iconic tower in the city wall. Anne worked as a tour guide and hotel administrator, enthusiastically showing her country to neighbouring Finns and other European visitors. Like most Estonians they had dreams of independence and had no time for rule by Moscow. Toomas in particular lived for independence even then and on one occasion I expressed scepticism about the prospects of a nation as small as Estonia becoming a viable independent state. His reply was simple – 'Trinidad and Tobago'. When he went to Moscow he stayed in the Estonian delegation building which he insisted on calling the Estonian Embassy even though, technically, Estonia was an integral part of the USSR at that point. History has rewarded his faith and contradicted my scepticism.

Other people who became close friends on later visits to Moscow starting in 1978, Lucy Lezhneva and Slava Nemodruk, illustrated the anomalies very well. Both spoke excellent English and worked as high-level interpreters and translators for leading publishers like Progress, the official publisher of materials in foreign languages. Slava also worked for the news agency TASS and, sometimes, translated items that went to the Central Committee. On one occasion in the perestroika years, among the latest western books I carried in for them on my visits, there was a signed copy of John le Carré's *Russia House*, which the author wanted to present to Lucy as thanks for help he had received from her while visiting Moscow when she acted as his interpreter. I am sure some of Lucy's characteristics can be found in the heroine of that book. Slava told me on another occasion that a number of years earlier he had been asked by the KGB, because of his contact with foreigners, to make reports on them. He neither refused nor complied with the result that no reports were compiled, for which he was rewarded by having all opportunities of foreign travel silently blocked for some fifteen years. Lucy did the same when she worked for the official travel company, Intourist. Both were regular readers of samizdat. Like Marina, Lucy was absorbed in art and literature rather than politics but Slava and I had many uninhibited discussions about Soviet and world affairs. He was a superb source of the latest and best political jokes of the era which were passed from one person to the next by word of mouth, thus evading censorship, though people could be and were informed on. Like Lucy and Slava themselves, the jokes were a wonderful guide to the real thoughts of many people at that time.[42] On one occasion, Slava asked me to meet a group of friends and acquaintances. This was unusual since meeting foreigners still had risks attached to it and trust between acquaintances and fellow workers was undermined by the informer system. One never knew who might be saying what to the authorities. Nonetheless, I met the group of half-a-dozen or so thirty-somethings (as we all were at that time) men and women with responsible jobs in ministries, in government and party agencies. None of them was the least bit interested in ideology though they were intensely interested in contemporary national and international politics. They exemplified the many party members, like Slava, for whom membership was a career necessity, not an ideological commitment. One particular experience exemplified the entire problem facing the authorities in their endless quest of 'winning over' the population. I asked Slava what he thought about Marxism-Leninism and he said that he, like his father, had been a believer until he realized those teaching him simply did not believe in it themselves. The circle was completed one day when he said 'Chris, you will not believe what I have been asked. The party people at work (TASS) want me to teach Marxism-Leninism.' Slava was about to become the kind of teacher who destroyed his own belief in the system.

Encounters with people working in the official ideological apparatus showed no more enthusiasm for the ideology they made their living from. On 13 March 1983, in a moment you will see why I remember the date so accurately, in response to a request from the British Cultural Attaché, who was himself responding to a request from a Soviet agency, I was meeting a reporter from Radio Moscow (an English language station which, like Voice of America or BBC World Service, broadcast to the outside world) who wanted to talk to foreigners visiting the USSR. When he arrived his first question was 'What shall we talk about?' which seemed an odd opening for an ideological specialist. 'Tomorrow', I said, 'is the centenary of Marx's death. Perhaps we could talk about some aspect of that.' 'Oh! Is it?' was the unexpected reply. The visiting bourgeois falsifier of history, i.e. me, was more aware of such a significant date than the official ideologist.

Of course there was still a handful of believers – we have already met the contrasting examples of Roy Medvedev and Suslov – but, literally, I did not meet any. I had a policy of keeping away from well-known dissidents. I believed I was doing more to help the situation by keeping good contact with my friends and wanted to go on visiting and doing what I could for them. It was also valuable to remember that there were many,

many people like my friends and acquaintances who were just as opposed to the system as those who were public about their refusal to accept it. Solzhenitsyn, ever the moral absolutist, was contemptuous of that vast layer of 'smatterers' who, he claimed, did not have the courage to do more than make rude gestures with their fingers at the authorities while their hands were in their pockets.[43] However, they were highly significant in their opposition and illustrated the emptiness of the ideological fuel tank.

Further striking examples showed me how deep the malaise had penetrated. Watching Soviet news reports from, say Washington, or New York, where the reporter would seek out an impoverished corner of the city to report from to show how awful capitalism was, I realized the Soviet students watching on the hostel TV were more interested in commenting on the new models of cars in the background rather than show repugnance at the harsh underbelly of American society.

Most striking of all, however, were friends of a friend. They were gilded children of the élite with high-flying careers. One was grandson of a well-known Red Cavalry general of the Civil War era, another was a member of the family whose paternal head was very high up in the state planning apparatus. They would not meet me as a foreigner. My friend told me their apartments in Moscow had no Soviet items whatsoever. The domestic appliances and entertainment systems were German and Japanese, the furnishings French and Swedish, the carpets were from Iran and so on. 'Surely', I said, 'they have vodka'. 'They only drink scotch' was the reply. One of the couples worked in foreign trade and could not wait to get back to a posting in Washington. Being in Moscow, a compulsory stay between postings, was a painful experience for them.

Such were the administrative pillars of the system by the early 1980s. The dreams of a socialist future were dissolving, even among many of the most privileged and powerful members of the party and state apparatus. The more perceptive observers had already noted it. As a student of the Columbia professor Seweryn Bialer recalls:

> At some point in the late 1970s he was giving a lecture in a large auditorium at Columbia, explaining the mentality of the then-current Soviet elite, their loss of ideological conviction. Looking over the 200–300 academics in the hall, he said, 'There are more people in this room who have seriously studied Lenin than in a meeting of the Communist Party Central Committee.'[44]

The Soviet transformation of the intelligentsia and managerial class had been extensive in many respects but it had clearly failed in its main objective. By the late Soviet period the intelligentsia was a mass phenomenon. In 1975 there were 856 higher education institutions including sixty-five universities and around 5 million students. Only the United States had a higher proportion of the population going through higher education. The Soviet Union had overtaken Britain, France, West Germany and Japan in this respect. The vast majority were scientists and engineers feeding into the continuing imperatives of productionism and in this respect the process was successful. It followed that the knowledge base of Soviet society had expanded exponentially in all areas, including history and the humanities as well as the highly favoured sciences. The Academy of Sciences had become an enormous institution and its leading figures won eleven Nobel Prizes between 1956 and 1980. By 1985 there were 274 academicians and another 542 Corresponding Members. The institution was composed of over 300 institutes employing a massive 57,000 researchers and a total of over 200,000 employees.[45]

However, as we have seen, the crucial political imperative of 'winning over' the population was faltering, even receding, as time passed and the ardour of revolution faded away. The late Soviet intelligentsia was very different from the pre-revolutionary years and the early Soviet era but there was still the instinct to return to the well-ploughed fields of westernizer versus slavophile; rationalist versus religious; nationalism; humanism; liberalism and democratic freedom and so on, as we have seen. There were some fascinating differences. The dissidents and late-Soviet intelligentsia more or less ignored social justice. Individual human rights and liberties were the main focus. One might, in their defence, say that they were pursuing these objectives to allow the opening up of themes of social justice, but it was rarely mentioned. Similarly the widespread populism and linkage of intelligentsia aims to the masses had almost completely disappeared. Most of the intelligentsia ignored the masses and did their best to distance themselves from the urban working class in particular. The gap between workers and dissidents was emphasized when, in late 1977, a group of workers led by Vladimir Khlebanov tried, after exhausting official channels, to set up an independent trade union. However, this crossed a line the authorities were keen to police. Khlebanov and others were arrested after talking to western reporters and, in 1979, he was confined to a psychiatric hospital for treatment following a 'mining accident'. Khlebanov and his associates emphasized they were not and had no links with dissident intellectuals whom Khlebanov characterized as 'renegades'. While there was some toleration of intellectual samizdat, worker dissent brought rapid retribution and imprisonment.[46]

Ironically, perhaps, it was among the intellectual descendants of the opponents of the populists, the Slavophiles, that remnants of idealization of the people could be found. Even here, however, it tended to be older, rural dwellers who were seen, like Solzhenitsyn's Matryona, as the embodiment of needed traditional values in a world of selfish privatization of life and lack of concern for others. These two features point to the striking, but once one reflects on it, all too likely a consequence of the Soviet experience, the marginalization of socialism and the weakening of pre-revolutionary collectivist solidarities. Very few socialists were left in the USSR, though a few, like Gorbachev, emerged from the reformist wing of the party, as we shall see, but, by and large, the Soviet system had managed to make socialism – which it did not embody – into a term with completely negative connotations. Marx and Marxism had become victims of the Soviet experience through false but completely comprehensible association of Marxist ideas with Soviet practices. Whatever elements of Marxism had inspired earlier revolutionary leaders and intellectuals had been sucked dry and turned into a parody by the time of Brezhnev.

By the early 1980s the ideological fuel tank was empty. From that perspective the Soviet Union was running on fumes. Its last high-priest, Mikhail Suslov, died in January 1982 and the revolutionary cause, as it had become understood in the USSR, more or less died with him. In a way, Suslov's passing was rather poignant. He was the embodiment of the system itself, having been born into a poor peasant family in

Saratov guberniya. He became a member of the village Committee of Poor Peasants when it was founded in 1918, and joined the party in 1921, when he was nineteen. He was educated in a rabfak in Moscow in the 1920s before graduating from the Plekhanov Economic Institute in 1928, followed by a higher degree (*kandidatura*) at the Communist Academy, an initiative of the new authorities in the mid-20s to circumvent the stranglehold still exercised by the Academy of Sciences. As well as lecturing in economics from 1931, when he was still only twenty-nine and a classic example of the positive discrimination of the era, he followed the career footsteps of Stalin himself in taking on positions in the party Control Commissions at the highest level and in the state supervisory body the Workers' and Peasants' Inspectorate. Later he was appointed to senior local positions in the provinces. During the war he was an organizer of partisans in occupied South Russia in the Stavropol' region. In 1946 he had his first major Central Committee appointment, becoming head of the International Relations Department linking up with foreign communist parties. From this position, he oversaw the anti-cosmopolitan campaign of the late 1940s. In 1949 he became chief editor of the party newspaper *Pravda* and in 1952 he was appointed to the Praesidium (Politburo by another name) just in time to be associated with Stalin just before his death and was, because of that, demoted back to the International Department. He did, however, come to support Khrushchev and was brought back into the fold. He was a senior figure dealing with the 1956 Hungarian crisis, eventually and reluctantly supporting armed intervention after an apparent settlement he and others had negotiated in Budapest fell apart. In 1968, he opposed intervention in Czechoslovakia and in 1980 supported the Polish leader General Jaruzelsky's view that armed intervention would be catastrophic, though the previous year he had voted in favour of sending troops to Afghanistan. He was, in effect, deputy leader in the Brezhnev years, though he seems never to have aspired to the leadership role itself. He was, as he has often been called, the *eminence grise* of the late Soviet leadership, working in the background to promote, as he saw it, the worker-peasant cause. In this respect, though different in almost everything else, he was reminiscent of Pobedonostsev. Suslov was, of course, an ideological zealot and was the architect of the attacks on the intelligentsia and dissidents, from his comments to Grossman to engineering the external and internal exiles of Solzhenitsyn and Sakharov, respectively. Although he was not a prominent public figure, his death, shortly before that of Brezhnev himself, seemed to bring to an end an era. He exemplified the first generation to emerge after the revolution, which opened the way for him to be transformed from a poor peasant background into a party intellectual and economics professor before he was thirty.

Many of the party's radical values died with him, as their last exemplar. The classical assumptions of the early revolution had lost almost all traction. A few diehards fought against perestroika but they found themselves in a weaker position than they, or most outside observers, thought possible. In terms of the battle of ideas the official party line had lost and the traditional values of the intelligentsia in their late-twentieth-century form seemed to be on the verge of triumph. But the outcome was such that, despite reaching a peak of influence in the late 1980s, it soon brought many to question whether the intelligentsia itself had survived in the new conditions for which it had performed an icebreaking role. The outcome was not a thaw, it was a tsunami.

10

The dissolution of the Soviet system and the intelligentsia

In the afternoon of 11 March 1985 Mikhail Gorbachev was named as the new General Secretary of the Soviet Communist Party in place of Konstantin Chernenko whose death had been announced the previous day. This was an unprecedentedly rapid transition. As my friend Slava pointed out, the TV announcers reporting Chernenko's passing were not wearing black ties, a sign he interpreted to mean that the audience should not be too concerned. Small gestures promised big changes. In his first, short, address to the nation, Gorbachev launched a discourse that resembled the language of dissidents rather than a party leader. The Soviet Union needed 'democratization', 'openness' (*glasnost*'), 'socialist legality' and a 'speed up' (*uskorenie*) of the economy, a package that soon came to be known as perestroika or (re-structuring). It sounded like an amalgam of Roy Medvedev and Sakharov. Most listeners and readers were sceptical. The terms could also be understood in a more neo-Leninist, even neo-Stalinist, way. That ambiguity was what enabled Gorbachev to keep a majority in the Politburo as he set about re-shaping it in his own image. Within two years, notably from the January 1987 Central Committee plenary meeting, it was clear that his political control was stronger and that what Gorbachev himself described as 'revolutionary changes' were on the way. The new direction was welcomed by intelligentsia icons.

> Nobel Peace Prize laureate Andrei Sakharov, in an interview today, hailed Gorbachev's speech last week as "an extraordinarily important" event.
>
> "He is going further down the road of democratic changes in our country," Sakharov said. "This was necessary. With such steps, the system either has to go forward or it will slip back. Now it is not possible to stand in one place."
>
> "These are sensible proposals, but not revolutionary," said dissident historian Roy Medvedev. Gorbachev "has created the mechanism. It still depends on the good will of those on a lower level" to implement it.[1]

By the end of the year censorship had practically disappeared and widespread freedom of speech was developing, inhibited more by people holding back, because they did not fully believe what was happening, rather than by restraints from above. Indeed, the message from above was, in the name of a popular play which captured the moment, *Go Further, Further, Further* (*Dal'she, Dal'she, Dal'she*). In October 1987, on the occasion of the seventieth anniversary of the October Revolution, Gorbachev said there should be 'no blank pages' in Russian history, that is the true history of the Stalin era should be brought out in the open. By 1989 voices from the Central Committee were querying why Lenin was not getting critical treatment. The works of 'unpersons' of the 1930s, notably Trotsky and Bukharin and earlier figures like Aleksandr Bogdanov and Iulii Martov, who had all been expunged from the historical record, became freely available. Touchingly, by 1989, perhaps the peak of openness when Russia had the freest possibilities of public expression in the world since there were no slander and libel restrictions at that moment, an informal garden of small crosses grew up under the Kremlin Wall in Revolution Square. Each cross bore the name of a 'lost' political party – Socialist Revolutionaries, Mensheviks and so on – or of leading political and religious individuals who had been repressed and even murdered by the regime. Symbolically, anarchists emerged and took over Kropotkin Square. Spectacularly the statue of Dzerzhinsky, founder of the Cheka, which stood in front of the Lubianka, was toppled by demonstrators in August 1991 as a sign of rejection of the attempted 'hardline' coup of that month against Gorbachev.[2]

The speed of cultural liberation was breathtaking. A whole variety of new magazines and journals in suppressed or ignored genres, from DIY to soft core pornography, appeared on newsstands. A wave of films, like the bleak *Little Vera* (*Malenkaia Vera* nb as well as being a name *vera* means faith in Russian), turned socialist realism on its head, retaining a kind of realism but stretching in the direction of the emptiness of provincial life in the late USSR, a sexually explicit, working-class *Madame Bovary*.[3] From the political and social point of view, however, perhaps the most revealing cultural intervention of the time was the extraordinary 1986 Latvian/Russian Documentary *Is It Easy to Be Young*? (*Vai viegli būt jaunam?* was the Latvian title and *Legko li byt molodim?* In Russian), directed by Juris Podnieks.[4] Made and released at a time when real insight into the lives of Soviet citizens was hard to come by it depicted a kaleidoscope of subcultures among young people, specifically in Latvia but, by association, as true of much of the rest of the European USSR, barely known to the outside world and to many Soviet citizens themselves. It opens with scenes from a banned rock concert and the trial of a young vandal who had smashed up a railway carriage on the way back from it. Other scenes depicted drug-taking, a returned Afghan veteran who worked in a mortuary, a Buddhist postman and many others. The film made two unprecedented points. First, that under the surface a wide variety of restricted but diverse cultures existed, a situation completely at odds with prevailing western Cold War descriptions of the USSR as 'totalitarian'. Second, the one feature the interviewees shared was a complete absence of interest in official ideologies. The point was emphasized by an interview with a group of young people in Riga, the capital of Latvia, sitting and possibly taking drugs, around a central city statue. The statue was of the main Latvian revolutionary heroes of 1917, the regiment of Latvian Riflemen who had, among other things, been Lenin's personal guard after October and, as such, the core around which the Cheka was formed in December 1917. When asked what the statue depicted, none of the teenagers knew or cared. Though it is not explicitly discussed in the film, it suggests a third message. In addition to the three reservoirs of non-Soviet values we encountered earlier, namely older people, the classics and thinking for oneself, the ideology was being undermined by knowledge of foreign cultures. Despite controls many foreign cultural items – films, books, tv programmes – and items of material culture with jeans and other fashionable clothing in the forefront were allowed because they depicted themes acceptable to the authorities and were also objects desired by the élite who could buy them on the black market. But, like the news broadcasts mentioned earlier, the messages received by the audience might be very different from those which the authorities wanted to point to. In addition, more and more Russians and other Soviet citizens were travelling abroad, some 2 million per year in the Brezhnev era, and increasing numbers of western visitors to the USSR – business people, engineers, exchange students and masses of tourists – inevitably brought greater knowledge of foreign living standards and ways of life.

Podnieks film was only possible so early in the reform period because, like Gorbachev and his associates at the time, it put out ambiguous signals. On one hand it showed the ideology was dead and on the other it was a useful tool to batter Brezhnev and his followers for allowing the situation to slip so badly. Both aspects called for reform, but in opposite directions. One way was to recognize failure, the other to try another round of tightening up cultural and political discipline, as Gorbachev's opponents in the leadership, 'hardliners' like Ligachev, wanted in order to, as it were, revive what Gorbachev's followers increasingly identified as a dead parrot. The ambiguity confused foreign analysts, especially those of the totalitarian persuasion who had nothing in their intellectual toolkit which could explain what was happening as anything but a public relations exercise – Gorbachev as Brezhnev but in a shiny suit.[5] Others interpreted exactly what was going on, including in their analysis, the audience for and subjects of *Little Vera* and *Is It Easy to Be Young?*

> While the people of the Soviet Union are highly literate and deeply interested in music, ballet, and literature, the officially sanctioned culture was wooden and banal and the most creative and independent spirits were suppressed or exiled. Even the enforced artistic standard of socialist realism, with its hollow, relentless optimism could no longer hide the sense of deep cultural pessimism permeating the educated strata of the society. This was the artistic expression of the feeling of hopelessness prevalent among the workers. The Soviet Union has probably been the only major country in the world where the youth neither rebelled nor expressed any youthful enthusiasm that could be channelled into creative public endeavours. The heroes of the youth were their own 'private' poets and balladeers (in particular, Vladimir Vysotsky) who were barely tolerated by the authorities, and their major public expression of dissatisfaction was the flaunting of the artifacts of western mass culture, such as blue jeans and popular records, officially permitted but never encouraged.[6]

The perestroika leadership was not content simply to have opened up intellectual freedom. They wanted to get the support of the intelligentsia to help promote their project. In 1986, Sakharov was allowed to return from Gorky (Nizhny Novgorod) to his apartment in Moscow. Not only that, he was consulted by Gorbachev on how to bring about lasting and effective change. Gorbachev and his team consulted widely among many branches of the intelligentsia. An international forum of intellectuals was convened in the resort of Issyk-Kul in the Tian Shan mountains of Kirghizia from (13–16) October 1986. Attendees included American futurologist Alvin Toffler and the novelist James Baldwin. Though it was largely a public relations exercise it was an extraordinary event, highlighting the completely unprecedented (in Soviet terms) nature of what Gorbachev was doing. It sent signals which could not be interpreted correctly through the Cold War-era decoding conventions.

It was not only the international community which was still divided over whether Gorbachev was an authentic reformer or a Leninist in a new guise. Gorbachev himself did not know how far the changes could go or what the outcome might be and what he was doing was so extraordinary that the confusion is not surprising. The Soviet population was harder to convince than the outside world and when, from 1987 onwards, the process resulted in a drop in living standards as a result of the almost inevitable massive rise in prices, disruption of work routines and practices and a rise in fragmentary nationalism, it was hard for them to see the positives. Perhaps more surprising, the initial beneficiaries of the process, the intelligentsia, still remained sceptical. The creative unions were riven with debates. One might have expected the new freedom of expression to be universally welcomed by them but that was not the case. Even some of the literary newspapers and journals were not only sceptical but highly critical of the whole process. The official newspaper of the writers' union, *Literaturnaia Gazeta* (Literary Gazette), which had had a reputation for limited independence of thought in the previous decades, became a platform for opponents of perestroika. In what one commentor correctly describes as a 'vicious attack' the twice-wounded war veteran, infantryman and war novelist Yuri Bondarev (1924–2020) launched a scathing attack in a speech at a conference of the Russian Republic affiliate of the Writers' Union held in 1987. He fulminated against what was happening:

> I am being asked by foreign correspondents whether a civil war has broken out in our literary circle. No, comrades, what has developed is not a civil war. It can be rather com-pared to the brutal onslaught on our country in the summer of 1941 by the forces of barbarism. If this onslaught is not halted it will endanger the very existence of our great Russian cultural heritage and of our Soviet way of life.[7]

Many other intellectuals from the nationalist and slavophile tendency shared Bondarev's outrage. On 23 July 1991, on the eve of the farcical attempted coup in August against Gorbachev, a group including Bondarev issued a 'Word to the People', its title reflecting the earlier 'Word to the Nation'. It repeated the main nationalist themes of the earlier item with a layer of anti-masonic and anti-Jewish conspiracy theories woven into the comments.

> Our homeland, our country, the great state, given to us in trust by history, nature and our glorious ancestors, perishes, disintegrates, plunges into darkness and nothingness ....with our connivance and consent ....What happened to us, brothers? Why are cunning and eloquent rulers, ... greedy and rich money-grubbers, mocking us, mocking our beliefs, taking advantage of our naivety,

> seizing power, taking away wealth, houses, factories and lands from the people, dividing the country into pieces?. .... Brothers, ... our house is already burning. .... Let us unite in order to stop the chain reaction of the disastrous disintegration of the state, economy, and individual; to help strengthen Soviet power, transform it into a truly people's power, and not into a feeding trough for the hungry nouveau riche who are ready to sell everything and everyone for the sake of their insatiable appetites.[8]

It was published in another conservative mouthpiece, *Sovetskaia Rossiia* (Soviet Russia). In addition to Bondarev its twelve signatories included the rural-school author Valentin Rasputin; several decorated veterans including Boris Gromov, later Governor of the Moscow Region and Deputy Minister of Defence; the folk singer Liudmila Zykina and the future presidential candidate and head of the Russian Communist Party, Gennady Zyuganov. Zyuganov commented that the article enraged Yeltsin who called for its signatories to be thrown into jail.[9] It was roundly rejected as 'demagogic', 'rabid' and 'vulgar' by Gorbachev's key associate Alexander Iakovlev in his memoirs.[10] The article could also proclaim a pedigree going back to 1973 when a group of intellectuals signed a letter published in *Pravda* aimed at Solzhenitsyn and Sakharov.[11] The thirty-one, all male, signatories included regime loyalists like Sholokhov and the longtime head of the Writers' Union, Konstantin Fedin and Sergei Mikhalkov who, among other things, co-wrote the words of the post-Stalin version of the Soviet national anthem. But there was also a number of more unexpected signatories, such as Chingiz Aitmatov, later a supporter of Gorbachev and convenor of the Issyk-kul forum. One of the earlier group, Vassil' Bykov, claimed in his post-Soviet memoirs that he had not agreed for his name to appear on it[12] reminding us this was a very different kind of letter from its successors. It was organized as part of the KGB campaign against Sakharov and Solzhenitsyn and, at the very least, many of the signatories were presented by the authorities with Hobson's choice. The letter was couched, of course, in official ideological terms, and primarily accused Sakharov and Solzhenitsyn of siding with the enemy at a critical moment in the Cold War, and as such was very different from the later letters. However, beneath the rhetoric there was subtext of Soviet patriotism as much as, or more than, Marxism-Leninism.

Numerous processes were occurring simultaneously in and to the intelligentsia during perestroika. In addition to it dividing into two camps of Slavophile nationalist and westernizer modernizers, each camp itself contained many subgroups and factions, which the explosion of free expression had made possible. At the same time, the economic effects of perestroika bore down on intellectuals as well as the rest of society. Public finances fell into disarray, salaries lagged further and further behind prices. Publication was easier than ever but making a living from it was increasingly difficult. Public sector employers such as universities, and even the Academy of Sciences, were falling into the clutches of economic crisis. Even the military could not guarantee its funding. Many of these features were appearing before 1991, with the two-stage transformation when the Communist Party was banned in August after the attempted coup and the Soviet Union itself broke up into fifteen independent successor countries in place of the fifteen federal republics. The splitting up of the unitary state and its constituent institutions – political structure, economy, military, judiciary, civil service and so on – was fractious and destructive. Meaningless borders between constituent republics became delimiters of national sovereignty overnight, leaving many anomalies in the Caucasus and Central Asia not to mention the thorny issue of Crimea. The deeply unsettled and unsettling conditions in most of the republics were not conducive to cultural, artistic or scientific life. For many *intelligenty* the conditions were a considerably less acute rerun of the civil war minus fighting, terror, hunger and disease. They were driven to desperate shifts in order to survive. Those in precarious temporary employment had to look for earnings wherever they could, often in manual and semi-skilled labour like driving lorries, buses and taxis. The Academy and other prestigious state institutions were kept afloat by injections of state subsidies, driven by the ever-more extensive printing of cash resulting in the rise of all-corrosive hyperinflation. A few lucky people got jobs with the increasing number of foreign enterprises, including western retailers including supermarkets, car dealers, law firms, the press and journalism, and often received their incomes in foreign currency which not only protected them, but in some cases made them more prosperous.

There was no single turning point but one extraordinary event of 1989 showed that the dams of official restraint on free speech had well and truly broken. We have already noted that 1989 was the peak of open expression. The peak of 1989 was the remarkable Congress of People's Deputies. In such tumultuous times it was not a perfect example of democracy. It was composed of three groups, each of 750 delegates. Two of the groups were elected according to the existing system of election to the supreme Soviet, which the new body replaced. The third group was composed of delegates of social organizations. The Communist Party itself had an allocation of 100 and the trade unions had a large bloc. Many other institutions, including the cultural unions, were represented. The Academy of Sciences had several seats, one of which was occupied by Sakharov who became a major figure in the new body which met from 25 May to 9 June. Although the vast majority of members were attached to the party, the opinions and positions of candidates ranged widely. The provision that the winning candidate needed over 50 per cent of the vote meant that old guard figures were largely defeated and numerous run-off elections had had to be held. The intended function of the Congress was to elect a subset of about half the total membership to become the permanent legislative body replacing the Supreme Soviet. However, its role as an outlet for pent-up criticisms dominated the first session. Like a herd of cattle turned out of their winter cowsheds which sprang out and ran around their spring meadow, the delegates exploded with ideas, debates, criticism, very much along the lines we have identified among the dissident underground. Russian nationalists clashed with liberals and representatives of national minorities. Party diehards demanded a return to 'discipline'. Experts denounced many specific grievances in local areas. Political chicanery was widely attacked. The congress met at a moment when the economy was in a complex transition from the old planning system to a very rough and ready market system and was at a delicate moment, when the costs of transition had severely reduced availability of goods and the hoped-for benefits of the system had not begun to flow. Unsurprisingly, there was a raucous exchange of views about economic inefficiency. Environmental degradation, with a focus on the purity of water in the world's largest body of fresh water, Lake Baikal, and a post-Chernobyl critique of nuclear power, precipitated numerous interventions. The whole nation was screaming for the microphone and the proceedings, broadcast live on TV, drew the attention of everyone. It is even argued that there was a traceable dip in economic activity during the Congress as workers paid more attention to the transmissions than to their tasks. It was an extraordinary phenomenon to see the recently exiled Sakharov leading debates. Notable speeches came from other intellectuals who had worked within the system such as the historian and archive head Yuri Afanas'ev who denounced the 'aggressive-obedient majority' for blocking the much-needed reforms for which the country had a deep thirst.

Was the Congress a triumph for the intelligentsia? Ironically, although it was the first time they had been able to speak openly in public, and many intellectuals took great advantage from that, the Congress also showed that all other sectors of society had been silenced and were intent on pursuing their own agendas. Secession from the Union was a major theme of delegates of national minorities, including some former dissidents but also many politicians and party members. As their predecessors had done since the rise of Muscovy, military leaders and spokespeople demanded the maintaining of what they considered adequate levels of armaments to police the Soviet Union's external borders and complained about the possible breakup of the Soviet armed forces into numerous successor bodies. In the national clamour, the once-clear and solitary voices of dissidents were being drowned out, not by state censorship any more, but by ruthless lobbies pursuing self and special interests. Sakharov, for example, had clashed directly with Gorbachev in the Congress by, for example, complaining that the Chair of the Supreme Soviet, namely Gorbachev who was elected to the post by the Congress, had excessive, even unlimited, personal powers, but he made one even more self-damaging error. Following unsubstantiated stories floated by the American right, he accused the Soviet armed forces in Afghanistan (which they had evacuated the preceding February) of having fired on its own men to avoid them being captured by the enemy. This provoked an avalanche of outrage at the unpatriotic accusation and a storm of refutation by the military leaders inside and outside the Congress.[13] Sakharov's error undermined much of his credibility and, already weakened by illness, he did not live long enough to fully restore it in the eyes of the Russian public. His error illuminated two major weaknesses of the dissidents and internal critics of the Soviet system. All too often they tended to be uncritical of the west and western sources for understandable but misleading reasons. It also showed up the naivety, not least in believing in the power of reason and that words and ideas alone would change the situation.

The Congress, which might have been expected to be a triumph of the intelligentsia, instead set the scene for what might be interpreted as the beginning of its decline and death or, more optimistically, the start of a transition to a very different kind of intelligentsia. Across the whole European communist world, together with echoes in China up to the Tien an Men repression in June, there seemed to be unprecedented opportunities for the various intelligentsias. At different points in the year intelligentsia voices like Jens Reich in East Germany, Jacek Kuron and Karol Modzelewski in Poland, Vaclav Havel in Czechoslovakia, Zhelu Zheliev in Bulgaria and many others had the attention of not only their nations when they addressed mass rallies but also the wider world. In all cases their influence did not survive transition. Some, like Havel and Zheliev, became presidents of their post-communist countries but they were soon by-passed by very different political forces. In the Soviet case, the collapse of communism opened opportunities for ruthless, demagogic and corrupt politicians like Yel'tsin and old-style dictators like Nazarbaev in Kazakhstan rather than the Sakharov's and Aitmatov's. In Ukraine, the candidacy in the presidential election of the distinguished dissident and former political prisoner, Viacheslav Chornovil, who spent years in solitary confinement in the Brezhnev era for promoting independence and civil rights in Ukraine, was swept aside with 23 per cent of the vote by Leonid Kravchuk, a former party agit-prop official and a leader of the Ukrainian Communist Party which had consigned Chornovil to the gulag, who garnered 61 per cent. Chornovil's untimely death in 1999 in a car crash, when he was poised to be a powerful opposition candidate to Leonid Kuchma in that year's presidential election, left many supporters suspicious that he had been murdered. Western media switched away from the dissidents almost as rapidly, since they were no longer useful spokespeople in the propaganda war against a now-collapsed Communist movement. History seemed to be moving beyond the intelligentsia, even submerging it in an outburst of unprecedented political freedom, a relatively open civil society and a popular turn to a consumer market economy with a priority for material welfare now that relative political liberty had been achieved.

In newly independent, or maybe one should say newly separated, Russia, another important focal, indeed turning, point came in August 1993 when Boris Yel'tsin, the president of the newly-fledged Russian Federation, sent troops, including tanks, to suppress the elected parliament. In a struggle between presidential and anti-presidential forces 147 people died, a figure not too far from some credible estimates of the victims of the much more widely known Tien an Men repression of July 1989 in Beijing. It is not our task to unravel this rather surreal confrontation in Moscow, which pitched a theoretically democratic parliament, ironically dominated by supposedly hardline opponents of 'shock' economic 'therapy' and deep political reforms, against a personally dictatorial president seen as guardian of democracy and guarantor of the new freedoms. For the intelligentsia, the Slavophile nationalists supported the so-called parliament, which was actually rooted in Soviet era institutions, while the westernizers, liberal and socialist, supported President Yelt'sin. At the time, about half the population seems to have done the same and supported Yel'tsin's coup, while about one-third opposed it. The intelligentsia and society had second thoughts to the extent that, in the early years of the new millennium, approval of Yel'tsin had fallen to some 20 per cent and disapproval to around 50 per cent as the consequences of the event – economic crisis in 1998 and a powerful, quasi-dictatorial, presidency – had become better understood. After 1993 an all-out privatization of many public assets was conducted. Employees in many institutions, from factories to hospitals, were presented with certificates of ownership, shares in effect, in their own institutions, without any real thought for the consequences. Many 'shareholders' sold them as quickly as possible to help survival in the difficult conditions. As a result, many of Russia's key assets were scooped up at bargain basement prices by ruthless, often gangster-related, 'businessmen' who were the original 'New Russians', as they were first called before they attracted the more enduring name of 'oligarchs'. It was the most devastating theft of a people's property since the American 'robber barons' of the late nineteenth century, many of whom looked like small time operators by comparison.

Be that as it may the intelligentsia was severely threatened, materially and intellectually, by the new situation. National unity was fracturing, education was under stress, unprecedented opportunities for consumerism were attracting the winners in the new economic race, privatization of personal life was undermining community solidarity. The intelligentsia foundations of democratic and human rights, service of the people and Slavophile nostalgia, looked hopelessly outdated or irrelevant. The question 'Has the intelligentsia survived into the new Russia?' became a real issue. Not since the time of *Vekhi* (*Landmarks/Waypoints*) in 1909 had such a debate engaged so much attention. Unlike the flash and burn two year *Vekhi* debate, the new discussion burned slowly through the first two decades of the millennium. Who belonged to the intelligentsia? What did it mean to belong? Did it exist in the traditional, moral sense? Was it now just a social class comprising intellectual brain workers in humanities, arts, engineering and sciences (though, unlike many western definitions, no one seriously included managers and bureaucrats as a whole)?[14]

One of the first to deny being an *intelligent* was Latvian-Russian essayist and critic Andrei Levkin who published an article entitled 'Why I am not an *intelligent*' in the controversial Latvian journal *Rodnik* around 1999.[15] Individuals put forward, for sometimes strange reasons, why they did not consider themselves to be *intelligenty*. Mikhail Gasparov, in a posthumous contribution to a collection of articles on the history of the intelligentsia published by the Academy of Sciences in 2010, also declined to call himself a member of the intelligentsia but rather 'I am a knowledge worker on a state salary'.[16] In a penetrating analysis of the words 'intelligentsia' and 'intellectuals' Gasparov argued that the classical identifiers of the intelligentsia, notably its 'service of the mind' which was applied to the living and non-living worlds, and its 'moral conscience' which directed its attention towards higher and lower spheres, the state and the people, had evolved into something different. In Gasparov's own words:

> (T)he era of the Russian intelligentsia of the 19th century is probably ending, which alone worked for art, and for philosophy, and for politics. Russian society is slowly and with difficulty, but, even so, democratising. (Intelligentsia) Relationships with higher and lower levels, with the authorities and the people, recede into the background compared to relations with one's peers. There is no need to fight for the truth, it is enough to tell the truth. It is not necessary to convince others to work well, but you need to show how to do so by example in your own work place. This is no longer intelligentsia, but intellectual behaviour. We have seen how the criterion of the classical era, moral conscience, has given way to two others, the old and the new: on the one hand, enlightenment, on the other, it is *intelligentnost'*/ intelligentsianess as the ability to consider one's neighbour to be an equal and to treat them with respect. This is good, as long as the concept of intelligent does not fuse into the idea of simply being a 'good person'.[17]

Gasparov's point emphasizes that the educated class no longer looked to oppose the state and serve the people. He does not specifically refer to the crucial absence of a sense of social justice which was integral to the classical intelligentsia of the nineteenth and early twentieth centuries but rather that members of the educated class measured themselves against each other, not simply for being good but also being 'enlightened' (*prosveshchennyi*) and 'cultured' (*kult'urnyi*). This he equates with the behaviour of 'intellectuals', a term he claims has only recently been imported into Russia in the form '*intellektualy*', rather than *intelligenty*, a term which, he rightly points out, has no equivalent in non-Russian languages.

There were numerous other contributions.[18] Can we throw light on the discussion from the perspective of the concerns of the present study? First and foremost we have seen that in the Soviet era, as well as a crude attempt to uproot elements of pre-revolutionary culture and raise communist consciousness, there was also an explosion of Russia's knowledge and skills base. Although it was constructed on a pre-existing base it grew vastly. A simple indicator shows this. In Russia in 1917 there were 15,000 engineers. By 1941 there were 250,000.[19] UN figures for 2021 indicate that Russia today produces more than 450,000 engineers per year, putting it in first place globally.[20] Even allowing for inflation in job titles, this is a very large increase. Since the fall of communism the country has been catching up with the worldwide digital revolution, comprising hardware, software and digital media development. Corresponding growth of education and cultural spheres has also taken place producing what some sources refer to as a 'mass intelligentsia', a complete antithesis to the select, élite nature of the mid-nineteenth-century intelligentsia. According to Galina Sillaste, the Russian intelligentsia at the end of the twentieth century comprised three strata:

> 'The highest intelligentsia' – members of the creative professions, developers in science, technology, culture and humanities. The overwhelming majority of representatives of this stratum are employed in the social and spiritual (*dukhovnyi)* spheres, a minority in industry (technical intelligentsia);
>
> 'Mass intelligentsia' – doctors, teachers, engineers, journalists, designers, technologists, agronomists and other specialists. Many representatives of the stratum work in social sectors (health care, education), slightly less (up to 40 per cent) in industry, the rest in agriculture or trade.
>
> 'Semi-intelligentsia' – technicians, paramedics, nurses, assistants, consultants, laboratory assistants.[21]

Such a broad definition brings into question, as Gramsci suggested in his *Prison Notebooks: The Origins of the Intelligentsia*, whether the intelligentsia constitutes a single group or an amalgam of separate layers. At the very least, the definition shows that the classical intelligentsia has transformed itself beyond recognition. There is very little suggestion from anyone that within the broader mass there is a core subgroup close to the original definition.

However, that may not be the end of the matter. There are many individuals in post-Soviet Russia who share characteristics with *intelligenty* of earlier periods. Most of them are in opposition to the government, as was the case in the past. However, by and large, from 1991 to the 2022 'Special Military Operation' against Ukraine whose long term consequences have yet to work themselves out, Russia has been in a phase where, although often hemmed in by underhand and barely legal and sometimes illegal and criminal tactics, opposition has remained open, widespread and accepted. Since the beginning of hostilities in February 2022 television has been subjected to the most severe political controls followed by a newspaper press which, even so, still covers a wide spectrum, and the internet which, so far, has remained relatively untouched. Up to the moment of writing (August 2023) there has been an explosion of social media and independent uploading of war-related videos on Telegram, VK (V Kontakte), Rumble, Rokfin and other platforms, though Facebook is mainly unavailable in Russia. Nonetheless, political opposition has never been allowed to reach the point where it threatens to defeat the ruling party and president. It is thought by many that Yel'tsin's re-election as president in 1996 was only achieved by election fixing. The west was not unhappy about this because the alternative candidate was Gennadi Zyuganov (b.1944) who represented the communist and social-democratic left and has been the leader of the second largest group in the Duma since 1995. From our perspective the election was a kind of coda to the 1993 suppression of parliament, ranging the forces of gangster capitalism and supposed western liberalism against the remnants of Soviet communism and democratic socialism. Both sides claimed to be nationalist.

However, opposition has included notable figures who fell foul of the regime and were imprisoned. One of the first prominent arrests in the Putin era, which began in 1999, was not of an *intelligent* opponent but an oligarch, Mikhail Khodorkovsky (b.1963), who served a jail term, was deprived of much of his wealth and, since his release, has re-styled himself in a more *intelligent* mode as a bearer of liberal values and rule of law. For westerners, the most prominent opponent, Alexei Navalny (b.1976), also has intelligentsia characteristics. His political pitch has had two main props. In the early stages he promoted limiting immigration (meaning largely the influx of Central Asian Muslims from post-soviet states) but in later years focused on accusations of personal corruption in high places on a colossal scale. His frequent YouTube channel broadcasts were compulsive viewing, especially for young Moscow and other metropolitan intellectuals. He continued for many years, until 2020, when some extremely provocative charges were made, notably that a massive, Disney/ Neuschwanstein-type chateau on the Black Sea coast – boasting swimming pools, sports facilities, extensive grounds, dozens of rooms and even a casino – had been built for Putin personally. Navalny then fell ill, was allowed to leave for treatment in Germany, where doctors asserted he had been poisoned with the deadly substance novichok, and was allowed back into Russia, an option he bravely chose despite the threat of imprisonment. He was, indeed, arrested and given a series of increasingly savage jail sentences. In many ways his career stands in the intelligentsia tradition as a former student, a lawyer as was Lenin, sacrificing himself in the cause of human rights. Critics, however, point not to his undoubted bravery and commitment, but to his political ambitions and desire to rule the system rather than change it. How that might play out in the future is hard to foresee.

During his first detention in Vladimir jail in December 2011, Navalny was not the only political prisoner. Another opposition leader, Sergei Udal'tsov (b.1977), had also been arrested and was on hunger strike to protest the conditions in which he was being held. The two of them had been arrested at the same Moscow rallies on several occasions. Despite that, and although very well-known in Russia, his case is hardly known in the west even though his political attachment is to an opposition group which rates higher than Navalny's in real and opinion polls. Much has been written about Navalny in the western press and his cause has been taken up officially by governments, a phenomenon which paradoxically both arouses Kremlin suspicion about him and partially protects him. No western government protested Udal'tsov's incarceration from 2014 to 2017 and no press campaign supports his stance. The proportion of column inches devoted to him in the western press compared to Navalny is minute. One does not have to look very far to find the probable answer to this question. Udal'tsov represents what he claims to be a democratic form of socialism and his political faction, the Vanguard of Red Youth, is affiliated to the bloc led by the Communist Party of the Russian Federation, the successor to the former Russian and USSR Communist parties which were dissolved in 1991. Where Navalny represents a post-Soviet version of liberalism, Udal'tsov and others in the Communist party represent the left. Unlike most dissidents from the late Soviet era, they highlight issues of social justice, wealth inequalities and economic structures as well as abstract, legal human rights. The Communist party has, unexpectedly perhaps, also wrapped the flag of Russian nationalism around itself and, ambiguously, claims to remain atheist but not militantly so as its Soviet era predecessor was. This has opened the way to rapprochement with the Russian Orthodox church, which has upset many of its own members. Udal'tsov also wants to renew the Soviet Union as a geopolitical entity by consent but not with the same command economy. Clearly these objectives, in a radically new mix, are rooted in the traditional intelligentsia left.

A third figure, often played up in the western press, is the extreme nationalist Alexander Dugin (b.1970) who is often attributed with more power over government than he actually has. Dugin's ideas are very hard to pin down as they are immensely eclectic and are constantly developing. In his early youth as a Soviet student he was violently anti-Communist to the extent he set up a neo-Nazi SS group. After the fall of communism he became more interested in aspects of Marxism and began to evolve a blend of left and right ideas. He often self-described as a fascist but what he meant by that notoriously imprecise term is hard to define. It seems to have incorporated the bedrock idea that the collective, the state, is everything, the individual nothing, though he substantially modified this later by adding that the vital inner content of the Russian state was the *narod* (people). He attached to this an aggressive Russian nationalism, the Old Believer branch of Russian Orthodoxy, a refusal to accept democracy as a good in itself (he said there had been good regimes that were not democratic and democratic regimes that were not good) and a fierce opposition to materialism, to liberalism and to their embodiment in the capitalist United States, which he came to describe as Nazi. By around 2009 his ideas were stabilizing around a 'fourth political theory' as he called it, which superseded liberalism, communism and fascism. He has often been described by western analysts, notably Andreas Umland, as fascist. However, the controversial specialist on fascism, A. James Gregor, pointed out that 'whatever Alexander Dugin is, he is not a fascist in the literal and historically meaningful sense of the term' in that he was influenced by so many views that he was not simply a fascist, but also a Bolshevik, a mystic, occultist, Sufi, samurai, 'neo-Eurasian', 'new socialist' and 'conservative revolutionary'.[22] He said his ideas came from the right but without zenophobia, racism or hierarchies between people; from the left without atheism and materialism, and he says yes to social justice and cultural identity.[23] His postmodernism has also come to the fore in his acceptance of the relativization of truth and his current philosophical starting point of the Heideggerian 'dasein', namely the existential experience of humans.

Fortunately it is not our task to untangle this skein of ideas. However, from our perspective of whether or not the intelligentsia has survived, Dugin is, perhaps paradoxically, one of Russia's current public intellectuals who is most closely integrated into the intelligentsia tradition. His association with the sacred and with the Old Believers is unusual but not unique in that tradition; but his two successive major political-organizational commitments reveal deep links to small groups on the intelligentsia fringe. These are National Bolshevism and Eurasianism. National Bolshevism emerged around 1919 among disillusioned White Guard officers who saw that their cause was heading for defeat. They were impressed by Bolshevik success in rapidly rebuilding a state capable of fielding a large army and fighting off Russia's enemies, a whole slew of whom were attempting to intervene in Russia for their own purposes. Since the Whites were reliant on the support of foreign powers it seemed, as already noted, to people like Nikolai Ustrialov and Yuri Potekhin that the Bolsheviks represented the White cause of 'Russia One and Indivisible' better than the Whites themselves.[24] The concept had been revived among 1970s dissidents by Mikhail Agursky, himself a fascinating figure who was a cybernetics specialist by training who became a dissident through, amongst other things, meeting the daughter of the pre-revolutionary religious philosopher and writer V.V. Rozanov, indicating the kind of channel by which non-Bolshevik cultures were flowing in informal channels throughout the Soviet period. Agursky, as a convinced Zionist who eventually emigrated to Israel and became a professor at the University of Jerusalem, had the unexpected notion that Zionism and Russian nationalism were not enemies but closely resembled each other, representing the will to survive of both nations. He wrote an account of this aspect of his ideas in *Ideologiia natsional bolshevizma* (The Ideology of National Bolshevism) published in Paris in 1980.[25] The ideas were taken up by another dissident, Eduard Limonov, who set up a political party of that name in 1991, inspired by Dugin's idea of uniting aspects of right and left, fascism and communism, against the new world monopoly of liberal capitalism.[26] Dugin left the National Bolshevik Party in 2009 and concentrated on a new Eurasian movement. Eurasianism had also emerged in the twilight of the tsarist era and the revolutionary struggle of 1917 and after. Figures like N. Trubetskoi and, for a time, George Fedotov associated themselves with the idea of Eurasianism while in exile in the 1920s and Blok's great poem *The Scythians*, which dramatically proclaimed: 'We are Scythians! We are narrow-eyed Asians!', could be considered Eurasian.[27] However, the modern stimulator of Eurasian ideas was the Soviet veteran of the Battle of Berlin, Lev Gumilev (1912–92) who became a maverick ethnographer in the post-Stalin era. Again illustrating continuities, he was the son of the executed poet Nikolai Gumilev and Anna Akhmatova. It was from Gumilev that Dugin adopted his new stance. In essence, Eurasianism stood for a crossover between westernizers and Slavophiles in identifying Russia as having an identity which was neither European nor Asian but a blend of both. In Blok's words:

> We've held the shield between two hostile powers –
> Old Europe and the barbarous Mongol horde.

Dugin argued that Russia stood against western liberal capitalism and materialism and proposed links with Iran, China and, surprisingly perhaps, Russia's persistent rival Turkey and a number of smaller, illiberal countries. He also reaches out to largely right-wing populist and extremist western writers, including Steve Bannon. The aim is to form an anti-western, anti-liberal capitalist, bloc and to gather lost Russian territories, notably Crimea but also Ukraine as a whole, back into the fold. Because of this, Dugin is usually presented in the west as the '*éminence grise*' behind Putin's throne, the architect of Putin's supposed expansionist ambitions. True, for a short period around 2009, Dugin appears to have had the ear of the speaker and chairman of the Duma, Gennadi Seleznev and Sergei Naryshkin, but he lost his posts at Moscow University in 2014. In late July 2020 his YouTube channel and email account were blocked by the state authorities. On the only occasion he stood to be elected to a public institution, the State Duma in 1996, he garnered less than 1 per cent of the vote, coming fourteenth out of seventeen candidates in the constituency. Despite this, his influence is frequently exaggerated in the west. His ideas can be used by Russophobes as evidence of a threat and he has had some access to media and high status events in western Europe and the United States including encounters with Francis Fukuyama, Zbigniew Brzezinski, Bernard-Henry Levy and an extended interview on BBC Newsnight, among others. He is usually presented, formally or implicitly, as a spokesperson for Russia though his influence is very limited. In an impromptu poll in 2009, at the peak of his public exposure, he came only thirty-sixth in a list of influential intellectuals.[28] In a tragic twist, when Dugin's daughter Darya was assassinated in Moscow in August 2022, by a Ukrainian death squad which probably mistook her for her father when she was unexpectedly driving his car, the western press immediately claimed it was because Dugin was 'the mind of Putin'. However, when it was realized this implied likely Ukrainian responsibility for her death, within two days and with no explanation, the press began to describe him as a leading opponent of Putin and possible opposition candidate in the 2024 presidential election so that they could blame Putin for the killing. Eventually Ukrainian responsibility was recognized.[29]

Naval'ny, Udal'tsov and Dugin do not 'typify' or 'represent' post-Soviet intellectuals but they do illustrate how the increasingly diverse civil society of Russia still has links which connect it deeply to the intelligentsia tradition. Comparing them with the earlier troika of Sakharov, Medvedev and Solzhenitsyn, we can see the ways intellectual life has moved on. The three more recent figures are more divisive and evoke respect only within their factions whereas the earlier dissidents were widely respected even by those who disagreed with them and, by and large, they respected each other, possibly because they were fighting the same enemy in the Soviet state. The post-Soviet dissidents are also competing more with each other for political influence in a way more comparable to their counterparts in liberal democratic societies.

Be that as it may, there are many other examples of public intellectuals in post-Soviet Russia who look back to the intelligentsia tradition. Boris Nemtsov (1959–2015) was a nuclear physicist before turning to liberal politics during perestroika. He had a fully western orientation and, after becoming Governor of the Nizhnyi Novgorod (formerly Gorky) province he made a success of the transition to a liberal market economy. He preceded Naval'ny in focusing on Kremlin corruption and focused sharply on Putin, whom he accused of being deeply involved in it. In 2015 he was assassinated near Red Square. A Chechen hit squad was convicted of his murder but there was no official word on who had paid their hefty commission for carrying out the dreadful deed. Another courageous victim was Anna Politkovskaya (1958–2006) who was an investigative journalist who specialized in highly critical reporting on the wars in Chechnya. Her criticism of Putin was extreme. In an interview with *The Guardian* after there had been an attempt, eerily foreshadowing a similar attack on Navalny fifteen years later, to poison her on a flight, she said

> Only a journalist who is loyal to the establishment is treated as "one of us". If this is a journalists' approach to the cause that we serve, then it spells an end to the basic tenet that we are working so that people know what is happening and take the right decisions … ….We are hurtling back into a Soviet abyss, into an information vacuum that spells death from our own ignorance. All we have left is the internet, where information is still freely available. For the rest, if you want to go on working as a journalist, it's total servility to Putin. Otherwise, it can be death, the bullet, poison, or trial—whatever our special services, Putin's guard dogs, see fit.[30]

Two years later she was shot to death in her apartment block hallway by contracted hitmen whose financer(s) remain unknown. Her bleak anxieties about the direction of change in Russia have not been borne out, though developments in 2020 and 2021, including the shutting down or state takeover of some media outlets and a campaign to force many independent organizations and NGOs to register as 'foreign agents', had ominous consequences. The career of another writer and publicist, Tatiana Tolstaya (b.1951), illustrates this. A classics graduate from Leningrad, Tolstaya turned to writing and became one of the most elegiac recorders of Russia's transition. Despite spending a considerable amount of time in the United States in the 1990s, when she returned to Russia she was able to host a television show, entitled *School for Scandal*, from 2002 to 2014 devoted to interviews with leading cultural and political figures. Since then she has been largely absent from Russian television screens. She is, perhaps, one of the few post-Soviet Russian writers whose works are widely translated in the west, though she is not widely known even among western *literati*. She has refused to endorse Russia's absorption of Crimea but, nonetheless, won a major prize of the Russian Writers' Union in 2020.

Tolstaya, in recent years, has promoted feminism in Russia. Women's equality, after broader social inequality and poverty in general, remains a major blight on contemporary Russian society. Women are massively under-represented in public bodies, especially the government and the Duma. They remain subjected to the quadruple burden of patriarchy, domestic duty, child-rearing and earning an income, all of which severely limit career opportunities. In Russia, the glass ceiling is more like concrete, but feminist movements are underdeveloped. Identity politics in general, especially discrimination on LGBTQ+ grounds, has attracted much attention in the west but is not something which moves Russian society beyond those directly involved. Postmodern protests include the provocative actions of the open to all, anarchist music group Pussy Riot. Three members of Pussy Riot – Nadezhda Tolkonnikova, Mariia Alyokhina and Yekaterina Samutsevich – were imprisoned for setting up an impromptu rock concert in Moscow's largest cathedral in 2012, as a protest against the Moscow Patriarchate supporting Putin's re-election to the presidency. This was typical of the kind of guerrilla, concept-art approach the group favours. It is hard to say what impact such activities have. Many people were repelled by the blatant sacrilege but their defenders included Sergei Udal'tsov and the former world chess champion-turned political activist Garry Kasparov. Both were arrested on separate occasions for demonstrating in support of the three women. Figures like the Soviet-era pop diva Alla Pugacheva and even Putin supporters, like the film director and actor Fyodor Bondarchuk, expressed a degree of support and Dmitrii Medvedev, the prime minister at the time, said after the trial that their pre-trial detention was sufficient punishment and they should be released. A number of other supporters of Putin expressed similar concerns, mainly because of the way such an affair affected the image of Russia in the west. However, religious leaders, notably Patriarch Kirill (not to mention Pope Benedict XVI), were horrified at the support for the women, especially from members of their churches. Putin also believed they had 'got what they were asking for' and that any disrespect to the church was completely unacceptable because 'the country has very grave memories of the initial period of Soviet rule, when a huge number of priests suffered. Many churches were destroyed and all our traditional faiths suffered huge damage.' The following year insulting people's religious feelings was made a specific crime but in December 2013, Putin also declared an amnesty which included the three women (and Mikhail Khodorkovsky and imprisoned Greenpeace activists) who were released three months early.

Do Pussy Riot have anything in common with the intelligentsia tradition? In some ways they are in the tradition of 'serving the people' and being 'the mind, honour and conscience' of the nation on issues of sexuality and gender as well as political and civic rights. Their immediate inspirations come from the western feminist tradition rather than Russia, where, although women's emancipation was an integral part of liberal and socialist discourse, commitment to it was often more rhetorical than practical. They do, however, reference Kropotkin, though what he would have made of their protest methods is hard to say. As an anarchist collective they recall some of the utopian communes of the revolutionary period, as well as the Dionysian energy of groups like the mystical anarchists, though Pussy Riot is not strongly spiritual despite using religious imagery from time to time. Interestingly, Pussy Riot were preceded in provocative protest in support of feminism by the Ukrainian Femen organization, led by Anna Khutsol, whose trademark is bare-breasted protest by women. Naked protests are not new in the Russian tradition. Before 1917 the Dukhobors (Spirit Wrestlers) protested by throwing off their clothes in public places, a practice some of them took with them when they emigrated to Canada.

While an intelligentsia group is hard to find in twenty-first-century Russia, specific continuities with the tradition are strong and continue to contribute to a specifically Russian mentalité, or perhaps selection of mentalités still revolving around those with a western orientation, slavophiles who denounce the west and interpret a culturally self-sufficient Russia and Eurasians who look to Russia as a bridge between the Atlantic and Pacific worlds and all that lies immediately to the south of Russia. Echoes of the deepest traditions and values from the past can appear in what, to the uninitiated, look like surprising anomalies but which, in actuality, lie deep within the remaining elements of 'the Russian soul'. Two striking examples, which emerged during the writing of this book, illustrate the point perfectly.

The first example is that of Vladimir Putin, a person whom everyone in the west thinks they know – as a ruthless and unimaginative, self-seeking and corrupt dictator. Many seem to think he is a communist, even a Stalinist, in light disguise. However, most such 'experts' would be surprised to learn that Putin professes a deep Orthodox faith and that the church is an integral part of Putin's rule. Sceptics argue that his faith is a cynical front tied to the nationalism which binds the country together. We cannot know for certain how accurate such assumptions are but we do know that what Putin actually says is rarely reported in any depth by western mainstream media and is simply set aside by Russophobic specialists who consider it to be mere propaganda. However, Putin's public utterances deserve to be taken into account. He often references the past and some of the great figures of the intelligentsia, usually from its spiritual rather than scientific wing. One of his frequent references is to the controversial historian/ethnologist Lev Gumilev (1912–92), the son of the executed poet Nikolai Gumilev and Anna Akhmatova. Gumilev's work has been taken up by Eurasianists. On 20 October 2021 Putin addressed the Valdai Club, an invited gathering of international figures many of whom support better relations between Russia and the west and the rest of the outside world, in the following terms, even catching out the chair who momentarily misquoted the title and theme of the discussion group:

> **Vladimir Putin:** I would start with the theme of today's Valdai meeting. What is it?
> **Fyodor Lukyanov:** The Return of the Future.
> **Vladimir Putin:** No, no. The slogan of today's meeting?
> **Fyodor Lukyanov:** Global Shake-Up.
> **Vladimir Putin:** It's longer.
> **Fyodor Lukyanov:** The Individual, Values. But 'individual' is rarely remembered.
> **Vladimir Putin:** Well, it should be, because this is the most important point.
>
> I have been remembering [Nikolai] Berdyaev. As you know, he wrote several major works, and they are still popular. He wrote about the new Middle Ages, as was relevant at that time, about freedom, how it was such a heavy burden. But he also said something else – that the individual should always be at the centre of development. The individual is more important than society or the state. I would very much like to see a future where all the resources of society and the state are concentrated around the interests of the individual. We definitely need to strive for this. It is difficult to say now how effective we will be in creating such a system, but this is what we should strive for.[31]

Putin reflects the central point of *Vekhi* proclaimed in the introduction by Gershenzon:

> Their common platform is the recognition of the theoretical and practical primacy of the spiritual life over the external forms of community. They mean by this that the inner life of the individual is the sole creative force of human existence, and that this inner life, and not the self-sufficient principles of the political sphere, is the only solid basis on which a society can be built.[32]

An even more striking continuity occurred, practically unnoticed in the West, when a Russian cosmonaut took with him into space a tiny but massively symbolic relic of St Serafim of Sarov, the hermit-saint whose canonization was attended by some 400,000 fellow-worshipers in 1903. The *Irish Independent* reported on its website on 12 April 2017:

> A cosmonaut who has returned to Earth after a mission on the International Space Station says he took a relic of a Russian Orthodox saint with him. Sergei Ryzhykov told Russian news agencies that he would give the tiny relic of St Serafim of Sarov's body to an Orthodox church in Star City outside Moscow, home to the cosmonaut training centre. Mr Ryzhykov, who landed with two other crew members on Monday after six months in space, said he would celebrate the relic's return at a church service in Star City on Thursday.[33]

This was not unique. On 9 January 2010 The Catholic News Agency passed on a story from Russia *Today* about another cosmonaut who had returned from the International Space Station:

> 'Writing on his blog at the website of the Russian Federal Space Agency (Roscosmos), Cosmonaut Maksim Suraev responded to readers' questions about religious symbols on the space station. "We have four holy icons on the Russia segment. We also have the Gospels and a big cross."'[34]

The monastery had come to the space station.

Notes

Introduction

1 Nahirny, V., *The Russian Intelligentsia: From Torment to Silence*, George, Allen and Unwin, London, 1966; Possony, S., *Lenin: The Compulsive Revolutionary*, London, 1965. Nozick, Robert, 'Why Do Intellectuals Oppose Capitalism?', *Cato Policy Report*, 20 (1) (January–February 1998), pp. 1, 9–11. Interestingly, Possony worked extensively for US military intelligence and has been credited with having devised the concept of the Strategic Defence Initiative (Star Wars).
2 Sadr, Ahmad, *Max Weber's Sociology of Intellectuals,* Oxford University Press, Oxford, 1995.
3 Marx, Karl, The International Workingmen's Association: General Rules, October 1864.
4 Lenin V. I. 'Letter to Gorky 15 September 1919', https://www.marxists.org/archive/lenin/works/1919/sep/15.htm
5 Read, Christopher, *Lenin: A Revolutionary Life*, Routledge, London and New York, 2003, p. 88.
6 Lenin V. I. 'Letter to Gorky 15 September 1919', https://www.marxists.org/archive/lenin/works/1919/sep/15.htm
7 Benda, Julien, *La Trahison des Clercs*, Grasset, Paris, 1927.
8 Burnham, James, *The Managerial Revolution,* John Day, New York, 1941.
9 Ibid., pp. 200–1.
10 Rizzi, Bruno, *La Bureaucratisation du Monde: le collectivisme bureaucratique, quo vadis America?* Paris, 1939. Extracts in English https://www.marxists.org/archive/rizzi/bureaucratisation/index.htm
11 Weil, Simone, *L'enracinement*, Gallimard, Paris, 1949.
12 See for example the locus classicus Kerr, Clark, Dunlop, John T., Harbison, Frederick and Myers, Charles A. *Industrialism and Industrial Man,* Oxford University Press (Galaxy), New York, 1960.
13 Quotations from Nozick (1998), p. 1 and p. 11. Nozick, Robert, 'Why Do Intellectuals Oppose Capitalism?', *Cato Policy Report*, 20 (1) (January–February 1998), p. 1 and 9–11.
14 Shils, Edward, 'Introduction', *The Intellectuals and the Powers, and Other Essays (His Selected Papers, 1),* University of Chicago Press, Chicago, 1972, p. vii.
15 Details in the Bibliography.
16 See for example Collini, Stefan, *Public Moralists: Political Thought and Intellectual Life in Britain 1850–1930*, Oxford University Press, Oxford, 1991.
17 Hamon, Hervé and Patrick, Rotman, *Génération*. t.1 *Les années de rêve (1958–68)* t.2 *Les années de poudre (1968–1975),* Le Seuil, Paris, 1987, 1988. Ory, P. and Sirinelli, J. F., *Les Intellectuels en France de l'affaire Dreyfus á nos jours,* Armand Colin, Paris, 1986; Debray, Régis, *Teachers, Writers, Celebrities: The Intellectuals of Modern France,* Verso, London, 1981; Bastié, Eugénie, *La Guerre des idées – Enquête au coeur de l'intelligentsia française,* Robert Laffont, Paris, 2021.

Chapter 1

1. They were animists; that is, they attributed a spiritual dimension to flora, fauna and inanimate objects such as rocks. Shamans were wise/holy men and women who led associated cults.
2. Other key words of Tatar/Turkic origin include *tamozhnia,* customs in the border, taxation sense; *deng'i* – money; *tiurm'a* – prison. A whole imperial system summarized in three words. Ironically, even the Russian word for 'yoke' – *iga* – was of Tatar origin.
3. A kind of prototype aristocracy, the next social group below the tsar and the princes. Unlike some of their western counterparts, the feudal barons of England, for example, their power declined in the face of increasing autocratic authority in the fifteenth and sixteenth centuries.
4. In the early years after the October Revolution of 1917, the philosopher Nicholas Berdyaev and others pointed to Russia's predisposition to communism in his *Origin of Russian Communism*, Geoffrey Bles, London, 1937 was the first English translation).
5. Moon, David, *The Russian Peasantry 1600–930: The World the Peasants Made,* Routledge, London and New York, 1999.
6. Zguta, Russell, 'Skomorokhi: The Russian Minstrel-Entertainers', *Slavic Review*, 31 (2) (June 1972), pp. 297–313.
7. Popova, Olga, *Russian Illuminated Manuscripts (English and Russian edition),* Thames and Hudson, London and New York, 1984. They are little known because they were rarely exhibited in Soviet times partly for ideological reasons but also because, as is obviously still the case, surviving examples are extremely fragile.
8. *Povest' vremennykh let* (*The Russian Primary Chronicle*), http://community.dur.ac.uk/a.k.harrington/christin.html
9. https://en.wikipedia.org/wiki/Theophanes_the_Greek
10. Many icons had a border of smaller images depicting stories from the life of the saint depicted in the main icon. Full-length figures could be found here but not in the central image.
11. Goldfrank, David M., 'Old and New Perspectives on Iosif Volotsky's Monastic Rules', *Slavic Review*, 34 (2) (June 1975), pp. 279–301.
12. Merezhkovsky, D. Gippius, Z. and Filosofov, D. *Le Tsar et la Révolution*, Paris, 1907.

Chapter 2

1. Billington, James, *The Icon and the Axe: An Interpretive History of Russian Culture*, New York, 1966, pp. 72–3.
2. Tolstoy, L., *The Kingdom of God Is within You*, Cassell, London, 1894.
3. There is an interesting and comprehensive summary of Ermolai's tract in Pashkov, A. I. (ed.), *A History of Russian Economic Thought from the Ninth Century through the Eighteenth Century* Institut ekonomiki (Akademiia Nauk Sovetskogo Soiuza) Gosizdat Moscow 1955. English edition Letiche, John (ed.), pp. 135–44, University of California Press, Berkeley and Los Angeles, 1964.
4. Nikitin, Afanasy, *Journey beyond Three Seas*. The manuscript was not published but was included in the *Sofiskaia vtoraia letopis*', a collection of manuscripts in multiple copies compiled in the first half of the XVI century and preserved in RGADA, the Russian State Archive of Ancient Documents. The text, in modern orthography, can be found at https://ru.wikisource.org/wiki/Хождение_за_три_моря_Афанасия_Никитина.

An English translation can be found in: Major, Richard H. (ed.), 'The Travels of Athanasius Nikitin,' in M. Wielhorsky, Mikhail (trans.), *India in the Fifteenth Century*, Hakluyt Society, ser. 1. vol. 22, Hakluyt Society, London, 1857.

5 Mogila (Mohyla in Ukrainian) (1596–1647) was Metropolitan (Archbishop) of Kyiv and Halich who wrote a number of influential works. His *Catechism* was adopted by many Orthodox patriarchates. A text in Latin from the Vatican archives, apparently by him, was first published in 1928. In it he acknowledges his own acceptance of papal supremacy and proposes a plan for bringing the eastern and western branches of Christianity back together.
6 http://www.vehi.net/florovsky/puti/02.html, Section 5 (in Russian).
7 Merezhkovsky, D., 'Revoliutsiia i religiia,' *Russkaia mysl'*, 2, pp. 64–85 and 3, pp. 17–34, 1907.
8 Hughes, Lindsey, *Peter the Great: A Biography*, pp. 90–2 describes the famous 'dwarves wedding'.
9 Osipov, Yu. S., 'Zarozhdenie traditsii,' in *Akademiia nauk v istorii Rossisskogo Gosudarstvo*, Nauka, Moscow, 1999. Extracts available at http://www.ras.ru/about/history/traditions.aspx. The publication publishes materials from the speeches of the President of the Russian Academy of Sciences Academician Yu. S. Osipov at the jubilee celebrations dedicated to the 275th anniversary of the Russian Academy of Sciences. The historical aspects of the creation and development of the Russian Academy of Sciences and its role in the history of the Russian state are highlighted.
10 Osipov ibid.
11 Osipov ibid.
12 Osipov ibid.
13 For a very enthusiastic endorsement of Herder's claim to philosophical centrality see his entry in *The Stanford Encyclopaedia of Philosophy* at https://plato.stanford.edu/entries/herder/
14 We will discuss the nuances of this key term below.
15 There is a well-received recent translation by Kahn, Andrew and Reyfman, Irina, *A Journey from St. Petersburg to Moscow*, Columbia University Press, 2020 (The Russian Library).
16 *Samizdat* means self-published and was a common way of unofficially circulating censored material in the late Soviet period from the 1960s on.
17 Skovoroda is the first figure we have encountered who raises the complex question of distinguishing Russian and Ukrainian identity.
18 Shevelov, George Y., 'Skovoroda's Language and Style,' in Marshall, Richard H. and Bird, Thomas E. (eds.), *Hryhorij Savyč Skovoroda: An Anthology of Critical Articles*. Canadian Institute of Ukrainian Studies, CIUS Press, Toronto, 1994, p. 131.

Chapter 3

1 For a very helpful guide see Harrison, E., 'The Image of the Jesuit in Russian Literary Culture of the Nineteenth Century,' *Modern Languages Open* (1) (2014): http://doi.org/10.3828/mlo.v0i1.38.
2 Gagarin, I. Prince, *La Russie sera-t-elle catholique?*, 1856.
3 The Russian terms were *Pravoslavie; samoderzhavie; narodnost'*. The last also echoes the German term 'volk' as much as nation and incorporates the supposedly simple, loyal peasant mass, a fanciful conceit to which we will return.

4 Note the Russian term for Minister of Education was literally Minister of Popular Enlightenment.
5 Kennedy, Paul, *The Rise and Fall of the Great Powers: Economic Change and Military Conflict from 1500 to 2000*, HarperCollins, London, 1988 and Pomeranz, Kenneth, *The Great Divergence: China, Europe, and the Making of the Modern World Economy*, Princeton University Press, Princeton NJ, 2000.
6 Fonvizin, M., *On Communism and Socialism*, n.p., n.d.
7 Hart-Davies, T., *The poems of K. F. Relaieff*, Remington & Co., New York, 1887, p. 132.
8 There were two earlier historians of Russia, Vassili Tatishchev (1686–1750) and Mikhail Shcherbatov (1733–90). They pioneered the more rigorous use of sources but their efforts were less comprehensive than Karamzin's. Like Karamzin, they believed autocracy was essential to Russian life.
9 Koniaev, N., *Rastsvet i gibel' dinastii*, Veche, Moscow, 2003, p. 465.
10 Sentimentalism derived morality from not only reason but also feeling. Among other consequences sentimentalism began a tradition of appealing to emotions to circumvent the rigours of reason. As such, it became a weapon of certain types of conservative. Unable to combat rationality head on in defence of their values many anti-enlightenment thinkers, political movements and leaders – from Dostoevsky to Nietzsche and, in debased versions, fascism and early twenty-first century so-called populism – emphasized the innate illogicality of human behaviour. For a short, sharp and engaging account of some of the central features of nineteenth-century Russian thought see Buruma, Ian and Margalit, Avishai, *Occidentalism: A Short History of Anti-Westernism*, Atlantic Books, London, 2005, especially pp. 78–99. Unlike much of the specialist literature the authors are steeped in other forms of resistance to 'western' reason and put Russian ideas into a broader context.
11 Chaadaev, P., *First Philosophical Letter*. The *Philosophical Letters* initially circulated from 1826 to 1831 in the form of multiple manuscripts. They were first published in the journal *Teleskop*, 15 (October, 1836).
12 Izgoev, A. S., 'Na perevale. Makhomakhiia v lagere marksistov', *Russkaia mysl'* (6), p. 106.
13 Gershenzon, M. O. (ed.), *Vekhi*, 1909, p. 18.
14 Camus acknowledged Berdyaev's influence in general terms in an article in *Alger-Republique*, 25 June 1939, p. 3.
15 The *Zemskii Sobor* was a gathering of representatives of the nobility, state officials and influential merchants and town leaders convened intermittently by the tsar or patriarch in the sixteenth and seventeenth centuries to confer on and resolve crises in national life. The best known was that of 1613 which resolved the central power vacuum by recognizing the succession of Mikhail Romanov as the first tsar of the Romanov dynasty which ruled until 1917.
16 Lossky, N. O., *A History of Russian Philosophy*, Allen and Unwin, London, 1952.
17 The concept of backwardness will be discussed below.
18 Haywood, Richard Mowbray, *The Beginnings of Railway Development in Russia in the Reign of Nicholas I, 1835–1842*, Duke University Press, Durham, 1969. Tupper, Harmon, *To the Great Ocean: Siberia and the Trans-Siberian Railway*, Little, Brown & Company, Boston, 1965; Westwood, J. N., *A History of Russian Railways*, George Allen and Unwin, London, 1964.
19 He also held the influential position of President of the Imperial Academy of Sciences from 1818 until his death in 1849.

20 Flynn, James T., 'Tuition and Social Class in the Russian Universities: S. S. Uvarov and "Reaction" in the Russia of Nicholas I', *Slavic Review*, 35 (2) (June 1976), p. 242.
21 Quoted in, for example, Chamberlin, William Henry, 'Turgenev: The Eternal Romantic', *The Russian Review*, 5 (2) (Spring, 1946), p. 17. See also Moser, Charles A. *Ivan Turgenev*, Columbia University Press, New York, 1972, p. 7.
22 http://pushkin-lit.ru/pushkin/stihi/stih-157.htm
23 Tyutchev, Fyodor, *Selected Poems*, Brimstone Press, Gillingham, 2014, p. 113.
24 Although the Russian title is straightforward enough it has multiple renderings in English translation including *A Sportsman's Sketches, Notes of a Hunter, Sketches from a Hunter's Album, a Sportsman's Notebook.*
25 Solzhenitsyn, Aleksandr, *The First Circle,* Chapter 57. First published in 1968. An extended version was published in 2009 with the title *V pervom kruge* translated as *In the First Circle* by Harper, New York and London, 2009.

Chapter 4

1 Troubetzkoy, A., *A Brief History of the Crimean War,* Constable and Robinson, London, 2006, p. 208.
2 Leikina-Svirskaia, V. R., *Intelligentsiia v Rossii vo vtoroi polovine XIX veka,* Mysl, Moscow, 1971, p. 94 and p. 96. Leikina-Svirskaia also points out that before the turn to reaction after 1881 several hundred army officers identified with the revolutionary intelligentsia. The military wing of *Narodnaia voliia* comprised some 400 officers but the professionalization of the army 'weakened the links between the officers and society' (p. 98) and by the 1890s 'many wanted to join the corps of gendarmes' something which would have seemed shameful not long before (p. 99).
3 Gregory Freeze has written a great deal to pinpoint the difficulties faced by the rural clergy including the pioneering studies *The Russian Levites: Parish Clergy in the Eighteenth Century,* no. 78 (Harvard Russian Research Center Studies) Harvard University Press, Cambridge, MA, 1977 and *The Parish Clergy in Nineteenth-Century Russia: Crisis, Reform, Counter-Reform* (Princeton Legacy Library), Princeton, NJ, 1983. See the memoir by I. S. Belliustin, *Description of the Clergy in Rural Russia: The Memoir of a Nineteenth-Century Parish Priest,* ed. and trans. Freeze, Cornell University Press, Ithaca and London, 1985 for an almost unremittingly bleak assessment of the rural clerical life.
4 For a superbly researched account see Manchester, Laurie, *Holy Fathers, Secular Sons: Clergy, Intelligentsia, and the Modern Self in Revolutionary Russia* (NIU Series in Slavic, East European, and Eurasian Studies), Northern Illinois University Press, 2008
5 On the massive challenge of surveying the immense territories of rural Russia from 1720–1861 see the fascinating article by Natalia Platonova, 'L'arpentage Général Des Terres En Russie Comme Projet Impérial (1765–1861)', *Histoire & Sociétés Rurales*, 50 (2) (2018), pp. 109–157 which depicts the difficulties of finding trustworthy surveyors, often chosen from among army officers, in the early stages, and the vast areas surveyed by the time of the completion of the second phase of the great land survey around 1860. Nonetheless, most of the western borderlands from western Ukraine to the Baltic States including Finland, not to mention Siberia and Turkmenistan, had still to be surveyed at that time. (pp. 133–4) Fortunately, from the point of view of emancipation, these were territories, by and large, in which serfdom was weak or absent. The author shows precisely the

stages in developing a key skill on which modernization had to be based. Land surveyors, like accountants, seldom attract the attention of historians but their function is crucial to keeping the economic and state taxation wheels turning.

6 Much of the influential historiography of the French Revolution at this time – the writings of Hippolyte Taine and Thomas Carlyle as prime examples – attributed the revolution in France to precisely this as a major feature. Also see Bergman, Jay, *The French Revolutionary Tradition in Russian and Soviet Politics, Political Thought, and Culture*, Oxford University Press, Oxford, 2019.

7 Blum, Jerome, 'Russia', in Spring, David (ed.), *Landed Élites in Nineteenth Century Europe*, Johns Hopkins University Press, Baltimore and London, 1977, p. 87

8 That is, a group of educated people dedicated to the moral task of improving the lot of the downtrodden in Russia. Note also, that though the 'Russian' is the standard descriptor it is used in the broad sense of *Rossisskii*, not the exclusively ethnic *Russkii*. Many *intelligenty* were Jewish, Polish, Finnish, Ukrainian, Armenian, Georgian and so on.

9 There have been multiple efforts to find a supposedly neutral vocabulary to describe these phenomena. Terms like 'underdeveloped' and later 'developing' or 'emerging' countries, the 'third world', the 'global south' and many others have been tried and rejected. The grounds for rejection were their teleological linearity, Eurocentricity, orientalist roots, geographical ambiguity, patronizing tone and so on. Today, much of this discussion is subsumed within the debate about 'postcolonialism' even though, like any word with the 'post' prefix, it is clearly linear. To reiterate, the term 'backwardness' was used extensively by Russians in Russia at the time and I am taking up that practice. Interestingly, when the idea of 'underdeveloped' countries emerged after the Second World War it was an economist of Russian background who became a professor at Harvard, Alexander Gerschenkron, who produced a seminal study entitled *Backwardness in Historical Perspective*, Harvard University Press, Cambridge, MA, 1962 based on ideas he had first published in 1951. Incidentally, when they were in use the terms 'First' and 'Third' worlds were well-defined but what exactly was the 'Second' world, a term rarely used? If anything it referred to the Soviet Union and the Soviet bloc but could also, if the terminology was accepted, fit Russia's situation at almost any time since about 1700. Russia has been the perennial 'second World' and this is what the intelligentsia pointed out and was a powerful component in their political commitment. Russia, its minority nationalities even more so, is also a fine example of a colonialist postcolonial power.

10 Note that Darwin's *Origin of Species by Natural Selection* was published in 1859 and was immediately taken up enthusiastically in Russia, becoming the intelligentsia's favourite book for at least the rest of the century. The implications of this are discussed later. Incidentally the full quotation from Bakunin is more clearly Hegelian and predates Darwin: 'Let us therefore trust the eternal Spirit which destroys and annihilates only because it is the unfathomable and eternal source of all life. The passion for destruction is a creative passion, too!' from *The Reaction in Germany* (1842). It is most commonly paraphrased as 'the urge to destroy is also a creative urge'.

11 First published in the thick journal *Russkii vestnik* (*Russian Messenger*) in instalments from 1871 to 1972 and as a book in 1873.

12 Offord, Derek, *The Russian Revolutionary Movement in the 1880s*, Cambridge University Press, Cambridge, 1986 (online ed. 2010), p. 122.

13 Valentinov, N., *The Early Years of Lenin*, University of Michigan Press, Ann Arbor, 1969, p. 135.
14 Weiner, Adam, 'The Most Politically Dangerous Book You've Never Heard Of', *POLITICO Magazine*, 26 December 2020. Amusingly, the author proposes that the modest Chernyshevsky had key responsibility not only for blowing up Russia through his influence on Lenin and the Bolsheviks but also US and global capitalism through his indirect influence on Alan Greenspan and his massive deregulation of the financial sector. Greenspan was deeply inspired by Rand and had invited her, alongside his mother, as one of only two permitted guests, to attend his swearing in as member of the Council of Economic Advisers in 1974, a step towards his eventual position as Chair of the US Federal Reserve where he presided over his regulatory bonfire which, according to a Congressional enquiry, precipitated the 2008 financial collapse.
15 Unfortunately, the most common use of the term 'populism' in English relates to demagogic, often right-wing and nationalist, political groups which are far removed from Russian *narodniki*.
16 Billington, James H., *Mikhailovsky and Russian Populism*, The Clarendon Press, London and Oxford, 1958.
17 The complexities of establishing the precise number of peasants are illuminated, mainly in connection with the 1897 census, in Moon, David, 'Estimating the Peasant Population of Late Imperial Russia from the 1897 Census: A Research Note', *Europe-Asia Studies*, 48 (1) (January 1996), pp. 141–53.
18 https://www.nobelprize.org/prizes/literature/1970/solzhenitsyn/lecture/
19 Venturi, Franco, *Roots of Revolution: A History of the Populist and Socialist Movements in Nineteenth-Century Russia*, Alfred A. Knopf, London and New York, 1972.
20 Note that the phrase 'survival of the fittest' is not from Darwin but is derived from the ideas of the Social Darwinist Herbert Spencer. Social Darwinism welcomed fierce competition rather than co-operation as the basis of modern society. For obvious reasons, it became popular in capitalist circles. Its critics, however, considered it to be the law of the jungle, not humanity.
21 Pobedonostsev, Konstantin *Moskovskii sbornik* Sinodalnaia tipografiia, Moscow 1896 translated as *Reflections of a Russian Statesman,* Grant Richards, London, 1898 (republished University of Michigan Press, Lansing, 1964) and available online at The Internet Archive, https://archive.org/details/reflectionsofrus00pobeuoft
22 Resis, Albert, 'Das Kapital Comes to Russia', *Slavic Review*, 29 (2) (June 1970), p. 221.
23 At this time women were officially excluded from Russian universities, nonetheless, higher education courses for women were available as early as 1872 when the so-called Guerrier Courses became available at what is now the Moscow State Pedagogical University and, from 1878, on the better-known Bestuzhev courses in St Petersburg. They were suspended from 1888 to 1900. Women could attend courses but no formal degree or overall qualification was issued. In 1911, universities opened their doors to women.
24 This is a significant theme in Gatrell, Peter, *Government, Industry and Rearmament in Russia, 1900–1914: The Last Argument of Tsarism,* Cambridge University Press, Cambridge, 1994.
25 Benkendorf, Aleksandr *Zapiska o Bulgarine* (*Notes on Bulgarin*), https://ru.wikipedia.org/wiki/%D0%A1%D0%B5%D0%B2%D0%B5%D1%80%D0%BD%D0%B0%D1%8F_%D0%BF%D1%87%D0%B5%D0%BB%D0%B0
26 It was revived in Moscow in 2012 and continues to the present day, testimony to the attraction of the old traditions.

27 Zhurnal 19 veka *Russkaia mysl'* – Russkaia Literatura 19 veka (28 Fevralia 2017).

28 On thick journals see 'Zhurnaly " Obychnogo russkogo tipa"' ('Typically Russian Journals') in Makhonina, S.Ia., *Istoriia russkoi zhurnalistiki*, http://www.evartist.narod.ru/text1/93.htm. On the contemporary significance of the tradition, see Bykov Leonid P., 'The "Thick Journal" in Russia: Yesterday, Today and Tomorrow', *Journal of Siberian Federal University. Humanities & Social Sciences*, 5 (9) (2016), pp. 1249–55. http://elib.sfu-kras.ru/bitstream/handle/2311/20274/22_Bykov.pdf?sequence=1&isAllowed=y

29 For excellent accounts of the Imperial theatre system and its impact see Frame, Murray, *The St. Petersburg Imperial Theaters: Stage and State in Revolutionary Russia, 1900–1920*, McFarland & Co., Jefferson, 2000 and *School for Citizens: Theatre and Civil Society in Imperial Russia*, Yale University Press, New Haven and London, 2006.

30 There is an informative article: Yurkina, Natalia Nikolaevna, 'Youth and Theatre in the Nineteenth and Early Twentieth Centuries', in Gorokhova, Anna and Read, Christopher (eds.), *Theatre through the Ages*, Moscow State Pedagogical University, Moscow, forthcoming.

31 There is no definitive number for the ethnicities inhabiting the Russian imperial space after the 1860s expansion into Central Asia. The figures depend on exactly how one defines an ethnic group. The general figure tends to be around 150. The smallest groups were from the Urals, Northern Siberia or the Far East and had only a few hundreds or thousands of members (Kets, Inuit, Sami, Chukhchi) to many millions (Russians 56m, Ukrainians 22m, Belarussians 6m – Great Russians, Little Russians and White Russians respectively in the official terminology of the time) Figures from 1897 census.

32 The library, in Moscow, became the Russian national copyright library (along with others in St Petersburg, Kiev and Helsinki). The name was changed to the Lenin Library in Soviet times but was renamed the Russian State Library in 1992. Note that there is also the National Library of Russia which is in St Petersburg.

33 Osipov, Yu. S., *Akademiia nauk v istorii Rossiskogo gosudarstva*, Nauka, Moscow, 1999.

34 Cooke, Roger, *The Mathematics of Sonya Kovalevskaya*, Springer verlag, Berlin, 1984, p. 13. Kovalevskaia, S., 'Vospominaniia o Dzhordzhe Eliote *Russkaia mysl'* (6) (1886), pp. 93–108.

35 Kovalevskaia, S., *Nigilistka*, Vol'naia Russkaiia Tipografiia, Geneva 1892. English translation: *Nihilist Girl*, translated by Natasha Kolchevska with Mary Zirin; introduction by Natasha Kolchevska. Modern Language Association of America (2001).

36 Cooke, Roger, *The Mathematics of Sonya Kovalevskaya*, Springer verlag, Berlin, 1984, pp. 12–13.

37 Gould, Stephen Jay, *Leonardo's Mountain of Clams and the Diet of Worms*, Harvard Belknap Press, Cambridge, MA and London, 2011, p. 150. Gould has a lively and engaging account of the Kovalevsky's. He says their life together was 'less colourful and extreme in their sentiments and actions' compared to the fictional Bazarov, but one wonders how much more adventure and achievement one could cram into two forty-year-long lives.

38 Her daughter, also named Sofia, maintained her mother's traditions well into the twentieth century. She was a strong-minded and independent woman who became a distinguished Moscow medical doctor and, taking advantage of her mother's later circumstances, used her knowledge of Swedish to translate numerous items from that language into Russian. Her eminence was such that she is buried in the élite Novodevichy Cemetery in Moscow.

39 Kuznetsov, Vadim B., *The Kowalewsky Property*, CRM Proceedings and Lecture Notes 32, American Mathematical Soc., 2002, p. 18.
40 Kovalevskaia, S., 'Vospominaniia o Dzhordzhe Eliote *Russkaia mysl*' (6) (1886).
41 As we shall see, this was equally true in the twentieth century. There is no better example than that of Lenin and his supportive entourage of wife, women friends and sisters, the infrequency of independent women in the leadership at that time (and later) and his reliance on women secretaries like Elena Stasova. All were devoted to him but Krupskaya for one, was in his shadow and her ideas never received the respect they were due, although, on the other hand, it is most likely that only her association with Lenin would have propelled her into the governing élite.

Chapter 5

1 Marx K., Preface to *A Contribution to the Critique of Political Economy*, Progress Publishers, Moscow, 1977. First published in 1859. https://www.marxists.org/archive/marx/works/1859/critique-pol-economy/preface.htm The 'antagonism' to which Marx refers is class struggle which he here prophesies will end with the overthrow of the bourgeois order.
2 Note that Marx was working within the prevailing labour theory of value – that is, the value of a product was arrived at mainly through the labour effort necessary to produce it – which he took from the classical economists, notably the Scot, David Ricardo. Later theories of value based on marginal utility and markets complicate this view but we are not critiquing Marx' theory per se here, but discussing its absorption into Russia.
3 For Marx and many others a 'feudal' peasant owned/shared enough land to meet the needs of subsistence rather than produce a surplus for the market. By contrast, an agricultural labourer on a capitalist farm owned no land and was dependent on wages, having thereby the same relationship to the landowner as an urban worker did to the factory owner. In the real-world complexity of rural society there were many intermediate peasants who had a little land, supplemented by wages and who might sell a small surplus, even, occasionally, employ someone (i.e. exploit, in Marxist terms).
4 See Magraw, Roger, *France 1815–1914: The Bourgeois Century,* Fontana, London and New York, p. 78 and, for a supremely well-informed analysis of the intertwining of traditional and radical elements in the mid-nineteenth-century French peasantry idem *France 1800–1914,* Taylor and Francis, London, 2002, pp. 129–39.
5 Marx, Karl, *The Class Struggles in France 1848–1850 Part II*. First published in *Neue Rheinische Zeitung* (January–October 1850). https://www.marxists.org/archive/marx/works/1850/class-struggles-france/ch02.htm
6 The argument has been refreshed by Thomas, Pikkety, *Capitalism and Ideology,* Harvard University Press, Cambridge, MA, 2019 and the debate around his theories.
7 See Gatrell, Peter, *Government, Industry and Rearmament in Russia, 1900–1914: The Last Argument of Tsarism,* Cambridge University Press, Cambridge, 1994 and the much-underestimated McKean, Robert, *St Petersburg Between the Revolutions: Workers and Revolutionaries*, Yale University Press, New Haven, 1990, notably Chapter 9.
8 One contemporary study of the Moscow guberniya by its *zemstvo* statistician V. I. Orlov found that between 1858 and 1878, 79.6 per cent of communes

repartioned arable land once or twice with 3 to 6 for the remaining 20 per cent. See Nafziger, Steven, 'Land Redistributions and the Russian Peasant Commune in the 19th Century', https://www.researchgate.net/publication/228550755_Land_Redistributions_and_the_Russian_Peasant_Commune_in_the_19th_Century

9 An excellent and wide-ranging discussion can be found in: Eaton, Henry, 'Marx and the Russians', *Journal of the History of Ideas*, 41 (1) (January–March, 1980), pp. 89–112. There are several illuminating pages on the discussion between V. P. Vorontsov, N. S. Rusanov and Daniel'son over what a Russian capitalism might look like. pp. 109–12. Prophetically, Vorontsov said that, because of the shortage of capital, exclusion from foreign markets and so on, only state-driven industrialization would work in Russian conditions.

10 Marx, Karl Letter to the editor of *Otechestvennyi zapiski*, November 1877. Marx 'finest chance' referred to the possibility of avoiding the capitalist stage.

11 Marx, Karl Letter to Vera Zasulich, 8 March 1881.

12 Marx, Karl and Engels, Friedrich, Preface to the Russian Edition of *The Communist Manifesto*, 21 January 1882. https://www.marxists.org/archive/marx/works/1848/communist-manifesto/preface.htm#preface-1882

13 Engels, Friedrich Letter to Daniel'son, 17 October 1893.

14 For a superb analysis of early Russian Marxism see White, James D., *Marx and Russia: The Fate of a Doctrine*, Bloomsbury Press, London, 2018.

15 This has been energetically argued by the present author in, for example, Read, Christopher, *Lenin: A Revolutionary Life,* Routledge, London and New York, 2004 and in Christopher Read, *Lenin Lives?* Oxford University Press, Oxford and New York, 2024 which examines the question of whether Lenin still has a living legacy. The 'populist' nature of the 1917 revolution is also at the heart of the same author's *From Tsar to Soviets: The Russian People and Their Revolution.*

16 See the excellent Ely, Christopher, *Russian Populism: A History,* Bloomsbury, London, New York, Dublin, 2022.

17 Read, Christopher, 'George Plekhanov and the Marxist Turn in Russia', in Hammersley, Rachel (ed.), *Revolutionary Moments: Reading Revolutionary Texts*, Bloomsbury Academic, London, 2015, pp. 125–32. *Bloomsbury Collections.* Web. 11 February 2021. http://dx.doi.org/10.5040/9781474252669.0022.

18 Skocpol, Theda, *States and Social Revolutions* (1980) pointed this out a generation ago. The theory certainly fits the final crisis of the Russian autocratic state in 1915–17.

19 Lenin, V. I., *The Development of Capitalism in Russia,* 1899.

20 Henderson, Robert, *Vladimir Burtsev and the Struggle for a Free Russia: A Revolutionary in the Time of Tsarism and Bolshevism,* Bloomsbury, London, 2018b.

21 For a much more detailed account, see Read, *Lenin* (2005). Chapters 3 and 5 in particular trace the interweaving of Menshevik and Bolshevik ideas and the wider context.

22 Essentially there were only two, Vyacheslav Ivanov (1866–1949) and Georgii Chulkov (1879–1939) but Ivanov was quite influential.

23 Merezhkovsky, D. Gippius, Z. and Filosofov D. I., *Le Tsar et la Révolution*, Paris, 1907.

24 Read, Christopher, *Religion, Revolution and the Russian Intelligentsia: The* Vekhi *Debate and Its Intellectual Background,* Macmillan, London and New York, 1979.

25 Fedorov N., *Vopros o bratstve, ili rodstve, o prichinakh nebratskogo, nerodstvennogo, t.e. nemirnogo, sostoianiia mira i o sredstvakh k vosstanovleniiu rodstva: zapiska ot*

neuchenikh k uchenym, dukhovnym i svetskim, k veruiushchim I neveruiushchim vol. 1 Vernay 1906; vol. 2 Moscow 1913.

26 Kozhevnikov, V. A., *Nikolai Fedorovich Fyodorov: Opyt izlozheniia ego ucheniia po izdannym i neizdannym proizvedeniiam, perepiske i lichnym besedam*, Moscow, 1908, p. 9.

27 Berdyaev, N. A., 'Religiya Voskresheniya ("Philosophiya obshego dela" N. F. Fedorova)' *Russkaya Mysl'*, July 1915, pp. 76–120. Article reprinted and included by YMCA Press Paris in 1989 in the Berdyaev Collection: 'Tipy religioznoi mysli v Rossii', (Tom III), pp. 242–301. Also available at: http://www.berdyaev.com/berdiaev/berd_lib/1915_186.html#7

28 Lukashevich, Stephen, *N. F. Fedorov (1828–1903): A Study in Russian Eupsychian and Utopian Thought,* Newark and London, 1977, pp. 9–10.

29 Starr, S. Frederick, *Melnikov: Solo Architect in a Mass Society*, Princeton University Press, Princeton New Jersey, 1978.

30 For a summary of ideas of death at this time see Coates, Ruth, *Deification in Russian Religious Thought: Between the Revolutions, 1905–1917,* Oxford University Press, Oxford, 2019 and the article by Christopher Read entitled 'Death and Resurrection in Russian Thought in Russia's Silver Age 1890–1930' in Gorokhova, Anna and Read, Christopher *Afterlife: The Life of the Dead* Moskovskii Gosudarstvennyi Pedagogicheskii Universitet', Moscow, 2021.

31 Tsiolkovskii, K. E., *Cherty iz moiei zhizni* Tula 1983 quoted in Fedorov, N. F., *Sobranie sochinenii v chetyrekh t-kh* Tom 1 Moscow, 1905, p. 5

32 Tomkeieff, S. I., 'V.I.Vernadsky', *Nature,* 10 March 1945, vol. 155, p. 29.

33 Ascher, Abraham, *The Revolution of 1905: Russia in Disarray*, Stanford University Press, Palo Alto, 1988, p. 19.

34 Note that the readership was much wider than the circulation as copies were passed around and were also consulted in public and private libraries.

35 Evoliutsiia tolstogo zhurnala in Makhonina, Svetlana, *Istoriia Russkoi Zhurnalistiki Nachal XX veka,* Nauka, Moscow, 2004; Bykov, Leonid P., 'The "Thick Journal" in Russia: Yesterday, Today and Tomorrow', *Journal of Siberian Federal University. Humanities & Social Sciences,* 5 (9) (2016), pp. 1249–55.

36 Kneen, Peter, 'Higher Education and Cultural Revolution in the USSR', SIPS Discussion Paper No. 5 Birmingham 1976, pp. 13–14.

37 Serengy, Scott, *Russian Teachers and Peasant Revolution. The Politics of Education in 1905,* Indiana University Press, Bloomington, 1989.

38 Leikina-Svirskaia, V. R., *Intelligentsiia v Rossii vo vtoroi polovine XIX veka*, Mysl Moscow, 1971, pp. 60–1.

39 Robbins, Jeremy plus more recent study of 1891 famine. Robbins, Richard G., *Famine in Russia, 1891–1892,* Columbia University Press, New York, 1965; Simms, J. Y., 'Economic Impact of the Russian Famine of 1891–92', *The Slavonic and East European Review,* 60 (1) (1982), pp. 63–74. Simms, J. Y., 'The Crop Failure of 1891: Soil Exhaustion, Technological Backwardness, and Russia's "Agrarian Crisis"', *Slavic Review*, 41 (2) (1982), pp. 236–50.

40 The official title was: 'Order on measures to preserve state order and public peace and to place certain areas in a state of enhanced security' (14 (26) August 1881). It initially applied to the ten most urbanized guberniyas.

41 Note that this form of discrimination was not based on race or ethnicity. A person of any ethnicity would be considered Russian if they were baptized.

42 Pobedonostsev, V. P., *Moskovskii sbornik Reflections of a Russian Statesman.*
43 Граф С. Ю. Витте. *Воспоминания. Царствование Николая II.* М-Пг., 1923, Т. I, с. 220 Witte, Count S. Iu., *Vospominaniia. Tsarstvovanie Nikolaia II*, Moscow-Petrograd 1923 t.1. Witte is quoting Pobedonostsev's actual words.
44 Read, Christopher, *From Tsar to Soviets: The Russian People and Their Revolution*, UCL, London and Oxford University Press, New York, 1976, pp. 30–1.
45 Baughman, John J., 'The French Banquet Campaign of 1847–48', *The Journal of Modern History,* 31 (1) (March 1959), pp. 1–15. Interestingly, in a reflective blog, leading social historian of France, Pamela Pilbeam, argues that the banquets were not instrumental in bringing down the monarch, Louis Philippe, and establishing the second French Republic. But once the monarchy had collapsed – as a product of economic crisis and political panic, 'an abdication not a seizure of power' – the banquet leaders began to assert themselves. It seems Tkachev's formula also fits France in 1848. Professor Pilbeam's conclusions have an uncanny echo in 1905 Russia, not to mention October 1917. Pilbeam, Pamela, 'The French Banquet Campaign of 1847–48', *Imagining Futures,* Plymouth University blog. http://blogs.plymouth.ac.uk/imaginingalternatives/2018/11/12/the-french-banquet-campaign-of-1847-48-by-pamela-pilbeam/
46 There is a brief account in Read, Christopher, *Religion, Revolution and the Russian Intelligentsia: The Vekhi Debate and Its Intellectual Background,* Macmillan, London and New York, 1979.
47 Bogdanov, A. A., *Vera I nauka. O knige V.Il'ina 'Materializm i empirio-krititsizm'* Moscow, 1910. Note: Lenin published *Materialism and Empirio-criticism* under the pseudonym V. Il'in.
48 A more nuanced view of Pavlov's ideas has been published in the superb Todes, D. P., *Ivan Pavlov: A Russian Life in Science,* Oxford University Press, New York, 2014. Todes summarizes his findings in the course of an interview published in the *Johns Hopkins University Magazine*, Winter 2014, https://hub.jhu.edu/magazine/2014/winter/daniel-todes-biography-of-pavlov/
49 Read, Christopher, *Culture and Power in Revolutionary Russia: The Intelligentsia and the Transition from Tsarism to Communism,* Macmillan, London and New York, 1991, pp. 115–18.
50 Lenin V. I., *Materialism and Empirio-criticism: Critical Comments on a Reactionary Philosophy*. The first edition, in Russian, was published in Moscow in 1909. An English translation is available at: https://www.marxists.org/archive/lenin/works/1908/mec/
51 Personal comment to author by Gleb Struve, Berkeley, July 1974.
52 Gershenzon, M. O., 'Introduction' *Vekhi: Sbornik statei o russkoi intelligentsii* Moscow 1909.
53 Ibid. 'Tvorcheskoe samopoznanie' (Creative Self-awareness) (section 4).
54 Struve, P. B., 'Otryvki ot gosudarstvo' *Russkaia mysl'* 1908. № 5. There is also a collection of his writings of the period with the evocative title *Patriotica. Politika. Kul'tura. Religiia. Sotsializm Sbornik statei za piat let (1905 – 1910),* St Petersburg, 1911.
55 Yurkina, N. N., 'Perception of Death by Russian Students of the 19th and Early 20th Centuries', in Gorokhova, Anna, Rallo G. E and Read, C. (eds.), *Afterlife: The Life of the Dead. Antropologiia smerti: Mental'nost', religiia, filosofii,* Moscow State Pedagogical University, Moscow, 2021, pp. 133–49.

56 For a survey of the debate and a bibliography and timeline of the major contributions see Read, Christopher, *Religion, Revolution and the Russian Intelligentsia: The Vekhi Debate and Its Intellectual Background*, Macmillan, London and New York, 1979.
57 Lenin, V. I., 'Leo Tolstoy as Mirror of the Russian Revolution', https://www.marxists.org/archive/lenin/works/1908/sep/11.htm
58 There is an interesting Timeline of Russian science at: https://en.wikipedia.org/wiki/Timeline_of_Russian_innovation
59 Graham, Loren R., 'Russian & Soviet Science and Technology', *History of Science Society Newsletter*, 18 (4) (Supplement, 1989), Introduction.
60 From Osipov, Iu. S., *Akademiia nauk v istorii Rossiiskogo gosudarstva*, Moscow, 1999 consulted at 'Ob akademii: Rossiia na pod'eme', Russian Academy of Sciences, http://www.ras.ru/about/history/ontherise.aspx
61 See Frame, Murray, *School for Citizens: Theatre and Civil Society in Imperial Russia*, Yale University Press, New Haven, 2006 and Frame, M., 'Russian Theater and the Crisis of War and Revolution, 1914–22', in Frame, M., Kolonitskii, B., Marks, S. G. and Stockdale, M. K. (eds.), *Russian Culture in War and Revolution, 1914–22: Book 2. Political Culture, Identities, Mentalities, and Memory*, Slavica Publishers, Bloomington Indiana, 2014 (Russia's Great War and Revolution series).
62 Figes, O., *A People's Tragedy: The Russian Revolution 1891–1924*, Jonathan Cape, London, 1996, p. 12.

Chapter 6

1 Read, Christopher, *War and Revolution in Russia 1914–22*, Palgrave, London, 2013 is a succinct summary of this extraordinary development.
2 For an excellent demographic analysis, see Blum, Alain, 'Of Populations and Wars', in Read, C., Lindenmeyer, A. and Waldron, P. (eds.), *Russia's Home Front in War and Revolution, 1914–22, Book 3: National Disintegration*, Slavica Publishers, Ann Arbor, pp. 133–56.
3 Ibid., p. 155.
4 Stites, Richard, *Revolutionary Dreams: Utopian Visions and Experimental Life in the Russian Revolution*, Oxford, 1987. There is also an unsurpassed collection of documents in translation edited by Rosenberg, William G. *Bolshevik Visions* (2 vols), 2nd ed., Ann Arbor, 1990. There is an engaging re-thinking of the theme covering topics across the whole Soviet era and beyond in Steinberg, Mark, *Russian Utopia: A Century of Revolutionary Possibilities*, Bloomsbury Academic, London, New York, Dublin, 2021 and also in Ree, Erik van, *Boundaries of Utopia – Imagining Communism from Plato to Stalin*, Routledge, London and New York, 2015.
5 Bukharin, N. and Preobrazhensky, E., *The ABC of Communism: A Popular Explanation of the Program of the Communist Party of Russia*, trans. Eden and Cedar Paul 1st English ed., Communist Party of Great Britain, London, 1922, p. 72. The *ABC* and the Party Programme are published together in this volume. A available at: https://www.marxists.org/archive/bukharin/works/1920/abc/ABC-of-Communism.pdf
6 Lenin, V. I., 'Immediate Tasks of the Soviet Government', *Pravda* (83) and *Izvestia VTsIK* No. 85, 28 April 1918. https://www.marxists.org/archive/lenin/works/1918/mar/x03.htm#sec7.

7 There is an account of the discussion in: Read, C., *Culture and Power in Revolutionary Russia: The Intelligentsia and the Transition from Tsarism to Communism,* Macmillan, London and New York, 1991, pp. 100–4.
8 Chagall, M., *My Life,* London, 1965, p. 137. In a curious repetition of history a police inspector, who was a student in one of my first ever seminars as a university lecturer, took one look at the poster reproduction of a Chagall hanging on my wall and asked exactly the same question.
9 Note: It was used as key image publicizing a British Museum exhibition in 2017 to be seen on many London buses and tubes at a time when, in Russian cities, there was little or no public indication that the centenary of the revolution was being experienced.
10 Dukes, Paul, 'The Russian Revolution in the Encyclopaedia Britannica', *Revolutionary Russia,* Special Issue in Honour of J. D. Smele 34 (2) (2021), p. 269.
11 Gorky, M., 'Otvet S. Budennomu', *Pravda,* 27 noiabriia 1928.
12 Got'e, I. V., *Time of Troubles: The Diary of Iury Vladimirovich Got'e*, trans and ed. T. Emmons, London, 1988, p. 466.
13 Ibid., p. 195.
14 See Holmes, Larry, *The Kremlin and the Schoolhouse: Reforming Education in Soviet Russia 1917–1931*, Indiana University Press, Bloomington and Indianapolis, 1991.
15 See Kneen, Peter, 'Higher Education and Cultural Revolution in the USSR', SIPS Discussion Paper No. 5 Birmingham 1976 and Ioffe, A. A., *Moia zhizn' i rabota – avtobiograficheskii ocherk*, Moscow and Leningrad, 1933. Read, *Culture and Power in Revolutionary Russia*, pp. 77–80.
16 Ransome, Arthur, in *Encyclopaedia Britannica* 13th ed., supplementary vol. III 'Russia' Section III 'The Revolution and After' [March 1921–March 1926], p. 421. For an illuminating discussion of Ransome and other contemporary writers' views on Russia and the Revolution, see Dukes, Paul, 'The Russian Revolution in the Encyclopaedia Britannica', *Revolutionary Russia,* 34 (2) (2021).
17 Zamiatin, E., *The Cave,* trans. D. S. Mirsky, *The Slavonic Review*, 2 (4) (June 1923), pp. 145–53.
18 Shentalinsky, V. A., 'Fragments of the Silver Age. Conclusion', *Novyi miir*, (6) (1998), pp. 184–5.
19 For an excellent account see Swain, Geoffrey, *The Origins of the Russian Civil War,* Routledge, London, 1995.
20 See Read, Christopher, *Lenin: A Revolutionary Life*, Routledge, London and New York, 2005, pp. 212–19 for a brief discussion.
21 Read, Christopher, *Culture and Power in Revolutionary Russia: The Intelligentsia and the Transition from Tsarism to Communism*, Macmillan, London and New York, 1990, p. 70.
22 Struve, Bulgakov, Izgoev, Frank and Berdiaev contributed to the new volume, Kistiakovsky and Gershenzon did not.
23 '*Predislovie izdatelia* (Publishers' Foreword)', *Iz glubiny,* 2nd ed., Paris, 1967.

Chapter 7

1 That has been expertly done by Matthew Rendle, Aaron Retish and William Pomeranz. See, for example, Rendle, Matthew, 'Revolutionary Tribunals and the Origins of Terror in Early Soviet Russia', *Historical Research,* 84 (226) (November

2011), pp. 693–721; Retish, Aaron, 'The Birth of Soviet Criminology: Mikhail Gernet's Vision of the Good State and the Dangers of the People in 1917,' *Journal of Modern Russian History and Historiography*, 13 (2020), pp. 184–213 and 'Judicial Reforms and Revolutionary Justice: The Establishment of the Court System in Soviet Russia, 1917–1922', *Russia's Home Front in War and Revolution, 1914–22*, 3, *Book* 4 (2018), pp. 369–99. Pomeranz, William, *Law and the Russian State: Russia's Legal Evolution from Peter the Great to Vladimir Putin,* Bloomsbury, London and New York, 2018.

2 Neumann, Matthias, *The Communist Youth League and the Transformation of the Soviet Union, 1917–1932*, Routledge, London and New York, 2011.

3 These included the Control Commissions, the Cheka, Political Commissars in the military and the party itself in wider society. See Read, Christopher, 'Values, Substitutes and Institutions: Cultural Roots of the Bolshevik Dictatorship', in Brovkin, V. (ed.), *The Bolsheviks in Russian Society: The Revolution and the Civil Wars*, Princeton University Press, Princeton and London, 1997.

4 Lenin, V. I., 'On Cooperation', 4–6 January 1923, https://www.marxists.org/archive/lenin/works/1923/jan/06.htm; Claudin-Urondo, C., *Lenin and Cultural Revolution: Marxist Theory and Contemporary Capitalism,* Branch Line, Hassocks, Sussex, 1977 and Read, Christopher, *Culture and Power in Revolutionary Russia: The Intelligentsia and the Transition From Tsarism to Communism,* Palgrave Macmillan, London, 1990, pp. 202–8.

5 For a summary of Bogdanov's ideas on Proletkul't, see Read (1990), pp. 111–33.

6 Read (1990), pp. 127–8.

7 Kunavin, V., 'Vserossiisskii s'ezd Proletkul'ta', *Proletarskaia kul'tura* (17–19) (1920), pp. 74–84.

8 Read (1990), pp. 145–56.

9 Gorky, M., *Vladimir Lenin*, https://www.marxists.org/archive/gorky-maxim/1924/01/x01.htm

10 Ibid.

11 Lenin, V. I., 'Leo Tolstoy as Mirror of the Russian Revolution', https://www.marxists.org/archive/lenin/works/1908/sep/11.htm

12 Lenin, V. I., Letter to Bukharin, 11 October 1920, https://www.marxists.org/archive/lenin/works/1920/oct/11.htmd

13 Todes, D. P., *Ivan Pavlov: A Russian Life in Science*, Oxford University Press, New York, 2014.

14 For example, he refers to NEP as a defeat seven times in Lenin, V. I., 'The New Economic Policy and the Tasks of the Political Education Departments', *Report To The Second All-Russia Congress of Political Education Departments,* October 17, 1921.

15 Andreev A. Iu and Tsygankov D. A., *Imperatorskii Moskovskii universitet 1755–1917: entsiklopedicheskii slovar'* ROSSPEN Moscow 2010. Covers to end of 1920s.

16 F.2306.1.595. Narkompros archive. Quoted in Read (1990), p. 180.

17 This curious incident has attracted considerable attention from scholars. Finkel, Stuart, *On the Ideological Front: The Russian Intelligentsia and the Making of the Soviet Public Sphere*, Yale University Press, New Haven, 2007; Baird, Catherine, *Revolution from Within: The YMCA in Russia's Ascension to Freedom from Bolshevik Tyranny*, 2013 (with biographical list of the deported); Chamberlain, Lesley, *Lenin's Private War: The Voyage of the Philosophy Steamer and the Exile of the Intelligentsia*, New York, St Martin's Press, 2007; Makarov, V. G. and Khristoforov, V. S., 'Passazhiry "filosofskogo parokhoda". (Sud'by intelligentsii, repressirovannoj letom-osen'ju 1922g.)', *Voprosy filosofii* (7) (2003), pp. 113–37 contains a list with biographical information on Russian intellectuals exiled 1922–. Kogan, L. A., '"Vyslat' za granitsu bezzhalostno" Novoe o izgnanii dukhovnoi elitii', *Voprosy filosofii* (9) (1993), pp. 61–84.

18 *Pravda*, 31 August 1922. It probably originated in the GPU (successor to the Cheka) which was handling the arrests and expulsions.
19 Osorgin, M., *How We Left – Fragments of a Memoir,* Paris, 1955, p. 81, http://old.ihst.ru/projects/sohist/document/deport/osorgin.htm
20 Yesenin, Sergei (1895–1925), *The Cradle Magazine,* 2019, https://thecradlemagazine.com/sergei-yesenin-1895-1925/
21 Heath, Nick (Battlescarred), https://libcom.org/history/bim-bom-bang-bang-chekists-clowns
22 Myers, Alan, 'Evgenii Zamiatin in Newcastle', *The Slavonic and East European Review*, 68 (1) (1990), pp. 91–9.
23 The film is about October in Petrograd. The statue of Alexander III was in Moscow and was pulled down in Spring 1918, nothing to do with the October revolution. See an illuminating article by Drubek, Natascha, 'Exegi Monumentum Revolutionis – On Eisenstein's October (1927)', in Balme, Christopher, Wessel, Martin Schulze and Brunnbauer, Ulf (eds.), *The Culture of the Russian Revolution and Its Global Impact: Semantics – Performances – Functions* (DigiOst 9), München, 2020, https://hcommons.org/deposits/objects/hc:30388/datastreams/CONTENT/content
24 For a fascinating discussion, see Tunzelman, Alex von 'The Toppling of Saddam's Statue: How the US Military Made a Myth', *The Guardian,* 8 July 2021, https://www.theguardian.com/world/2021/jul/08/toppling-saddam-hussein-statue-iraq-us-victory-myth
25 There is an extensive list at: https://en.wikipedia.org/wiki/List_of_monuments_and_memorials_removed_during_the_George_Floyd_protests
26 For a perceptive account of Vertov's career see Hicks, Jeremy, *Dziga Vertov: Defining Documentary Film*, London and New York: I.B. Tauris, 2007.
27 Leyda, Jay, *Kino: A History of the Russian and Soviet Film*, Macmillan, New York, 1960 is still a very useful starting point for delving further into Soviet cinema. For excellent recent accounts see the work of Joan Neuberger, especially *This Thing of Darness: Eisenstein's Ivan the Terrible in Stalin's Russia* Cornell University Press, Ithaca, 2017.
28 S. Frederick Starr discusses death and resurrection in Melnikov's philosophy in *Melnikov. Solo Architect in a Mass Society,* Princeton University Press, Princeton, NJ, 1978. The theme of death in the Silver Age and 1920s is the subject of a brief essay by the present writer 'Death and Resurrection in Russian Thought in Russia's Silver Age 1890–1930', in Gorokhova, Anna, Rallo, G. and Read C. J., *Afterlife: The Life of the Dead,* Moscow State Pedagogical University, Moscow, 2021, pp. 115–32. Cross ref Ch 5 p. 111.
29 Read (1990), p. 225.
30 Cross ref Ch 5 p. 150.
31 Read (1990), pp. 191–2.
32 Jasny, Naum, *Soviet Economists of the Twenties: Names to Be Remembered,* Cambridge University Press, Cambridge, 1972, sketches many of the employees at *Vesenkha* but not Florensky. Most accounts of Florensky's extraordinary life lean towards his theological, philosophical and aesthetic ideas. A broad selection of his writings have been published in post-Soviet Russia as well as several biographies, notably Pyman, Avril, *Pavel Florensky: A Quiet Genius: The Tragic and Extraordinary Life of Russia's Unknown da Vinci,* Continuum International Publishing Group (now Bloomsbury), London and New York, 2010. There is a Russian website which contains his main works and a number of major articles on his thought: http://www.vehi.net/florensky/
33 Developed at several points in Read, Christopher, *Lenin: A Revolutionary Life,* Routledge, London and New York, 2005, for example pp. 13–14; 21–2; 58–9.

34 There are numerous editions in English translation including Trotsky, L., *Literature and Revolution,* Haymarket Press, Chicago, 2009. It can also be found at https://www.marxists.org/archive/trotsky/1924/lit_revo/
35 *Voprosy kul'tury pri diktature proletariata,* Moscow, 1925, p. 3 quoted in Read, Christopher, *Culture and Power in Revolutionary Russia: The Intelligentsia and the Transition from Tsarism to Communism,* Macmillan, London, 1991, pp. 213.
36 *Voprosy kul'tury* (1925), p. 109 quoted in Read (1991), pp. 21–5.
37 For a more detailed account of party policy and its effects see Read (1991) chapters 4 and 5 and especially pp. 200–20 on the debates.
38 Russian language Wikipedia has a brief summary and references to the weak theory that he was murdered: https://ru.wikipedia.org/wiki/%D0%95%D1%81%D0%B5%D0%BD%D0%B8%D0%BD,_%D0%A1%D0%B5%D1%80%D0%B3%D0%B5%D0%B9_%D0%90%D0%BB%D0%B5%D0%BA%D1%81%D0%B0%D0%BD%D0%B4%D1%80%D0%BE%D0%B2%D0%B8%D1%87#%D0%92%D0%B5%D1%80%D1%81%D0%B8%D1%8F_%D1%83%D0%B1%D0%B8%D0%B9%D1%81%D1%82%D0%B2%D0%B0
39 On the mentality of young people in the 1920s see Neumann (2013) and Healy, Dan, *Bolshevik Sexual Forensics: Diagnosing Disorder in the Clinic and Courtroom, 1917–1939,* Northern Illinois University Press, DeKalb, 2009.
40 For more detail see Read, Christopher, *Stalin: From the Caucasus to the Kremlin,* Routledge, Historical Biographies. London and New York, 2017, pp. 71–3.
41 Ree, Erik van, *The Political Thought of Joseph Stalin: A Study in Twentieth Century Revolutionary Patriotism,* Taylor and Francis, London, 2006; Roberts, Geoffrey, *Stalin's Library: A Dictator and His Books,* Yale University Press, New Haven and London, 2022; Brandenberger, David and Zelenov, Mikhail, *Stalin's Master Narrative: A Critical Edition of the History of the Communist Party of the Soviet Union (Bolsheviks), Short Course,* Yale University Press, New Haven, 2019, https://weeklyworker.co.uk/worker/1309/stalin-as-historian/
42 Most recently by: Read (2017); Suny, Ronald, *Stalin: Passage to Revolution,* Princeton University Press, Princeton, NJ, 2020 takes the story to October while Kotkin, Stephen, *Stalin: Volume I: Paradoxes of Power, 1878–1928,* Penguin Books, 2014; vol. 2, *Stalin: Waiting for Hitler 1929–1941,* Penguin, 2017 goes up to the onset of the Second World War on the Eastern Front; vol. 3 forthcoming.
43 Not least by Sheila Fitzpatrick in her excellent pioneering works especially Fitzpatrick, S. (ed.), *The Cultural Front. Power and Culture in Revolutionary Russia,* Cornell University Press, Ithaca, 1992.
44 The concept remains alive, most recently in connection with the development of Skyway in Abu-Dhabi, http://sky-way.org/en/skyway-linear-city-in-abu-dhabi/
45 Schultz, Kurt S., 'Building the "Soviet Detroit" the Construction of the Nizhnyi-Novgorod Automobile Factory 1927–32', *Slavic Review,* 49 (9) (1990), pp. 200–212 reproduced in Read, Christopher (ed.), *The Stalin Years: A Reader,* Palgrave Macmillan, London, 2003, pp. 70–83.
46 Khan-Makhomedov, Selim O., *Pioneers of Soviet Architecture,* Rizzoli, New York, 1987 is a wonderful survey by a scholar who is himself a pioneer in the study of this topic.
47 Peasants were still few and far between but tended to be classed in the worker category with some of 'kulak' origin classified with the 'bourgeois' elements.
48 'Dizzy with Success' can most easily be found at https://www.marxists.org/reference/archive/stalin/works/1930/03/02.htm

49 Stalin, J. V., 'The Tasks of Business Executives: Speech Delivered at the First All-Union Conference of Leading Personnel of Socialist Industry', 4 February 1931, https://www.marxists.org/reference/archive/stalin/works/1931/02/04.htm

Chapter 8

1 Hellbeck, Jochen, *Revolution on My Mind: Writing a Diary under Stalin*, Harvard University Press, Cambridge, MA, 2006 opened up a whole raft of studies of diaries and memoirs to expand our insight into the mentalité of Soviet citizens in the 1930s. For a thoughtful analysis of the value of diaries to the historian see: Paperno, Irina, 'What Can Be Done with Diaries?' *The Russian Review*, 63 (4) (October 2004), pp. 561–73 and Shaw, Claire, 'Soviet Memoir Literature: Personal Narratives of a Historical Epoch', in Gilbert, George (ed.), *Reading Russian Sources: A Student's Guide to Text and Visual Sources from Russian History*, Routledge, London, 2020, pp. 212–28.
2 For a helpful discussion of Timasheff's thesis, see Lenoe, Matthew, 'In Defense of Timasheff's Great Retreat', *Kritika: Explorations in Russian and Eurasian History*, 5 (4) (Fall 2004) (New Series), pp. 721–30.
3 Timasheff, Nicholas, *The Great Retreat*, E. P. Dutton, New York, 1946.
4 Hoffmann, David L., 'Was There a "Great Retreat" from Soviet Socialism? Stalinist Culture Reconsidered', *Kritika: Explorations in Russian and Eurasian History* 5 (4) (Fall 2004) (New Series).
5 Martin, Terry, *The Affirmative Action Empire: Nations and Nationalism in the Soviet Union, 1923–1939*, Cornell University Press, Ithaca, 2001, p. 415.
6 Stalin, J. V. Conversation with Writers at Home of Maksim Gorky, 26 October 1932.
7 'On the Re-structuring of Literary-Artistic Organisations', Politburo decree of 23rd April 1932.
8 Barry, Donald D. and Berman, Harold J., 'The Soviet Legal Profession', *Harvard Law Review* 82 (1) (November 1968), pp. 8–9. For an excellent and more recent study based on greater archive access see Huskey, Eugene, *Russian Lawyers and the Soviet State: The Origins and Development of the Soviet Bar*, Princeton University Press, Princeton, 1986.
9 Kepley, Vance, Jr., 'Federal Cinema: The Soviet Film Industry, 1924–32', *Film History*, 8 (3) (1996), pp. 344–56.
10 Stalin, Iosif, *Marksizm i natsional'no-kolonial'niy vopros*, Partizdat, Moscow, 1934, p. 194. For an extraordinarily detailed account of early language policies see: Shelestiuk, Elena Vladimirovna, 'National in Form, Socialist in Content: USSR National and Language Policies in the Early Period', *SHS Web of Conferences* 69 (157) (January 2019), p. 00104. DOI: 10.1051/shsconf/20196900104.
11 In recent years increasing attention has been paid to telling the history of the period through these buildings and their inhabitants. There is a wonderful satire on the process of getting such an apartment by the writer Vladimir Voinovich (1932–2018) with the self-explanatory title: *The Ivankiad: or, The tale of the writer Voinovich's installation in his new apartment*, Jonathan Cape, London 1978 or (in Russian). Ardis Publishing, Ann Arbor, Michigan 1976. Historians musing evocatively on the histories within the apartment blocks include a pioneering study by Rachel, Polonsky,

Molotov's Magic Lantern; A Journey in Russian History, Faber & Faber, London, 2010 (The subtitle of the paperback edition is the rather more sensationalist *Uncovering Russia's Secret History*) and the blockbuster Slezkine, Yuri, *House of Government: A Saga of the Russian Revolution*, Princeton University Press, Princeton, NJ, 2017. A less well-known doctoral thesis – Sigler, Krista, *Ksheshinskaia's Mansion: High Politics and the Culture of Modernity in Revolutionary Russia*, University of Cincinnati, 2009 – also makes imaginative use of the former Bolshevik HQ in 1917 and later museum of the revolution as an entry point into broader speculation.

12 Famous for his controversial monuments like the massive ship commemorating Peter the Great, with a giant Peter standing at the prow and, symbolically if not realistically, with his hands on the ship's wheel, situated at the confluence of the Moscow River and the Otvodnoi Canal in the centre of Moscow. 1997.

13 James, C. Vaughan, *Soviet Socialist Realism: Origins and Theory*, Macmillan, Basingstoke, 1973.

14 It would be more accurate to translate them as classness, partyness and peopleness but they sound odd in English.

15 Iudin, P. (ed.), *Ob ustave soiuza sovetskikh pisatelei*, Gosizdat, Moscow, 1934, p. 26. A number of the major speeches, in English, can be found at: https://www.marxists.org/subject/art/lit_crit/sovietwritercongress/

16 For anyone able to read French, Michel Aucouturier's *Le réalisme socialiste* Presses Universitaires de France, Paris 1998 in the '*Que sais-je*' series, provides an excellent overview of the cultural politics of Soviet literature from the revolution to perestroika.

17 Moroz, Valentyn, *Report from the Beria Reserve: The Protest Writings of Valentyn Moroz, A Ukrainian Political Prisoner in the USSR*, ed. and trans. John Kolasky, Peter Martin Press, Toronto, 1974, pp. 21–2. Emphasis by Moroz.

18 Medynsky, Eugene, 'Schools and Education in the U.S.S.R.', *American Sociological Review* 9 (3) (June 1944), Recent Social Trends in the Soviet Union (June 1944), pp. 287–95. Statistics on schools from p. 288 and on higher education from pp. 289–90. It is worth noting that this article itself is evidence of the mini-thaw in Soviet-Western relations during the war when items from East and West appeared in each other's publications.

19 Lewin, Moshe, 'Society and the Stalinist state in the Period of the Five Year Plans', *Social History* 1 (2) (1976), p. 171.

20 Ibid., pp. 173–4.

21 Osipov, Yu. S., *The Academy of Sciences in the History of the Russian State*, Nauka, Moscow, 1999, http://www.ras.ru/about/history/revolution.aspx

22 Ibid., http://www.ras.ru/about/history/sovietcountry.aspx

23 There is a great body of work on Soviet science produced by Loren Graham which includes: Graham, Loren, *The Soviet Academy of Sciences and the Communist Party, 1927–1932*, Princeton University Press, Princeton, 1967; *Science and Philosophy in the Soviet Union*, Alfred Knopf, New York, 1972; *Science in the New Russia: Crisis, Aid, Reform* (with Irina Dezhina), Indiana University Press, Bloomington, 2008 and *Lysenko's Ghost: Epigenetics and Russia*, Harvard University Press, Cambridge, Mass, 2016

24 There are only 30 women under the rubric 'Soviet women scientists' who have a Wikipedia page devoted to them compared to 143 men (English Wikipedia: 5 July 2021). There were eleven Nobel Prizewinners in the Soviet era, all male.

25 See the excellent MacTutor website from the University of St. Andrew's devoted to biographical sketches of leading mathematicians. Shmidt is listed under the German version of his name, Otto Schmidt, and can be accessed at: MacTutor History of Mathematics Archive – MacTutor History of Mathematics (st-andrews.ac.uk), https://mathshistory.st-andrews.ac.uk/. There is a fine monograph on Arctic exploration and its role in the political culture of the 1930s in the USSR: McCannon, John, *Red Arctic: Polar Exploration and the Myth of the North in the Soviet Union 1932–39,* Oxford University Press, Oxford, 1998.

26 Aucoutourier, Michel, *Le realisme socialiste,* Que sais-je, Presse Universitaire de France, Paris, 1998; Ruhle, Jurgen, *Literature and Revolution,* Frederick A. Praeger, Pall Mall Press, London, 1969; Thomson, Boris, *The Premature Revolution: Russian Literature and Society, 1917 1946,* Weidenfeld & Nicolson, London, 1972; Fitzpatrick, S. (ed.), *The Cultural Front. Power and Culture in Revolutionary Russia,* Cornell University Press, Ithaca, 1992; Fitzpatrick, S. (ed.), *Cultural Revolution in Russia 1928–1932,* Indiana University Press, Bloomington, 1978.

27 Bulgakov, M., *Diaries and Selected Letters,* Richmond, Surrey, 2013, p. 200 (This a translation by Roger Cockrill, funded by the Arts Council of England, of the short Russian edition edited by V. I. Losev, *Mikhail and Yelena Bulgakov: Dnevnik Master I Margarity,* Vagrius, Moscow, 2004. This is a selection from the more extensive Bulgakov, M., *Dnevnik, pis'ma 1914–1940,* Sovremennyi Pisatel', Moscow, 1997).

28 First published in English in 1968 as *The First Circle.*

29 See Kerber, L. L., *Stalin's Aviation Gulag: A Memoir of Andrei Tupolev and the Purge Era,* Smithsonian Institution Press, Washington, DC, 1996. Expanded and published in Russian as Kerber, L. L., *Tupolev,* Politekhnika, St. Petersburg, 1999.

30 For a good summary of the sharashka system see the blog by Asif Siddiqi at: https://russianhistoryblog.org/2011/03/the-sharashka-phenomenon/

31 Siddiqi ibid. Siddiqi also plausibly suggests the original idea for sharashkas may have come from certain scientist prisoners themselves with the mixed motives of keeping themselves out of the gulag proper and using their talents more productively for the nation.

32 McKie, Robin, 'Sergei Korolev: The Rocket Genius behind Yuri Gagarin', *The Guardian,* 13 March 2011, https://www.theguardian.com/science/2011/mar/13/yuri-gagarin-first-space-korolev

33 Kumanev, V. A. (ed.), *Tragicheskie sud'by: repressirovannye uchenye Akademii nauk sssra,* Nauka, Moscow, 1995.

34 That is, giving more attention to the form of a work of art than to its content.

35 These lines are much-quoted. See, as an example, Hingley, Ronald, *Pasternak: A Biography*, George Weidenfeld and Nicholson Ltd, London, 1983. Republished as an e-book and kindle edition by Routledge 2021 ch.6.

36 The number of churches had fallen from 55,000 at the time of revolution to about a 1,000 in 1940. By 1958, when Khrushchev began to close them down once more, the number had reached 22,000.

37 There were a few reciprocal concessions which, for example, allowed a Soviet-edited newspaper to be published in London which survived until the end of the Soviet system. Admirers of the actor Gregory Peck will know that his first starring role was as a Russian guerrilla commander fighting Nazi invaders in a Jacques Tourneur movie celebrating Russian partisans (*Days of Glory* 1944).

38 *Foreign Relations of the United States: Diplomatic Papers, 1942, Europe,* vol. III, p. 643.
39 Harrison, Richard W., *The Russian Way of War: Operational Art 1904–1940,* University Press of Kansas, Lawrence, Kansas, 2001, p. 204.
40 See Chapter 5 p. 113.
41 For two complementary and extremely thoughtful explorations of the topic, see Perrie, Maureen, *The Cult of Ivan the Terrible in Stalin's Russia,* Palgrave, London and New York, 2001 and Neuberger, Joan, *This Thing of Darkness: Eisenstein's Ivan the Terrible in Stalin's Russia*, Cornell University Press, Ithaca, 2019
42 *Pravda,* 28 January 1936. In the days of the Cold War the anonymous article was attributed to Stalin but archive evidence suggests it was written by a journalist named David Zaslavsky. (Efimov, E., *Sumbur vokrug 'Sumbura' i odnogo 'malenkovo zhurnalista,* Flinta, Moscow, 2006.) Whoever wrote it, the article certainly conveyed Stalin's sentiments.
43 The story has been told a number of times. See Moynahan, Brian, *Leningrad: Siege and Symphony,* Quercus, London 2014; Fay, Laurel, *Shostakovich: A Life*, Oxford University Press, Oxford, 1989; Reid, Anna, *Leningrad: Tragedy of a City under Siege 1941–44,* Bloomsbury, London, 2011; Salisbury, Harrison, *The 900 Days: The Siege of Leningrad,* Pan Books, London, 1969.
44 Significant elements of this painting – the head-down figure and the anti-tank barrier – reference his earlier works *The Parachutist over the Sea* (1934) and *The Defence of Moscow* (1941).
45 A glance at the Getty Images catalogue of almost 45,000 items related to Russia – from Russian, German, American and other sources – shows the wide range and immediacy of Russian war photography. Select 'Most Popular' for a more manageable subgroup. https://www.gettyimages.co.uk/photos/world-war-ii-russian# See also the volume of photos by Vladimir Karpov for many striking images including harrowing photos of women and men breaking through ice to get water during the siege of Leningrad, munitions workers in factories and building – to – building fighting in Stalingrad Karpov, Vladimir et al., *Russia at War 1941–45,* Stanley Paul, London and Vendome Publishers, New York, 1987.
46 This was also the time of the mass campaign to end illiteracy in the USSR.
47 For an excellent bilingual edition of war poetry from leading writers and amateurs, see the 500-page anthology: Bloshteyn, Maria (ed. and trans.), *Russia Is Burning: Poems of the Great Patriotic War*, Smokestack Books, Ripon, 2020. This remarkable collection includes published and 'desk drawer' items and poems by front-line soldiers, war and gulag prisoners, Leningraders and many others.
48 Faminsky, Valerii, A painter of the Grekov Studio in Berlin, 1945. From the *New York Times* archive courtesy of Arthur Bondar.
49 There is not very much material on wartime newsreels. A welcome exception is Spring, Derek W., 'Soviet Newsreel and the Great Patriotic War', in Pronay, Nicholas and Spring, D. W. (eds.), *Propaganda, Politics and Film, 1918–45*, Palgrave Macmillan, London, 1982, pp. 270–92. See also the informative Smirnov, V. *Dokumental'nye filmy o Velikoi Otechestvennoi Voiny,* Moscow, 1947.
50 There are several collections of his war correspondence and other writings in English including: Grossman, Vassilii, *The Road, Stories, Journalism, and Essays*, translated by Robert and Elizabeth Chandler with Olga Mukovnikova, commentary and notes by Robert Chandler with Yury Bit-Yunan, afterword by Fyodor Guber, New

York Review Books, New York, 2010 in *'The War' and Other Stories*. Trans Andrew Glikin-Gusinsky. Sovlit.net and *A Writer at War: A Soviet Journalist with the Red Army, 1941–1945,* edited and translated by Antony Beevor and Luba Vinogradova from Grossman's wartime notebooks. New York: Vintage Books, 2013. His works in Russian can be found at: lib.ru.

51 There is a massive literarure on the origin of the Cold War. See Read, Christopher, *Stalin: From the Caucasus to the Kremlin,* Routledge, 2017, chapter 8 especially pp. 259–93 for a brief account which locates the events within the framework of Stalin's life and career and Roberts, Geoffrey, *Stalin's Wars: From World War to Cold War 1939–1953,* Yale University Press, New Haven and London, 2008 for a more detailed account.

52 Priestley, J. B., *Russian Journey*, Writers Group of the Society for Cultural Relations with the USSR, London, 1946, p. 5.

53 Ibid., p. 5.

54 Ibid., p. 38.

55 All quotations from Zhdanov, A., *On Literature, Music and Philosophy*, Lawrence and Wishart, London 1950 Chapter II, accessed via https://www.marxists.org/subject/art/lit_crit/zhdanov/lit-music-philosophy.htm#s2

56 Ibid., chapter II.

57 Gorlizki, Yoram and Khlevniuk, Oleg, *Cold Peace: Stalin and the Soviet Ruling Circle, 1945–1953,* Oxford, Oxford University Press, 2005.

58 Capital punishment had been abolished in 1947 but was re-instated to enable these sentences to be passed.

59 https://www.ft.com/content/ede1e5c6-e0c5-11e5-8d9b-e88a2a889797

60 Zhdanov, chapter II.

61 The Gopak (Hopak) and Komarinsky (Kamarinskaya) are folk dances.

62 Zhdanov Chapter III.

63 Ibid, chapter IV.

64 An interesting illustration of this, together with brief but excellent descriptive essays can be found in connection with the University of Chicago Library exhibition of 2011 devoted to *Adventures in the Soviet Imaginary: Children's Books and Graphic Art* accessible at https://www.lib.uchicago.edu/collex/exhibits/soviet-imaginary/

65 Ibid, chapter II.

66 Gorlizki, Yoram and Khlevniuk, Oleg, *Cold Peace: Stalin and the Soviet Ruling Circle, 1945–1953,* Oxford University Press, Oxford, 2004. Watson, Derek, *Molotov: A Biography,* Palgrave, London and New York, 2005. Still useful are Pethybridge, Roger, *A History of Postwar Russia,* Allen and Unwin, London, 1966; Dunmore, Timothy, *Soviet Politics 1945–53*, Palgrave Macmillan, London and New York, 1984 and Hahn, Werner G., *Postwar Soviet Politics: The Fall of Zhdanov and the Defeat of Moderation, 1946–53,* Cornell University Press, Ithaca and London, 1982.

67 The *New York Times* claimed confirmation of this on 17 January 1963 but its Lithuanian source was not revealed: https://timesmachine.nytimes.com/timesmachine/1963/01/17/89514480.html?pageNumber=5]

68 Medvedev, Zhores, *Stalin i evreiskaia problema: novyi analiz,* Izdatel'stvo Prava Cheloveka, Moskva, 2003.

69 Holloway, David, *Stalin and the Bomb: The Soviet Union and Atomic Energy 1939–1956,* Yale University Press, New Haven and London, 1996.

70 There is one former closed town within the borders of the European Union. Sillamäe, on the Estonian north coast near Narva and the Russian border, was a centre for the

production and processing of uranium. Its wide avenues and large-scale majestic buildings testify to its former privileged status. A beautiful theatre, under which an atomic shelter was constructed, have been restored to their Soviet-era glory, including decorations featuring Lenin and Marx, an unusual project for the EU. Only around 5 percent of its population is ethnically Estonian. Like its neighbour, Narva, it is 85 percent Russian by ethnicity.

Chapter 9

1. Ehrenburg, Ilya, *Ottepel' (The Thaw)* Sovetskii Pisatel', Moscow, 1954. It was initially published in *Novyi mir*. English editions were published by H. Regnery Co, Chicago, 1954 and Harvill Press, London, 1955.
2. Alexeyeva, Ludmila and Goldberg, Paul, *The Thaw Generation: Coming of Age in the Post-Stalin Era,* Little, Brown and Company, Boston, Toronto, London, 1990, p. 4.
3. Gorbachev, Mikhail and Mlynar, Zdenek, *Conversations with Gorbachev: On Perestroika, the Prague Spring and the Crossroads of Socialism*, Columbia University Press, New York and Chichester, West Sussex, 2002.
4. Tromly, Benjamin, *The Making the Soviet Intelligentsia: Universities and Intellectual Life under Stalin and Khrushchev*, Cambridge University Press, Cambridge and New York, 2005.
5. A transcript of Khrushchev's remarks as he went round the exhibition was originally published in *Encounter* (London) April 1963. The source is unclear. Although the journal was part-funded by the CIA at the time the remarks are widely agreed to be genuine. Extracts can be found on the *Seventeen Moments in Soviet History* website at: http://soviethistory.msu.edu/1961-2/khrushchev-on-the-arts/khrushchev-on-the-arts-texts/khrushchev-on-modern-art/
6. 'Ernst Neizvestny, a Russian Sculptor Who Clashed with Khrushchev, Dies at 91', *New York Times*, 18 August 2016, https://www.nytimes.com/2016/08/18/arts/international/ernst-neizvestny-a-russian-sculptor-who-clashed-with-khrushchev-dies-at-91.html
7. Ibid.
8. For an excellent account of the affair, including fascinating comments from the Visitors' Book, see Reid, Susan Emily, 'In the Name of the People: The Manège Affair Revisited', *Kritika: Explorations in Russian and Eurasian History*, 6 (4) (Fall 2005) (New Series), pp. 673–716.
9. Neizvestnyi, Ernst, *Govorit Neizvestnyi*, Possev-Verlag, Frankfurt am Main, 1984, pp. 37–49.
10. Trump and his entourage have perfected this technique along with the Murdoch press and its clones, so it is not such an un usual development. There is an added deliciousness in that the western right uses a tactic shared with Soviet Communists to counter what they see as the Marxist-inspired culture of 'political correctness'.
11. *Seventeen Moments in Soviet History.*
12. For an excellent account which brings the story into the twenty-first century, see Beumers, Birgit, *A History of Soviet Cinema*, Bloomsbury, London and New York, 2008. Leyda, Jay, *Kino*, Collier Books, New York, 1973 remains iconic for the earlier period.
13. For an excellent account of psychiatric hospital incarceration see Reddaway, Peter and Bloch, Sidney, *Psychiatric Terror: How Soviet Psychiatry Is Used to Suppress*

Dissent, Basic Books, New York, 1977 (British edition: *Russia's Political Hospitals: The Abuse of Psychiatry in the Soviet Union*, Gollancz, London, 1977) and *Soviet Psychiatric Abuse,* Westview Press, Boulder Col., 1984. The authors worked tirelessly to expose the practice and to isolate Soviet psychologists in international organizations and conferences.

14 See Frankel, Edith Rogovin, 'The Tvardovsky Controversy', *Soviet Studies*, 34 (4) (October, 1982), pp. 601–15, esp p. 609.

15 Solzhenitsyn, A. *Letter to Soviet Leaders* (*Pismo Vozhdiam Sovetskogo Soiuza*), Index on Censorship and Fontana Books, London, 1974.

16 A text of the speech and a recording of it can be found at https://www.americanrhetoric.com/speeches/alexandersolzhenitsynharvard.htm

17 See, for example, Bukovsky, V., 'The Peace Movement and the Soviet Union', *Commentary,* May 1982, https://www.commentary.org/articles/commentary-bk/the-peace-movement-the-sovietunion. The text, from which the quotation is taken, is largely a long line of non sequiturs, misconceptions, errors and wishful thinking. It makes a multitude of assertions but adduces next to no evidence.

18 Sakharov, A., *Progress, Co-existence and Intellectual Freedom*, Pelican Books, Harmondsworth, 1968.

19 Sakharov, A., *Memoirs,* Hutchinson, London, Sydney, Auckland, Johannesberg, 1990, p. 281. 'Convergence' was a theory propounded in the west and taken up unofficially in the USSR which suggested that the imperatives of an industrial society would bring capitalist and socialist societies to increasingly resemble each other. One of its fullest developments can be found in Galbraith, John Kenneth *The New Industrial State* 1967. See Kelley, Donald R., 'The Soviet Debate on the Convergence of the American & Soviet Systems', *Polity*, 6 (2) (1973).

20 Sakharov, A., *Memoirs,* Hutchinson, London, Sydney, Auckland, Johannesberg, 1990, p. 326.

21 It should be noted that Sakharov and Solzhenitsyn were writing at a time when the USSR had broken off its assistance to China around 1960, relations had worsened during the Chinese cultural revolution and in 1969 there had been open skirmishing on the frontier over Damansky (Zhenbao) Island, which was a wetland of less than one square kilometre in the Ussuri river.

22 From *Chronicle of Current Events* no. 26, 5 July 1972. Accessible at: https://chronicle-of-current-events.com/2021/04/12/sakharovs-memorandum-june-1972-26-17/ There are also a number of editions of the text. For an excellent compilation of writings and speeches by Sakharov up to his Nobel Prize see Salisbury, Harrison E. *Sakharov Speaks*, Collins/Harvill, London, 1974.

23 Rubinstein, Joshua and Gribanov, Alexander, *The KGB File of Andrei Sakharov*, Yale University Press, New Haven and London, 2005, p. 171.

24 Editor's comment in ibid.

25 Andropov to Central Committee, 7 March 1974. Proposals on how to handle Sakharov in ibid., pp. 174–5.

26 Gordon, Dmitrii, *Bul'var Gordona,* no. 2 (402), 7 January 2013, http://bulvar.com.ua/gazeta/archive/s2_65879/7902.html

27 The English edition is Medvedev, R., *Let History Judge: The Origins and Consequences of Stalinism,* Random House, New York and London, 1971. An expanded version was published in 1989 by Oxford University Press.

28 Medvedev, Roy, *On Socialist Democracy*, Albert A. Knopf, New York, 1972. There is an excellent review of the original Russian language edition by Frederick Barghoorn

which summarizes the main points of change – political, social and economic – proposed by Medvedev which, from today's vantage point, look like a recipe for perestroika. Barghoorn considers Medvedev to be more important than either Solzhenitsyn or Sakharov not least because his proposals are rooted in the actually existing condition of the Soviet system. Barghoorn, Frederick C, 'Medvedev's Democratic Leninism: *Kniga O Sotsialisticheskoi Demokratii.* by Roy Medvedev', *Slavic Review,* 32 (3) (September 1973), pp. 590–4.

29 Presumably Osipov is thinking of the Lenin of NEP. Prior to the 'turn towards the middle peasant' in 1919 Lenin and the party's views were strongly anti-peasant, a tendency tragically and viciously revived by Stalin.

30 For an excellent and authoritative account of the main ideas of Osipov and *Veche,* to which the present author is much indebted, see Duncan, Peter J. S., 'The fate of Russian Nationalism: The Samizdat Journal *Veche* Revisited', *Religion in Communist Lands*, 16 (1) (1988), pp. 36–53. https://www.tandfonline.com/doi/pdf/10.1080/09637498808431347?needAccess=true

31 The English edition was published in 1971. The original Russian title was *Chernyi doski: Zapiski nachinaiushchego kollektsionera* (Black Boards: Notes of a Starting-out Collector).

32 There was an unwritten expectation that if you received something in samizdat format, including unavailable literature from *Doctor Zhivago* to the 1920s science fiction of the Strugatsky brothers, there was responsibility to try to make an extra copy and pass both on.

33 Personal observation by the author.

34 Others associated with the New Direction included academicians and senior figures among historians from universities. Among the leading exponents of the new approach were K. Tarnovskii, I. F. Gindin, L. M. Ivanov, A. Ia. Avrekh, V. Bovykin.

35 Nekrich, Aleksandr, *1941. 22 iunia* Nauka, Moscow 1965. Published in English as: *June 22, 1941: Soviet Historians and the German Invasion*, University of South Carolina Press, Columbia SC, 1968.

36 Kam-Az was the brand name of a Soviet and Russian manufacturer of heavy trucks for large cargoes and special purposes like open-cast mines.

37 Eremenko, Alexey 'Monument to Soviet Space Program Put Out to Pasture in Moscow's VDNKh' *Moscow Times*, 7 July 2014.

38 Baikonur, actually in Kazakhstan, was the main Soviet space launch facility but after the breakup of the Soviet Union Russia retains it by leasing it from Kazakhstan.

39 Facebook 05/08/21 Kluber account.

40 Alexeyeva and Goldberg, p. 11. Pavlik Morozov was a young boy who informed to the authorities on the illegal activities of his parents who murdered him as a result. He became an official icon of social duty taking priority over family ties.

41 Roberts, Geoffrey, *Stalin's Library: A Dictator and His Books*, Yale University Press, New Haven and London, 2022.

42 There are a number of excellent studies and compilations of Soviet-era jokes but most of them focus on the Stalin era. For a sample including the Brezhnev years see Dolgopolova, Zhanna, *Russia Dies Laughing: Jokes from Soviet Russia,* Allen and Unwin, London, 1983. An excellent study which brings out the importance of jokes under Soviet conditions is Waterlow, Jonathan, *It's Only a Joke, Comrade!: Humour, Trust and Everyday Life under Stalin (1928–41)*, Self-published, Oxford, 2018, who reminds us of the key point that 'The joke contradicted the idea that the population had been suffocated or brought under the regime's control' (Introduction p. 3).

For an excellent anthology of Stalin-era jokes, see Brandenberger, David, *Political Humor under Stalin: An Anthology of Unofficial Jokes and Anecdotes,* Slavica Press, Ann Arbor, 2009. The tradition of Bim and Bom satirizing the system lived on underground.

43 Solzhenitsyn, A., 'The Smatterers' (*Obrazovanshchina*), in Solzhenitsyn, A. (ed.), *From under the Rubble,* HarperCollins and Fontana, London and New York, 1976.

44 From his obituary in the *New York Times,* 21 February 2019.

45 Khromov, Gavriil, 'The Russian Academy of Sciences: History, Myth, Reality', *Otechestvennye zapiski*, 7 (2002).

46 Ziegler, Charles E., 'Worker Participation and Worker Discontent in the Soviet Union', *Political Science Quarterly*, 98 (2) (Summer, 1983), pp. 249–50.

Chapter 10

1 Lee, Gary and Bohlen, Celestine 'Gorbachev Steps Up Drive for "Revolutionary Change"', *Washington Post,* 1 February 1987.

2 In fact, the job was completed by a crane brought in by the local authorities who feared a falling statue of such size and weight threatened to crash through into the metro line beneath.

3 *Malenkaia Vera* 1988. Directed by Vassili Pichul and filmed in Zhdanov (Mariupol'), Ukraine.

4 *Is It Easy to Be Young*? 1986. Directed by Juris Podnieks (1950–92) and filmed in Latvia with Latvian and Russian dialogue. Podnieks was beaten up and two of his collaborators shot dead by snipers in 1991 while filming a violent incident at the Riga television tower. Podnieks drowned while scuba diving a year later. Much less well known than the original but also inordinately interesting and revealing, there were two documentary sequels directed by Antra Cilinska in 1998 (*Is It Easy to Be?*) and 2010 (*Is It Easy?*) which followed up the stories of as many of the interviewees from the original film who were still alive and could be traced.

5 Nonetheless, they soon switched into arguing it was the economic pressure and the arms race they had imposed on the USSR which had caused it to crack and switched to congratulating themselves and perform apparently endless victory laps over a process they did not fully understand.

6 Bialer, Seweryn, 'Gorbachev's Program of Change: Sources, Significance, Prospects', *Political Science Quarterly*, 103 (3) (Autumn 1988), p. 405.

7 Ibid., p. 439. Note the interesting juxtaposition of heritage and Soviet values.

8 Translated from original extracts in https://ru.wikipedia.org/wiki/%D0%A1%D0%BB%D0%BE%D0%B2%D0%BE_%D0%BA_%D0%BD%D0%B0%D1%80%D0%BE%D0%B4%D1%83

9 'Chetyre voprosa Gennadiiu Ziuganova', *Zavtra,* no. 7 (554) 30 iiunia 2004.

10 'Sumerki Rossii' *Lebed' Al'manakh* No. 450 6 Noiabr' 2005.

11 'Open Letter of Well-known Soviet Writers to the Editor of *Pravda* in connection with the Anti-Soviet Activities and Speeches of A. I. Solzhenitsyn and A. D. Sakharov', *Pravda*, 31 August 1973.

12 Bykov, Vassil', *Dolgaia doroga domoi*, AST Moscow, 2005, p. 324.

13 Clines, Francis X, 'Sakharov Draws Wrath in Stormy Soviet Congress', *New York Times,* 3 June 1989, https://www.nytimes.com/1989/06/03/world/sakharov-draws-wrath-in-stormy-soviet-congress.html

14 The western debate includes: Burnham, James, *The Managerial Revolution*, John Day, New York, 1941; Benda, Julien, *La Trahison des Clercs*, Grasset, Paris, 1927; Rizzi, Bruno, *The Bureaucratisation of the World*, The Free Press, New York, 1985 (originally published in France, 1939), https://www.marxists.org/archive/rizzi/bureaucratisation/index.htm; Djilas, Milovan, *The New Class: An Analysis of the Communist System*, Harcourt, Brace, Jovanovich, New York, 1957; Shils, Edward, *The Intellectuals and the Powers, and Other Essays (His Selected Papers)*, University of Chicago Press, Chicago, 1972
15 I have not found a precise reference to this item though several sources quote it.
16 Gasparov, M. L., 'Intellektualy, intelligenty i intelligentnost', in Likhachev, D. S. and Kniazevskaia T. B. (eds.), *Russkaia Intelligentsiia: istoriia i sud'ba*, Russian Academy of Sciences Scholarly Committee for the History of World Culture, Nauka, Moscow, 1999, p. 188.
17 Ibid.
18 For example: Gidrinskii, V. I., *Russkaia intelligentsia v istorii Rossii*, Moscow, 2005; Isaev, I. A., *V poiskakh puti: russkaia intelligentsia i sud'by Rossii*, Moscow, 1992: Klimova, Svetlana, *The Russian Intelligentsia: In Search of an Identity*, Brill, Leiden, 2020; Kapustin, M. P., *Kul'tura i vlast': puti i sud'by russkoi intelligentsia v zerkale russkoi poezii*, Moscow, 2003.
19 Smith, S., 'Bolshevism, Taylorism and the Technical Intelligentsia in the Soviet Union, 1917–1941', *Radical Science Journal* (13) (1983), p. 4.
20 Chatterjee, Debasmita, 'Top 10 Countries That Produce the Most Engineers', 4 May 2021, https://www.embibe.com/exams/top-10-countries-that-produce-the-most-engineers/
21 Sillaste, Galina, 'Podgotovka novoi ekonomicheskoi intelligentsia kak factor restrukturatzii ekonomikii: spetsifika i perspektivy', *Dialog*, 3 (2006) (e-journal of Tsenov Academy), p. 225, https://dialogue.uni-svishtov.bg/title.asp?title=225
22 There is a full debate about this between Umland and Gregor, with some references to Roger Griffin, in 'Dugin Not a Fascist? A Debate with A. James Gregor (6 texts)', *Erwägen Wissen Ethik*, 15–16 (3–4) (January, 2005), pp. 424–429, 591–595, 566–572. The comments by Gregor can be found on pp. 594 and 570. The texts are accessible at https://www.researchgate.net/publication/255970590_Dugin_Not_a_Fascist_A_Debate_with_A_James_Gregor_6_texts
23 Youtube, Luis Razo Bravo, 'Alexander Dugin on Donald Trump and the Fourth Political Theory' (at 55 mins). Recorded 3 October 2020. https://www.youtube.com/watch?v=uCkw_20R04Y. There are a number of YouTube videos where Dugin discusses his ideas. For example 'Bernard-Henri Lévy vs. Aleksandr Dugin' – Nexus Symposium, 21 September 2019, Amsterdam, https://www.youtube.com/watch?v=x70z5QWC9qs
24 For a summary of National Bolshevism (*Smena vekh*) and its ideas in the 1920s see Read, Christopher, *Culture and Power in Revolutionary Russia: The Intelligentsia and the Transition from Tsarism to Communism*, Macmillan, London, 1991, pp. 189–200.
25 Agursky, M. *Ideologiia national bolshevizma*, YMCA Press, Paris, 1980. It was reprinted in Moscow in 2003 by Algoritm publishing house.
26 Brandenberger, *David National Bolshevism. Stalinist Mass Culture and the Formation of Modern Russian National Identity, 1931–1956* interprets Stalin-era culture as a form of National Bolshevism.
27 The Scythians were a Siberian nomadic warrior tribe who settled in the territory of present-day Ukraine and Russia in the eighth and seventh centuries BCE.
28 http://os.colta.ru/society/russia/details/15155/

29 See almost any major western newspaper or broadcaster at that time for examples of this extraordinary U-turn. On Ukrainian responsibility see, amongst many accounts, Bertrand, Natasha and Lillis, Katie Bo 'US Believes Elements within Ukraine's Government Authorized Assassination near Moscow, Sources Say', *CNN*, 6 October 2022, https://edition.cnn.com/2022/10/05/politics/us-intelligence-ukraine-dugina-assassination/index.html
30 "Poisoned by Putin", *The Guardian*, 9 September 2004.
31 Source: Valdai Discussion Club 'Vladimir Putin Meets with Members of the Valdai Discussion Club. Transcript of the Plenary Session of the 18th Annual Meeting', *Global Shake-up in the 21st Century: The Individual, Values and the State*, 22 October 2021, Sochi, Russia. https://valdaiclub.com/events/posts/articles/vladimir-putin-meets-with-members-of-the-valdai-discussion-club-transcript-of-the-18th-plenary-session/
32 Gershenzon, M. O. (ed), *Vekhi: sbornik statei*, Sablina, St Petersburg, 1909. Introduction.
33 https://www.independent.ie/world-news/russian-cosmonaut-takes-relics-of-saint-to-space-35617127.html
34 https://www.catholicnewsagency.com/news/18349/relics-icons-and-crosses-are-onboard-international-space-station-cosmonaut-says

Bibliography and sources

Adventures in the Soviet Imaginary: Children's Books and Graphic Art. https://www.lib.uchicago.edu/collex/exhibits/soviet-imaginary/

Agursky, M. *Ideologiia national bolshevizma,* YMCA Press, Paris, 1980 and Algorithm publishing house, Moscow 2003.

Alexeyeva, Ludmilla and Goldberg, Paul, *The Thaw Generation: Coming of Age in the Post-Stalin Era*, Little, Brown and Company, Boston, Toronto, London, 1993.

Alexievich, Svetlana, *In Search of the Free Individual: The History of the Russian-Soviet Soul*, Cornell Global Perspectives, Ithaca, 2018.

Andreev, A. Iu and Tsygankov, D. A. *Imperatorskii Moskovskii universitet 1755–1917: entsiklopedicheskii slovar*', ROSSPEN, Moscow, 2010.

Aron, Raymond, *L'Opium des Intellectuels*, Calmann-Lévy, Paris, 1955 (English edition: *The Opium of the Intellectuals* Norton, New York and London 1957).

Aucouturier, Michel, *Le réalisme socialiste*, Presses Universitaires de France, Paris, 1998 ('*Que sais-je?*' series).

Avineri, S. 'Marx and the Intellectuals', *Journal of the History of Ideas*, 28 (197), pp. 269–78.

Baird, Catherine, *Revolution from within: The YMCA in Russia's Ascension to Freedom from Bolshevik Tyranny*, 2013.

Barghoorn, Frederick C. 'Medvedev's Democratic Leninism: Kniga O Sotsialisticheskoi Demokratii. by Roy Medvedev', *Slavic Review*, 32 (3) (September, 1973), pp. 590–4.

Barry, Donald D. and Berman, Harold J. 'The Soviet Legal Profession', *Harvard Law Review*, 82 (1) (November, 1968).

Bastié, Eugénie, *La Guerre des idées - Enquête au coeur de l'intelligentsia française,* Robert Laffont, Paris, 2021.

Benda, Julien, *La Trahison des Clercs*, Grasset, Paris, 1927.

Berdyaev, Nicholas, 'Religiya Voskresheniya ("Philosophiya obshego dela" N. F. Fedorova)', *Russkaya Mysl*', July 1915, pp. 76–120. Article reprinted and included by YMCA Press Paris in 1989 in the Berdyaev Collection: 'Tipy religioznoi mysli v Rossii', (Tom III), pp. 242–301. Also available at: http://www.berdyaev.com/berdiaev/berd_lib/1915_186.html#7

Berdyaev, Nicholas, *Origin of Russian Communism*, Geoffrey Bles, London, 1937.

Bergman, Jay, *The French Revolutionary Tradition in Russian and Soviet Politics, Political Thought, and Culture*, Oxford University Press, Oxford, 2019.

Bernard-Henri Lévy vs. Aleksandr Dugin – Nexus Symposium 21 September 2019, Amsterdam, https://www.youtube.com/watch?v=x70z5QWC9qs

Bertrand, Natasha and Lillis, Katie Bo, 'US Believes Elements within Ukraine's Government Authorized Assassination near Moscow, sources say', *CNN* Thu, 6 October 2022, https://edition.cnn.com/2022/10/05/politics/us-intelligence-ukraine-dugina-assassination/index.html

Besançon, Alain, 'Un point de vue nouveau sur l'Intelligentsiia russe', *Revue Historique* (1963).

Beumers, Birgit, *A History of Soviet Cinema,* Bloomsbury, London and New York, 2008.

Bialer, Seweryn, 'Gorbachev's Program of Change: Sources, Significance, Prospects', *Political Science Quarterly*, 103 (3) (Autumn, 1988).
Billington, James, *The Icon and the Axe: An Interpretive History of Russian Culture*, Random House, New York, 1966.
Billington, James H. *Mikhailovsky and Russian Populism*, The Clarendon Press, London and Oxford, 1958.
Bloshteyn, Maria (ed. and trans), *Russia Is Burning: Poems of the Great Patriotic War*, Smokestack Books, Ripon, 2020.
Blum, Jerome, 'Russia', in Spring, David (ed.), *Landed Élites in Nineteenth Century Europe*, Johns Hopkins University Press, Baltimore and London, 1977.
Bogdanov A. A. *Vera I nauka. O knige V.Il'ina 'Materializm I empirio-krititsizm'*, izd. S. Dorovatovskago i A. Charushnikova, Moscow, 1910.
Bourdieu, Pierre, *The Field of Cultural Production*, Polity Press, Cambridge, 1993.
Brandenberger, David, *National Bolshevism. Stalinist Mass Culture and the Formation of Modern Russian National Identity, 1931–1956*, Harvard University Press, Cambridge, MA, 2002.
Brandenberger, David and Zelenov, Mikhail, *Stalin's Master Narrative: A Critical Edition of the History of the Communist Party of the Soviet Union (Bolsheviks), Short Course*, Yale University Press, New Haven, 2019, https://weeklyworker.co.uk/worker/1309/stalin-as-historian/?fbclid=IwAR2F25HOQX0gw8-wnf4WagCkLlHt9xFBSWwI093QGMBREq VulBDAZ8BPauYccccccccc
Brandenberger, David, *Political Humor under Stalin: An Anthology of Unofficial Jokes and Anecdotes*, Slavica Press, Ann Arbor, 2009.
Bravo, Luis Razo, 'Alexander Dugin on Donald Trump and the Fourth Political Theory' (at 55mins). Youtube. Recorded 3 October 2020, https://www.youtube.com/watch?v=uCkw_20R04Y
Brooks, Jeffrey, *'The Firebird' and 'The Fox': Russian Culture under Tsars and Bolsheviks*, Cambridge University Press, Cambridge, 2019.
Bukharin, N. and Preobrazhensky, E. *The ABC of Communism: A Popular Explanation of the Program of the Communist Party of Russia*, 1st English edition (trans. Eden and Cedar Paul) Communist Party of Great Britain, London, 1922, p. 72.
Bukovsky, V. 'The Peace Movement and the Soviet Union', *Commentary*, May, 1982, https://www.commentary.org/articles/commentary-bk/the-peace-movement-the-sovietunion
Bulgakov M. *Dnevnik, pis'ma 1914–1940*, Sovremennyi Pisatel', Moscow, 1997.
Bulgakov, M. *Diaries and Selected Letters*, Alma Classics, Richmond, Surrey, 2013.
Burke, Peter *What Is Cultural History?* Polity Press, London, 2018.
Burnham, James, *The Managerial Revolution*, John Day, New York, 1941.
Buruma, Ian and Margalit, Avishai, *Occidentalism: A Short History of Anti-Westernism*, Atlantic Books, London, 2005.
Bykov Leonid, P. 'The "Thick Journal" in Russia: Yesterday, Today and Tomorrow', *Journal of Siberian Federal University. Humanities & Social Sciences*, 5 (2016), pp. 1249–55, http://elib.sfu-kras.ru/bitstream/handle/2311/20274/22_Bykov.pdf?sequence=1&isAllowed=y
Bykov, Vassil', *Dolgaia doroga domoi*, AST, Moscow, 2005.
Chaadaev, P. *First Philosophical Letter*.
Chamberlain, Leslie, *Lenin's Private War: The Voyage of the Philosophy Steamer and the Exile of the Intelligentsia*, St Martin's Press, New York, 2007.

Chamberlin, William Henry, 'Turgenev: The Eternal Romantic', *The Russian Review*, 5 (2) (Spring, 1946).
Chatterjee, Debasmita, 'Top 10 Countries That Produce the Most Engineers', 04 May 2021, https://www.embibe.com/exams/top-10-countries-that-produce-the-most-engineers/
Chronicle of Current Events, https://chronicle-of-current-events.com
Claudin-Urondo, C. *Lenin and Cultural Revolution: Marxist Theory and Contemporary Capitalism*, Branch Line, Hassocks, Sussex, 1977.
Clines, Francis X, 'Sakharov Draws Wrath in Stormy Soviet Congress', *New York Times*, 3 June 1989, https://www.nytimes.com/1989/06/03/world/sakharov-draws-wrath-in-stormy-soviet-congress.html
Coates, Ruth, *Deification in Russian Religious Thought: Between the Revolutions, 1905–1917*, Oxford University Press, Oxford, 2019.
Collini, Stefan, *Public Moralists: Political Thought and Intellectual Life in Britain 1850–1930*, Oxford University Press, Oxford, 1991.
Confino, M. 'On Intellectuals and Intellectual Traditions in Eighteenth- and Nineteenth-Century Russia', *Daedalus* (Special issue: *Intellectuals and Change*), Summer, 1972, pp. 117–49.
Cooke, Roger, *The Mathematics of Sonya Kovalevskaya*, Springer verlag, Berlin, 1984.
Coser, L. *Men of Ideas. A Sociologist's View*, The Free Press, New York, 1975.
Debray, Régis, *Teachers, Writers, Celebrities: The Intellectuals of Modern France*, Verso, London, 1981.
Djilas, Milovan, *The New Class: An Analysis of the Communist System*, Harcourt, Brace, Jovanovich, New York, 1957.
Dolgopolova, Zhanna, *Russia Dies Laughing: Jokes from Soviet Russia*, Allen and Unwin, London, 1983.
Drubek, Natascha, 'Exegi Monumentum Revolutionis – On Eisenstein's October (1927)', in Balme, Christopher, Wessel, Martin Schulze and Brunnbauer, Ulf (eds.), *The Culture of the Russian Revolution and Its Global Impact: Semantics – Performances – Functions*, (DigiOst 9) München, 2020, https://hcommons.org/deposits/objects/hc:30388/datastreams/CONTENT/content
Dukes, Paul, 'The Russian Revolution in the Encyclopaedia Britannica', *Revolutionary Russia*, 34 (2) (2021) Special Issue in Honour of J. D. Smele, pp. 259–75.
Duncan, Peter J. S. 'The Fate of Russian Nationalism: The samizdat journal Veche Revisited', *Religion in Communist Lands*, 16 (1) (1988), pp. 36–53. https://www.tandfonline.com/doi/pdf/10.1080/09637498808431347?needAccess=true
Dunmore, Timothy, *Soviet Politics 1945–53*, Palgrave Macmillan, London and New York, 1984.
Eaton, Henry, 'Marx and the Russians', *Journal of the History of Ideas*, 41 (1) (Jan.–Mar., 1980), pp. 89–112.
Ehrenburg, Ilya, *Ottepel' (The Thaw)* Sovetskii Pisatel', Moskva 1954. English editions were published by H. Regnery Co., Chicago 1954 and Harvill Press, London, 1955.
Ely, C. *Russian Populism: A History*, Bloomsbury, London, New York, Dublin, 2022.
Engels, Friedrich, 'Letter to Daniel'son', 17 October 1893.
Eremenko, Alexey, 'Monument to Soviet Space Program Put Out to Pasture in Moscow's VDNKh', *Moscow Times*, 7 July 2014.
Fay, Laurel, *Shostakovich: A Life*, Oxford University Press, Oxford, 1989.
Fedorov N. *Vopros o bratstve, ili rodstve, o prichinakh nebratskogo, nerodstvennogo, t.e. nemirnogo, sostoianiia mira i o sredstvakh k vosstanovleniiu rodstva: zapiska ot*

neuchenikh k uchenym, dukhovnym i svetskim, k veruiushchim i neveruiushchim, vol. 1, Vernay, 1906; vol. 2 Moscow, 1913.

Feuer, S. *Marx and the Intellectuals*, Anchor Books, New York and London, 1969.

Figes, O. *A People's Tragedy: The Russian Revolution 1891–1924*, Jonathan Cape, London, 1996.

Finkel, Stuart, *On the Ideological Front: The Russian Intelligentsia and the Making of the Soviet Public Sphere*, Yale University Press, New Haven, 2007.

Fitzpatrick, S. (ed.) *Cultural Revolution in Russia 1928–1932*, Indiana University Press, Bloomington, 1978.

Fitzpatrick, S. (ed.), *The Cultural Front. Power and Culture in Revolutionary Russia*, Cornell University Press, Ithaca, 1992.

Florensky, Pavel, Website of works and commentaries, http://www.vehi.net/florensky/

Flynn, James T. 'Tuition and Social Class in the Russian Universities: S. S. Uvarov and "Reaction" in the Russia of Nicholas I', *Slavic Review*, 35 (2) (June, 1976).

Fonvizin, M. *On Communism and Socialism*, n.d., n.p.

Foreign Relations of the United States: Diplomatic Papers, 1942, Europe, Volume III (eds. Noble, G. Bernard and Perkins E.R.) Office of the Historian, United States Government Printing Office, Washington 1961.

Frame, Murray, 'Russian Theater and the Crisis of War and Revolution, 1914–22', in Frame, M., Kolonitskii, B., Marks, S. G. and Stockdale, M. K., *Russian Culture in War and Revolution, 1914–22: Book 2. Political Culture, Identities, Mentalities, and Memory*, Slavica Publishers, Bloomington Indiana, 2014 (Russia's Great War and Revolution series).

Frame, Murray, *The St. Petersburg Imperial Theaters: Stage and State in Revolutionary Russia, 1900–1920*, McFarland & Co., Jefferson, 2000.

Frame, Murray, *School for Citizens: Theater and Civil Society in Imperial Russia*, Yale University Press, New Haven and London, 2006.

Frankel, Edith Rogovin, 'The Tvardovsky Controversy', *Soviet Studies*, 34 (4) (Oct., 1982), pp. 601–15.

Freeze, G. *Description of the Clergy in Rural Russia: The Memoir of a Nineteenth-Century Parish Priest*, Cornell U, Ithaca and London, 1985.

Freeze, G. *The Parish Clergy in Nineteenth-Century Russia: Crisis, Reform, Counter-Reform*, Princeton Legacy Library, Princeton, NJ, 1983.

Freeze, G. *The Russian Levites: Parish Clergy in the Eighteenth Century*, no. 78 (Harvard Russian Research Center Studies) Harvard University Press, Cambridge, MA, 1977.

Gagarin, Prince I. *La Russie sera-t-elle catholique?*, 1856.

Galbraith, John Kenneth, *The New Industrial State*, Penguin Books, London, 1967.

Gasparov M. L. 'Intellektualy, intelligenty i intelligentnost', in Likhachev, D. S. and Kniazevskaia T. B. (eds.), *Russkaia Intelligentsiia: istoriia i sud'ba* Russian Academy of Sciences Scholarly Committee for the History of World Culture, Nauka, Moscow, 1999.

Gatrell, Peter, *Government, Industry and Rearmament in Russia 1900–1914: The Last Argument of Tsarism*, Cambridge University Press, Cambridge, 1994.

Gatrell, Peter, *Government, Industry and Rearmament in Russia, 1900–1914: The Last Argument of Tsarism*, Cambridge University Press, Cambridge, 1994.

Gershenkron, Alexander, *Backwardness in Historical Perspective*, Harvard University Press, Cambridge, MA, 1962.

Gershenzon, M. O. (ed.), *Vekh: Sbornik Statei*, 1909.

Gidrinskii, V. I. *Russkaia intelligentsia v istorii Rossii*, Moscow, 2005.

Goldfrank, David M. 'Old and New Perspectives on Iosif Volotsky's Monastic Rules', *Slavic Review*, 34 (2) (Jun. 1975), pp. 279–301.
Gorbachev, Mikhail and Mlynar, Zdenek, *Conversations with Gorbachev: On Perestroika, the Prague Spring and the Crossroads of Socialism*, Columbia University Press, New York and Chichester, West Sussex, 2002.
Gordon, Dmitrii, *Bul'var Gordona*, no. 2 (402), 7 January 2013, http://bulvar.com.ua/gazeta/archive/s2_65879/7902.html
Gorky, M. 'Otvet S. Budennomu', *Pravda*, 27 noiabriia, 1928.
Gorky, M. *Vladimir Lenin*, https://www.marxists.org/archive/gorky-maxim/1924/01/x01.htm
Gorlizki, Yoram and Khlevniuk, Oleg, *Cold Peace: Stalin and the Soviet Ruling Circle, 1945–1953*, Oxford University Press, Oxford, 2005.
Got'e, I. V. *Time of Troubles: the Diary of Iury Vladimirovich Got'e*, trans. and ed. T. Emmons, London, 1988.
Gould, Stephen Jay, *Leonardo's Mountain of Clams and the Diet of Worms*, Harvard Belknap Press, Cambridge, MA and London 2011.
Graham, Loren (with Irina Dezhina) *Science in the New Russia: Crisis, Aid, Reform*, Indiana University Press, Bloomington, 2008.
Graham, Loren, *Lysenko's Ghost: Epigenetics and Russian Science*, Harvard University Press, Cambridge, MA, 2016.
Graham, Loren R. 'Russian & Soviet Science and Technology', *History of Science Society* Newsletter, 18 (4) (Supplement 1989). Introduction.
Graham, Loren, *Science and Philosophy in the Soviet Union*, Alfred Knopf, New York, 1972.
Graham, Loren, *The Soviet Academy of Sciences and the Communist Party, 1927—1932*, Princeton University Press, Princeton, 1967.
Griswold, Wendy, *Cultures and Societies in a Changing World*, Pine Forge Press, Thousand Oaks, 2004.
Grossman, Vassilii, *A Writer at War: A Soviet Journalist with the Red Army, 1941–1945*, Vintage Books, New York, 2013.
Grossman, Vassilii, *'In The War' and Other Stories*. Sovlit.net.
Grossman, Vassilii, *The Road, Stories, Journalism, and Essays*, New York Review Books, New York, 2010.
Hahn, Werner G. *Postwar Soviet Politics: The Fall of Zhdanov and the Defeat of Moderation, 1946–53*, Cornell University Press, Ithaca and London, 1982.
Hamon, Hervé and Rotman, Patrick, *Génération*. t.1 *Les années de rêve (1958–68)* t.2 *Les années de poudre (1968–1975)*, Le Seuil, Paris, 1987, 1988.
Harrison, E., 'The Image of the Jesuit in Russian Literary Culture of the Nineteenth Century', *Modern Languages Open* (1) (2014). https://modernlanguagesopen.org/articles/10.3828/mlo.v0i1.38
Harrison, Richard W. *The Russian Way of War: Operational Art 1904–1940*, University Press of Kansas Lawrence, Kan., 2001.
Hart-Davies, T. *The Poems of K. F. Relaieff*, Remington & Co., New York, 1887.
Healy, Dan, *Bolshevik Sexual Forensics: Diagnosing Disorder in the Clinic and Courtroom 1917–1939*, Northern Illinois University Press, DeKalb, Il., 2009.
Heath, Nick (Battlescarred) https://libcom.org/history/bim-bom-bang-bang-chekists-clowns
Hellbeck, Jochen, *Revolution on My Mind: Writing a Diary under Stalin*, Harvard University Press, Cambridge, MA, 2006.

Henderson, Robert, *Vladimir Burtsev and the Struggle for a Free Russia: A Revolutionary in the Time of Tsarism and Bolshevism*, Bloomsbury, London, 2018.
Hicks, Jeremy, *Dziga Vertov: Defining Documentary Film*, I.B. Tauris, London & New York, 2007.
Hingley, Ronald, *Pasternak: a Biography*, George Weidenfeld and Nicholson Ltd, London, 1983. Republished as an e-book and kindle edition by Routledge 2021.
Hoffmann, David L. 'Was There a "Great Retreat" from Soviet Socialism? Stalinist Culture Reconsidered', *Kritika: Explorations in Russian and Eurasian History*, 5 (4) (Fall, 2004) (New Series).
Hoffmann, David L. *Stalinist Values. The Cultural Norms of Soviet Modernity 1917–1941*, Cornell University Press, Ithaca, 2003.
Holloway, David, *Stalin and the Bomb: The Soviet Union and Atomic Energy 1939–1956*, Yale University Press, New Haven and London, 1994.
Holmes, Larry, *The Kremlin and the Schoolhouse: Reforming Education in Soviet Russia 1917–1931*, Indiana University Press Bloomington and Indianapolis, 1991, https://dialogue.uni-svishtov.bg/title.asp?title=225
Hughes, Lindsey, *Peter the Great: A Biography*, Yale University Press, New Haven, 1998.
Huskey, Eugene, *Russian Lawyers and The Soviet State: The Origins and Development of the Soviet Bar*, Princeton University Press, Princeton, 1986.
Iakovlev, Alexander. 'Sumerki Rossii', *Lebed' Al'manakh*, No.450 6 Noiabr' 2005. https://lebed.com/2005/art4373.htm
Ioffe A. A. *Moia zhizn' I rabota – avtobiograficheskii ocherk*, Gos. tekhniko-teoreticheskoe izd-vo, Moscow and Leningrad, 1933.
Is It Easy to be Young? 1986. Directed by Juris Podnieks (1950–1992).
Is It Easy to be? Directed by Antra Cilinska, 2010.
Is It Easy? Directed by Antra Cilinska, 1998.
Isaev, I. A. *V poiskakh puti: russkaia intelligentsiaiI sud'by Rossii*, Russkaia kniga, Moscow, 1992.
Iudin, P. (ed.), *Ob ustave soiuza sovetskikh pisatelei*, Gosizdat, Moscow, 1934, https://www.marxists.org/subject/art/lit_crit/sovietwritercongress/
Iz glubiny, 2nd edition, Paris, 1967.
Izgoev, A. S. 'Na perevale. Makhomakhiia v lagere marksistov', *Russkaia mysl'* (6) (1910), p. 106.
James, C. Vaughan *Soviet Socialist Realism: Origins and Theory*, Macmillan, Basingstoke, 1973.
Jasny, Naum *Soviet Economists of the Twenties: Names to Be Remembered*, Cambridge University Press Cambridge, 1972.
Johnston, Gordon, 'Revisiting the Cultural Cold War', *Social History*, 35 (3) (2010), pp. 290–307.
Kapustin, M. P. *Kul'tura i vlast': puti i sud'by russkoi intelligentsia v zerkale russkoi poezii*, Moscow, 2003. http://capustin.narod.ru/culture/intro.htm#6
Karpov, Vladimir et al. *Russia at War 1941–45*, Stanley Paul, London and Vendome Publishers, New York, 1987.
Kelley, Donald R. 'The Soviet Debate on the Convergence of the American & Soviet Systems', *Polity*, 6 (2) (1973).
Kelly, Catriona and Shephard, David, *Constructing Russian Culture in the Age of Revolution: 1881–1940*, Oxford University Press, Oxford, 1998.
Kennedy, Paul, *The Rise and Fall of the Great Powers: Economic Change and Military Conflict from 1500 to 2000*, Random House, New York, 1987.

Kepley, Vance, Jr. 'Federal Cinema: The Soviet Film Industry, 1924–32', *Film History*, 8 (3) (1996), pp. 344–56.
Kerber, L. L. *Stalin's Aviation Gulag: A Memoir of Andrei Tupolev and the Purge Era*, Smithsonian Institution Press, Washington, DC, 1996.
Kerber, L. L. *Tupolev* Politekhnika, St. Petersburg, 1999.
Kerr, Clark, Dunlop, John T., Harbison, Frederick and Myers, Charles A. *Industrialism and Industrial Man*, Oxford University Press (Galaxy), New York, 1960.
Khan-Makhomedov, Selim O. *Pioneers of Soviet Architecture*, Rizzoli, New York, 1987.
Khromov, Gavriil, 'The Russian Academy of Sciences: History, Myth, Reality', *Otechestvennye zapiski*, 7 (2002).
Klimova, Svetlana, *The Russian Intelligentsia: In Search of an Identity*, Brill, Leiden, 2020.
Kneen, Peter, 'Higher Education and Cultural Revolution in the USSR', SIPS Discussion Paper No. 5, Birmingham, 1976.
Kogan L. A. '"Vyslat' za granitsu bezzhalostno" Novoe o izgnanii dukhovnoi elitii', *Voprosy filosofii* (9) (1993), pp. 61–84.
Kolakowski, L. 'Intellectuals against Intellect' Daedalus' (Special issue: *Intellectuals and Change*), Summer, 1972.
Kolonitskii B. I., Kitanina, T. M. and Smirnov, N. N. (eds.), *Intelligentsiia i Rossiiskoe Obshchestvo V Nachale XX Veka: Sbornik Statei*, Rossiskaia Akademiia Nauk, Moscow, 1996.
Koniaev, N. *Rastsvet i gibel' dinastii*, Veche, Moscow, 2003.
Kotkin, Stephen, *Stalin*: *Volume I: Paradoxes of Power, 1878–1928,* Penguin Books, 2014; vol. 2 *Stalin: Waiting for Hitler 1929–1941* Penguin 2017 (vol. 3 forthcoming.)
Kovalevskaia, S. Vospominaniia o Dzhordzhe Eliote *Russkaia mysl'*, no. 6 (1886), pp. 93–108.
Kovalevskaia, S. *Nigilistka* Vol'naia Russkaiia Tipografiia, Geneva 1892. English translation: *Nihilist Girl*, translated by Natasha Kolchevska with Mary Zirin; introduction by Natasha Kolchevska. Modern Language Association of America (2001).
Kozhevnikov, V. A. *Nikolai Fedorovich Fyodorov: Opyt izlozheniia ego ucheniia po izdannym i neizdannym proizvedeniiam, perepiske i lichnym besedam*, Moscow, 1908, p. 9.
Kumanev, V. A. (ed.), *Tragicheskie sud'by: repressirovannye uchenye Akademii nauk sssr*, Nauka, Moscow, 1995.
Kunavin V. 'Vserossiisskii s'ezd Proletkul'ta', *Proletarskaia kul'tura* (17–19) (1920), pp. 74–84.
Kuznetsov, Vadim B. *The Kowalewsky Property*, Providence, Rhode Island, American Mathematical Soc., 2002.
Labedz, L. 'The Destiny of Writers in Revolutionary Movements', *Survey* 18 (1972).
Lee, Gary and Bohlen, Celestine, 'Gorbachev Steps Up Drive For "Revolutionary Change"', *Washington Post,* February 1, 1987.
Leikina-Svirskaia, V. R. *Intelligentsiia v Rossii vo vtoroi polovine XIX veka*, Mysl, Moscow, 1971.
Lenin, V. I. 'Leo Tolstoy as Mirror of the Russian Revolution', 1908, https://www.marxists.org/archive/lenin/works/1908/sep/11.htm
Lenin, V. I. 'Letter to Bukharin', 11 October 1920, https://www.marxists.org/archive/lenin/works/1920/oct/11.htmd
Lenin, V. I. 'Letter to Gorky', 15 September 1919, https://www.marxists.org/archive/lenin/works/1919/sep/15.htm
Lenin V. I. *Materialism and Empirio-criticism: Critical Comments on a Reactionary Philosophy*. The first edition, in Russian, was published in Moscow in 1909. An English translation is available at https://www.marxists.org/archive/lenin/works/1908/mec/.

Lenin, V. I. 'Immediate Tasks of the Soviet Government', in *Pravda*, no. 83 and *Izvestia VTsIK* No.85, April 28, 1918. https://www.marxists.org/archive/lenin/works/1918/mar/x03.htm#sec7.
Lenin, V. I. *On Co-operation,* 4–6 January 1923, https://www.marxists.org/archive/lenin/works/1923/jan/06.htm
Lenin, V. I. *The Development of Capitalism in Russia* 1899, 2nd edition, 1908, https://www.marxists.org/archive/lenin/works/1899/devel/index.htm
Lenoe, Matthew, *Closer to the Masses. Stalinist Culture, Social Revolution and Soviet Newspapers,* Harvard University Press, Cambridge, MA, 2004.
Lenoe, Matthew, 'In Defense of Timasheff's Great Retreat', *Kritika: Explorations in Russian and Eurasian History*, 5 (4) (Fall, 2004) (New Series), pp. 721–30.
Lewin, Moshe, 'Society and the Stalinist state in the Period of the Five Year Plans', *Social History*, 1 (2) (1976), pp. 139–75.
Leyda, Jay, *Kino: A History of the Russian and Soviet Film*, Macmillan, New York, 1960.
Lichtheim, G. 'Alienation', *International Encyclopaedia of the Social Sciences,* 1, New York, 1968.
Likhachev, D. S. and Kniazevskaia, T. B. (eds.), *Russkaia Intelligentsiia: istoriia i sud'ba* Russian Academy of Sciences Scholarly Committee for the History of World Culture, Nauka, Moscow, 1999.
Linoln, W. Bruce, *Between Heaven and Hell: The Story of a Thousand Years of Artistic Life in Russia,* Viking, New York, 1998.
Lipset, S. M. and Dobson, B. 'The intellectual as critic and rebel: With special reference to the United States and the Soviet Union', *Daedalus* (Special issue: *Intellectuals and Change*) Summer, 1972.
Losev, V. I. (ed.), *Mikhail and Yelena Bulgakovy: Dnevnik Master i Margarity*, Vagrius, Moscow, 2004.
Lukashevich, Stephen, *N. F. Fedorov, (1828–1903): A Study in Russian Eupsychian and Utopian Thought,* Newark and London, 1977.
Major, Patrick and Mitter, Rana, 'East Is East and West Is West? Towards a Comparative Socio-Cultural History of the Cold War', in Mitter, Rana and Major, Patrick (eds.), *Across the Blocs: Cold War Cultural and Social History*, Frank Cass, London, 2004, pp. 1–22.
Makarov, V. G. and Khristoforov, V. S. 'Passazhiry "filosofskogo parokhoda". (Sud'by intelligentsii, repressirovannoj letom-osen'ju 1922g.)', *Voprosy filosofii* (7) (2003), pp. 113–37.
Makhonina, S. Ia. *Istoriia russkoi zhurnalistiki*, http://www.evartist.narod.ru/text1/93.htm.
Malenkaia Vera, 1988, Directed by Vassili Pichul.
Malia, M. 'The Intellectuals: Adversaries or Clerisy', *Daedalus* (Special issue: *Intellectuals and Change*) Summer, 1972.
Manchester, Laurie, *Holy Fathers, Secular Sons: Clergy, Intelligentsia, and the Modern Self in Revolutionary Russia,* Northern Illinois University Press, DeKalb, 2008.
Mannheim, Karl, *Essays on the Sociology of Culture*, Routledge, Kegan and Paul, London, 1956.
Marks, Steven G. *How Russia Shaped the Modern World – From Art to Anti-semitism, Ballet to Bolshevism*, Princeton University Press, Princeton, 2002.
Marks, Steven G. *The Information Nexus: Global Capitalism from the Renaissance to the Present*, Cambridge University Press, Cambridge, 2016.
Martin, Terry, *The Affirmative Action Empire: Nations and Nationalism in the Soviet Union, 1923–1939,* Cornell University Press, Ithaca, 2001.

Marx, Karl, Preface to *A Contribution to the Critique of Political Economy*, Progress Publishers, Moscow, 1977. First published in 1859. https://www.marxists.org/archive/marx/works/1859/critique-pol-economy/preface.htm
Marx, Karl and Engels, Friedrich, Preface to the Russian Edition of *The Communist Manifesto,* 21 January 1882, https://www.marxists.org/archive/marx/works/1848/communist-manifesto/preface.htm#preface-1882
Marx, Karl, 'Letter to Vera Zasulich', 8 March 1881.
Marx, Karl 'Letter to the editor of *Otechestvennyi zapiski'*, November, 1877.
Marx, Karl, *The Class Struggles in France 1848–1850 Part II*. First published in *Neue Rheinische Zeitung* (Jan.–Oct., 1850), https://www.marxists.org/archive/marx/works/1850/class-struggles-france/ch02.htm
Marx, Karl, *The International Workingmen's Association: General Rules,* October, 1864.
McCannon, John, *Red Arctic: Polar Exploration and the Myth of the North in the Soviet Union 1932–39*, Oxford University Press, Oxford, 1998.
McKean, Robert, *St Petersburg between the Revolutions: Workers and Revolutionaries*, Yale University Press, New Haven, 1990.
McKie, Robin 'Sergei Korolev: The Rocket Genius behind Yuri Gagarin', *The Guardian*, 13 March 2011, https://www.theguardian.com/science/2011/mar/13/yuri-gagarin-first-space-korolev
Medvedev, R. *Let History Judge: The Origins and Consequences of Stalinism*, Random House, New York and London, 1971, 2nd edition, 1989.
Medvedev, Roy, *On Socialist Democracy*, Albert A. Knopf, New York, 1972.
Medvedev, Zhores, *Stalin i evreiskaia problema: novyi analiz*, Izdatel'stvo Prava Cheloveka, Moskva, 2003.
Medynsky, Eugene, 'Schools and Education in the U.S.S.R', *American Sociological Review*, 9 (3), Recent Social Trends in the Soviet Union Jun., 1944, pp. 287–95.
Merezhkovsky, D. 'Revoliutsiia I religiia', *Russkaia mysl'*, 2, pp. 64–85 and 3, pp. 17–34, 1907.
Merezhkovsky, D., Gippius, Z. and Filosofov, D., *Le Tsar et la Révolution*, Société du Mercure de France, Paris, 1907.
Moon, David, 'Estimating the Peasant Population of Late Imperial Russia from the 1897 Census: A Research Note', *Europe-Asia Studies*, 48 (1) (Jan., 1996), pp. 141–53.
Moon, David, *The Russian Peasantry 1600–1930: The World the Peasants Made*, Routledge, London and New York, 1999.
Moroz, Valentyn, *Report from the Beria Reserve: The Protest Writings of Valentyn Moroz, A Ukrainian Political Prisoner in the USSR*, ed. and trans. John Kolasky, Peter Martin Press, Toronto, 1974.
Moser, Charles A. *Ivan Turgenev*, Columbia University Press, New York, 1972.
Mowbray, T. *The Beginnings of Railway Development in Russia in the Reign of Nicholas I 1835–1842*, Duke University Press, Durham, North Carolina, 1969.
Moynahan, Brian, *Leningrad: Siege and Symphony*, Quercus, London, 2014.
Nahirny, V. *The Russian Intelligentsia: From Torment to Silence*, George, Allen and Unwin, London, 1966.
Neizvestnyi, 'Ernst Neizvestny, a Russian Sculptor Who Clashed with Khrushchev, Dies at 91', *New York Times*, 18 August 2016, https://www.nytimes.com/2016/08/18/arts/international/ernst-neizvestny-a-russian-sculptor-who-clashed-with-khrushchev-dies-at-91.html
Neizvestnyi, Ernst, *Govorit Neizvestnyi,* Possev-Verlag, Frankfurt am Main, 1984.

Nekrich, Aleksandr, 1941. *22 iunia* Nauka, Moscow 1965. Published in English as: *June 22, 1941: Soviet Historians and the German Invasion* University of South Carolina Press, Columbia SC 1968.

Neuberger, Joan, *This Thing of Darkness: Eisenstein's Ivan the Terrible in Stalin's Russia*, Cornell University Press, Ithaca, 2019.

Neumann, Matthias, *The Communist Youth League and the Transformation of the Soviet Union 1917–1932*, Routledge, London and New York, 2011.

Nikitin, Afanasy, *Journey beyond Three Seas*. An English translation can be found in: Major, Richard H., ed., 'The Travels of Athanasius Nikitin,' tr. Mikhail M. Wielhorsky. in *India in the Fifteenth Century*. Hakluyt Society, ser. 1. volume 22 Hakluyt Society, London 1857.

Nozick, Robert, 'Why Do Intellectuals Oppose Capitalism?', *Cato Policy Report*, 20 (1) (Jan.–Feb. 1998, pp. 1, 9–11.

Offord, Derek, *The Russian Revolutionary Movement in the 1880s*, Cambridge University Press, Cambridge, 1986.

'On the Re-structuring of Literary-Artistic Organisations' Politburo decree of 23rd April 1932.

'Open Letter of Well-Known Soviet Writers to the Editor of *Pravda* in connection with the Anti-Soviet Activities and Speeches of A. I. Solzhenitsyn and A. D. Sakharov', *Pravda*, 31 August 1973.

Ory, P. and Sirinelli, J. F. *Les Intellectuels en France de l'affaire Dreyfus à nos jours*, Armand Colin, Paris, 1986.

Osipov, Yu. S. *Akademiia nauk v istorii Rossiskogo gosudarstva*, Nauka, Moscow, 1999 consulted at 'Ob akademii: Rossiia na pod'eme', Russian Academy of Sciences, http://www.ras.ru/about/history/ontherise.aspx

Osipov, Yu. S. *The Academy of Sciences in the History of the Russian State*, Nauka, Moscow, 1999, http://www.ras.ru/about/history/revolution.aspx

Osipov, Yu. S. 'Zarozhdenie traditsii', in *Akademiia nauk v istorii Rossisskogo Gosudarstvo*, Nauka, Moscow, 1999, http://www.ras.ru/about/history/traditions.aspx

Osorgin, M. *How We Left –Fragments of a Memoir*, Paris, 1955, http://old.ihst.ru/projects/sohist/document/deport/osorgin.htm

Paperno, Irina, 'What Can Be Done with Diaries?' *The Russian Review*, 63 (4) (Oct., 2004), pp. 561–73.

Pashkov, A. I. (ed.), *A History of Russian Economic Thought from the Ninth Century through the Eighteenth Century*. Institut ekonomiki (Akademiia Nauk Sovetskogo Soiuza) Gosizdat Moscow 1955. English edition Letiche, John (ed.), University of California Press, Berkeley and Los Angeles, 1964, pp. 135–44.

Perrie, Maureen, *The Cult of Ivan the Terrible in Stalin's Russia*, Palgrave, London and New York, 2001.

Platonova, Natalia, 'L'arpentage Général Des Terres En Russie Comme Projet Impérial (1765–1861)', Association d'histoire des sociétés rurales *Histoire & Sociétés Rurales*, 50 (2) (2018), pp. 109–57.

Pobedonostsev, Konstantin, *Moskovskii sbornik* Sinodalnaia tipografiia, Moscow 1896 translated as *Reflections of a Russian Statesman* Grant Richards, London 1898. Reprintedition by University of Michigan Press, Lansing, 1964 and available online at The Internet Archive, https://archive.org/details/reflectionsofrus00pobeuoft

'Poisoned by Putin', *The Guardian*, 9 September 2004.

Polonsky, Rachel, *Molotov's Magic Lantern; A Journey in Russian History*, Faber and Faber, London, 2010.

Pomeranz, Kenneth, *The Great Divergence: China, Europe, and the Making of the Modern World Economy*. Princeton University Press, Princeton NJ, 2000.

Pomeranz, William, *Law and the Russian State: Russia's Legal Evolution from Peter the Great to Vladimir Putin*, Bloomsbury, London and New York, 2018.

Popova, Olga, *Russian Illuminated Manuscripts* (English and Russian edition), Thames and Hudson, London and New York, 1984.

Possony, S. *Lenin: The Compulsive Revolutionary*, Allen Unwin, London, 1965.

Povest' vremennykh let (*The Russian Primary Chronicle*), http://community.dur.ac.uk/a.k.harrington/christin.html

Poznanski, R. *Intelligentsiia et Révolution: Blok, Gorkii et Maiakovskii face à 1917* Editions Anthropos, Editions Anthropos, Paris, 1981.

Priestley, J. B. *Russian Journey*, Writers Group of the Society for Cultural Relations with the USSR, London, 1946.

Pyman, Avril, *Pavel Florensky: A Quiet Genius: The Tragic and Extraordinary Life of Russia's Unknown da Vinci*, Continuum International Publishing Group (now Bloomsbury), London and New York, 2010.

Radishchev, A. *A Journey From St. Petersburg to Moscow*, Columbia University Press, New York, 2020.

Ransome, Arthur, in *Encyclopaedia Britannica* 13th ed, supplementary vol III 'Russia' Section III 'The Revolution and After' [Mar. 1921–Mar. 1926], 1926.

Read, Christopher, *Lenin Lives?* Oxford University Press, Oxford and New York, 2024.

Read, Christopher, 'George Plekhanov and the Marxist Turn in Russia', in Hammersley, Rachel (ed.), *Revolutionary Moments: Reading Revolutionary Texts*, Bloomsbury Academic, London, 2015, pp. 125–32. *Bloomsbury Collections*. 11 February 2021. http://dx.doi.org/10.5040/9781474252669.0022

Read, Christopher, 'Death and Resurrection in Russian Thought in Russia's Silver Age 1890–1930', in Gorokhova, Anna and Read, Christopher, *Afterlife: The Life of the Dead*, Moskovskii Gosudarstvennyi Pedagogicheskikh Universitet', Moscow, 2021.

Read, Christopher, *Stalin: From the Caucasus to the Kremlin*, Routledge Historical Biographies, London and New York, 2017.

Read, Christopher, 'Krupskaya, Proletkul't and the Origins of Soviet Cultural Policy', *International Journal of Cultural Policy*, 12 (3) (2006), pp. 245–65.

Read, Christopher, *Lenin: A Revolutionary Life*, Routledge, London and New York, 2005.

Read, Christopher, 'Values, Substitutes and Institutions: Cultural Roots of the Bolshevik Dictatorship', in Brovkin, V. (ed.), *The Bolsheviks in Russian Society: the Revolution and the Civil Wars*, Princeton University Press, Princeton and London, 1997.

Read, Christopher, *Culture and Power in Revolutionary Russia: The Intelligentsia and the Transition from Tsarism to Communism*, Macmillan, London and New York, 1990.

Read, Christopher, *Religion, Revolution and the Russian Intelligentsia: The Vekhi Debate and Its Intellectual Background*, Macmillan, London and New York, 1979.

Read, Christopher, 'Cultural Policy', in Frame, M., Kolonitskii, B., Marks, S. and Stockdale M. (eds.), *Russian Culture in War and Revolution, 1914–22: Book 1. Popular Culture, the Arts, and Institutions*, Slavica Press, Bloomington, Indiana, 2014, pp. 1–14. (Vol. 1 of *Russia's Great War and Revolution 1914–1922*).

Reddaway, Peter and Bloch, Sidney, *Psychiatric Terror: How Soviet Psychiatry Is Used to Suppress Dissent*, Basic Books, New York, 1977 (British edition: *Russia's Political Hospitals: The Abuse of Psychiatry in the Soviet Union* Gollancz, London 1977).

Reddaway, Peter and Bloch, Sidney, *Soviet Psychiatric Abuse*, Westview Press, Boulder Col., 1984.
Ree, Erik van, *Boundaries of Utopia - Imagining Communism from Plato to Stalin*, Routledge, London and New York, 2015.
Ree, Erik van, *The Political Thought of Joseph Stalin: A Study in Twentieth Century Revolutionary Patriotism*, Taylor and Francis, London, 2006.
Reid, Anna, *Leningrad: Tragedy of a City under Siege 1941–44*, Bloomsbury, London, 2011.
Reid, Susan Emily, 'In the Name of the People: The Manège Affair Revisited', *Kritika: Explorations in Russian and Eurasian History*, 6 (4) (Fall, 2005) (New Series), pp. 673–716.
Rendle, Matthew, 'Revolutionary Tribunals and the Origins of Terror in Early Soviet Russia' *Historical Research*, 84 (226) (November, 2011), pp. 693–721.
Resis, Albert, '*Das Kapital Comes to Russia*', *Slavic Review*, 29 (2) (Jun., 1970), pp. 219–37.
Retish, Aaron, 'Judicial Reforms and Revolutionary Justice: The Establishment of the Court System in Soviet Russia 1917–1922', in *Russia's Home Front in War and Revolution, 1914–22*, Book 3, 2018, pp. 369–99.
Retish, Aaron, 'The Birth of Soviet Criminology: Mikhail Gernet's Vision of the Good State and the Dangers of the People in 1917', *Journal of Modern Russian History and Historiography*, 13 (2020), pp. 184–213.
Rizzi, Bruno, *La Bureaucratisation du Monde: le collectivisme bureaucratique, quo vadis America?* B. Rizzi, Paris, 1939.
Roberts, Geoffrey, *Stalin's Library: A Dictator and His Books*, Yale University Press, New Haven and London, 2022.
Rosenberg, William G., *Bolshevik Visions*, 2 vols, 2nd edition, The University of Michigan Press, Ann Arbor, 1990.
Rubinstein, Joshua and Gribanov, Alexander, *The KGB File of Andrei Sakharov*, Yale University Press, New Haven and London, 2005.
Ruhle, Jurgen, *Literature and Revolution*, Frederick A. Praeger, New York, Washington, London and Pall Mall Press, London, 1969.
Sadr, Ahmad, *Max Weber's Sociology of Intellectuals*, OUP, Oxford, 1995.
Sakharov, A. *Memoirs*, Hutchinson, London, Sydney, Auckland, Johannesberg, 1990.
Sakharov, A. *Progress, Co-existence and Intellectual Freedom*, Pelican Books, Harmondsworth, 1968.
Salisbury, Harrison E. *Sakharov Speaks*, Collins/Harvill, London, 1974.
Salisbury, Harrison, *The 900 Days: The Siege of Leningrad*, Pan Books, London, 1969.
Sartre, J. P, *Plaidoyer pour les Intellectuels*, Gallimard, Paris, 1972.
Sartre, J. P, *Qu'est-ce que la literature?* Gallimard, Paris, 1948.
Schapiro, L. 'The Vekhi Group and the Mystique of Revolution', *Slavonic and East European Review*, 32 (85) (December, 1955), pp. 56–76.
Schultz, Kurt S. 'Building the "Soviet Detroit". The Construction of the Nizhnyi-Novgorod Automobile Factory 1927–32', in *Slavic Review*, no. 9, 1990, reproduced in Read, Christopher (ed.), *The Stalin Years: A Reader*, Palgrave Macmillan, London, 2003, pp. 70–83.
Scott-Smith, Giles and Krabbendam, Hans, 'Introduction. Boundaries to Freedom', in Scott-Smith, Giles and Krabbendam, H., *The Cultural Cold War in Western Europe, 1945–1960*, Frank Cass, London, 2003, pp. 1–10.
Serengy, Scott, *Russian Teachers and Peasant Revolution. The Politics of Education in 1905*, Indiana University Press, Bloomington, 1989.

'Sergei Yesenin (1895–1925)', *The Cradle Magazine*, 2019, https://thecradlemagazine.com/sergei-yesenin-1895-1925/

Seventeen Moments in Soviet History: An Online Archive of Primary Sources, https://soviethistory.msu.edu/

Shaw, Claire, 'Soviet Memoir Literature: Personal Narratives of a Historical Epoch', in Gilbert, George (ed.), *Reading Russian Sources: A Student's Guide to Text and Visual Sources from Russian History*, Routledge, London, 2020, pp. 212–28.

Shelestiuk, Elena Vladimirovna, 'National in Form, Socialist in Content: USSR National and Language Policies in the Early Period', *SHS Web of Conferences*, 69 (157) (Jan., 2019), p. 00104. DOI: 10.1051/shsconf/20196900104.

Shentalinsky, V. A. 'Fragments of the Silver Age. Conclusion', *Novyi mir* (6) (1998). https://new.nm1925.ru/articles/1998/199806/oskolki-serebryanogo-veka-4745/

Shevelov, George Y. 'Skovoroda's Language and Style', in Marshall, Richard H. and Bird, Thomas E. (eds.), *Hryhorij Savyč Skovoroda: An Anthology of Critical Articles*, Canadian Institute of Ukrainian Studies, Toronto, CIUS Press, 1994.

Shils, E. 'Ideology', *International Encyclopaedia of the Social Sciences,* 7, New York, 1968

Shils, E. 'Intellectuals', *International Encyclopaedia of the Social Sciences,* 7, Macmillan Reference USA, New York, 1968.

Shils, Edward, Introduction *The Intellectuals and the Powers, and Other Essays (His Selected Papers, 1)*, University of Chicago Press, Chicago, 1972.

Sigler, Krista, *Ksheshinskaia's Mansion*: *High Politics and the Culture of Modernity in Revolutionary Russia,* Ph.D. Thesis University of Cincinnati, 2009.

Sillaste, Galina, 'Podgotovka novoi ekonomicheskoi intelligentsia kak factor restrukturatzii ekonomikii: spetsifika i perspektivy', *Dialog*, 3 (2006) (e-journal of Tsenov Academy).

Skocpol, Theda, *States and Social Revolutions*, Cambridge University Press, Cambridge, 1979.

Slezkine, Yuri, *House of Government; A Saga of the Russian Revolution*, Princeton University Press, Princeton New Jersey, 2017.

Smirnov, V. *Dokumental'nye filmy o Velikoi Otechestvennoi Voiny*, Goskinoizdat, Moscow, 1947.

Smith, S. 'Bolshevism, Taylorism and the Technical Intelligentsia in the Soviet Union, 1917–1941', *Radical Science Journal*, 13 (1983).

Soloukhin, Vladimir, *Searching for Icons in Russia*, Harvill/Collins, London, 1971.

Solzhenitsyn, A. 'The Smatterers' (*Obrazovanshchina*), in Solzhenitsyn, A. (ed.), *From Under the Rubble*, HarperCollins and Fontana, London and New York, 1976.

Solzhenitsyn, A. *Letter to Soviet Leaders* Index on Censorship and Fontana Books, London, 1974.

Solzhenitsyn, Aleksandr, *The First Circle*, Harper, New York and London, 1968. An extended version was published in 2009 as *In the First Circle* by Harper, New York and London, 2009.

Solzhenitsyn, Alexander, Harvard Speech, text of the speech and a recording of it can be found at https://www.americanrhetoric.com/speeches/alexandersolzhenitsynharvard.htm

Spring, Derek W. 'Soviet Newsreel and the Great Patriotic War', in Pronay, Nicholas and Spring, D. W. (eds.), *Propaganda, Politics and Film, 1918–45*, Palgrave Macmillan, London, 1982, pp. 270–92.

Stalin, J. V. 'The Tasks of Business Executives' Speech Delivered at the First All-Union Conference of Leading Personnel of Socialist Industry 4 February 1931, https://www.marxists.org/reference/archive/stalin/works/1931/02/04.htm

Stalin, J. V. 'Dizzy with Success', https://www.marxists.org/reference/archive/stalin/works/1930/03/02.htm

Stalin, J. V. *Marksizm i natsional'no-kolonial'niy vopros*, Partizdat, Moscow, 1934.

Starr, S. Frederick *Melnikov. Solo Architect in a Mass Society*, Princeton University Press, Princeton, New Jersey, 1978.

Steinberg, Mark, *Russian Utopia: A Century of Revolutionary Possibilities*, Bloomsbury Academic, London, New York, Dublin, 2021.

Stites, Richard, *Revolutionary Dreams: Utopian Visions and Experimental Life in the Russian Revolution*, Oxford University Press, Oxford, 1987.

Struve P. B. *Patriotica. Politika. Kul'tura. Religiia. Sotsializm. Sbornik statei za piat let (1905–1910)*, St Petersburg, 1911.

Suny, Ronald, *Stalin: Passage to Revolution*, Princeton University Press, Princeton, New Jersey, 2020.

Szamuely, T. *The Russian Tradition*, Secker and Warburg, London, 1974.

Thomson, Boris *The Premature Revolution: Russian Literature and Society, 1917 1946*, Weidenfeld & Nicolson, London, 1972.

Timasheff, Nicholas, *The Great Retreat* 1946.

Todes D. P. *Ivan Pavlov: A Russian Life in Science*, New York, Oxford University Press, 2014.

Tolstoy, L. *The Kingdom of God Is within You*.

Tomkeieff, S. I. 'V.I.Vernadsky', *Nature*, 155, 10 March 1945.

Tromly, Benjamin, *The Making the Soviet Intelligentsia: Universities and Intellectual Life under Stalin and Khrushchev*, Cambridge University Press, Cambridge and New York, 2005.

Trotsky, L. *Literature and Revolution*, Haymarket Press, Chicago, 2009, https://www.marxists.org/archive/trotsky/1924/lit_revo/

Troubetzkoy, A. *A Brief History of the Crimean War*, Constable and Robinson, London, 2006.

Tsiolkovskii, K. E. *Cherty iz moiei zhizni*, Priokskoe knizhnoe izdatel'stvo, Tula, 1986.

Tupper, Harmon, *To the Great Ocean: Siberia and the Trans-Siberian Railway*, Little, Brown & Company, Boston, 1965.

Tyutchev, Fyodor, *Selected Poems*. Translated with an Introduction and Notes by John Dewey, Brimstone Press, Gillingham, 2014.

Umland, Anders and Gregor, A. James, 'Dugin Not a Fascist? A Debate with A. James Gregor (6 texts)', *Erwägen Wissen Ethik*, January 2005, 15;16 (3;4), pp. 424–9, 591–5, 566–72. The comments by Gregor can be found on pp. 594 and 570. The texts are accessible at https://www.researchgate.net/publication/255970590_Dugin_Not_a_Fascist_A_Debate_with_A_James_Gregor_6_texts

Valdai Discussion Club, 'Vladimir Putin Meets with Members of the Valdai Discussion Club. Transcript of the Plenary Session of the 18th Annual Meeting', *Global Shake-Up in the 21st Century: The Individual, Values and the State*, 22.10.2021, Sochi, Russia, https://valdaiclub.com/events/posts/articles/vladimir-putin-meets-with-members-of-the-valdai-discussion-club-transcript-of-the-18th-plenary-session/

Valentinov, N. *The Early Years of Lenin*, University of Michigan Press, Ann Arbor, 1969.

Venturi, Franco, *Roots of Revolution: A History of the Populist and Socialist Movements in Nineteenth-Century Russia*, Alfred A. Knopf, London and New York, 1960.

Voinovich, Vladimir, *The Ivankiad: or, the Tale of the Writer Voinovich's Installation in His New Apartment*, Jonathan Cape, London, 1978 or (in Russian). Ann Arbor, Michigan: Ardis Publishing, 1976.

Voprosy kul'tury v diktature proletariata, Gosizdat, Moscow, 1925.
Vowinckel, Annette, Payk Marcus, M. and Lindenberger, Thomas, 'European Cold War Culture(s)? An Introduction', in Vowinckel, Annette, Payk Marcus, M. and Lindenberger, Thomas (eds.), *Cold War Cultures. Perspective on Eastern and Western European Societies*, Berghahn, New York, 2012, pp. 1–17.
Waterlow, Jonathan, *It's Only a Joke, Comrade!: Humour, Trust and Everyday Life under Stalin (1928–41)*, Self-Published, Oxford, 2018.
Watson, Derek, *Molotov: A Biography*, Palgrave, London and New York, 2005.
Weil, Simone, *L'Enracinement*, Gallimard, Paris, 1949.
Weiner, Adam, 'The Most Politically Dangerous Book You've Never Heard of', *POLITICO Magazine*, https://www.politico.com/magazine/story/2016/12/russian-novel-chernyshevsky-financial-crisis-revolution-214516/
Westwood, J. N. *A History of Russian Railways*, George Allen and Unwin, London, 1964.
White, James D. *Marx and Russia: The Fate of a Doctrine*, Bloomsbury Press, London, 2018.
Williams, Raymond, *Culture,* Fontana New Sociology Series, Collins, Glasgow, 1981. (US edition, *The Sociology of Culture* Schocken Books New York, 1982).
Yurkina, Natalia Nikolaevna, 'Perception of Death by Russian Students of the 19th and Early 20th Centuries', in Gorokhova, Anna, Rallo, G. E and Read, C. (eds.), *Afterlife: The Life of the Dead. Antropologiia smerti: Mental'nost", religiia, filosofii,* Moskovskii Gosudarstvennyi Pedagogicheskikh Universitet', Moscow, 2021.
Yurkina, Natalia Nikolaevna, 'Youth and Theatre in the Nineteenth and early Twentieth Centuries', in Gorokhova, Anna and Read, Christopher (eds.), *Theatre Through the Ages* Moskovskii Gosudarstvennyi Pedagogicheskikh Universitet', Moscow, forthcoming.
Zamiatin E., 'The Cave' (trans. D. S.Mirsky) *The Slavonic Review*, 2 (4) (Jun., 1923), pp. 145–53.
Zguta, Russell, 'Skomorokhi: The Russian Minstrel-Entertainers', *Slavic Review*, 31 (2) (Jun., 1972), pp. 297–313.
Zhdanov, A. *On Literature, Music and Philosophy* Lawrence and Wishart, London, 1950, https://www.marxists.org/subject/art/lit_crit/zhdanov/lit-music-philosophy.htm#s2
Ziegler, Charles E. 'Worker Participation and Worker Discontent in the Soviet Union', *Political Science Quarterly*, 98 (2) (Summer, 1983), pp. 249–50.
Zyuganov, G. 'Chetyre voprosa Gennadiiu Ziuganova', *Zavtra*, 7 (554), 30 iiunia 2004.

Index

Printed in the USA
CPSIA information can be obtained
at www.ICGtesting.com
LVHW021014171024
794074LV00001B/4